THE

PRINCIPLES OF NATURE,

HER DIVINE REVELATIONS,

AND

A VOICE TO MANKIND.

THE

PRINCIPLES OF NATURE,

HER DIVINE REVELATIONS,

AND

A VOICE TO MANKIND.

BY AND THROUGH

ANDREW JACKSON DAVIS,
THE "POUGHKEEPSIE SEER," AND "CLAIRVOYANT."

IN THREE PARTS.

PART FIRST.
Any theory, hypothesis, philosophy, sect, creed, or institution, that fears investigation, openly manifests its own error.

PART SECOND.
Reason is a flower of the spirit, and its fragrance is liberty and knowledge.

PART THIRD.
When distributive justice pervades the social world, virtue and morality will bloom with an immortal beauty; while the Sun of Righteousness will arise in the horizon of universal industry, and shed its genial rays over all the fields of peace, plenty, and HUMAN HAPPINESS!

VOL. II.

LONDON:
JOHN CHAPMAN, 142, STRAND.

MDCCCXLVII.

STEREOTYPE   EDITION.

NATURE'S
DIVINE REVELATIONS.

§ 94. Before I proceed to speak of the origin of the opinion concerning the universality of the flood, I will speak of the flood itself, in connexion with what has already been said on the same subject.

In previous remarks upon the formation of the Pacific ocean, Caribbean sea, gulf of Mexico, and Guatemala—also on the confirmation of the Atlantic and Mediterranean waters in their present forms—I spoke of the valley which now forms the bed of the Pacific ocean; of the inhabitants of those portions now known as the Sandwich and Philippine islands; and also of those of the fertile portions now known as the West-India islands, of the portion which now forms the Mexican gulf, and of the extent of the tribes into the inland fertile locations. I have in general terms described how these portions became populated; and a more particular relation is not necessary. Keeping in memory, then, all the conditions of which I have previously spoken, I proceed to some general considerations concerning the phenomenon, cause, and result of the deluge which was at this period about transpiring.

It is unnecessary here to explain the primary physical causes engaged in producing this awful catastrophe: I have before spoken at length concerning the transformation of particles of inferior substances into the watery element and into the atmosphere, and of the equilibrium between the external and internal portions of the earth. I have also spoken of the stupendous icebergs that were formed in the arctic regions. And I have intimated that the upper portions of the two hemispheres were as yet concealed by the water, because the land there was lower than at any other portion of the earth, with the exception of the beds of the Atlantic and Mediterranean which then were partly formed, according to the level-seeking tendency of the watery element. So about these things I relate no more.

It was by the loss of the equilibrium between the interior and exterior forces that the molten contents of the centre of the earth became excited in an inconceivable manner. And as was the case in previous instances, the Andes, Vesuvius, and the many other relieving vents, were inadequate now to restore the equilibrium. So the voice of the earthquake thundered through the bowels of the earth.

It was mightier than the mightiest earthquake, and louder than the loudest thunder. It burst forth, and the earth trembled to its centre. Fire, smoke, mist, and rain, surrounded the whole earth. The tribes that were existing on the portions intermediate between what are now called the eastern and western hemispheres were nearly all destroyed; and those that survived fell stupified, as if dead, to the ground. Thought can not clothe itself in words sufficiently expressive to describe the sufferings and exclamations of the inhabitants. And about three days elapsed before the equilibrium was restored — at the end of which time the northern portions being elevated, and other portions depressed, the water rushed from the former regions and filled valleys which had previously been dry land, and the oceans, seas, lakes, gulfs, and rivers, became established as existing at the present day.

I am now impressed to notice the surviving inhabitants, and the effect which this great occurrence produced upon their minds.

The tribe which remained up to this time in the valley of Shinar, together with five small, detached tribes, were destroyed: but those that separated from the former, and located in China and Japan, remained unharmed. They retained the theology and doctrines taught them by the chieftain of whom I have spoken. And I will proceed to notice the effect which this event produced upon them, and the interpretation of the occurrence as given by their head and ruler.

Soon after all things became quiet, they sent messengers to ascertain how it had fared with their elder brethren in the valley of Shinar. But discovering them not, and seeing a river where once they had lived, they returned and related this to their governor. And as they knew of no other nations existing upon the earth, they concluded that they were the only people saved from the great catastrophe. So the chief began to instruct them that as the others had not been good, and had not offered sacrifices to satisfy the demands of Brahma — "Brahma seeing that the wickedness upon the earth was great, and the imaginations of the thoughts of their hearts were only evil continually, began to repent that he had directed Vishnu to create their forefathers and them. And seeing that the earth was filled with wickedness and abomination in the sight of Brahma, he said he would cause the great waters, of which he had made the ground and them, to sweep them off the face of the land."

So the governor and prophet of this eastern tribe gave the impression that it was because he himself, and his tribe, were better than their forefathers, that Brahma let them live. He represented these ideas by sounds and hieroglyphics. He instructed them to build a brazen image that would represent, as he said, the god of the Sun. The head of this being was very much like that of the unicorn, and the body like that of a fish; and they placed it within a stone tent, and every year visited it and offered up sacrifices. To this they were prompted because they had been preserved. And from this time they began to worship the sun, the moon, the stars, and the milky way, which they supposed were the habitations of spirits, the number of which they represented as being thirty-three thousand, each one of these being a god to its respective sphere or planet.

They as yet did not designate each other by *names*, but merely by families or states of association. But the person who was their governor and prophet, yet unnamed, was, by subsequent writers, named *Fohi*. This may be verified in the Chinese record of the present day. And this person has been supposed by still more modern writers to be the Noah spoken of in the " primitive history."

The Chaldeanic Persians, or the Japan tribe of which I have spoken, preserved in their mythology the whole account, with very little modification. But the father of the family who was permitted to live by Brahma, they named *Xisuthrus*. This also has been supposed by modern historians to be the person named in the Jewish account of the deluge.

The sects known as the Budhists and Jaina preserved with great care the same traditional account, and the same ultimately became a portion of the Greek oriental history and theology: and in this the same being is named *Deucalion*. This is the termination of the tradition concerning the deluge as the account and interpretation of it were given by the leader of the eastern isolated tribe of which we have spoken.

§ 95. I now proceed to speak of the aborignal inhabitants of America, and of the effect produced upon their minds by the same catastrophe.

By the formation of the Pacific ocean they were separated from, and lost all communication with, the tribes that were existing upon the present Sandwich islands: and they knew not of the tribes and nations in the southern continent. And there were but few Indians who escaped the inundation, which was by them supposed to be universal; for they dwelt more upon the portions now covered by the Pacific than they did east of the present limits of that ocean. So they believed that they were the only tribes that were saved, and that they dwelt upon the only land in the earth, supposing that all other portions had sunk beneath the great waters.

And now I have occasion to speak of their original conceptions of the Great Spirit.

They were unlike their brethren in disposition and social condition; for they were united by a well-directed affection, and by a unity and harmony in all their plans and proceedings. They were exceedingly fond of hunting, and this employment they supposed was right, or else their forefathers who followed it would not have dwelt in such a beautiful garden. So they invented instruments, and cultivated the disposition to roam and hunt through the wilds of the forest, and would pitch their bark tents wherever they pleased.

Being thus socially united, they were not led to conceive of gross errors: for errors spring from social disunity and disorganization, and from a misapprehension of the cause of existing evil. Having imbibed and retained the impression received by their early forefathers, they proceeded to reconcile this impression with the manifestation of all things about and above them. So they saw that the "breaths" were not evil to them as their fathers had taught, but instead of this they supposed that they proceeded from a good spirit, who desired to fan their heated brows after they had toiled and travelled excessively in the light of the Good Spirit. So when fatigued and exhausted by toilsome travels, they would rest confidingly under the protection of the Great Spirit who had formed their world, and would joyously receive his refreshing breath, that came, as they supposed, from some of the good subordinate spirits. They saw that these "breaths" were generally good for them; and this manifestation of goodness unfolded the tender dispositions of their nature, and they dwelt in love one with another. And these truthful conceptions, and their tranquillizing influences, descended through all the succeeding generations of this people down to the present time.

They believed that the eye, the tongue — that plants, animals, and all the celestial orbs — had spirits in attendance. They believed that the power of speaking was communicated to them by the spirit of the tongue, and so also the power of seeing by the spirit of the eye. They loved, adored, and worshipped, the Sun: for it made their earth fertile in all the things which they cultivated. They worshipped the Moon: for it was a good spirit to give them light while the warm and better spirit had gone to rest. They beheld the stars with awe and admiration : because they were little lights held out by the good spirits to give them light, and to make their earth look beautiful when the sun and the moon had retired to rest. They believed that when they should lie down and die, the spirit of their eyes and tongue would convey the spirit that was within them to the beautiful habitations of the spirit-land. They felt conscious that the spirit-land was analogous to the one on which they dwelt, in all its productions, so that there they might hunt, adore the good spirits, and love one another; and it was therefore to them a land of transcendent beauty and grandeur. There they would not see any more the spirit of the waters. And there they would not die any more, neither dislike nor injure one another; but would be near the placid waters, and the meandering streams, and in the forests and gardens of beauty and delight. There they would see the shining fish, the gilded birds, and the gentle animals, that would not resist their grasp. There they would behold the Good Spirit, while the vaulted chambers above would be illuminated by all the grandeur and magnificence possible to conceive.

This truthful conception and its accompanying influences became established immoveably in the minds and affections of each succeeding generation down to the present time. Here is the first instance, from the moment the human form first obtained an existence, in which human thought took a proper, truthful, and natural direction. It was the spontaneous teaching of Nature about them, and the corresponding prompting of the principle within, that taught them of the spirit-land. Disunity was not in their midst; and therefore wickedness and abomination were to them unknown. Their thoughts were natural, spontaneous, true, and celestial. Learn from this, ye men of erudition, and let your lofty aspirations sink to the lowest degree of abasement. Learn from this, ye theologians, philosophers, and metaphysicians, and let your now-ambitious thoughts sink so low that generations yet unborn will be unconscious of their existence. Learn from this, ye traditional historians, ye governors, chieftains, prophets, and potentates, and promptly discard all that has been and begin again, and travel the path of wisdom and virtue. Learn from this, ye classifiers, ye commentators, ye external and unnatural teachers, and let the ink which has been wasted in penning your thoughts be naught in comparison to the abundance of tears shed by you in the act of humiliation! Let external pride and consequent arrogance fall for ever. Let highmindedness and pretended enlightenment cease to trammel your spiritual principle, and let this then seek *true* wisdom, derivable from the inexpressible beauties of a smiling NATURE!

The Indians supposed that none but themselves were preserved upon the earth; and they believed that the spirit of the great waters had swallowed up their brethren because of their wickedness, and left *them* because they were good, and favored in the sight of the Good Spirit. They named the chief existing among them at the time of this occurrence *Sottavarata*. This tradition, with a very little modification, has descended through the minds of every subsequent generation. And this person has been supposed by some modern chronological and biblical writers to be the Noah of the " primitive history."

I will now proceed to speak of the nation and collateral tribes that dwelt in Central America and southern Europe. Inasmuch as they had advanced more in all the arts and sciences than any other nation, their language and theology were necessarily more sublime. I am now speaking of the fleeting, evanescent sublimity that is always connected with an unreal idealism. It will be remembered that they had removed the origin of evil to an abyss below, of which the sun was a representative: but it now became necessary for their inspired chieftain to interpret and account for this wonderful catastrophe by the theological materials in his possession. I am now speaking of a chieftain who superseded the one of whom I last spoke. He said (as the inhabitants of the city wherein they dwelt were the only ones known to be preserved, with the exception of three tribes that dwelt on the more inland portions) that the angry being who had made that great fiery gulf was exasperated because of the short-coming and wicked transactions of their brethren, the tribes that dwelt upon the gulf of Mexico and other portions leading to the West-India islands. And he said this angry being had conversed with their previous governor, for the sake of whose presence the tribes had long been saved. And as he was the only good person among all the tribes, he was permitted to converse with the spirit who was opposed to these abominations. And he entered into a covenant with this angry being (for the latter lamented that he had created so many tribes) to let that tribe and himself live, because it was necessary that the earth should be peopled by those who were as good as he and they were. So one of their vortical edifices contained the hieroglyphical promise or covenant made with the potentate of whom I have spoken, and which was confirmed by the one of whom I am now speaking. It is well to remark that I am now speaking of a chieftain who taught and established the traditions of three generations before him — the one living when occurred the deluge. For the theology was not definitely confirmed and promulgated until the third generation after the occurrence. But this vortical edifice contained hieroglyphical representations which the then-present chieftain interpreted into a demonstration that the forefather had conversed with the angry being. And it was owing to this, he taught, that they were saved; while their brethren, who were wicked in the sight of their god, descended into the burning realms below. I will now trace this idea until it makes its appearance in modern days.

It will be remembered that this nation believed that they were the only human beings saved, because they knew not of any other inhabitants — and believed that their god had repented of making so many tribes, because of their wickedness, and destroyed them on that account. The chieftain who transferred this traditional account from the time of the deluge, was not named until many generations after him. And I find no absolute trace of a name until I trace these ideas into the manuscripts of which I have spoken, in the Jews' possession: and there he is named *Noah*.

I have thus traced the Chinese mythology to the Greek — and the mythology of these southern tribes to the Jews; and I find the accounts in this manner: The good, saved, and favored, of the Chinese, were *Fohi* and his family; of the Chaldeanic-Persians, *Xisuthrus* and his family; of the Greeks, *Deucalion* and his family. In the Indian mythology, the saved were *Sottavarata* and his family: and each believed that the whole world was drowned, with the exception of themselves. In the Jews' manuscripts, I find that the saved were *Noah* and his family.

And in the writings of modern commentators upon oriental and heathen mythology, these various traditions are generally referred to, to establish the truthfulness of the relation as contained in the "primitive history" — it being supposed that the account in the possession of each nation originated from one source, and from the actual, traditional experience of a man and family as is therein related. Such a supposition is not warrantable; for all the traditions that are in possession of the different nations can not be traced to one source.

In the Jewish record, the general account is as follows: "And the wickedness of man was great upon the earth, and the imagination of the thoughts of his heart was only evil continually. And God repented that he had peopled the earth;—but Noah found favor in his sight." And the latter was directed to construct an ark of gopherwood, with specific and required dimensions: and Noah and his family, and the beasts of the earth, and the fowls of the air, entered, sexually conjoined, into the ark, and were saved. After this, dry land appeared, as Noah inferred from evidence conveyed by a dove. And soon the ark rested upon Mount Ararat, and the animals therein contained went forth to multiply and reanimate the face of Nature; and Noah and his family went forth to multiply, and to populate the whole earth.

In the Chinese mythology, or rather in that of the more recent tribes of that nation, the following account may be found: "And Brahma seeing the wickedness of the forefathers, did lament because they did not sacrifice their offerings, and began to lament that he had directed Vishnu and Narasayana to awake them from the depths of the great waters. But Fohi could speak with Brahma because of his goodness. And he directed Fohi to journey to that high land and live. Then Vishnu broke up the bottom of the great deep, and opened the places above: and the great waters covered all the land, together with our forefathers, who were taken by the evil spirits."

I have related the mythology of the southern tribes, together with the modification of the Chinese into the Chaldeanic-Persian and Greek. And the impression that was conveyed to the early Jewish tribes, and the account contained in the Persian tradition, were blended together; and being afterward written and re-written, compiled and re-compiled, through the successive languages, it has appeared in the English version as it may be found by perusing the " primitive history." The account is well preserved, considering the innumerable contingencies which govern all circumstantial things. And it is only an exaggerated and poetical representation of that which is substantially true: and for its truth the history demands the highest respect.

§ 96. I am impressed to proceed to another class of ideas and to speak of their origin and successive modifications until they appear in their present form. The first of these may be found in the early manuscripts of the " primitive history," clothed in the following words: "And God said, Let us make man in our own image and likeness."

In establishing a superficial interpretation of this subject, many noble and highly-cultivated intellects have been engaged. Time, talents, and wealth, have been employed in disseminating such superficial opinions, sufficient to have instructed and cultivated the moral and intellectual powers of many a nation. The desires and prejudices of men have warred against the promptings of their judgment, and have circumscribed the range of their own and others' reasoning powers to the limited circle of a sectarian and hereditary belief. In endeavoring to establish preconceived opinions, men have severed the affectionate ties of congeniality, which should unite mankind as one vast brotherhood; and they have established a deep-seated impression that only breathes sectarian contention and local hostility. They have not proceeded to investigate the interior origin of *thoughts*, of which *words* are merely *sheaths;* but they have presumed upon the divineness of the sheathings themselves, and warred against the teachings of judgment, of Nature, and of her Author!

But let the mind search well into the *cause* of thoughts, and then it will be able to judge of the external clothing of these, whether it be of man, or of that Divine Principle which speaks only by manifesting, at a single expression, millions of systems, decked with life, beauty, and grandeur! Let it search well into the internal real reality of all things: and if qualities and principles are found that are good, divine, and indestructible, then such will be approbated by the judgment, and Nature will seal their truth with her universal concurrences.

I am deeply impressed that volume after volume has been written upon this and similar subjects, without producing the least relief to a depressed and ignorant world. Thoughts like unto the ones under consideration, clothed in words, have occupied the attention of an innumerable host of theological writers. Their labor, time, and talents, have thus been employed in building upon a superficial foundation a theological superstructure which has not in the *least* degree ameliorated the unhappy social and national condition of mankind their brethren! The many theories of this nature that are in the world are external, interruptive, and unholy invasions upon the human affections and judgment. They are unprofitable and injurious to the race; they are local, isolated, sectarian, and entirely opposed to the highest good of every living creature. They are unreal, impure, wicked. They are corrupting and vitiating to all the pure affections of man's nature. They are the foundation of universal sectarian hostility and superstition. They are at war with all the pure, social, and moral interests of man, that would, if undisturbed, join in one the whole race of intelligent beings. In the promulgation of these external and evanescent thoughts, the physical world has been left uncared for, and still remains a comparative wilderness. If those men who have been thus engaged had been employed according to the design and intention of an unchangeable Governor, the uninhabited deserts would have been rendered fertile, blooming, and fragrant; and then would their talents and powers have been appreciated. And then the peace and unity of feeling which would have pervaded the whole race of mankind, would have spoken to them with a voice of thankfulness, and great would have been their reward.

The tribes that had become consociated in the valley of Shinar, according to previous description, received the early impression of their forefathers concerning the creation, and also the improvements that were made upon it by their supposed inspired chieftain. In his cosmogony, he called to his assistance from the depths of the water, the deity of whom I have spoken, subsequently named Parama, Vishnu, and Siva. This chieftain first conceived of an original spirit. This conception suggested the idea of a second spirit; and this of a third. The first he supposed to be the great good spirit that had reposed from the remotest period of eternity to the time of the creation, in the bosom of the great waters. And he conceived that as this spirit awoke to activity, he breathed forth another spirit to do the work which he (Parama) had designed. Vishnu was the subordinate spirit thus created; and he was, according to the chieftain, *a part of Parama's soul.* He moved the waters, and continued to do so until he created, from the superior materials of the egg, the earth and man. Then he supposed that the spirit Siva was the cause of those "breaths" which inspired the bosoms of themselves and their elder brethren with envy, hatred, and deception. Here, then, originated the thought which has clothed itself in the word TRINITY.

I do not discover any essential change in this part of the oriental mythology for many centuries; and it ultimately fell into the possession of the Persianic tribes, who preserved it until Zoroaster systematized it and other existing traditions, in his *Zend Avesta.* He changed the deities into the characters of Ormuzd, Amshaspands, and inferior spirits. Thus he formed from the three, a trinity of good, celestial, and holy spirits, among which *Ormuzd* was supreme.

Seeing so much evil and wretchedness among the inhabitants of the earth, and seeing war, persecution, and tyranny, existing, he began to reason upon their causes. And this suggested to his mind a corresponding trinity of infernal spirits. The greatest of these was *Ahriman;* and he was attended by subordinate and inferior spirits, and millions of *deevs*.

Thus Zoroaster presented the trinity in a new form; and from this it was transplanted into the Jewish manuscripts, in the brief and comprehensive expression which reads, "And God said, Let us make man in OUR own image." It was also subsequently expressed, "Father, Son, and Spirit." The expression, "Let us make man," is derived from the early myth in which the "*us*" means Brahma, Vishnu or Narasayana, and Siva. It corresponds also to the Greater, the Lesser, and the Least; Father, Son, and Spirit; Ormuzd, Amshaspands, and superior subordinates.

In the original conception, the characters were distinct and singular; but they were classified and divided by Zoroaster into plurals. And they were comprehensively expressed in the primitive, Jewish transcript, according to the original conception.

§ 97. But it is given me to know through the medium of superior impressions that the expression, "*in our image and likeness,*" does really shadow forth a substantial and truthful idea, verified in the natural and spiritual spheres. The terms "image and likeness" have suggested to a most exalted intellect* a conception in which, after spiritual research and investigation, he became confirmed; and the general features of his impressions were correct. This will appear as I proceed to a comprehension of the spiritual spheres — from which, I am deeply impressed, flowed high and truthful impressions into the expanded internal of this Swedish philosopher. But it is impossible to find in these words, as originally employed in the "primitive history," one particle of spiritual signification. It is not true that he, with all his enlightenment, unfolded an interior truth as expressed in these primitive sayings. Instead of this, he unfolded a stupendous correspondence — not from their interior, but from their external suggestions. And it is now demonstrated by the unreal external of things, which he so deeply opposed, that these primitive

* Swedenborg.

records do not contain, as divinely originated, a minute spiritual meaning or application. It is absolutely demonstrated in his philosophical and analytical investigations, that externals are the mere superficial and evanescent indications of the interior, and therefore are to be regarded only as the deceptive garments or sheathings of truths. Therefore to give an internal signification to a passage which the external of the same does not indicate, is indeed to fabricate that which is unreal and absolutely unprofitable. The external of the written record, when viewed by a purely spiritually-exalted intellect, shows not the least indication of a spiritual signification. And if the external gives evidence of the interior, why endeavor to give to a passage a different signification from that which the external manifests?

The external clothing of the "primitive history" interprets its own internal signification. It professes to be a truthful and comprehensive history of opinions concerning creation before the flood, and of the customs, manners, dispositions, and movements, of subsequent nations; of the repopulation of the earth, and the distribution of the early tribes; of their leaders, chieftains, prophets, kings, and emperors. It professes to give the history of wars; of the subjugation and captivity of tribes; of the upbuilding and downfall of kingdoms and empires; of the vice, misery, and imaginations, of many nations of the earth. These things are therein recorded in the usual style of the early writers, the forms of expression employed being such as were adapted to the education of the early inhabitants of the earth. It professes to be this; its external proves its profession, and its interior is its own expositor. If more is professed, then such profession has arisen from its promulgators, and is not in accordance with its own intentions. So while I am deeply impressed to venerate the truthfulness of those historical traditions, I am at the same time impressed to expose and discard all untrue theological interpretations, and all unreal and unholy pretensions. Things of this nature should be loved according to the truthfulness of their professions, and not according to the misinterpretations of their pretensions, such as have clothed those simple mythological and primitive writings with a mysterious and impenetrable garment.

The next in the class of ideas the origin of which is to be traced, is the traditional opinion concerning *Cain* and *Abel*. It will be recollected that I have spoken comprehensively concerning the branch tribes as the offspring of the early family, and have related that one conquered and destroyed the other—the triumphant nation subsequently journeying to the European continent. The history of this was transferred, with other and similar impressions, through successive generations and centuries, until we find it first expressed by a writer among the early Egyptians. A correspondence was connected with this tradition, which was of the following import (for the early inhabitants knew things by their obvious correspondences and representatives): The younger and weaker tribe (which was Abel) corresponded to light, purity, and innocence. Cain (which was the stronger and grosser nation) corresponded to darkness, wickedness, and abomination. For, according to the early theology, darkness was the first principle in being, and therefore was the oldest and most powerful; while light was subsequently created, and was consequently weak and unmatured. And thus the comparison was written among the Egyptians as follows:—

"And from the forefathers sprang two children, whose names were Osiris and Typhon. Osiris was a good and gentle brother, and was loved by Brahma. Typhon was a strong brother, and cultivated the things of the earth. For Typhon is the child of darkness which was over all and for ever: but Osiris was a child of light, because light was permitted by Vishnu the good spirit." But Typhon, which is darkness, was represented as attacking and overpowering Osiris, which is light and innocence. This is the first written correspondential account of this primitive tradition.

I find that this was admitted into other manuscripts, and appeared among the Chaldeanic writings. Afterward it was transcribed into Greek, and ultimately into the Hebrew oracles and manuscripts; and through this medium it was conveyed to subsequent generations who admitted it into the " primitive history :" and in this the characters are named *Cain* and *Abel*.

§ 98. The next idea to be analyzed and traced to its origin is concerning the *seven days* that are represented as elapsing during the formation of the earth and all things therein, the seventh day being spoken of as smiling on the consummation of the grand work, and giving rest to Brahma, who blessed it.

Many centuries elapsed before the early inhabitants began to make astronomical observations. But from the indications of the winds, atmosphere, heat, light, sun, moon, stars, and all visible objects which were supposed to be gods, they at length began to learn to enumerate, to determine upon the seasons, to know their approach, and also to know when to visit one another. The first inhabitants knew well when to expect darkness, by the periodical recession of the sun behind the western lands. They also knew when to expect light, by the illumination of the eastern hills. They were uncertain for a time whether these things would continue so or not; but they were soon confirmed in the opinion that they would continue, by the unvarying appearance and disappearance of the sun. Hence they made one of the first detached tribes to represent darkness, and the other light. So far, then, they had advanced in astronomical knowledge — they knew the periodicity of days and nights.

But they could as yet only perceive *general* correspondences, and these they represented in hieroglyphical characters. And so they continued for several centuries, until they discovered a new and valuable truth — that the moon was made and destroyed twelve times while the sun was passing once through the circle of the zodiac. This established in their minds the first idea of a *year* with its subdivisions. And they had a god constructed to represent, and to correspond precisely to, this occurrence: and at the end and beginning of this period they had great festivities, and offered up to the god of the year innumerable sacrifices.

The twelve periods of the moon's destruction and reproduction corresponded to *months* — though these divisions were the work of generations subsequent to the discovery of the year. And thus they continued for many seasons, until their faculties of discernment became improved and they discovered that the moon was large, diminished, half destroyed, nearly destroyed, entirely annihilated, at regular periods, which were afterward found to be just seven days and nine hours. But the hours were unnoticed, as they could only distinguish bold numerals. This gave the conception of *weeks;* and thus this division of time became established among the Egyptians, Chinese, Persians, and Jews.

Succeeding generations reduced weeks to *days*, because there were seven of these in one of the periods of the moon's transition. Days became classified into *hours*, by the changing shadow of an immoveable object situated in the light of the sun. In this manner, years, months, weeks, days, and hours, became established.

And *Sunday* is a *name* of more recent date, and was instituted by the Danes, adopted by the Saxons, and transplanted to the English language. In the Saxon, the word was *Sunnedag: sunne* signifying the sun, and *dag* signifying day. In the Danish, it is written *Sonedag*, meaning day of the sun. And this was applied to the first day of the changed moon, in glorification of the sun. And the next day, the moon having advanced, was called *Moon's*-day — it being a day attributed to the moon. And *Tuesday* received its name from the god *Tuisco;* and *Wednesday* from the god *Wednos;* and *Thursday* from the god *Thursco:* and the remaining days were in like manner allegorically named.

In a similar manner the division of days became introduced into the Jewish historical writings — where the days were only designated by the phrase, " the evening and the morning." And as the seventh day was the last, or the great Sun-day, it was looked upon by the Jews as being of divine origin. And they imbibed the impression that the light on that day was peculiarly pure and serene. So six days were observed as times for labor, and the seventh was appropriated to rest — as had reposed the good spirit Parama, after he had finished the creation of the world and man, according to oriental mythology.

But I was impressed in describing the geological epochs of the creation of the globe, and of the plants and animals, to use the expression " evening and morning," &c., because the correspondence between the expression and the physical reality was complete.

In the manner above related, the inhabitants in all early and subsequent ages made the starry heavens their field of observation ; and they received from it unfailing instruction and wisdom, which imbodied itself in the language of correspondences.

So likewise has the system of *enumeration* become established. All nations and tribes upon the face of the earth manifest a sameness in their rules of counting, their highest number of the unit series never exceeding ten. The reason why this became so general and confirmed among all nations is manifest: for it appears that the early tribes counted their fingers, which were for a long time their only arithmetic. And the same rule being subsequently recognised in the written records of all nations, formed the established mode of enumeration among all, and is perfectly universally recognised by the nations of the present day.

---

§ 99. The next idea in the class before mentioned is that of the *origin of language* as intimated in the mythological tradition contained in the "primitive history," that "the whole earth was of one language and of one speech."*

When the early family perceived that they possessed the power of vocal communication, and began to convey their thoughts to one another through that medium, they supposed that this power was given to them by the "breaths," and that therefore it should be used and cultivated. But succeeding generations, discovering that this faculty had produced a disunion among their forefathers, believed, according to the tradition transmitted from their previous brethren, that the "breaths" were *evil spirits*, and had given to the world one language and one speech so that they might deceive and dislike one another. This was the prevailing opinion for many ages, both before and after the deluge, and among all the tribes of the earth. All admitted this as a part of their sacred theology, because it was told by their forefathers, and was confirmed by the sacredness which their minds associated with its age.

This opinion continued to prevail until they had gained, from hieroglyphics and terrestrial and astronomical correspondences, instruction sufficient to enable them, according to previous description, to construct a language which was the parent of the subsequent Sanscrit.

At this time they used the soft bark of trees, and palm-tree leaves, as materials whereon to impress, in this language, their thoughts. This art continued in this condition for a long period, and meanwhile was mostly in possession of governors, chieftains, and lawgivers, who believed and taught, according to early impression, that their language was of divine origin.

I find the next development of this idea (which is strictly mythological) among the Chinese, Chaldeans, Brahmins, and other Hindostanic tribes. They believe that the *Vedas* and *Brahmanas* in their possession are sacred oracles, written by celestial beings in divine language; and these collectively are known as the *Shaster*.† The *Vedas* compose the first part of the Shaster—which signifies and represents life, light, truth, fire, wit, law, ordinance, and celestial knowledge. And the *Brahmanas* are the second part, and are composed of Orphic hymns, which they believe to be heavenly, and which are like the poetical songs of the early Egyptian tribes. These they would sing to the deities, raising their voices in thanksgiving and praise to the great and good spirit who had formed the Sanscrit

---

* Genesis xi. 1. † This is the Hindoo Bible.

language. For a clearer idea of the character of these Orphic hymns, it would be well to read the Psalms, and the book of Job, as these were an imitation of the Orphic hymns of the Shaster, which were in manuscript among the Egyptians and Chaldeanic-Persians. The early Hindostanic tribes believed that their language was given to Brama* from heaven, by the Deity: and hence their supposition that the Shaster, which is composed of the Vedas and Brahmanas, was an emanation from heavenly spheres, and was an embodiment of the thoughts of the celestial beings.

For many continuous ages, the Sanscrit was the most perfect language known among mankind. Being so nearly perfected by earlier generations, it was afterward improved, cultivated, and rendered copious, by successive chieftains, and finally it was perfected by Brama their lawgiver and holy prophet, who was supposed to hold intercourse with the deities.

A further development of this theological tradition is found among the Persians. I am obliged to pass over many centuries, during which time other tribes migrated from the southern portions of the earth into Asia and Africa, bringing with them a different mode of expression. For the Chaldean or Persian language is from a root consisting of a different form of speech, and this afterward became perfected and established by uniting with its rudimental form a dialect of the Sanscrit. And about the time this language became thus established and confirmed, those who employed it were equally confirmed in the belief that it was of a spiritual origin, according to the sacred tradition of their forefathers. Zoroaster now lived, and was the Persian lawgiver. He wrote the *Zend Avesta*, which he said was a gift from the gods: and the people believed that this was given to Zoroaster, as the Brahmin believes of the Shaster, by a communication with the Deity. They supposed that their language originated in the same way.

The Jews also believed that the knowledge and direction received by Moses, their lawgiver, was directly from the Deity. So likewise the followers of Mohammed supposed that the Koran was written in celestial spheres by God, and was given to Mohammed while in a cave.

So in giving an opinion concerning the original state of language, it is said that " the whole earth was of one language and of one

---

* This Brama was a lawgiver among the ancient Hindoos, and the founder of the sacerdotal order known as Brahmins. So said the author in an incidental remark.

speech. And it came to pass that as they journeyed from the east, they discovered a plain in the valley of Shinar, where they dwelt."* It is well to remark that this is from a manuscript the substance of which sustains a position in the " primitive history" *after* the relation of the flood. But the account should not be thus placed, as it relates a circumstance that occurred *before* the flood some ages.

And I feel deeply impressed that the inhabitants of the earth at the *present* day are not generally any better informed concerning the origin of language than were the early tribes of China, Egypt, and Hindostan. For they are believing, like the Brahmin, the Egyptian, the Chaldean, the Persian, the Jew, and the Greek, that language was communicated to the forefathers by the Deity himself. Very many learned and enlightened men still maintain this heathen and unadvanced idea. They can not, because of their early education, properly conceive of natural and progressive development. But if they could only recognise and understand this divine and unchangeable principle of the Universe, they would discard all further belief in the mythological idea of direct instruction from the Deity.

Instead of exerting your powers to sustain these superficial chimeras, investigate the interior reality of which all natural endowments and developments are the representatives. Suspend your preconceived opinions, and ask the more interior and rational element of your being whether language is of celestial origin, or whether it does not naturally unfold itself, commencing in a rudimental form in the animal kingdom, and being perfectly developed by man? Consider whether effects do not always correspond to their interior and inciting causes; and then deeply consider the question, "If language was an effect of a celestial cause, and if its origin is divine, should not language be pure, celestial, and undeceptive?"

The nature of the mental and physical constitution of mankind is divine, perfect, and harmonious. This never will deceive. It is perfectly good, and represents the divineness of its great Origin and Cause. Deception, however, exists in the world, and all descriptions of dissimulation. But these things do not flow from the interior of man's nature, but arise merely as a consequence of his unholy, imperfect, and vitiated situation, in reference to his fellow-beings. Unholy situations produce unholy effects. But the interior principle, which is of *divine origin*, can not be made evil, nor can it be contaminated. And all evil is of external and superficial origin, and

* Genesis xi. 2.

is felt by all as external; and hence, in order to banish evil from the earth, a change must occur in the social condition of the whole world. Among other superficial things, *language* is existing; and as its effects are manifestly imperfect, it is evident that it must have originated from a source correspondingly imperfect.

§ 100. The next idea in the series is the mythological theory of the *origin of evil*. I have spoken at length concerning the general and natural cause of the existence of evil in the world. But as what I have said does not correspond with the prevailing theological conception of its origin, it becomes necessary to speak of the *early* conception, and to briefly notice its subsequent developments.

The first inhabitants believed that the "breaths" inspired them with evil thoughts; which suggested and confirmed a belief in the existence of a malignant deity who was opposed to them, and who destroyed their social love and breathed among them a spirit of envy, hatred, and deception. This conception was modified by the southern tribes, by transferring the origin of evil to the light and warmth of the atmosphere, and even to the sun itself—and also by conceiving that the sun was the representative of a corresponding fount of undiminishing fire. But the idea proceeded no further than this among these nations.

But the eastern tribes conceived that a spirit was existing between them and the good deity, which prevented their having divine commerce. This belief existed in a similar form among all the tribes of the east up to the time of Zoroaster, who established in the world a belief in two antagonistic, eternal, unconquerable deities: one the god of evil, and the other the god of goodness. The throne of each of these beings was surrounded by subordinate spirits of a character corresponding to the deity to which they were respectively attached. So he conceived of an innumerable host of *deevs*, which were associated with the evil deity, and were his agents to disseminate evil imaginations and unrighteous thoughts and desires in the minds of all mankind.

The Jewish rabbinical writers are no more free from these mythological imaginations: for they adopted the Persianic opinion and put it forth in their writings. Hence the origin of the passage in the "primitive history" which speaks of the appearance of an evil spirit in the form of a serpent in the garden of Eden, and asserts that the woman, being gentle and unsophisticated, became deceived thereby, and was induced to partake of the fruit of the tree of evil; that she transmitted the forbidden fruit to her associate Adam, who, being equally delighted and enchanted, partook thereof—and that they were thus both made sinful, whereas before, they were pure and unpolluted.

These rabbins also have conveyed the idea that God planted the garden of Eden, and made man and placed him there, and then directed him not to eat of the fruit of the tree of evil, without telling him the full consequences which would result from a participation thereof. They represented the Deity as placing before the youthful minds of the first pair an irresistible temptation, without giving them constitutional strength to resist its captivating influence. They have represented the Deity as saying, "In the day thou eatest thereof, thou shalt surely die," and represented one of the deevs of Zoroaster's infernal deity as contradicting the words of the Divine Being, saying to them, "Ye shall not surely die." Notwithstanding the promises of this evil spirit, they are represented as falling from a state of innocence to the depths of evil, from which it is supposed that the world at the present day has not experienced a resurrection. They are also represented as being driven out from the beautiful garden and from the Deity's presence, to roam uncared for throughout the wilds of an uncultivated earth. This is a comprehensive description of the contents of the Zend Avesta of Zoroaster, and does not much transcend the mythology of the first oriental and heathen tribes.

The word *diabolos** is only another name for Zoroaster's *deevs*; and *deevs* is another name for "breaths." In the English version the same is expressed by the words *darkness, death, sin, devil, Satan,* and *evil.*

It is to be deeply lamented that this simple history of the oriental mythology has been the foundation of so vast an amount of improper theological speculation. Men have not investigated the origin of the *ideas,* and their internal signification, but have descended into the foreign languages to ascertain the original application of the mere *words.* And thus the ideas of "temporal death," "moral death," and "spiritual death," have been recognised in all theological speculation growing out of that simple verse of the traditional account, which says, "Ye shall not surely die"—and its opposite declaration by the Deity.

* Devil.

By a law governing all organized substances, every particle composing these must of necessity undergo a specific change and decomposition. And when matter forms an organization in any department of Nature, that organization is supported and perpetuated by the law of association, or by a reciprocal change of particles with other substances. Therefore the particles which flow into an organization must be extracted and received from other substances, of which these particles previously formed a part. And when they enter into the new organization, they receive new life, according to that contained in the body of which they then become a part. Thus bodies or organizations are incessantly produced, sustained, developed, and perpetuated, in every department of the Universe. Therefore there is no such thing in existence as *natural death*: for an exchange of particles from one form of life to another, is nothing more than the necessary requirement of every organized substance in being. So what is called natural death, is not death, but a mere change of organization. Why have ye not analyzed the interior workings of Nature and her immutable laws, and from them learned to discard for ever all chimerical and unnatural theological speculations? Natural death has been the basis of many a controversy: but now it is made plain to a demonstration that such discussions were based on a misapprehension, and were unprofitable, because such a thing as natural death never occurred in any of the recesses of the great Universe.

I now proceed to speak of *moral* death. The idea of moral death has arisen from a superficial view of social disunity, and of disunity of thought and action. The innate *divineness* of the spirit of man prohibits the possibility of *spiritual* wickedness or unrighteousness. The desires and affections of the spirit proceed from within and from without. Desires spring from the material relation which man sustains to his brother and the Universe. These desires proceed from sensation, which creates inclination, which demands gratification. Then there is another class of desires, which are affections springing up within and directing and controlling the outer. These affections are the elements of the spirit, which desires purity and perfection. It is the principle within that illuminates the external, whenever any pure and divine thought or principle is presented for contemplation. This is the element that recognises goodness, gentleness, and purity; it is the element of love; it is the immortal principle. Its workings and effects are the morals and affections of man, and they are immortal and can not die. Morality, then, is a consequence of the unchanging divinity of the spirit, and is as undying as the immutable laws that govern all subordinate organizations. "Moral death" is therefore a manufactured expression, meaning *nothing*.

Spiritual death is only another form of the latter expression: and it never had and never can have the least particle of signification. The word *death* may be used as corresponding to the conventional idea of *darkness*, and the figure is good. But natural, moral, or spiritual darkness, is impossible: for darkness is an expression presupposing the existence of *light*. And man has not retrograded from perfection in his spiritual and natural organization toward the lowest point of imperfection; for this, again, would be an absolute impossibility. Retrogression is a word, like death, having no meaning. Everything is unfolding life and beauty, according to the law of progressive and eternal development.

Let Nature, then, be heeded as she proclaims her divine instructions, though all artificiality be sacrificed by her omnipotent authority. Love that which is lovely, and deal gently with that which has been misdirected or imperfectly developed. At the same time, love, adore, and express the truth, because Truth is a principle which unites and harmonizes an entire Universe!

---

§ 101. I now proceed to consider the origin of the ideas concerning *oracles and prophets*, as these are spoken of in the "primitive history," and understood by the theological writers of modern days.

The reasoning faculties of the early inhabitants were for many ages uncultivated, undisciplined, and undeveloped; while their powers of imagination and love of the marvellous were highly susceptible of influence, and consequently became very prolific. The products of their imaginations have afforded materials for speculation among all sacred and theological writers who have bestowed any attention on mythology. Their imaginative and conceptive powers were exceedingly susceptible to impressions from, and liable to misconstrue, all remarkable physical occurrences and manifestations within the sphere of their observation. They believed that each external appearance was either a good or bad indication, and that all such appearances were produced by the invisible yet innumerable spirits and deities which they believed to be existing. From the time the opinion became established that the "breaths" were evil spirits, they conceived that all other manifestations were ominous of evil, or indicative of good. Their imaginative powers, and the rudimental elements of their judgment, were excited and developed by all things about them; and their very perfect powers of memory enabled them to form almost any description or chimerical conception. Whatever became impressed upon their susceptible imaginations sank deeply into the recesses of their memory, and from this general source sprang all traditional mythology.

Thus, among the primitive family, as has been stated, one whose organization qualified him for the office of a governor and admonisher, conceived that the cause of the disunity and contention existing among them was the influence of the evil spirits of the "breaths." He believed that he received this information through the medium of an impressive *dream*. Believing that this was made known to him because he was better and wiser than any other, he promulgated the same to the pre-impressed minds of the people. He was at once elevated by his brethren, and was thought to be a person of superior holiness, holding intercourse with the deities.

Dreaming, then, was believed to be the medium of celestial intercourse and communication. And whoever dreamed an important dream was called upon to relate the same, and this was then interpreted by their governor. They also beheld the various objects in the vegetable and animal kingdoms either as omens of appalling catastrophes or as indications of great good. And the character of the omen was always determined by the governor, by inquiring of those who beheld the animals, in what direction they were going, in what position they were seen, what were their color, size, general appearance, &c. The flight of huge birds they believed to portend evil, and this was to be in accordance with the direction, manner, height, and distance, of their flight. So also the internal organs of animals were supposed to represent various good or evil things that would ultimately occur. Also they believed that the clouds, sun, moon, and stars, were all evident indications, and the things which they represented were decided upon by their chieftain and governor. Their reasoning faculties were not employed, and they admitted into their minds precisely that which was promulgated by their leader. Everything to them was a correspondence or representation; and by the means of correspondences and representations, they became acquainted with the thoughts and intentions of one another, and with the interpretations of their governor concerning all physical manifestations.

For many ages this mode of interpretating physical appearances continued; and it would be proper to consider this as the *age of imagination*.

After this, in various portions of the earth, men of highly-cultivated powers discovered that these things were unreal: but they could not instruct the world concerning this important discovery. And thus general ignorance continued to prevail among all the nations of the earth; and the governor and chieftain of each nation, possessing more intelligence than the rest, could exert any amount of power and influence over the people.

And at this time, kings were in the habit of having persons who professed to interpret dreams, as their counsellors; and these persons were also believed to be in communication with celestial beings, and enabled thereby to foretell events, and interpret all occurrences. This was a general custom among the eastern tribes and families; and they also still retained all the traditional impressions of early generations. The persons who claimed to be in possession of these peculiar powers were not deceiving, but were deceived, concerning the extent of their knowledge, and the reliableness of their imaginative impressions.

Each king had counsellors, who would prophesy favorably in regard to the prosperity and perpetuation of his kingdom, and the peace and happiness of his dominions. If there were strong indications of war and hostility, they would indefinitely prophesy concerning the conflict and its termination. When any of the kings dreamed, these counsellors or prophets were called to reveal the signification of his dream. And they were very indefinite in their interpretations, but sufficiently distinct to have the generals of their remarks establish in the minds of those seeking their services, the probability of soon-occurring events.

Subsequently many prophets arose among the Persians, Chinese, Chaldeans, and Egyptians, who recorded their pretended communications with the deities upon impressible substances, and these were safely preserved for the sake of their divine and celestial contents. This state of things continued for many ages, and may properly be termed the *era of oracles*.

---

§ 102. But the world at length became generally more enlightened, and more confirmed as to the unceasing manifestations of Nature. They therefore began to discard many of their original conceptions, and to exercise their reasoning faculties, which led them to a more truthful and exalted conception of the Great Spirit which created and controls the Universe. At this time some very noble and expanded minds, availing themselves of the improvements in the art of writing, reasoned profoundly, and recorded their thoughts; and their productions afford the first indication of a mental resurrection. Many Chinese, Egyptian, Persian, and Greek philosophers, conceived and promulgated pure principles of morality, and high and truthful conceptions concerning the great first and essential Cause of the Universe — and also believed and taught the doctrine of immortality. These minds were, however, trammelled by early impressions derived from their forefathers, and it was with exceeding difficulty that they unfettered their faculties and followed their natural judgments to the extent which their productions indicate.

At the same time, in other portions of the earth, persons were still existing who pretended to prophesy, and to be divinely instructed. And it was at this time that the Egyptians and other eastern tribes discovered the power and art of inducing *abnormalness*, by various gestures and manipulations. Persons who were very susceptible of being thus influenced, were selected and brought into the presence of the king's counsellors, who would affect them physically, and make them appear as if dead — inducing the sleep which they supposed was necessary in order that they might have direct intercourse with, and receive advice from, the deities. For they could not always dream when they chose: and so in order that a dream might be had whenever desired, they would throw these persons into a state corresponding to death, and receive from their lips while in that state the indefinite expression of their dreams, which would be interpreted by those counsellors or prophets, and sent forth as being true and divine. This custom continued until they discovered that they were employing these agents to no good purpose. For the visions and conceptions of the persons in that condition were unreal and unprofitable, because these persons were improperly used; and thus the power and sympathy (which were real) were made the agents of perpetual deception. Thus dreams, visions, and prophecies, were the agents and causes, in early generations, of an immense amount of disunity, deception, and wickedness.

I am impressed that some of these oriental prophecies have been immersed into, and at the present time form a part of, the Primitive History. And it is well to remark that the *urim* and *thummim* among the Egyptians was nothing more than a modified medium of obtaining knowledge of the future, and was thus a means of sustaining those whose lives and talents were spent in the occupation of prophecy.

All physical manifestations in Nature were understood by the primitive nations (according to the interpretation given them by their prophets) to be indications of future occurrences according to the pleasure or displeasure of the deities. Not understanding that light possessed the property of refraction and of resolving itself into different colors when subjected to certain conditions, they conceived that the rainbow was the expression by the Deity of a promise that the land should not again be overflown with water. So they looked upon the rainbow as an unfailing indication and everlasting promise that the race should never again be drowned.

Notwithstanding all the deeply-seated opinions concerning the truthfulness of this original conception, it is clearly demonstrated to those in possession of knowledge concerning the qualities and properties of light, that the rainbow has no signification, but is merely a meteoric phenomenon. And it is also evident that the early inhabitants, not comprehending these things, would have been very likely to account for this phenomenon, and interpret its signification, on some imaginary hypothesis. For the human mind will investigate all manifestations, and attribute every physical occurrence to some cause; and if it can not discover the *real*, it will ascribe to the phenomenon an *unreal* cause. Hence the word "*supernatural*" has had its origin. But as those original conceptions are without the least interior truth, so this word is without the least signification.

Another species of prophecy is also derived from the same source; and this is exemplified in the saying that "summer and winter, seedtime and harvest, shall never fail." In order that we may have a foresight of the future, it is necessary that we should understand the immutable laws governing Nature and all things which are *unfailing*. So in order to prophesy that summer and winter, seedtime and harvest, shall never fail, it is necessary for the mind to be perfectly familiar with the unvarying principles on which depend the vicissitudes of the seasons. This prophecy, therefore, is true and perfectly natural, being the decision of a convinced judgment that that which is now and has been from time immemorial, will be perpetuated throughout eternity.

There are several other species of prophecy, some of which are faithfully represented in the "Primitive History." Some of the authors of these were engaged in protecting kings and kingdoms from the invasions constantly expected from other nations. They would prophesy evil and discomfiture as the fate of the opposing nation, while they would stimulate their own with flattering prospects of prosperity and by promises of ultimate triumph. Others were engaged in performing various marvellous works in order to inspire confidence in the minds of kings and nations, by convincing them that they were assisted by the deities, and that they possessed unsurpassed wisdom. Others would lead families and nations on tedious and protracted expeditions, prophesying for, and governing and controlling them, until they at length, by the direction of their prophet, would fall upon other nations and tribes, and destroy or disperse them, and then make their city and home the place of their own habitation. Other prophets or chieftains would prophesy against and for kings and kingdoms, and incite war and bloodshed, all for the sake of praise and emolument. Some who were sufficiently ingenious, would only prophesy that which was within their power to fulfil and make true. Others would consign all disbelievers, or persons whose minds were too well organized to be governed by them, to the fires of that gulf of which the sun was the representative. But *sheol, hades, tartarus,* and *gehenna,* were originally used by them to express death, darkness, the grave, pain, wretchedness, and sepulchrous abodes. And as these words now stand in the Primitive History, they express merely the things to which they were applied by the Jews and Greeks, and who would represent by them a dark and loathsome valley, impassible and dreadful gulfs, the dark and gloomy grave, and darkness, death, ignorance, and wretchedness. Prophets would consign unbelieving and refractory persons to the hideous and dreadful valley of *gehenna,* and also to the pit, sepulchre, or *hades.* And some prophets continued to speak of the gulf that was conceived of and promulgated by the potentate of those southern tribes which were the origin of the Jews.

§ 103. All prophecies that are contained in the Primitive History are such as have been retained from the innumerable manuscripts of the ancient prophets, and which seemed to have a connexion with one another and with the doctrines which the Jews felt very anxious to sustain, so that the Gentiles might be entirely overcome by the influence of their preconceived mythology. More than are now contained in the Primitive History were rejected as useless and irrelevant; and this occurred before those which now form the record were collected for arrangement. And the second part of the Bible, some of which has no connexion whatever with the primitive records, is also composed of a selection of manuscripts made by the councils of bishops convened at Nice and Laodicea.

The sacred writings of each nation during the era of oracles were almost innumerable. And after the age of prophecy, selections were made from these materials by the various nations, and each nation thus formed its own sacred records. And from all of them the Jews copied extensively; and such writings as were in perfect unity with their own preconceived mythological theology, they preserved; and those that were not, were thrice rejected and consigned to the flames. Those manuscripts were without name and date, and disconnected from all circumstances indicating their origin. They were written upon the soft bark of trees, and in hieroglyphical and pictorial characters.

The Jewish rabbins are well informed concerning the origin of the Talmud; the Mohammedans are well aware of the origin of the Koran; the Brahmins know the origin of the Shaster; the Persians know the origin of the Zend Avesta: but modern theological speculators do not know of the origin of the "history" which they have defended by the pen, the stake and flame, and most powerfully and effectually by the potency of the sword.

For many centuries the Primitive History was uncondensed into its present form; and there were manuscripts collected sufficiently numerous to form a volume three times as large as the present book. Each of these was without name, but nearly all were written by different persons; and the periods at which they were written vary from six thousand to fifteen hundred years anterior to the *present* time.

The original manuscripts in possession of the Jews were written in the Greek language. In addition to these, manuscripts of other nations and writers were collected, and their contents were in like manner transcribed. And it was at this period that many portions of the Primitive History were conveyed into Persia; and they were there retained for several centuries, until the Jews were taken into captivity, at which time the latter transcribed some of them, and the remainder they brought with them when they returned to their own country. This was the period of which I have spoken, when many of the original writings, being opposed to their peculiar opinions, were rejected. And those that were saved constituted the last will and testament of the Deity as recognised by the Jewish rabbinical writers.

This collection remained unchanged for nearly one century and a half—after which a new revision occurred, which resulted in a rejection of some of the then-existing manuscripts, and also in the division of those which were retained, into books. These were subsequently divided into chapters, each book being named according to the person who was supposed to have written the manuscript. Chapters were subsequently divided into verses; but all these divisions are the work of recent date.

And in some passages in the Old Testament which seem to be prophetical, and appear to correspond to that which actually did occur, the compilers occasionally changed the tense, to make the prophecy appear more definite. Many instances might be shown in which the present tense has been changed to the past, and where the future tense is used both instead of the past and present. This may be properly termed an era of heterogeneous theology, interspersed with folly, ignorance, prejudice, and fanaticism.

The origin of oracles and prophets is, then, plainly understood. They are an effect of ignorance, and uncultivated judgment, and imagination. I have been impressed to speak *briefly* concerning them, as they are unimportant in respect to the great end which these sayings are designed to accomplish.

§ 104. But it is proper that I should speak briefly concerning the possibilities and probabilities of *truthful* prophecy.

The mode of oriental prophecy was to interpret *signs* as indications of future occurrences. But their signs seldom corresponded to the thing anticipated. The sign must always correspond to that which it is made to signify, or else it is no sign. The prophets and dreamers were in the habit of producing simple and unmeaning signs to represent great and glorious occurrences, or terrific and appalling catastrophes. Therefore their prophecies were unreal, even if the thing foretold occurred: for there was not and could not be any connexion between the occurrence and its representative. Many prophecies were apparently substantially fulfilled; —but these were particular and occasional occurrences, and did not necessarily follow the prophecies in the form of fulfilments. Things prophesied according to existing *probabilities*, did sometimes occur; but there is no evidence of the actual fulfilment of *all* those ambiguous prophecies, many of which are contained in the Primitive History. Besides this, many of their prophecies were impure and unholy, destructive to the morals and happiness of their own nation, and tended to excite hostility, envy, and sectarian vengeance, in the bosoms of those to whom their prophecies were unfavorable. They breathed forth no celestial purity and refinement, but all their deeds and expressions were blackened by sectarian fanaticism. They were not deceiving, but were deceived. They should not be condemned, but it should be regretted that they were not delivered from the bondage of sectarian corruption into the congenial atmosphere of light, reason, and happiness.

To prophesy or foretell truly an event, the person must be in communion with the original design of the Divine Creator, and with the laws which are fulfilling design. The mind, in correctly apprehending these, is enabled to foretell occurrences throughout eternity. There can be no truthful prophecy unless the laws fulfilling design are familiarly comprehended by the person prophesying. It is impossible to foretell an occurrence absolutely by the indications of any external event or circumstance. It is a thing which never has been done, and can not be done by any being in the Universe. All things that are truly foretold, occur as the result of *immutable laws*, and not of any mere fleeting and evanescent circumstances.

I am impressed to briefly appeal to the character of my own prophetical impressions as these are presented to my mind by being in communion with the interior reality and producing causes of all things. When I speak of that which shall be, I adduce no sign or external evidence in confirmation of my prediction. I present no indication in order that the prophecy may be believed by those hearing it. The reason is plain why I do not: I can not conceive of any external sign as demonstrating the thing or occurrence prophesied. For it is impossible for an external sign to be in being as corresponding to the thing foretold; and the only external indication of the truthfulness of any prophecy, must be its own actual accomplishment. Prophecies are truly made concerning the movements of the planetary system, and concerning eclipses that are to occur; but there can be no *sign* to demonstrate the occurrence of an eclipse before it actually takes place: and when it occurs, it is its own external demonstration. But the prophecy is governed by unvarying *laws;* and it is for this reason alone that it is infallibly true.

Moreover, it is impossible for any mind to be enlightened from the higher spheres concerning incidental, external circumstances; for all incidental and external circumstances are evanescent and changeable, connected with no design, produced by no interior cause, and governed by no general principles. Hence they are alike unknown to the expanded powers of mind existing in higher spheres, and to the uninformed minds of the present state of existence. To definitely foretell war, an accident, or any incidental circumstance, is positively an impossibility; for it is not in the power of any *internal* and general principle to foreshadow to the mind a merely incidental circumstance. It is upon *interior principles* alone that a prophecy can be made with an absolute certainty of its accomplishment; and therefore if it were possible for these to foreshadow external and incidental circumstances, then prophecy concerning such might be relied upon. But as this is not in the nature of general principles, and is beyond the power of individual influence, it is impossible for any being, either in this or higher spheres, to proclaim the particular circumstances of an event, with the *absolute* certainty of their occurrence.

I am not impressed to speak concerning the innumerable volumes that have been written on this subject; because these have sprung from an understanding of the prophecies contained in the Primitive History still more superficial than the character of the prophecies themselves.

§ 105. Before I speak concerning many true prophets and truthful prophecies, I will briefly appeal to the truths unfolded in the Key, concerning immutable laws and their effects as the unvarying manifestations of Nature and the Universe — and also concerning the *artificial* causes which are continually producing unreal effects, which latter are the fleeting and evanescent circumstances connected with social and physical existence.

By immutable laws, I mean that universal tendency of all things, which can not by any possible means be interrupted, changed, or frustrated.

The process by which man may become acquainted with these laws, is by analyzing external, physical manifestations, and discovering their interior cause and governing principle. It has been established that external and visible effects can not be depended upon as indicating their own *interior* cause; but that to become acquainted with the cause, the effect or form must be *analyzed*. By becoming acquainted with the interior and moving principles of Nature, we become acquainted with the elements of the Divine Mind, and also with the universal designs of the latter. These designs are the effects and developments constantly manifested throughout Nature.

By becoming acquainted with the cause, we become correspondingly familiar with the effect; and if it is upon *laws* that the mind rests, effects and external manifestations may be prophesied with the utmost certainty, millions of years in advance. For laws and principles are the producing *causes* of all effects; and all physical effects, developments, and manifestations, are the real and inevitable consequences of the interior, divine, and creative Cause. Thus, in the beginning, a Cause produced an Effect, which became the cause of another; and so cause and effect became universal and eternal, according to the promptings of the interior or divine Cause, which will produce one general, external, celestial Effect. I have been impressed to speak thus much on this point, so that theologians may know the only basis upon which rests all truthful and infallible prophecy.

Many conditions which surrounded the first types of mankind were unfavorable to the proper unfolding of their mental faculties. The consequence was, an improper tendency of those faculties and inclinations which otherwise would have been perfect and righteous in their operations. From this youthful tenderness sprang all the gross and imaginative impressions which are at the present day clothing the minds of mankind with a most unreal and unfortunate garment. The first misdirection sprang from unfavorable conditions, and was connected with no law, design, or principle, which governs the Universe.

Therefore those things which I term unreal and superficial are circumstances which are created by prior and corresponding conditions, such as are within the power of mankind to produce, control, and annihilate. If superficial effects and circumstances such as mark the incidental movements of society and the vicissitudes of government, or if any other exterior, obtrusive circumstances that have produced so much poverty and wretchedness in the world, were the results of Law, Design, and established Principles — then the world of mankind would for ever be in bondage, because these deleterious influences would be beyond the possibility of human control. But the truth is, *Man* has created these circumstances, and he has the power to remove them. Therefore, as these circumstances happen only as thousands of contingencies conduce to their development, it is positively impossible to foretell them with an absolute certainty of their fulfilment.

What I mean by *circumstances*, then, are those contingent occurrences which are entirely disconnected from Design or Law, being created and developed by man. And what I mean by external physical manifestations are the unvarying effects and consequences of an *interior* divine and unchangeable Cause.

Many of the early prophets did pretend to foretell wars, famines, and pestilences, and would produce simple signs, which they taught corresponded to and foreshadowed the occurrence prophesied. Others would in the same manner foretell the destruction of cities and downfall of nations, and speak of many things that were to occur in future, and that would conduce to the advancement and emolument of themselves and of those for whom they prophesied. Many of these prophecies are contained in the Primitive History. Some of them were fulfilled; but this affords no evidence of the divine instruction of their authors: for all external circumstances, which are dependent upon favorable contingencies, are entirely beyond the reach of all prophetical minds or divinely-instructed persons, because these things are not *destined*, but flow from the corrupted and evanescent tendencies of human society and of physical existence. Therefore I am deeply impressed with the truthfulness of the proposition, that it is absolutely impossible for any being, either in this or any higher sphere, to be instructed concerning evanescent contingencies, so as to foretell their occurrence with certainty.

§ 106. The object of making these things plain, is to establish the probability of truthful prophecy, and to defend the Primitive History against the many false and imaginative interpretations that have been imposed upon it. The latter gives a very simple and concise account of the prophecies of men who lived antecedent to its compilation, but many of these made no pretensions to prophecy beyond the limits of their own era. Another object in making these things plain, is to establish a division between real and unreal prophecy. For there are prophecies contained in the Primitive History that are true, divine, and righteous; and those who prophesied thus were instructed concerning the interior workings and tendencies of Nature, and proclaimed, upon the unchanging principles of cause and effect, many grand and holy truths—occurrences which will transpire—effects that will be accomplished. These men had their internal, thinking principles so expanded that they were able to recognise the interior workings of all divine law, and thus could with certainty proclaim great and glorious truths. Some of the teachings of these men have been, by modern commentators and theologians, most unrighteously misrepresented. For the latter, being misdirected in their religious education, have not been able to discover the real, simple, and unadulterated truths which are contained in many of the prophecies gracing the pages of the Primitive History.

But these prophecies have been misplaced and imperfectly apprehended; while among them are interspersed many unholy sayings, and records of many unrighteous deeds that transpired among the early inhabitants of the earth. There are very many interpolations, though these were not introduced with any evil intentions, but because the compilers seriously supposed that those additions should be made in order that the whole history might present a connected and comprehensive account of the things to which it contained allusions.

Another object in making this clear is that the mind may thus be freed from unnatural affection and sectarian prejudice (which is the first necessary step toward a reorganization of society and the world), and be inspired with the love of truth and truth only.

This, then, it is well to understand: that many local prophecies which are to be found in the Primitive History concerning circumstances some of which were fulfilled, do not necessarily afford any evidence of the celestial instruction of their authors, or of their superior theology. And inasmuch as they are external and superficial, they should be disregarded by those who are pressing forward to the attainment of a higher order of things. And it is well to understand, also, that many prophecies of this nature which are true, have their own proof, and further than that they are positively useless.

Then, on the other hand, it is well to remark that those prophecies which are founded upon the principles of Nature, and will be fulfilled, should be regarded as substantial evidence of an enlightened judgment and lofty spirituality on the part of their authors, and these should be admired and appreciated. And it is proper that these prophecies should be proclaimed to the world: but only as mankind are brought to a comprehension of the causes to bring about the event predicted, and as they are disposed to put forth powerful exertions for its accomplishment.

When those noble and enlightened intellects proclaimed that " an end shall be made of sin and transgression, and everlasting righteousness shall be brought in," they were inspired with the grand and brilliant truth of a universal resurrection from all immorality and from all unnatural social conditions. And that mind which foresaw that " death would be destroyed, and he that hath power over death, which is the evil," was inspired with a high and truthful conviction, of the truth of which Nature everywhere contributes evidence. And that mind also conceived that this mortal and evanescent corruption which mars the happiness and peace of society, would be exchanged for the genuine principles of Nature, and that mankind would thus be made incorruptible. He also saw that there would be a time when those corrupting and vitiating influences that shroud the whole mental and social world, would be done away, and when society and the world would be clothed with happiness and immortality.

And these things were proclaimed by all the pure and inspired prophets since the world of social disunity began — even the final restitution of all intelligent beings to primitive innocence and universal harmony. And they plainly saw that when this occurred, there would be no more sorrow nor pain, for the old and corrupted things that destroyed the peace of society would have passed away, and all things would have become new. And they saw that this great renovation would constitute "a new heaven and a new earth, wherein would dwell righteousness." They saw the evils of society — the immoral and corrupt situations of mankind — and proclaimed, according to the unchangeable law of progressive development, that evil would ultimately be banished from the earth, that the " sun of righteousness would rise with healing in his wings," and that goodness and brotherly kindness would reign universally. These minds associated with the interior of all things, and received divine impressions of eternal truths. They spoke not of higher spheres, because the world was not yet sufficiently enlightened to receive the truth concerning these. But they spake concerning present evil and mortality, and concerning future goodness and the permanent restitution of the whole race to peace and harmony.

They foresaw that a great Exemplifier of the true moral and spiritual qualities of man would ultimately appear. They saw that he would, because of his superior qualifications, manifest all that purity and gentleness of disposition, and all that loving kindness and consociality, that would be to the world a type of social harmony and spiritual perfection. They saw that he would possess all the natural abilities and superior endowments to which the whole race would ultimately progress. They saw that in him would be *developed* all that high moral purity and spirituality which every human being possesses *undeveloped*. He was to be a simple type of spiritual goodness and perfect social qualification. This they proclaimed to the world, because they were impressed thus to do by the teachings of their internal principles which communed with the *divine* Principles that sustain and control the Universe, and which emanate from the inexpressible Vortex of celestial Love and Wisdom.

These prophecies show that their authors had a truthful knowledge of the Principles of Nature, and of the divine Design which those principles are constantly manifesting. They prove that their minds were maturely developed, and were fit receptacles for the influx of wisdom and knowledge.

It was thus that they foresaw that which has been fulfilled, and that which shall be in future. And their prophecies are susceptible of demonstration, because they are based upon those unerring laws that must of necessity ultimate in the effects predicted. They saw (what was spoken of in the Key) that Truth is a positive principle, and that Error is negative and superficial; and they saw that that which is positive and eternal must transcend and subdue that which is merely fleeting and superficial.

§ 107. I now proceed to consider another idea in the series, which is concerning the birth and use of that being who was the highest personification of virtue, purity, and goodness. But before I proceed to speak of the prophecies and accounts concerning this noble personage which are given in the Primitive History, I will introductively insert some highly-important reflections concerning the divine origin of Truth, and its unchangeableness and omnipotence.

It must be distinctly evident to every mind that man did not create himself, nor the vegetable and animal kingdoms: and also that he did not plan and execute the creation of the earth or solar system. Nor was he in any way connected with the production, and the establishment of the harmony, of the Universe. Nor is he engaged in developing any new divine Principle, or unfolding from the Vortex of the Divine Mind, laws or principles which never before existed.

Moreover, he can not, with all his pride and presumption, annihilate or change one feature or quality of a single particle that enters into the composition of an harmonious Universe. Nor is he competent to alter Truth by reposing confidence in its opposite. And while he is capable of believing or disbelieving, and exercising an affection for, pre-impressions and all ideas which he considers truth, Truth itself remains the same, and is not affected, either favorably or unfavorably, by the fleeting opinions of Man.

Truth is an element of the Divine Mind, and is developed by the wisdom, uniformity, and harmony, which characterize and render perfect all that is created. It is therefore of divine and celestial origin, and is made manifest to the mind of man by the manifold expression of Nature and the Universe. Being an internal and controlling element, it pervades alike every department of the Univercœlum. It is therefore a necessary and unchangeable Principle, and hence also is ETERNAL. And while all created forms dwell in unity and harmony as arranged in their respective spheres of existence; while all rudimental productions are continually breathed forth and perpetuated by Nature and her laws; and while all the celestial spheres and systems of life, beauty, and perfection, continue to manifest and develop the same order and harmony, Truth will continue to proclaim her divine and eternal omnipotence. When all things that are created are restored to unity and stand in their proper and reciprocal relations, then may man perceive the full manifestation of that Truth which emanates from the celestial Vortex of Love and Wisdom.

Thus Truth is divine in its origin, eternal and unchangeable in its nature, and omnipotent in its constitution.

The early inhabitants of the earth conceived that they lived upon a flattened sphere, sustained by as many huge living monsters as imagination could well conceive. They endeavored to comprehend, as the human mind is wont to do, the causes of things manifested. So they formed these chimerical conceptions; for they were not enlightened sufficiently to comprehend the truth, or to understand the principles upon which they and the Universe existed. So it became a universal belief that the earth was entirely motionless, not only because all external evidences seemed to demonstrate that conclusion, but because they could not believe that such a sphere could possibly revolve, and still remain in the same position, sustained by *nothing*.

Many writers of the books of the Primitive History believed this conception most sincerely, and occasionally imbodied it, in poetical descriptions, in their sacred compositions. It was an opinion that was not for a moment doubted, until a Grecian and an Egyptian philosopher expressed their conviction publicly that the earth revolved. This opinion gained many advocates; but they were few in comparison to those who sacredly believed in all the traditions of their forefathers.

So the same impression continued to prevail almost universally for many generations, until a well-known philosopher of modern times discovered those interior moving principles which were to his mind an incontestable demonstration that the earth and all kindred bodies revolved unceasingly in harmony around the sun, their parent. He thus *discovered* the truth; *but that truth had existed the same from all eternity!*

The nations of the earth opposed him; for they had sacred oracles and prophets who taught a different doctrine. All the ecclesiastics and potentates of the land, incited by an unreal and superficial abhorrence of his heresy, opposed his efforts, and came near consigning him to the flames. These men were believing what they supposed to be sacred truth, and felt that as truth sustained them, they should in return sustain truth. This false impression clothed their minds with a fanatical hostility against all new theories and discoveries, which might in any way attract the attention of mankind from those things which they were so firmly defending.

It is well to remark that the earth revolved before any being believed it, and that a discovery of the fact did not make it any more true. The *information*, however, was profitable, inasmuch as a knowledge of Nature and her laws inspires in the enlightened understanding confidence in the Universe and her Creator. At the present time, the modes and habits of thinking among mankind are changed in many particulars and upon various important subjects; but the *people* in general have improved in their intellectual attainments very little beyond those who opposed the promulgation of the new astronomical discoveries.

Then while I am impressed to speak of the Primitive History with caution and gentleness, I am also impressed that it deserves no more veneration than do the teachings of many other good minds that have lived and written. And while I discover interior and immortal truth in many of the expressions, precepts, and examples, therein recorded, I am impressed that they should be loved and admired for their *reality* and *usefulness*— not merely because this truth is found in those written or printed pages, but because it IS Truth, and always WAS, and always WILL BE.

§ 108. The reason why I am impressed to speak concerning this " history" particularly, is, that there have arisen from its existence in the world, huge monuments of ignorance, superstition, and misapprehension. For this reason I have shown that some of its parts are compendiums of oriental mythology — Jewish, Egyptian, and Persianic poetry — and of the productions of the brilliant imaginations of minds uninformed. There are many noble and enlightened persons represented in those written pages, whose powers of thought and capabilities of imagination justly demand the deepest esteem and admiration. Many allegorical and symbolical representations therein contained are exceedingly beautiful, and are capable of being interpreted in a most brilliant and magnificent manner. But the world clothes this history with more divinity than *it itself* claims, and thus shrouds the whole in a garment of gloom and impenetrable mysticism, which does violence to the judgment, and distorts the faculties of the mind from their natural condition and mode of action.

When good and enlightened men put forth their thoughts to the world, and when their noble works appeal to mankind for respect and approbation, a due distinction should be made between these and the unrighteous. But men should love only that which they are compelled to love from the force of truth, and repulse that which is repulsive and uncongenial to their nature and mental susceptibilities. The Primitive History makes us acquainted with some of the former class of men and teachings : and these should be admired according to that which is intrinsically worthy of approbation.

But good men and deeds should be as much beloved *out* of those pages as *in* them. And no distinction of a superficial character should be established between any members, classes, or nations, of the human family. Therefore, for those writers to be respected more than is allowable according to the universal principles that govern Nature and Man, would be to violate the plainest laws of equity, and to forsake the divine principles of harmony for that which is disunited, unreal, and confused.

While I am in a situation to recognise the causes of things, I can not let that escape notice which is sowing the seeds of disunity and corruption throughout the world. And when I investigate the origin of allegorical and mythological theology, I am compelled to speak of the same in a style agreeing with the nature of my impressions. And while I am conscious that the feelings, affections, and judgments of men, are deeply involved in this subject, and that for this book men exercise love and admiration as if it were far more true than the very Elements and Body of the Divine Mind, I am nevertheless constrained to speak seriously and unreservedly concerning the truth or falsity of many parts of the same. Yet notwithstanding these affections for erroneous principles are created only by early impressions, it is proper that they should be gently appealed to, so that the judgment may be brought to recognise the important truth that if all those prophecies and sayings are divine and eternal, they will remain unchanged, and be perpetuated through all generations; while all invasive theories and hypotheses will be destroyed to be known no more.

Let what I am impressed to state, then, be received as true or rejected as false, according to its appeals to your judgments. And if what I relate is *not* true, it will not injure that which *is* truth. Be not afraid, then, that truth will suffer from these investigations, but repose confidence in its immortality and omnipotence, and be assured of the weakness and evanescence of error. Be cautious, however, in your decisions, and do not receive that which does not address your affections and judgment in the voice of reason, and which does not receive spontaneous approbation from your interior principles.

If the Primitive History is an Oracle of Truth, no assistance from man can render it more so. Fear not, then, that truth may suffer from the invasions of error and unrighteousness. Those who are strenuous to defend the sayings contained in that book are persons who have an affection for early impressions, more than they have for progressive discoveries in the unexplored labyrinths of wisdom and righteousness. Such as are apprehensive concerning the results of a strict investigation, not only of this subject, but of many others, and are not seeking to know what truth is, but are merely anxious to have their present convictions prevail.

In view of these considerations, I find it proper to enforce the necessity of investigating all things, without entertaining the least doubt as to the incorruptibility and immortality of truth. And it is proper to forsake all *denunciation;* though it may be that the world will oppose the truth now presented with the same ungrounded hostility and prejudice as was manifested by those who opposed the distinguished and venerable astronomical philosopher. But remember that the earth continued to revolve, though the fact was wholly disbelieved by mankind. Remember also that truth will always continue to live, whether believed or disbelieved, either by the educated or uneducated classes of mankind. And let those who tremble for the truth, whether this be such as is supposed to exist in the Primitive History, or in any other department of the Universe, arrest their agitation and excitement for one moment, and behold their own folly and imbecility — while Truth itself illuminates its features with a smile of undying beauty! Let Nature, the Universe, and the Divine Mind, then, be the source of your instruction. But if you desire to behold examples of human weakness, read this History's commentators.

Search, explore, and discover truth, then, and place your affections upon it, because it is an element of Divine Wisdom. Place not your affections upon that which judgment disapproves, or against which your spiritual sensibilities revolt. Believe not a truth because it was believed and taught before you lived, but because it *is* truth, leading the mind onward and upward to higher spheres of grandeur and beauty. Remember that the mind in its true state is free to think and act — free from all sectarian bondage and superstition. Meanwhile consider that the mind does not now act freely, or express its serious convictions, because it has fettered itself, and seems to have no desire to become untrammelled.

Mythology has resulted from prior ignorance and misconception; and superstition, sectarian affection, and prejudice, have arisen out of mythology. All these have affected the uninformed minds of generations past, and are inherited by millions of the freeborn minds of the present era. Hence your strenuous adherence to early impressions; to what your parents have taught; to the sectarian interpretation of the Primitive History; and to sanctimonious and unmeaning ceremonies all of which have been, and are at the present time, establishing walls of distinction between husband and wife, parent and children, brothers and sisters, nation and nation, and Nature and theology, and destroying the happiness of mankind. And these effects afford living evidence to the enlightened understanding that whatever system has caused them is not divine — is not born of Nature or of her Creator, and is consequently injurious and positively unrighteous. Learn from these things, then, to modify your early affections, so that reason may bring forth good and truthful sentiments, and that you may be rendered suitable receptacles of the spontaneous breathings of the Divine Mind, which is Love and Wisdom, and is incessantly evolving the Omnipotent Principle of Eternal Truth.

These reflections are presented as an appeal to your interior affections, and more especially to that divine principle, REASON, which constitutes the interior nature of every man.

---

§ 109. I now proceed to communicate my impressions concerning the prophecies and opinions relating to that lovely personage who existed upon the earth, and whose history is so imperfectly and unrighteously related by many writers. His birth and life have been clothed with many unjust descriptions — unjust because they are not true. The writers spoke as men speak at the present day, from early-imbibed convictions. Many accounts that are given of him are interspersed with plain contradictions of the fundamental principles of Nature. It is well to elucidate the *origin* of these many accounts before I proceed to consider specifically the superior purity and majestic greatness of him who came to enlighten the world.

In order that we may properly understand the origin of many doctrines relating to this subject that have been derived from the teachings of men called prophets, it is necessary to institute some considerations concerning the five books ascribed to Moses, and also concerning other writings that have a connexion with the subject.

The first book, called GENESIS, was not written by Moses, but the first part of it consists of traditional allegories of primitive ages, and which existed in the world before Moses lived. The description of the formation of the world, of the creation of Adam, of the garden of Eden, and the tree of knowledge, are figures that were used by the previous eastern nations. This book bears external evidence of its own origin.

But theologians have supposed that Moses must have been instructed in the knowledge of these things many ages after they transpired. Some have supposed that the earth is no older than is indicated by the chronology of the Primitive History. They also have believed, and have endeavored to prove, that the allegories recorded in the book of Genesis were actual, literal truths. It is well to bear this in mind; for on this supposition all Christian writers have based their interpretations of accounts in Genesis as relating to the birth, life, and office of JESUS, the great Moral Reformer. They have thus endeavored to form a connexion between the fall of man in the garden of Eden, as related in Genesis, with a restitution which they suppose was to be accomplished by the ultimate triumph of the divine principles taught by Jesus of Nazareth.

It is distinctly evident that this idea could not have been entertained by those who wrote the books of either of the Testaments. The apostles, in giving an account of the birth, life, and preaching of Jesus, did not, in all their writings, even once intimate any such idea. They do not speak of the original purity of man, and of his fall, in connexion with the use of the birth, life, and preaching, of the one they so much loved. They do not even intimate that Jesus was a means by which the race would be restored to any degree of refinement which they *once* possessed. They say nothing of the garden of Eden, of the fall of man, nor of any of the allegorical sayings contained in the book of Genesis. Those who wrote concerning Jesus must have known the object of his birth and preaching, and therefore if the "plan of redemption" manufactured by theologians represents the truth, it would have been mentioned by them as one of the first and most important points to be understood when speaking of the birth and life of him who labored for a moral resurrection.

It is clear, from many expressions in Genesis, that this book could not have originated with Moses. But it was written by a man who sacredly compiled the traditional mythology of the forefathers. I am perfectly convinced, from the nature of my impressions, that the other books which are ascribed to Moses were in reality written by him. The history as contained in those four books is generally very true; and for their truthfulness the books should be esteemed and appreciated.

An account is given of the birth of Moses, or rather of the circumstances of his infancy. This account, whether true or untrue, has no possible bearing on the general history contained in these books. It appears that the romantic account of his birth, and of his singular position in early life, is true. And the fact of his being discovered in that novel situation excited among the inhabitants of the land a great deal of astonishment; and as the account thereof was related in a marvellous manner by those who discovered him, he soon became a distinguished youth: and the marvellous things that were told of him were believed and improved upon by many tribes of the east, including the Egyptians. He thus became notorious among all, and he was consequently inclined to endeavor to sustain the general impression which prevailed concerning his superior abilities. He was thus led to form a studious habit, which unfolded and greatly improved his mind. It was for him, indeed, a happy circumstance that those marvellous things were connected with his birth; for as all believed he was destined for some high and sacred office, he had no desire to forfeit the regards bestowed upon him on that account, and he was also led finally to believe as much as others, the idea of his high destiny. So these things operated upon his self-love, and he consequently pressed forward to the attainment of wisdom and knowledge, transcending, if possible, that of any other man living in those times.

It is well to remark that the expression was in those times almost universally prevalent among the eastern nations, that "the Lord directed"—"the Lord spake," &c., and that they employed this phrase to express the evolution of a thought. The early inhabitants believed that the "breaths" created their thoughts; and so they would say that the "breaths" taught them to do thus or so, to accomplish this or that, or to undertake a journey—all of which promptings they implicitly obeyed if they were distinct and forcible. This expression was modified by the subsequent generations into many forms, until it became a cant phrase; and owing to the commonness of its usage, it became abundantly dispersed throughout the sacred writings. The early inhabitants of the earth, and indeed the nations existing upon the earth for many hundred years after, could not possibly conceive how thoughts could exist within them without an influx of some exterior but invisible spirit. The phenomenon of thought led them into more imaginative speculations than any other thing which attracted their attention. So also it became a universal expression among the prophetical writers, that the Lord spake unto them—constructed plans—instituted questions—suggested signs, &c.: for these they supposed came by direct influx from the thoughts of the Divine Mind. The conception of the invisible origin of thoughts was a natural result of the uninformed state of their minds concerning the causes of mental phenomena. They used the term "Lord" in the same sense as I use the term "impression;" for their thoughts were caused by associations with similar truths to those with which I associate. So if, instead of using the expression "the Lord spake," they had said, "I am impressed with such or such a thought," then would theologians of the present day have comprehended the mystery.

Moses, ascending to manhood with a healthy and athletic constitution, and in possession of many superior intellectual endowments, soon began to teach learnedly, attributing his impressions to the influence of the Lord's invisible spirit, in accordance with the general conviction of those times. This, in fact, was the first opinion that was enstamped upon his mind in youth; and in manhood the same became fully developed. Notwithstanding this error, he was far more intellectual than almost any other person at those times.

§ 110. It is unnecessary for me to enter into details concerning his long and protracted expedition at the head of the Israelites, or to consider particularly the accounts given of his many miraculous performances. But my main object is to notice some theological opinions that have been derived from his writings.

Whether he was designed to be a leader and governor of the Israelites, is a question that should not excite discussion, as it neither involves any important truth nor any principle of useful application. But there are many erroneous impressions received from the miracles which he is said to have accomplished while journeying with the Israelites. The account of his passing with the hosts of Israel through the Red sea on dry land, is very truthful. But what is said concerning the *causes* which produced the separation of the waters, is entirely figurative, only expressing an external form of procedure which Moses observed in praise to the Origin of the impressions which led him onward, believing as he did that the Lord was the suggester. The passage of the Red sea on dry land, the waters being upon each side, was not only effected by the Israelites under Moses, but was accomplished *before*, and has been *since* Moses lived.* For at that time the water had merely receded from the elevated portion of the sea-bottom over which they crossed: for when the tide ebbed, this place, being a sandbar, was left dry, like a beach, and therefore it was possible to effect a safe passage across.

It was a custom to wave a rod over, or to kiss, or to smite anything from which assistance was desired. These formalities were also intended to express obligation and gratitude. The account in-

---

* The author here remarked to those present when this was delivered, that he perceived that this passage of the Red sea had been effected in the same manner as it was by the Israelites, by one of the five kings, accompanied by his army, spoken of in the fourteenth chapter of Genesis. He also stated that *Bonaparte*, in a similar manner and at the same place, crossed the dry bottom of the sea on the recession of the tide. Since that period, however, the sea-bottom at the same locality had materially altered by the shifting of the sand.

dicates nothing more than this; as the rod was waved, and the waters were smitten with the garment, because the beach was dry so that they could pass over in safety.

The account of their being followed by Pharaoh and his hosts is also true, as is likewise that of the destruction of his army: for in attempting to cross, they were, because of their numbers, very much impeded; and when they were nearly all upon the passage, the tide returned, and they were drowned. Moses ascribes this deliverance from their enemy to a direct interposition of the Divine Mind; and so the event has been considered by many theological writers.

Other remarkable things are also related, such as obtaining water by the smiting of a rock; the rod being changed into several forms; their being fed by manna which fell from above; and also many other things of like marvellous nature. Whether any of these accounts are true or untrue, is a question which should not engage the time and talents of mankind, inasmuch as a solution of this question would not produce the least possible good toward promoting a physical and moral renovation of the human race.

Moses also speaks of receiving some divine commandments while upon Mount Sinai, and of receiving instructions from the Lord from a dark and immoveable cloud. He relates that a voice came out of the cloud to him while on the mount, which spake those stern commandments which were to constitute the law to govern the Israelites. There are many very beautiful figures and allegorical representations that have been suggested by the account of this very novel and mysterious interview; but it is my object at the present time to speak concerning the origin of this account, which in its *general* features is substantially true.

Moses, after having been with the Israelites for many years, and finding that many of them were exceedingly desirous of changing their situation and government, conceived it proper that they should have some specific and rigid laws. Finding it impossible to inspire their minds with any real and substantial moral principles, he conceived it proper to obtain by some means a code by which they might be governed, derived from a source not known to them. For as they were fanatical and superstitious, he could not instruct them as he desired; for they were believing every species of phantasy—and in these they reposed more confidence than they subsequently at times reposed in their leader himself.

Moses, in view of these things, felt that he was divinely impressed to leave the people for a time, and find some solitary and sequestered place in the mount that was near them, where he might listen to the influx from the Divine Being, of such principles as would form a law to those he was leading. He obeyed the suggestion, and repaired to the mount in silence. In ascending he would occasionally arrest his steps, and meditate upon the proper requirements of those whom he saw spread over the plains below; and before he arrived at the top of the mountain, many important thoughts were suggested to his mind by the impressiveness of the scene that lay before him. So he sat down and was absorbed in contemplation for many hours, at the end of which time the ten commandments were framed in his mind, and he wrote them upon stones such as could be conveyed to the valley below, and such as were easily impressible. At the time he began to write, a *cloud* was seen on the mount, which moved not, because of the stillness of the atmosphere, until he completed the ten commandments. Believing from youth that thoughts were caused by an influx from invisible, celestial beings, he supposed that at this time all these suggestions proceeded from the Lord, who was clothed with the cloud. He accordingly wrote his opinion concerning the whole divine instruction, and concerning the means by which he obtained the commandments. Moses, being more enlightened than any other person, was capable of conceiving and forming those commandments, from the knowledge he had of the wants of those whom he governed.

Some theological writers conceive that these commandments must have divinely originated; and in support of this opinion, they say that had these laws, which are of the very highest morality, been instituted by Moses alone, or forged in those books by any other writer, they would not have been so just or so severe: because if they had been composed by man, they would have consisted of the easy rules that man's inclinations always invent for his own government. This reasoning is not conclusive. For it is well known that nations often create laws that are severely binding and compulsory, and that the Hindoo tribes have codes and legal requirements eminently more severe than those instituted by Moses.

It was the prevailing policy of the nations, before Moses lived, to have the most severe and stringent laws, the violation of which was punished with death as a sacrifice to the gods, whom they supposed to be their lawgivers. Moses also imbibed hereditarily the opinion that these arbitrary forms of government were necessary; and his was the most judicious and appropriate code of laws that ever was framed by any governor in those times. So the account which Moses has written is truthful, and it is written precisely according to his belief. It was the very best code of moral and social laws that could possibly have been invented under the existing circumstances of those times, and the potency of those commandments has been exemplified in all subsequent ages.

§ 111. Many writers have supposed that the law of Moses was instituted to govern the world until the great Moral Reformer should make his appearance. This opinion is in one sense true — though the two systems of moral government are not so intimately connected as many are led to believe. I do not perceive that it was the intention of the Divine Mind to call into being a purer spirit for the purpose of doing away with the old law, and to establish the new. Instead of this, it was by the progress of refinement and intellectual attainment that the new reformation was determined. It would have been unnecessary to have higher or more refined principles to govern the Israelites than those instituted by Moses; because if his commandments had been mild, gentle, and highly refined, the gross and imperfectly-developed intellects of those times would have disregarded their teachings: and disunity and disorganization would have been the consequence. But the principle requiring "an eye for an eye, and a tooth for a tooth," they could readily apprehend, and could obey its requirements without misunderstanding its meaning; and this was a high moral law compared to that by which they had previously been governed. So this was one more step in the progress of intellectual development, and was an improvement in the mode of government which before that period was grossly imperfect.

The law of Moses, therefore, has no real connexion with any theological system, except so far as it indicates a steady moral, intellectual, and social progression in the condition of man. I can not conceive of any other use that it has accomplished besides that it has served as a curved line to lead past generations to more truthful and righteous government; and it should even now be to the world a lesson of instruction. It is merely a chart in which are represented various courses of social policy, some of which led to evil and others to good results — all of which have been pursued, and should not be again. Therefore the writings of Moses are useful to the world at the present day: yet only as a means of enlightening the uninformed, and preventing improper adventures in the establishment of arbitrary moral laws and government.

The ancients were in the habit of understanding all things by correspondences and allegories; and in relating accounts of things and occurrences, they would often speak as if their correspondents and allegorical representatives were themselves true. This custom is evidently observed by the writers of the Primitive History, and particularly by the writer of the book of Genesis; for the writings of the Old Testament are much characterized by allegorical and highly-figurative descriptions, the figures being related as though they themselves were true, instead of being said to represent things according to the intention of their writers.

This, then, is my impression concerning Moses: that being discovered as he was among the rushes; being believed by all to be destined to some high office, and growing up in the knowledge of these things, in order to make good the opinions that were entertained of him, and which he himself believed, he obtained great intellectual acquirements. His natural faculties being thus developed, he was capable of conceiving more truths than others, and thus became the chieftain and governor of the tribes of Abraham. These he led out of Egypt, crossing the pass of the Red sea into the wilderness, where one generation passed away; and the subsequent generation, imbibing all the opinions of their fathers, became fanatical and enthusiastic. Moses being inspired with more brilliant and truthful thoughts than others, owing to his natural capabilities, produced the law and ten commandments, supposing that he was assisted by a divine influx. He was also capable of foretelling some occurrences (which capacity was surprising to his brethren), because he was sufficiently enlightened to infer the same with accuracy, from the tendencies of existing circumstances. He also received information from his assistant JOSHUA, on whom he would, by manipulations, produce *abnormalness*, so that he might dream and relate his visions.

In general, Moses's prophecies were true, and he did that which he seriously felt to be his duty; although many of his wars, persecutions, and invasions, are repulsive to the more refined feelings of an enlightened mind. He wrote the four books in a language suited to the customs of that age, and intended no forgery or imposition, but believed he was inspired with divine teachings emanating from the fire, smoke, and thunder, on Mount Sinai. And for his historical and prophetical relations, he should be approved, admired, and appreciated, because they are substantially true. But further than this, his writings are disconnected from any theological system that has been subsequently invented. Therefore he who would be wise, should free his mind, if possible, from all theological systems that have been founded upon a basis thus absolutely unallowable.

These writings, then, so far, have no use in common with the birth and teachings of the Great Reformer, of whom I shall hereafter speak.

Moses used the forms of expression and the singular modes of allegorical representation which were customary among the Egyptians and other eastern tribes. And what should be particularly remarked is, that this custom was to relate the allegory in such a manner as to convey the impression that that itself was the thing signified. He also, as was the case with other writers, was accustomed to use the *third person*, which would naturally convey the impression that it was not Moses who wrote, but some other person. Also there are many instances in the book of Deuteronomy where the pronoun, first person singular, has been stricken out by compilers, and the third person singular inserted in its stead. Also, the present tense has in some instances been changed to the future; and so from the present English version it is impossible, according to our grammatical rules, to decide whether Moses was the writer, or whether the books were originally anonymous, and subsequently named.

I find upon investigation that the last chapter of Deuteronomy was written by another person, who intended to relate the traditions concerning Moses's discovery of the promised land, his divine instructions, and his death and burial. The generals of this account are strictly true, and need no qualification.

AARON, who was a contemporary and assistant of Moses, was, according to the relation given, nearly as useful a functionary as Moses himself, in leading and governing the children of Israel. But the account given of Moses, as written by himself, displays more magnanimity than was possessed by any other person then living; and he was declared to be the greatest prophet that ever arose in Israel, and that the Lord knew him face to face. (Deut. xxxiv. 10.) Notwithstanding this is an exaggerated description of his powers of mental conception, and susceptibility of internal prompting, he *was* the most enlightened person then existing, either among the Egyptians or Israelites.

So Moses led the children of Israel through innumerable vicissitudes and deep afflictions, until they came near to the land of their contemplated future abode. But before he realized all of his prophetical anticipations, he ceased to live ; and Joshua, who was prequalified, advanced to his position as prophet and governor.

§ 112. JOSHUA was naturally well constituted, both physically and spiritually ; and his mind was rendered the more fertile and susceptible of correct instruction by his being influenced by the manipulation of Moses. This, I find, is clearly expressed in the last chapter of Deuteronomy, and ninth verse, which speaks of Joshua, the son of Nun, as being " full of the spirit of wisdom, because Moses had laid his hands upon him." He was therefore rendered capable of discharging the duties of his new station with as much exactness and promptitude as characterized the proceedings of his predecessor. So Joshua now became the chieftain and governor of that expedition.

An account is given concerning the attacks made upon the inhabitants of the promised land, and how the Israelites felt convinced that as the Lord sustained them and their movements, they would be eminently successful. Actuated by this unholy belief, they fought desperately, and apparently at the sacrifice of all natural sensibilities, brotherly kindness, and affection. This spirit characterized their movements while with Moses, and was still persisted in under the sanction and jurisdiction of Joshua.

The object of referring to this account is, to exhibit to a class of men who are supposed to be true theologians, the absurd and destructive tendency of that doctrine which supposes that these bloody and inhuman invasions were sanctioned by that Divine Intelligence which knows no thought contrary to the indestructible indications of Nature. It is also to impress the conviction that such plans and means as were employed to obtain the promised land, could only have originated in the imperfectness of the uneducated intellects and in the false direction of the affections of men. It is blasphemous to believe and preach that these inhuman proceedings were sanctioned by a *Divine intention.*

By some expressions used by Moses, Joshua, and other writers of the Old Testament, one would be led to suppose (admitting their divine origin) that these wars, persecutions, and devastations, were not only incited, but were pronounced good, by the Omnipotent Mind. But this idea has arisen from a misinterpretation of the peculiar form of expression contained in those books. And it is proper that men should not presume upon that which is doubtful, or endeavor to establish a system of theology without even inquiring whether the basis is competent to sustain the superstructure.

Joshua being rendered susceptible to interior impressions by being subjected to abnormalness, could with ease and precision prophesy many things that would and did occur, for and against the children of Israel. I discover no use that would arise from a further account of the doings of Joshua and those whom he governed.

But as there exists an apparent uniformity in the prophetic succession, it is proper to glance generally at each one in the order in which they occur in the Old Testament.

Whether Joshua wrote the book ascribed to him is not at this time clear; but that the things therein related as appertaining to Joshua and the Israelites are true, appears evident, and the account requires no comment. In those days the Israelitish nation had no king. So after Joshua died, they were governed by a number of Judges; and hence the BOOK OF JUDGES, which follows Joshua.

It appears that there existed great animosity of feeling among the Canaanites, Ammonites, Edomites, and others, toward the children of Israel. This was the cause of frequent wars between the former tribes and the latter. Notwithstanding the usurpation of the Judges, and the advice of many prophetical counsellors, the tribes were not adequately defended against invasion, but instead thereof, suffered some of the most inconceivable afflictions. I perceive that nothing occurred during the reign of the Judges that is remarkable, with the exception that the Israelites became idolatrous and enthusiastic, which led to a fanatical hostility between the governors and various portions of the nation. And the tribes were subsequently compelled to admit that they had been worshipping gods that were not true, but false and imaginary. It was the general belief among the Israelites that only one God existed, whom they called the God of Abraham, Isaac, and Jacob; but where or how he existed, was to them a profound mystery.

Moses had taught them that it was by the assistance of the Deity that he turned the waters into blood, and that his rod assumed the form of a serpent, which was to be to Pharaoh a sign of power. And he taught that the magicians were assisted by the same Deity to perform the wonders which he for a time accomplished. The design of the magicians was that Pharaoh might disbelieve Moses's superior power, seeing that they performed the same things by magic, which he professed to perform by the assistance of Divine power. But in order to display his pre-eminence, his rod, while a serpent, was made to swallow all the serpents of the magicians, with the utmost ease and convenience! By what principles of motive power the rod assumed life, is not explained; and how the serpent of Moses could swallow and digest all the other serpents, is likewise a mystery not unfolded to the rational mind by theological speculators. And how water was decomposed and transformed into blood, is also a physiological problem yet remaining unsolved.

Moses also taught that he conversed with the God of Abraham, Isaac, and Jacob, face to face; that God manifested himself in a burning bush; that he was enveloped in the cloud on Mount Sinai; and that he was always at his command, whenever he desired his Divine Presence. Aaron continued to give the same kind of instruction, which was subsequently promulgated by Joshua, and believed by the Judges and all the children of Israel.

Here, then, are striking examples of allegorical expression. The relation concerning the serpents, and the manifestation of Divine power in turning water into blood, were representations which Moses conceived of the pre-eminence of his own position and qualifications over those of all others; and of his supposed supernatural assistance and Divine instruction which established his authority over the people. But in writing these things, he related *the figure* as being a literal truth, which was the universal custom among the eastern nations.

It was a belief also among the Jews and Israelites that good and evil both proceeded from the same Divine source. Hence in their expressions they would convey the idea that *the Lord* would say that they should do so and so, and then afterward would *repeal* the command, as if he had *repented* for what he had before said. So they would say that "when a prophet is deceived, it is *the Lord* that deceiveth him."* And they would also at times lose all confidence in the Lord because of their oppressive afflictions, and burst out in a flood of exclamations, saying unto the Lord — "Wilt thou be unto us altogether false, deceiving us, and leading us into deep afflictions?" So they would represent the Lord as instituting laws on one day, and repealing them with sorrow on the next. They would charge all their weaknesses, afflictions, persecutions, and disconsolations, to the Lord, believing that all evil proceeded from the same Fount from

* Ezekiel xiv. 9.

which all goodness also flows. And they supposed that the Lord was the originator of all thoughts, feelings, and sentiments, whether good or evil, pure or impure; for, as I have stated, they could not account for the evolution of thought upon any other conceivable hypothesis. It was very natural, therefore, for Moses, Joshua, and the Judges, to have the history of their afflictions, proceedings, and expeditions, interpersed with all descriptions of allegorical language and conventional forms of expressions. Further than these remarks would indicate, no instruction that would be of any use at the present day could possibly be derived from the theology and movements of the Jews, or children of Israel, and their governors.

§ 113. The book that follows Judges appears to have been written by the same person who wrote Judges and Joshua: because the connexion is clear, and the composition uniform and historical. As to its truthfulness, nothing needs to be said; for I find no such discrepancies in the expressions and punctuation between the original manuscripts of this book and our present mutilated versions, as appear so conspicuous in other books.

The BOOK OF RUTH is useful, inasmuch as it contains some very beautiful manifestations of devotion, kindness, and refined affection. It represents the peculiar customs relating to matrimonial engagements which then prevailed universally, but which were subsequently reformed and essentially modified. It represents also the custom of maidens gleaning the fields, together with the customs of the husbandmen, which prevailed in those days. It gives a description of the separation and affliction of the mother and daughters; of the marriage of Ruth to Boaz; and of the unity and affectionate friendship which subsisted between the mother and her daughters-in-law.

The object of this book appears to be, not only to illustrate these customs of the eastern nations, but to establish the genealogy of DAVID and his successors down to the Babylonish captivity. This is continued in the first book of Chronicles. It is clear that the compilers misplaced those books, and also their chronology; for the book of Ruth is nothing more than an introduction to the book of Chronicles. It speaks of circumstances connected with chronology and genealogy, and seems to have been intended as an introduction to a concise history of the Jews, from David to Nebuchadnezzar, who overpowered Jerusalem, and led the Jews captive into Babylon.

After Ruth, is the book ascribed to SAMUEL.* Samuel was also a child of Jewish birth, and was much beloved, because he was supposed to be the chosen of the Lord, who, it was supposed, strengthened and caressed him during his childhood and youth. During his life, the Judges gave room to the establishment of Kings, like unto those who reigned in various other portions of the eastern hemisphere.

The transition of Samuel from infancy to youth appeared surprising; and so he was soon elevated to a high degree of honor, and his position conduced not only to his pleasure, but to his emolument. Samuel, however, was a refined person, because he possessed a combination of high moral and social qualities. But I discover nothing important to relate concerning him, save that he was one of those who are supposed to belong to a perpetuated line of prophets. This, however, is unimportant, as the book of Samuel is, like Ruth to the book of Chronicles, a mere introduction to the book of Kings and a continuation of historical information closely following the book of Judges.

The book of KINGS is indeed an index that points all human governors to the fount of terrible wretchedness as the result of tyranny and oppression, or to the pure and silvery streams of well-ordered social government, and a pure and refined morality. The book of Kings bears distinct evidence of being a compilation from abundant materials, among which were existing the book of Isaiah. For the thirty-seventh chapter of Isaiah is perfectly identical with the nineteenth chapter of the second book of Kings; which latter appears to have been copied from Isaiah, who must have written previously, and whose writings must have been associated with those that precede his book.

I discover that the book of Kings is a confused, though concise description, of the movements and jurisdictions of the kings of the Israelites and Jews; and was written by the same person who wrote Joshua and Judges. The thirty-seventh chapter of Isaiah is not derived from Kings, but is inserted as the nineteenth chapter of second Kings, from a serious conviction of the compiler that it belonged there; and it appears that the books were originally compiled at the time the Jews were under Babylonish bondage.

There are no prophecies contained in the books of Samuel and

---

* It will be observed that the author in speaking of the *books* of Samuel, and also of Kings, employs the *singular number*, intending in each case to include the two books in one.

Kings that can be of any possible use as applying to the world at the present day; for all the prophecies therein contained are confined to the age in which they were made, and relate to the movements of kings and nations, and to wars, devastations, famines, and pestilences. All of these prophecies were true, because of their authors' superior power of interior perception and understanding; and they were, as I have intimated, an advancement of those gross and imperfect prophecies that were common among eastern nations, many accounts of which were contained in those books that were rejected at the councils of Nice and Laodicea as being undivine and uncanonical. However, as the books display truth, they can be read with profit by those desiring information on the subjects to which they relate.

Next follow the books of CHRONICLES, which explain themselves, and therefore require few remarks. The things therein chronicled are also generally true, with the exception of some particular and isolated expressions which are so insignificant and unimportant that it is not necessary to pursue a general investigation. It however appears that the last verses of the second book of Chronicles have an intimate connexion with the book of Ezra, which follows.

The writings of EZRA contain some very valuable instruction. The book bearing his name, as presented in the Primitive History, is devoted particularly to a relation of events and occurrences connected with the return of the Jews from Babylon, and the rebuilding of their city and temple.*

---

* It will be recollected that the author in previous pages speaks of his being in the "sphere of *causes*," or in a condition to recognise the "internal reality" or "germinal principles" of the things on which he speaks. Accordingly, in speaking of the various books of which the Bible is composed, the most forcible tendency of the author's mind was to observe the *original manuscripts*, rather than the writings in the form in which they are now presented in the Bible. Hence his remarks on the primitive records and traditions from which the first part of the book of Genesis was compiled. For the same reason, in speaking of the book of Ezra, and of those of three or four of the minor prophets, the author's attention was attracted to the *writers themselves* with whom these books originated: and in speaking of these, he has spoken briefly of some things which they wrote which are not recorded in the Bible in its present form. Some intimations, for instance, were given concerning the productions of Ezra, which can only be verified by a reference to the books of *Esdras*, which claim to be written by the same author. But on reviewing the manuscripts previously to committing them finally to my charge for publication, the author remarked in substance that although he saw the object of his being impressed to speak as he did concerning three or four of the less important writers of the Old Testament, he saw that it would not be necessary to publish anything he had said of their productions, except what had reference to their books in their *present form* as recorded in the Bible. He therefore only authorizes me to publish such remarks as *appear*:

§ 114. Next follows the book of NEHEMIAH. This is a continuation of the Ezraite history which speaks of the rebuilding of the temple and other national occurrences, and sustains the character of profane and ecclesiastical history. Nehemiah was a good and amiable man, and was beloved by the people, notwithstanding his unhappy situation. And he was also interiorly enlightened concerning many events and occurrences which in reality transpired many years after he ceased to live.

But as the book of Nehemiah is connected only with the circumstances of the times in which it was written, it is unnecessary that I should enter into further explanations concerning it, or point out the interpolations which it subsequently underwent from the hands of the compilers of sacred books. And had it not been for the meditations and history contained in Nehemiah, I am distinctly impressed that it never would have been seen by subsequent generations: for as it was, it barely escaped the same fate that many of its associate manuscripts experienced.

For a truthful understanding of the contents of some of the previous books, this, and *following* ones, I would refer the reader to the theological writings of SWEDENBORG, the enlightened philosopher — especially to a valuable work entitled "*Summaria Expositio Sensus Prophetici.*" I will remark, however, that in reading the above work, in order to comprehend properly the meaning of the author, great caution should be observed in distinguishing the *prominent principles* which he develops. For there will be observed an apparent discrepancy between the things I relate and those written by this Swedish philosopher: and this discrepancy will appear conspicuous when the *external* of the account only is viewed, but not when his interpretations and correspondences are properly comprehended. His writings do not unfold a germ of spiritual truth in those primitive pages, because it is impossible for them to contain such, inasmuch as they are only historical accounts, and not spiritual revelations. So he does not unfold an *interior* meaning from these writings, but develops a novel *exterior* application and signification, which robs the Old and New Testaments of their present garb, and clothes them in a garment of spiritual beauty of which they are unworthy. So apprehend the things which I relate, and know that I am speaking concerning the

and the main object of this explanatory note is to exclude any idea of unlawful suppression that might otherwise possibly arise in the minds of those who may now, or may hereafter, be but *partially* informed in reference to the above facts.

origin of certain biblical accounts, and not concerning the thousands of creeds, doctrines, and commentations, that have been based upon a still more superficial view of the subject.

Then follows the book of ESTHER. This is also connected with the national history of the times to which it relates. But as it is connected with no theological system, and affords no prop or foundation for the support of any theological speculation, it is proper that I should forbear further remark upon it.

Next comes the book of JOB. This book presents conspicuous examples of hope, praise, and worship, together with distrust, disconsolation, and oppressive afflictions. The book bears external evidence of Egyptian origin; for in it a distinction is made between the evil spirit, or tempter, and the Lord, which distinction is not recognised in books preceding. This was according to the traditional Egyptian theology — Osiris being the spirit or Lord of light, goodness, and prosperity, and Typhon the spirit of darkness, evil, and adversity.

The book of Job presents a character suffering inexpressible afflictions. With this, many other characters are introduced, who play respectively the parts of consolers, tempters, and persecutors — some endeavoring to add more pain and create more distress, while others would act as moderators, manifesting sympathy and spiritual affection, and endeavoring to console the sufferer.

This book is imperfectly derived from the original manuscript; yet it answers the purpose for which it was intended, which was to represent allegorically the great afflictions and oppressions to which man was liable, and how he must look to the Good Spirit, or the Divine Mind, for succor and consolation. It teaches submission, purity, and humiliation. It also advises affectionate devotion to truth and virtue, and an immoveable confidence in that Divine Mind who breathed into being the earth, plants, and animals, as well as Man and the starry heavens. It teaches the evil consequences of vitiated and unholy situations; the horribleness of unrighteous thoughts; and the slavery and imprisonment of that mind and conscience which know no good. Meanwhile, it teaches a devotional resignation to the Divine Love and Wisdom universally prevailing, and to the Divine Design, or laws ånd principles, that create, govern, and control, all things. It teaches that meekness, charity, patience, perseverance, and virtue, should characterize the disposition and actions of every being who is susceptible to the pains and pleasures ordinarily connected with human life.

Such evidently was the intention of the book of Job. Its instructions are pure and good; its style, though forcible, is gentle and attractive, and its tendency is evidently proper and useful. The book of Job, however, introduces some characters into notice that are subsequently neglected and forgotten; while others are retained throughout the historical and allegorical relation. Viewed in this light, the book of Job may be made useful. But this book is incoherent with every other part of the Old Testament.

I do not discover in any of these books any prophetic sayings that have the slightest allusion to him who came to inform the world concerning their sins, and to bring peace on earth, and good-will to men.

§ 115. Should I proceed further with the present subject without presenting some reflections in review of previous sayings and primitive customs, the matter would be left in some obscurity.

It will be remembered that in speaking concerning the nations that existed upon the earth about the time of the deluge, and especially those that dwelt in Central and South America, I stated that they conceived the sun to be the face of a deity who disseminated evil among them because of their abominations. They believed the sun to be the great vortex of central power, around which the Universe revolved; and this constituted their peculiar conception of the great Creative Cause. It is not necessary that I should enter into details concerning the various movements of this nation, or concerning their division into tribes and families—and how, after their discovery of the art of navigation, they migrated to the eastern hemisphere, where (as I am distinctly impressed) they formed settlements in Egypt and also near ancient Jerusalem.

The Bible does not give a connected account of the origin of the Jewish nation after the flood, but simply speaks of Abraham being instructed by the Lord in a dream, to journey, with his wife, to another portion of the land, whence sprang the various tribes of the Israelitish nation. This account is generally correct: for it speaks of one of those tribes which came from the south and settled in the east near Egypt, of which Abraham was a distinguished member. From him forward, the history is correct in all its essential particulars.

The first account of building and architecture after the flood, and when the earth had become dry, was that concerning the building of the tower of Babel. This account represents the descendants of

Noah as congregating upon a beautiful plain, where all materials for building and establishing a city were abundant and accessible. Retaining their impression concerning the flood and all its horrors, they conceived the idea of building a tower so high, if possible, that the waters could not ascend to their exalted habitation. It seems from this that they were not altogether convinced of the unchangeableness of the promise which Noah believed to be indicated by the bow in the heavens. The world was represented as being " of one language and of one speech;" and so among these tribes there was a unity of intention, and this was easily communicated vocally to each other. They are represented as saying, " Go to, let us build a tower whose top may reach unto heaven;" and it is supposed that the object of this tower was to protect them from being again destroyed. The account represents that the Lord sanctioned this movement by promising that whatsoever they desired and undertook should not be prohibited, and that there should be no interference in the accomplishment of their intentions. The building then progressed, and massive stones were conveyed to the spot, and were adjusted with a uniformity characterizing a superior order of architecture. And while they were pleased and elated with their progress, and exulted in the probability of the fulfilment of their anticipations, the account represents the Lord to say, " Go to, let us confuse their language"!

Thus the account makes the Lord to sanction their proceedings, and to promise that they should not receive from him the least interruption ; and then represents him as repealing his promise, and sending forth his power to destroy their means of vocal communication! And this is understood by theologians and their followers to be the origin of the great variety of tongues and languages among mankind.

Those who have perused the theological writings of Zoroaster, are aware that six thousand years are spoken of in his Zend Avesta, in connexion with his Cosmogony, in such a manner as to render the affinity plainly visible between his account and the account of the six days of creation spoken of in the book of Genesis. Among the writings of the Grecians, the Persian magi, and the Egyptian priests of the sun, may be found allegorical allusions to an oriental tradition concerning the building of a Jaina temple, and how it was constructed in order that the inhabitants might escape another inundation. I am now distinctly convinced that the account of the building of this tower is derived from an oriental allegory ; for I can not find in all my researches a single indication that such an occurrence as the literal account would represent, actually took place.

After the time of the building of the tower of Babel, as spoken of in the book of Genesis, many cities and temples are spoken of in various portions of the books upon which I have briefly commented.

My object is now to show the origin of the sect called the ZENDS, or the fire and sun worshippers.

It was the theology of those southern nations, after they became thus subsequently settled, that the sun was not only the centre of the whole Universe, but that it was the throne and habitation of the Omnipotent Governor of all things. Such was the theology of the Egyptians, Jews, Chaldeans, and some of the Persians. In confirmation of these statements I would refer the reader to the historical works of Herodotus.

There was generally much antipathy existing between the Israelites and the Egyptians, because of the dissimilarity of their beliefs: one believing that the Lord resided in one place, and the other in another; while the Zends and other sects were worshipping the sun, and paying homage to the various celestial bodies. There was also a sect of DRUIDS who were similar to the Druids of the Germanic tribes which were originally called Teutons. This sect had much formality in their mode of worship; for they wore badges, and were appareled with clothing bearing representations of the sun, moon, and stars, together with the signs and characters of the zodiac. These would secretly worship the sun in their temples or the sequestered sanctuaries in which they would congregate. Their form of compact and mode of recognition were made up entirely of allegorical representations of the tower of Babel, of the various materials employed in its construction, and of the various degrees of mechanical and masonic labor. So each member of the sect or association was made to correspond to the men who were engaged in building the temple (or tower) and the institution corresponded to the temple itself. And after the building of Solomon's temple, the associations of this sect changed their institution to a representation of the temple built by Solomon. This sect, then, arose upon a foundation entirely allegorical. But as time will sacredize any institution, they were finally led to suppose that their origin was of a divine nature.

It may be seen, in the fifth chapter of the first book of Kings, that the Jews were not of themselves capable of building the temple according to the desire of Solomon; and that he was obliged to send to Hiram, king of Tyre, for some of the Sidonians to come (for they were skilled in masonry) and build the temple. Solomon declares that the Jews were not skilled in the art of architecture, and were unfit to construct the temple as he desired.

So it was by the assistance of the Sidonians that Solomon had his temple built. The interior of this temple displayed all the grandeur and magnificence which the art of man could possibly produce from the sublimest conceptions of architecture. In the dome or centre was a resplendent sun, glittering with the finest gold, and throwing out radiations of the most exquisite beauty. Also the interior represented the moon and stars, and the signs and constellations of the zodiac. Together with this, there was a general representation of the most gigantic and pusile animals that were then known and worshipped; also of such portions of the vegetable and floral kingdom as were most esteemed by the forefathers of Solomon, and of those who built the temple. So it may be said, according to the account of Herodotus, that the temple was a complex representative of the whole creation, and of the sun, as the central power of the Universe.

In the twenty-third chapter of second Kings, it may be read that Josiah commanded that all the abominations of the temple and its builders, and of those who worshipped the sun and moon, should be destroyed and abolished. All this he did because he had no sympathy with the sects of the Druids and Zends, or with any other heathenish abominations.

My object in speaking of these things, as related in the Primitive History, is to make plain the affinity existing between the opinions of those southern tribes whose origin I have revealed, and the modifications of the same opinions as existing among the Jews and Egyptians. Of this the Primitive History itself affords a confirmation.

§ 116. While Josiah reigned, the law of Moses is said to have been discovered, and its rules adopted and applied to the nation over which Josiah was king. Hilkiah and others were engaged in establishing and promulgating the law of Moses.* In the books of Kings, mention is frequently made of the heathen worship and abominations that prevailed, and also concerning the worship of the sun. The Pleiades (mentioned in the book of Job) were also in those days the object of worship and adoration. For a classification and concise application of numbers, as anciently suggested by the movements of

* See Second Kings xxii. 8, 10, *et seq.*; also chap. xxiii. 4, 5.

the heavens, it would be well to consult a work published by Scaliger, a writer who discovered the Julian period.

All these sects were existing, and consequently their innumerable correspondences and allegorical representations, before Homer or any other Grecian poet imbodied any of their thoughts in verse. But Hesiod, who was a contemporary of Homer, conveyed many of those demonic personages to the prolific imagination of Homer, and hence the demonology and allegory so much interspersed throughout the writings of that poet. I would also refer to the account given by Josephus concerning Solomon's temple and the magnificence of its exterior and interior. So it is clear to a demonstration, that very many of the things related in the books that have been examined, must have been derived from oriental tradition and demonology, which, at the time those books were written, formed the foundation and theology of many sects, and were consequently alluded to by Moses, Joshua, Solomon, Hezekiah, Josiah, and others.

In confirmation of what has been said upon this subject, I would refer explorers of the labyrinths of antiquity to the images and hieroglyphics of Egypt, and also to their primitive records, which descend into the interior of time many ages antecedent to the chronology of the Primitive History. I would also refer to the traditions and writings of the Chinese, and to their records, which extend in an unbroken manner thirty-four thousand years beyond the chronology of the Bible. I would also recommend a close observation of the matter and style of the writings of the Old Testament, which will be found to exhibit undeniable indications of figurative and allegorical conception, which fact accounts for the many indefinite and ambiguous expressions which occur among the writings of those books.

It is also clear, from various external evidences which all point to the same conclusion, that the accounts contained in those books are generally founded upon actual historical facts, notwithstanding the vast amount of skepticism which has arisen from the ambiguous style in which these books are written. But it is no wonder that skepticism has existed in reference to such a combination of impossibilities as a literal view of these writings would present. And it would be equally natural to expect that an immense amount of *superstition* and theological speculation would grow out of a superficial view of such marvellous revelation. The skepticism has arisen because some minds are superiorly enlightened, and can not repose confidence in that which neither addresses their judgment nor their affections. And by being led to discard these teachings, they have also become incredulous concerning the great truth of *immortality*. This is unwarrantable: and that mind which, from such premises, rushes to such a conclusion, is as much devoid of reason as he who *believes* in immortality merely because it was taught by his forefathers. And minds of the latter class have been led to believe in the divinity and sacredness of *every word* recorded in those ancient writings which now compose the Bible. And they believe this not from *reason* or *understanding*, but from early *education* and from the sacredness which *antiquity* has thrown around these records. More believe in the divine origin of these writings from education, than do for any other reason; and more thus believe who can not comprehend the contents of a single chapter, than there are believers of the same things among those who are superficially enlightened. Such implicitly believe in all the sayings of this book and in the many doctrines which it appears to them to teach, together with the flattering scenes of immortality which they imagine to be therein set forth, without being competent to give a substantial reason for their hope. So persons of one class have reasoned improperly and arrived at illegitimate conclusions, and have no hope for which to give a reason; while others have not reasoned at all, but implicitly receive the whole, which is beyond the capacity of the mental powers to digest, and hence have no reason whereon may be founded a hope. I would, then, refer to THE KEY, for a proper exposition of the true course of reasoning; and the correctness of this may be perceived by observing the superiority of its tendency and application.

When passages occur in the Old Testament which make the Lord say one thing and do another; when, as in the case of Saul, an *evil spirit* is represented as proceeding from the Divine Mind; and when many expressions of like character occur, some of which are found in Jeremiah, it is well to know that these have their explanation in the fact that the different tribes and nations originally supposed that the evolution of *thoughts* proceeded from an influx of the spirit of the Lord. Therefore they would in their writings use the expressions, "The Lord spake"—"The Lord directed," &c., to signify this opinion, and would always write as if they actually believed in this manner of receiving instruction.

When Saul desired the presence of the witch of Endor, he merely desired to have an experiment performed that would surprise and terrify those who would hear of, or witness, the occurrence. It is clear to every reflecting mind, that neither Samuel nor any other physical organization, after it had given forth its interior moving principle or spiritual essence to associate with higher spheres, could actually experience a resurrection, with a return of those vital powers and mental faculties that before characterized the organization. It may be inquired, "How does any one know, from his limited acquaintance with natural laws, that such an occurrence never took place?" In answer to this, I would remark that the laws of Nature and the Universe are the mediums by which *designs* are accomplished — and that each law which exists at the present time, must have *always* existed: for otherwise the unity of plans and designs would not have been complete. Therefore, if such an event ever did occur, it must have been *designed*, and therefore was a result of an *eternal law*. And if that law in that instance accomplished an eternal design, other instances of like nature would have subsequently been numerous, according as all things in Nature gradually assumed higher degrees of refinement. And that law which was impregnated with any ultimate intention of this kind, would produce unceasing developments of like nature, as the consequent and inevitable result.

I have presented these reflections with the design that they should serve not only as a commentary upon the things spoken of, but as an interpretation of all things that may follow in the course of my remarks in connexion with these writings and with the speculations of theologians.

This account of Saul, Samuel, and the witch of Endor, was derived from an occurrence which is distinctly presented to my mind, but which it would be useless to explain. But I will say, by permission of my impressions, that the account of the transformation of sand in Egypt into a certain insect which infested the whole nation, and of many other things as being accomplished by the intervention of the Divine Power, should be attributed only to the style of expression and to the prevailing opinions of the nations and writers whose thoughts are communicated in the Primitive History.

§ 117. I now proceed to a consideration of the book succeeding Job, entitled "The Psalms of David."

It appears that soon after the decline of King Saul, David became the chosen of the people, and was generally beloved. David possessed many superior social and moral qualifications. He was generally inclined to ideal and sublime thoughts, which proceeded from his high moral and spiritual goodness, and social affection and friendship. His meditations were entirely a reflux of his moral susceptibilities. He possessed much of the spirit of wisdom and understanding. His interior faculties were very much expanded, and he was thus rendered a suitable receptacle of pure sentiment and prophetical knowledge. He loved the silent and undisturbed groves, wherein he could retire and commune with those more interior and truthful associations of thought and sentiment which breathed praise to the Divine Intelligence. He esteemed it a great privilege to be alone, and at such times he would compose and address his psalms of praise and thanksgiving to the Divine Mind. These psalms were wafted upon the serene air of the shady forest by his selected and favorite musicians. He saw that the heavens proclaimed the wisdom of the Lord, and that day unto day showed forth his handy-works. He loved man, and adored and worshipped Nature, the Universe, and the Creator. He was a good man, and was an exemplifier of good and proper deeds. His goodness imparts instruction, and is worthy of imitation.

Thus I am impressed to speak of DAVID, because he uttered many truthful prophecies concerning the prosperity of Zion, and the ushering into the world of a great Reformer, who would possess combined all the physical and spiritual perfections contained in this rudimental sphere.

I would direct the reader's attention to a prophecy contained in the second psalm, seventh, eighth, and ninth verses. It can be proved to an absolute demonstration, that a prophecy like unto this, concerning the birth, preaching, and spiritual kingdom of Jesus, was made before the chronological period of creation as set forth in the book of Genesis, and consequently more than four thousand years before Jesus was born. But before I speak further of David's prophecies concerning this exalted personage, I will say that many portions of the Psalms are very imperfect, irrelevant, and unprofitable; and that the present book of Psalms contains but a very small portion of those Orphic hymns that were composed by David. The Egyptian Orphic praises are all similar to those of David, but are not so grand. And that David composed much poetry and many Orphic praises, can be clearly proved by research among primitive manuscripts. Many of David's sayings were not procured by the Jews: and some that were, were voted uncanonical, and committed to the flames.

There are some things related in the books of Kings and Chronicles concerning the life, government, and deeds of David, which are inconsistent with the superior goodness that is related of him in other places. He was said to be a type of the heart of the Deity, and yet the purity of his character is destroyed in the minds of many readers by some deeds which are ascribed to him. He was at times unfortunately situated; and this fact led to a development of some gross sensualities that would not have occurred under superior circumstances.

David alludes more definitely to the birth and kingdom of Christ than any previous writer in the Old Testament, and therefore he demands more attention; for his allusion is distinct and obvious, and it could not have had reference to any king who arose subsequently in Israel. When David, in the seventh verse of the second psalm, declared the decree, he himself (in language supposed to be uttered by the Divine Mind) impersonates the Son that was to be born. And he goes on to state that his kingdom would comprehend the heathen, who would come into his possession, and that he would inherit the uttermost parts of the earth. He relates this in an ambiguous manner, but the language is sufficiently distinct to apply only to the spiritual kingdom of Jesus, which was peace and righteousness. David also alludes to this period in subsequent chapters, although with less distinctness; yet his allusions afford decided evidence of his own spiritual love and wisdom.

David was a man given to devout meditation, and possessed the most refined and exquisite feeling, affection, and friendship. His meditations in the last three chapters of the Psalms are concerning the praise that should ascend from every heart to Him who rules with a Divine majesty, the Universe. He calls upon all things to praise the Lord. He considered the heavens as presenting evidence of His great goodness and everlasting endurance. He contemplated the sun as displaying His wonderful works to the children of men. He would sing of the silvery moon; for it was to his mind evidence of the greatness and indulgence of the Creator. The stars of the firmament, and all visible objects, proclaimed to his mind that the Lord was good to all, and that his tender mercies were over all his works. In his songs of praise and adoration, he would also sing concerning the temple and the spiritual Zion. He calls emphatically upon all to praise the Lord, because He is abundantly righteous, and his mercy endureth for ever; and he closes by exclaiming with the deepest emotion, "Praise ye the Lord!"

When David spoke concerning the mercy of the Lord enduring *for ever*, it was from an unavoidable conviction that rested upon his mind from his serious and truthful contemplation of Nature around him. He, like others, had been led to suppose that the apparent evil existing in the world had been disseminated by an evil spirit proceeding from the Divine Mind—the result of an obedience to which would banish the transgressor from His presence for ever. But he was constrained to acknowledge, from the ten thousand voices arising from every department of Nature, that this opinion could not be entirely true: so he frequently proclaimed with great fervency that "the mercy of the Lord endureth for ever."

The book of Psalms contains many imperfections; but in general it is of useful application. There is no importance to be attached to it beyond the truthful prophetic instructions it contains, its superior expressions of thanksgiving and praise, and its well-directed and useful contemplations. Viewed in this light, the book of Psalms may be read with profit. But it is a book void of all *general principles*, such as are necessary to create a confidence in the mind of man in the unchangeableness of Nature, of her laws, and of their Creator.

§ 118. Following the book of Psalms, are the very useful and wise PROVERBS OF SOLOMON. This writer had experience of the most diversified and instructive nature, reflection upon which created knowledge and rendered him wise. He was a man of superior abilities, having a perfect organization, which was characterized by health and physical energy. He did not possess those refined and elevated qualities, that characterized his father David, to any very high degree. But some of his faculties were greatly unfolded, which gave him great power of discernment, and disposed him to meditation. His social and natural affections were fully unfolded and exercised. This fact, together with his peculiar temperament, rendered him susceptible to all influences that arose from his peculiar and in a measure vitiating situation. He had great powers of construction, which enabled him to plan and direct the building of the temple; and also great highmindedness, which was displayed in the exceeding grandeur, perfectness, and magnificence, which characterized the temple, from the very base to the dome, and rendered it a work of superior design and architecture.

It was necessary for him to experience all that he did, in order to unfold that wisdom and understanding which he possessed beyond any other king existing either before or since he lived. Taking into consideration, therefore, the particular temperament and organization of Solomon — his elevated and vitiating situation, the physical influences with which he was surrounded, and the vast experience which he possessed — he should be considered truly an enlightened man in social and general affairs, the study of which is profitable to all men.

His proverbs are concerning the attainment of wisdom, and the advantages of sobriety, both in early and advanced life. He gives much proper and truthful advice, the good results of which will be experienced, but only when the world discards all arbitrary and superficial government, and becomes reorganized upon the principles governing Nature and mankind with an unerring government.

It is scarcely possible for any one to obtain the same wisdom and understanding that Solomon possessed; because that would require the same situation, influences, and physical constitution, that surrounded and characterized him. All men are differently constituted, and their external experiences are exceedingly dissimilar; but all experience the promptings of their internal principle alike, and all would cheerfully obey its teachings if it were possible. Ask not, then, why all are not righteous, but search for the reason among the thousands of vitiating and wretched situations occupied by the various classes of the human family. In order to remove these destructive influences with their unholy effects, learn from Solomon to be wise; for thus alone the world may become sensible of the causes that are productive of so many direful and unrighteous results.

In the book of Proverbs there are one or two very slight intimations concerning the time when wisdom and goodness shall become universal; but this is spoken of in an ambiguous and indefinite manner, and therefore no comment or application is required.

The book of Proverbs is a concise embodiment of the results of the experience of Solomon; and being a compendium of practical thoughts and teachings, it is useful to be read as such, and its teachings should be applied to the human race. Further than this, I discover no use to be derived from this book. And that this is its intention is made evident from its style of expression, from the nature of its contents, and from its position among the books of the Old Testament.

Then follows ECCLESIASTES, OR THE PREACHER. This book displays a vast amount of erudition and absolute knowledge. It appears to be a continuation of the book of Proverbs. It contains much important and valuable instruction, and may be read with profit and pleasure; and the scraps of truthful expression which it contains are worthy of serious consideration. But I observe nothing in this book especially applicable to the ushering-in of the great Reformer, or as relating to his spiritual teachings or kingdom. The use, then, of this book, consists in some valuable instructions and admonitions that will be fulfilled when society is reformed.

The book following this consists of poetical meditations similar to those contained in the book of Psalms, with the exception of their imperfectness and sensual character. The SONGS OF SOLOMON are supposed to have some slight reference to the beauty and harmony that would result from the principles of Jesus and from the establishment of his spiritual kingdom. I do not, however, discover any such reference; for Solomon possessed not the spirit of prophecy. There are many ambiguous and inflated expressions contained in this book, which neither involve any useful figure, nor any principle of truth or morality. Some of the songs are well composed, partaking greatly of the Orphic style of David, and also displaying the spirit of wisdom. The book, however, is useless, for it is void of any exalted principles which can instruct the race and lead them to a more perfect degree of social unity and mental refinement. Therefore the Songs of Solomon might have shared the fate that many kindred books did, without being the least loss to the world.

§ 119. Following these is the book of ISAIAH. I experience an influx of higher veneration for this writer, and am attracted to him more strongly than to any other whom I have examined. I feel constrained to speak of him with the highest respect. He possessed naturally a good and well-constituted organization. His temperament was warm, and he possessed affectionate social feelings; and all his moral and intellectual faculties were also highly developed. His endowments were of such a character as to render him a fit receptacle of the spirit of prophecy. His mind was so constituted that he was not only able to receive knowledge of, but to associate with, the principles of the Divine Mind existing in Nature, which are the agents and mediums through which eternal Design is accomplished. By being thus spiritually qualified, he could and did prophesy that which was fulfilled only when the Messiah came to breathe purity, social unity, and consequent righteousness. Isaiah spoke not concerning the day and hour of, or the circumstances that would be connected with, the birth and the establishment of the spiritual reign of this noble personage. He spoke not concerning any contingent, external, and circumstantial events, that would serve as an indication of this occurrence; because it would have been impossible for him or any other human being to speak with certainty concerning these. But he could speak with the utmost confidence concerning any event that would result from the manifestations of Divine intention respecting the nature of which he became enlightened.

He, then, like all other prophets, was fitted for the use for which he was intended. It was not a *merit* in him or in any other person to be at times in possession of the spirit of prophecy, inasmuch as an influx of Divine intention is a result of a superior organization, not rendered so by the person himself, but by the superior *influences*, both internal and external, that have governed and developed him from birth. Considering the inseparable connexion which is sustained between the Universe and the Deity, the whole forming one grand System, it is impossible for any rational mind to conceive of such a thing as "*free will*," or independent volition. For if such a thing existed, then would the Universe be disunited, and the Divine Mind would be incapable of communicating life and animation to its various recesses and labyrinths. The chain of cause and effect, and the bond of unity, harmony, and reciprocation, would be broken, and the Universe would be no longer an organized system of beauty and grandeur, but an incomprehensible ocean of chaos and confusion.

The Universe must be animated by a LIVING SPIRIT, to form, as a Whole, ONE GRAND MAN. That Spirit is the Cause of its present organized form, and is the Disseminator of motion, life, sensation, and intelligence, throughout all the ramifications of this one GRAND MAN. That Spirit is the Spirit of Truth, of Love and Wisdom, and of inexpressible Knowledge; and this is the GREAT POSITIVE MIND. Then, again, this interior Spirit must have a Form, through which its attributes may be developed, in order that it may be called a perfect Organization; and that Form is the expanded Universe. Therefore, there are only two Principles existing: one the BODY, the other the SOUL; one the DIVINE POSITIVE MIND, the other the UNIVERCŒLUM. Man is a *part* of this great Body of the Divine Mind. He is a gland, or minute organ, which performs specific functions, and receives life and animation from the interior, moving, Divine Principle.

Here, then, is the result of these considerations: that Man is an organ produced and developed by a law pervading the whole organization of the Divine Mind, which law will therefore continue to govern him throughout eternity. And if it were possible to conceive of a gland or any organ of the human form as existing independently of other parts, then it would be possible to conceive of the propriety of the term *independence* as applied to man, viewing him in connexion with the vast Organization of the Divine Mind. If it can be proved that there are organs in the human form not dependent on the form for motion, life, or existence, then it may be proved that man is an independent being, and exercises what has been termed "free will." But if the first can not be proved, then the conclusion is irresistible that the Divine Mind has created the universal organization of His Own Essence, and instituted laws to govern the same, with the positive design that every particle should have a dependence upon the whole, that all particles should sustain reciprocal relations, and that the whole should thus form one united, harmonious System. If this conclusion is denied, it would be well for the one who denies it to prove the existence of an actual independence in any part of the human form. When this is done, the great question may be considered as everlastingly decided respecting the doctrines of *indefinite free will* and of *absolute necessity*.

The many high and noble qualities of which Isaiah was in possession rendered his mind suitable for the influx of prophetic knowledge, which he proclaimed with great perspicuity to the world. But this was not a *merit* of his, but a natural consequence of the relations which he sustained to those laws which he felt impressed would develop the event he was constrained to prophesy. I would that all ideas of *merit* were for ever dissipated from the human mind, and that the mind might become rationalized on this subject. Then much knowledge concerning the Laws of Nature, and the Designs of the Divine Mind, would be unfolded; and this would elevate the general mind, and produce a concert in the human family sanctified by Nature as being in accordance with her immutable laws.

§ 120. Isaiah being superiorly enlightened, was enabled to speak with prophetic assurance concerning the beauties that will arise from a social and spiritual elevation of the race as determined by the triumph of moral and natural principles. He was convinced, from his prophetical meditations, that the world of mankind would undergo such a change, as that unity, peace, and righteousness, would spread over the whole earth. His thoughts were not circumscribed by any sectarian dogma, or any outward form of worship, but were as expansive as the wide-spread fields of Nature and the unfolded heavens. He spoke concerning the mountain of the house of the Lord, and the holy magnificence that will characterize the great temple of Mankind, after goodness and virtue shall have become fully developed. He saw that the *germ* of righteousness was deposited in Nature, and existed also in Man. He saw that this would unfold its divine qualities into roots, and that these, again, would produce a body, which would ascend and put forth branches throughout the world — which, again, would bud and blossom on the mount of the Lord, on the hill of Zion. Thus would be unfolded the beauty of the tree of righteousness whose everlasting branches would ascend through all the celestial spheres, with continually-increasing beauty, until they became immersed into the celestial Fount wherein dwell unbounded Love and Wisdom.

He saw that one would come who would "judge among many nations," and who would deposite a germ whose growth would produce a social and moral resurrection of all the world to harmony and righteousness. He saw that one would come who would "rebuke many people," unfolding the proper principles that belong to the nature of man, on the full accomplishment of which, error and false instruction would be for ever annihilated. He saw that this would cause all nations to "beat their swords into ploughshares, and their spears into pruning-hooks;" and that then would exist peace on earth and universal industry. He saw that when this would be accomplished, "nation would not again rise up against nation, and that they would learn war no more." He saw that error and ignorance, which are the causes of the various systems that exist, would be banished from the earth, and that all sectarian and local hostility would be annihilated. He saw that when this unity of intention and action became universal, "the wilderness and the solitary places would be made glad, and that the deserts would be made to blossom as the rose." He saw that the world would be no longer dreary and uncongenial from the prevalence of sectarian artificiality, but that it would be converted into an Eden whose fragrance would diffuse universal happiness. He saw that this would be accomplished as an inevitable result of the moral and spiritual teachings of those principles which have existed in Nature ever since the Universe had a being. He saw that social unity would unfold spiritual righteousness, which would become as a great mountain, a sanctuary in which the whole world might congregate, and where the true worshipper might worship the Divine Mind in spirit and in truth. He saw that the time would come when neither Jerusalem nor any other city nor temple wherein sectarian teachings are promulgated, would be the sanctuary of the true worshipper, but that his sanctuary would be the expanded earth and the unfolded heavens. He saw that man would worship because every flower would invite; and saw that every countenance would be illuminated with brotherly kindness, such as would cause the aspiring elements of the soul to ascend to that Divine Spirit who seeketh such to worship him. He saw that Nature would sanction the then-existing social government and spiritual condition of the world, and that in the excellency of her superior beauties all men would be united and happy.

Isaiah spoke kindly of the kings and kingdoms that then existed, and of those that would exist upon the earth, and meanwhile admonished them to be wise, with all gentleness, meekness, and humiliation. For he saw that one would come who would " neither fail nor be discouraged," but would " exercise judgment among the nations, and that the isles would wait for the fulfilment of this law." He saw that this great moral Reformer would " see the travail of his soul," that is, the development of his social and spiritual government, and " would be satisfied." And he saw that the time would come when unto these divine principles " every knee should bow, and every tongue confess that in them they had righteousness and strength."

Isaiah exerted his influence to console kings, as many nations then anticipated invasion and destruction. He was considered by all as a general consoler, and would endeavor to convince their minds by external representations, which, though having no connexion with the thing prophesied, satisfied them of the truthfulness of his consolatory assurances. All such signs were considered by Isaiah merely as external representations, but not as confirmations of the occurrence foretold. But being in possession of the spirit of prophecy, because of the influx of divine principles, he knew that the many occurrences of which he prophesied would inevitably be accomplished. He foresaw the birth, the life, and the preachings of Christ, and the ultimate triumph of the principles which he would inculcate, but was unable to speak of time, or any incident or circumstance that would be connected with the occurrence of the things which he absolutely foresaw.

§ 121. Highly enlightened indeed must have been that mind which amid all the artificialities of the world, and all the sectarian hostility and local and national wretchedness which then prevailed, could see that all this would be destroyed to be known no more for ever, and that then the earth and the Universe would be the great worshipping Temple, in which there would be but one Eternal Preacher and Admonisher, and He — the Divine Mind! He saw that this great and unfailing Shepherd would disseminate through the world by his teachings, the principles of love, unity, and reciprocation ; and that he would make every silent stream eloquent ; every flower inviting ; every grove a sanctuary of prayer and devotion ; and the whole earth a fold of peace and safety in which all might be gathered, and from which no one could possibly go astray.

Nature breathes forth her interior and immortal teachings, because she is a child of the great Divinity. She communicates these teachings to man, who feels them as the inexpressible promptings of his internal being, because he is a child of Nature, even as she is of the Divine Mind. The spirit thus receives the truth, because of its susceptibility to divine influx. And yet in the world the spirit has become encompassed with every species of gross materiality, and therefore has not as yet unfolded its deep internal qualities, as it ultimately will when new and superior influences are unfolded in the social world. Nature, according to the prophecies of Isaiah, is performing the ultimate design of the Divine Mind through her eternal laws, the accomplishment of which will conspicuously display the infinite perfection of the Divine attributes.

Thus I am constrained to speak of the prophecies of Isaiah : for they are true and steadfast ; and if the world will receive wisdom, they will all be accomplished. Will you not, then, abandon all sectarian affection and impure highmindedness? Will you not seek to become enlightened, and strive to banish all ignorance, superstition, and hostility, from the earth? Do you not desire to become suitable receptacles for the influx of Divine intention, so that this may unfold your interior nature, and enable you to associate with the knowledge of higher spheres, and be for ever happy? Will you not discard the unholy and vitiating influences that are now connected with your social relations, so that swords and spears may become implements of industry by which the physical requirements of mankind may be supplied, and that the world may thus be elevated to the highest degree of social unity and spiritual goodness? Ye who are defenders of the prophecies, will you not put forth powerful exertions to verify their teachings, and thus prove your defence to be pure and genuine, by an actual manifestation? Ye who wield the pen of theological discussion and the sword of sectarian bigotry — will you not forsake these useless instruments, and go forth into the world and preach the doctrine of the Divine Theologian, and thus become useful instruments in accomplishing the designs of the Creator as manifested in his unchangeable laws?

Here, then, is a test: He who loves and appreciates the prophecies of Isaiah (or any others of similar nature), will no longer endeavor to sustain sectarian institutions, or to perpetuate that state of things which is necessarily productive of disunity, sorrow, and social wretchedness — but will go forth and preach universal redemption from mental poverty, imbecility, and social disunity, so that the prophecy *may be fulfilled.*

---

§ 122. The book following Isaiah is JEREMIAH's prophecies and historical records. Jeremiah was very unlike Isaiah in his physical and mental organization; for he did not possess so much of that spiritual refinement and devotedness to truth and knowledge as did the latter. Yet his social qualities were very active, and his attachments were exceedingly strong. His affections comprehended the whole race, but his prophecies referred mostly to the events of that era, and contain but little allusion to the great and glorious period of which Isaiah so feelingly prophesied. His moral powers were not so unfolded as that truth of a very elevated character might enter; but his powers of observation were full, and adequate to the fulfilment of the office which he sustained.

His time and talents were chiefly employed in admonishing, instructing, and consoling, the Jews, whose bondage he very correctly foretold. As may be perceived by various expressions found in his book, he felt constrained to prophesy of the invasion, subjugation, bondage, and suffering, of the Jews, under the severe and powerful administration of Nebuchadnezzar. Jeremiah lived until the time this awful occurrence took place, and was consequently involved in the trials and sufferings of the Jews incident thereunto; and this circumstance of necessity confined his prophetic visions mostly to then-transpiring occurrences.

I find only one allusion in this book to the great Moral Reformer and his social and spiritual kingdom, and this is very brief. It is sufficiently definite, however, to demonstrate his prophetic knowledge and power of spiritual perception. This may be found in the twenty-third chapter, fifth and sixth verses. The allusion here to the things that were to occur in future, was not perceived by Matthew, or any of the other historians of Jesus. There is a passage in the thirty-first chapter, fifteenth verse, which has been supposed to refer distinctly to the coming and reign of the Messiah. Even Matthew quotes this in speaking of the children said to have been destroyed under the reign of Herod, intending to convey the impression that this occurrence was referred to by the prophet Jeremiah in the above chapter, where he speaks of "a voice being heard, and lamentations and weeping; Rachel weeping for her children, and could not be comforted, because they were not." Matthew must have mistaken the allusion made by Jeremiah to the return of the Israelites to their own land, for the occurrence said to have taken place under Herod the king.

In this book I discover no useful or expansive principles, nor any absolute allusion to the great and glorious era now before the world in anxious anticipation. Jeremiah, however, speaks very plainly concerning false prophets and prophetesses. And this may be offered as a confirmation of what I have stated concerning the practice that was general in those days, of kings having counsellors who could prophesy, and these having in their charge persons who were susceptible to *abnormalness*, and who would utter in the name of the Lord many false and deceptive prophecies. For a confirmation of this, read chap. xiv. 14–16, and xxiii. 25–35. These passages will show that Jeremiah became very much exasperated, and felt constrained to speak and prophesy against false and deceptive prophets which were engaged in promulgating and perpetuating vice and wretchedness. Each would prophesy in the name of the Lord, believing as they did that the Lord spake unto them by the influx of his spirit. Read also other portions of Jeremiah: and then bear in mind that many of these prophecies became immersed into the Bible, and that they are at the present time interspersed throughout various books of the Old Testament. No one certainly will disbelieve what I have related concerning matters of this kind, when he can find the same confirmed in the book of Jeremiah.

This book contains many expressions of deep and heartfelt sorrow for the afflictions imposed upon the Jews and other tribes by wars, persecutions, famines, and captivity. He speaks very feelingly concerning the destruction of Jerusalem, typifying its downfall by many significant and striking representatives, which most certainly proves his prophetical pre-vision. He in like manner prophesied concerning the Babylonish captivity, and also the ultimate restoration of the Jews to liberty and their own land.

Many parts of this book were revised by subsequent writers, and the future tense was exchanged for the past, which would seem to convey the impression that many things in this book were written after the Jews were restored to freedom.

NEBUCHADNEZZAR, the great king of Babylon, was to Jeremiah one of the most uncongenial and disagreeable of men on earth. Therefore he spoke indignantly concerning him and his kingdom; while he manifested great social affection toward the Jews, for which nation he possessed an hereditary affection and friendship.

The book following is named LAMENTATIONS OF JEREMIAH— being occasioned by the realization of anticipated captivity, and containing contemplations of relief to be given the Jews. These lamentations sprang mostly from Jeremiah's social sympathies, which were exceedingly excited by the sufferings and afflictions then being experienced by his brethren and nation. In view of the many horrible occurrences which had befallen the Jewish nation, he could only utter his lamentations and weep in sympathy. And being much depressed in view of these scenes of desolation, he endeavored to chase away sorrow by indulging in prophetic hope, which is expressed in different places in the book of Lamentations.

The writings of Jeremiah are not useful or important in respect to the object contemplated in this book. They relate mainly to the wars and sufferings of the Jews, to their captivity in Babylon, to the fall of Babylon, and to many shocking catastrophes that would befall various kingdoms and nations of the east. They are written in a figurative and indefinite style, nearly in the imperfect language of correspondences. They are connected with no theological system, and are absolutely unimportant to the world at the present day, with the exception of a few figurative historical records contained in them, which are true, and which, if read understandingly, may not be unprofitable.

§ 123. We next come to the book of EZEKIEL. This writer was similarly situated from youth to manhood with Jeremiah, and with him possessed very many of the same physical and spiritual qualifications. He, however, possessed but little of the true spirit of prophecy; yet in a few instances he bursts forth under the excitement of spiritual elevation, and utters many indefinite yet truthful sayings concerning the Zion of the Lord, and the Tree of Righteousness whose germ would be deposited by Jesus — the fair Example of purity and refinement — and whose qualities and principles would be unfolded by generations to come, even by those of the nineteenth century.

The things written in this book also appertain mostly to the period during which they were written, and to the period just preceding. I am not attracted to the contents of this book; for it contains many gross and blasphemous sayings — more than would be permitted in any other book so generally read. In the ninth chapter some things are expressed which are very repulsive to any mind of refinement, or to any person who has an affection for spiritual edification.

And Ezekiel also exhibits what has been before stated: that those who prophesied were in the habit of making the Lord say what they themselves said and wrote, and that they would attribute false and deceptive prophecy to the prompting influence of the Divine Mind. Ezekiel speaks in the fourteenth chapter concerning prophets real and unreal, and says, "If a prophet be deceived in a thing, I, the Lord, deceive that prophet." Ezekiel also writes as if he received instruction from the Lord concerning the baking of bread — and how they should procure, boil, and eat a lamb — and how they should choose the color, cut the cloth, and make garments, for the priests, &c.

It is well to remark that there is to be attached no blame to the writer of this book for these unprofitable expressions, as he, like others, was habituated to such modes of speaking. But what is unjust and unwarrantable, is the arbitrary interpretations of those sayings, and the unreal garment of *divinity* which has been imposed upon them by speculative theologians, and which conceal their meaning from the mind. This book professes to be nothing more than a collection of figurative descriptions, prophetic allusions, and historical records, concerning the numerous afflictions experienced by the

Jews, both in Babylon and at Jerusalem. This book is also useful so far as it presents a truthful history of occurrences and afflictions experienced by bygone generations, and of the mode of prophecy and expression that was then universally customary.

The book of DANIEL, which succeeds, contains more historical, allegorical, and mythological representations and prophetical visions, than either of the books on which we have commented. Daniel was very eccentrically organized. He possessed some good social qualities, but was characterized more by the perceptive and moral faculties, which latter were highly developed. He was but little above the rudimental state of mental development, and thus perceived and taught only that which was external and material. His visions were of the most eccentric and ambiguous character, some of which were sufficiently definite not to apply to things then transpiring, and others were sufficiently *indefinite* to apply to almost *any* material catastrophe — corresponding in this respect to various portions of the Apocalypse.

Daniel, whose powers of analogy and comparison were strong, prophesied concerning the rise and downfall of various kings and kingdoms, representing the things of which he spoke by very singular animals, some of which would resemble the ichthyosaurus and the iguanodon more than any other species. Some of his metaphorical beasts had more horns than any animal that ever existed upon the earth. Nevertheless the comparisons were true, though *beastly*. He symbolized some vast monarchies that should subsequently extend over the earth, by an image composed of various metals, which signified the character of as many kings, and the different ages in which they would reign. His prophecies all related to kings that were to arise and pass away, and new ones that would arise in their stead. These prophecies are very true, inasmuch as they have been actually fulfilled in the successive tyrannical governments that subsequently existed upon the earth.

The prophecies contained in this book are so exceedingly ambiguous and superficial that they do not demand that high and spiritual interpretation which has been given them by many biblical commentators and spiritualizers. They are, however, capable of being interpreted as representatives of almost anything that may suit the fancy of the commentator. There are some rather beautiful yet terrific figures, which have indeed a great deal of signification; but they can not be made to represent those grand and divine principles which alone can produce a resurrection of mankind to social unity and spiritual happiness. Therefore they are unprofitable so far as the knowledge is concerned which the world requires for the accomplishment of this great and desirable end.

It is humiliating to reflect upon the very many false and imaginative interpretations that have been placed upon the crude images and imperfect correspondences contained in the book of Daniel. Many have been led, even in the present century, to suppose that a general conflagration of this terrestrial sphere is therein typified and absolutely asserted. They have believed this, too, when Nature, her laws, and the immutable teachings of the Divine Mind, have promulgated a different truth, of which everything is a demonstration. It is not to be wondered that persons not understanding the structure of the Universe, nor perceiving the unchangeable laws that govern her in harmony, should be imbued with this imaginative belief as derived from theological interpretations of the book of Daniel, in connexion with others in which sayings of like nature are contained. But Divine Love and Wisdom have developed the still more exalted Principle of *Truth*—which will outlive all errors and imperfections of the outer world, and preserve its omnipotence for ever and ever. Let him, then, who is capable of receiving the consoling truths which Nature everywhere manifests, rest confidingly: and he may thus rest, because that upon which he reposes confidence is divine, celestial, and eternal. Such principles are not derived from the books last commented upon; and hence, though these books should be regarded as true considered in an historical point of view, they should not be considered as developing the celestial purity and greatness of Him who reigns eternal and omnipotent.

Much time and talent has been expended in elucidating the vast number of figures and correspondences contained in the books of Jeremiah, Ezekiel, and Daniel. The latter book, however, contains more local and figurative prophecy, and more ambiguous and unprofitable matter, than either of the others. Nevertheless there are some very conspicuous and positive assertions in this book, which have been rendered more so by revisers and compilers than the assertions of any other writers upon which I have thus' far been impelled to speak. I need not mention any particular figures therein recorded, or proceed to prove their non-allusion to the "Sun of Righteousness," so brilliantly spoken of in Malachi, and so perfectly exemplified in the life and teachings of JESUS. For it is unnecessary to prove that which has no opposers : and when these sayings *are* opposed, then it will be time to verify them by further considerations.

§ 124. I now proceed to speak concerning the book following Daniel, entitled HOSEA. This book commences with an account of a command of the Lord to Hosea to choose him a conjugal associate. The representation here recorded concerning the Lord's direction how he should marry, and how his children should be named, is very unprofitable, and is indeed revolting to the feelings of every person of true refinement. It will appear in the highest degree improbable to every person of interior and truthful reflection, that Hosea ever received an influx of Divine instruction to choose a wife as is herein recorded, or concerning the names by which his children should be known. For these things would tend to withdraw from the exalted character of the Divine Mind much of that veneration which it is proper for every being to entertain, and for every child to be instructed in. From these considerations, it is clear that these expressions must have been untrue, or rather must have corresponded to the primitive mode of written expression.

It is not necessary to speak particularly concerning Hosea, as he makes no pretensions to prophecy, but was only a general observer, contemplator, admonisher, and instructor. He observes the depression and disconsolation that were then enshrouding many kingdoms within the circumference of his knowledge, and especially the Jews and the house of Israel, which were within his immediate observation. He saw the gloomy forebodings of vengeance from the Medes, Persians, and Babylonians, upon the Jewish nation : and on seeing every tie which had previously united one nation with another exchanged for vengeance and retaliation, he trembled in prospect of what was to follow. From these things he felt constrained to speak against the idolatries of his nation, and their many eccentricities, which were opposed to the commands of the Divine Mind, and were against their future peace and prosperity. He felt also that it was his duty to speak indirectly and comparatively concerning the Jews and Israelites, and to endeavor to enforce upon their minds a deep and serious conviction that if they did not leave the worship of idols and the practice of abominations, they would be ultimately subdued, their nation dispersed, and their beautiful city overthrown. In confirmation of these things he offered many typical illustrations, and spoke parables, as he professes to be commanded to do, in order that their minds might be duly impressed with the awful catastrophe that was then hovering over their nation. In contemplating these things, he, as all minds are wont to do under similar circumstances, prophesied ultimate amelioration, such as was suggested by the yearnings of hope.

There are some indefinite allusions in this book to the Zion of righteousness that was thereafter to exist; but they are so much intermingled with the occurrences then impending, that they are unimportant. Besides, they are disconnected from the general chain of prophecy under special review. So I find nothing in this book capable of a decided application to anything beyond the period in which the book was written. For the writer's feelings were involved in, and his judgment exceedingly trammelled by, the many unhappy circumstances of the times, and this fact prevented the development of higher and more spiritual qualifications.

The book of JOEL, which succeeds, is mainly a recapitulation of things contained in Hosea, with the exception of the introduction of new figures, and a dissimilarity of expression. Joel also exhorted the children of Israel to repentance, and enforced upon them the necessity of being reformed in order to escape the direful judgments of the Lord of Israel, who, he taught, would visit their land with a consuming vengeance, and disperse their nation even to the lands in possession of the heathen. He introduced new and convincing representations of the great and awful day when the land that was then fertile, yielding beauty and abundance, would be a forsaken and uninhabited wilderness; and when their city, along whose streets and in whose well-constructed edifices happiness dwelt, and no fear or consternation was indicated, would be destroyed and left desolate. It was to be an awful revolution, and therefore many, like Joel, felt it a duty to speak and prophesy concerning the best and most expedient means to escape the terribleness of the calamity, and also to speak concerning the great and glorious day when bondage would be unknown to them, and the nation would be restored again to prosperity, unity, and brotherly affection.

He presents descriptions also of some very appalling manifestations of Divine judgment, which are calculated to operate strongly upon the sentiments of fear and marvellousness, and to excite superstition to the highest possible degree. Thus he spoke of a day which should come when the Lord would pour out his Spirit upon them, and their sons and daughters should have visions, and their aged men should dream dreams; when the sun would cease to give its light, and the moon be darkened and changed into blood, and the stars refuse to shine, and the earth shake to its centre, and darkness reign universally.

This very indefinite yet powerful representation bears all the appearance of a literal prophecy yet to be fulfilled. But it will be perceived by any enlightened understanding that all these physical transformations are entirely opposed to all law and to the harmony of the Universe; and therefore if understood in a *literal* sense, the figures are untrue and insignificant. But this was a mode of expression only intended to awaken the apprehensions of the Jewish nation, and to impress them with the terribleness of the calamities which then evidently awaited them.

Joel also says, " The Lord will show forth wonders in the heavens and in the earth — blood, and fire, and pillars of smoke." It is indeed unprofitable to consider these sayings as ever having proceeded from the Divine Mind; for it is infinitely beneath his supreme dignity and divine majesty to condescend to present to man such terrific figures and sublime panoramas. I find nothing in this book absolutely relating to or foretelling the coming of the great Reformer.

The book of AMOS is a prophetic document concerning various kingdoms and cities which are prophesied against in the book of Daniel. This book also may be considered as a collection of private meditations and reflections on historical events intimated in previous books, which books existed at the time this was written. And as it is connected with subsequent records and prophecies, it is unnecessary to remark further upon it.

Therefore I proceed to the book entitled OBADIAH — which contains the impressions and prophecies of a herdsman, who, evidently being excited by the then-existing circumstances, could not, because of his peculiar mental constitution, refrain from uttering his opinions and contemplations also. He also spoke symbolically, but very briefly and comprehensively, concerning things referred to in previous books. So as there exists no apparent use in these sayings, or capability of a profitable application, it is not necessary that I should remark further upon this book.

§ 125. The succeeding book is entitled JONAH. This book, in an abrupt and broken manner, commences speaking of Jonah as being commanded by the Lord to go to Nineveh and preach against it, denouncing its destruction. It represents the inhabitants of Nineveh as being ignorant, idolatrous, and wicked, insomuch that the Lord became exasperated because of their continual abominations, and determined in his vengeance to destroy the city. To prophesy concerning them, Jonah was selected. It appears that the Lord spake to Jonah, and gave him his directions; and Jonah, to escape him, proceeded to the seaside, where he beheld a ship, in which he took passage for Tarshish.

It appears from this that Jonah was much opposed in heart and affection to the thing commanded by the Lord: and this would appear to convey external evidence that the Lord was incapable of selecting a proper person to do his will. After Jonah had paid his passage and embarked, he fell asleep under the weight of a heavy conviction of transgression. After this followed an interference of the Lord, which is represented as destroying the equilibrium of the atmosphere, and causing a most severe and tempestuous storm. Jonah is represented as being the one who occasioned this terrible storm, on which discovery he was, at his own request, cast upon the agitated waves.

The relation also represents the Lord as preparing a fish, the capacity of whose stomach would admit Jonah, in order that his life might be preserved. How the fish was caused to move near the ship where Jonah was cast into the sea, is not made plain; for it is only by desire arising from the sensation of the body, that any form possessing sensation is attracted toward the thing desired: and therefore the fish must have had a knowledge of Jonah's immersion, to have been there at the time, and to have swallowed him so deliberately.

Several things are related concerning the conscientious convictions of Jonah while in the "belly of hell," or hades, and also how he was finally landed unharmed upon the beach. After passing through so many trials and transitions, he felt persuaded that he had better proceed on his three days' journey to Nineveh, and there preach what he was commanded, which was, "Yet forty days, and Nineveh shall be destroyed."

Such a novel declaration, not the least anticipated by the inhabitants, excited their fear and superstition to such a degree, that they, at the command of their king and rulers, forsook all labor, and while fasting, deeply repented in sackcloth and ashes. Meanwhile, Jonah withdrew to a short distance from the city, and reposed under a booth with the greatest self-complacency, and with the prospect of witnessing a *beautiful* display of Divine vengeance, such as would be to him a gratification, because of the sublimity of the spectacle. But it was not long before his prophecy was proved untrue, and he raged with anger and disappointment. He was very much vexed that the Lord had repented, and indeed was absolutely angry at his relenting weakness. So a gourd was created and destroyed before his eyes, which typified the forgiveness, and this led to a discussion between Jonah and the Lord. But the latter is represented as soothing the disordered feelings of Jonah, and leaving him to learn, from what he had seen, submission and forgiveness.

The book represents the Divine Mind as *repenting* — and as cursing a people who, as he afterward acknowledged, knew not their right hand from their left. It represents his incompetency to judge of the proper agents to execute his commands, and makes Jonah desire to have his prophecy and opinions prove true — for the fulfilment of which he had a heart to see that city, filled with ignorance, and yet with beauty and animation, absolutely annihilated!

I am not impressed that such a being as Jonah ever existed. I, however, distinctly perceive the origin of the book; but as this is not particularly necessary to reveal, I let it pass, and proceed to some useful considerations concerning the *spirit* which is said to have actuated Jonah in his preaching, and to the application of the account.

Mankind at the present day are much like the citizens of Nineveh. They are ignorant, not knowing the interior from the outward, or their right hand from their left. They have a most idolatrous superstition, and a most distorted imagination. They are existing among grand and beautiful external things. They have beautiful and well-constructed cities. They have arbitrary and vitiating laws and governments, which require of man that which his nature and the constitution of the Universe absolutely prohibit. They have temples for the worship of imaginary beings, not transcending those of Zoroaster. They have idols and graven images, such as convey to the mind superstitions and mythological thoughts not much above the worship of the Ganges or of the Juggernaut. They have, because of this ignorance and disorganization, sinks and dens of loathsome iniquity, wherein dwells every species of abomination and wretchedness; and thus the whole race is most dangerously diseased — even like the inhabitants of Nineveh.

There are those who proclaim in these outward sanctuaries, day after day and year after year, " Repent, or you will be speedily visited with Divine and consuming vengeance ;" and if they are told that the Lord repenteth, and will save the race because of their want of proper instruction, they show by their expressions of indignation that they would rather have the whole race sink to the lowest depths of eternal darkness, than to have their preaching and proclamations prove untrue ! Behold, then, ye who thus preach, your own insignificance ! Behold your dark and unnatural ingratitude to that Divine and Unchangeable Mind who breathes in every department of his united System, forgiveness and reconciliation ! Behold, also, your likeness, by observing Jonah in his self-complacency and in his disappointment, for he is a correct mirror to convey the reflection of your insignificance.

These teachers, then, are like Jonah : they would rather have the great Nineveh of the world and the inhabitants thereof experience all the calamities which they have been led to preach, than to have their prophecy prove false, or their present impressions demonstrated to be unfounded. So much instruction, then, may be derived from the book of Jonah ; and thus far it is a most perfect representation of the mental condition of the race in the nineteenth century. But further than this the book is unprofitable, and might have been destroyed, like many of its kindred books, without the least injury or loss to the world.

§ 126. Next follows the book of MICAH—which is devoted to meditations similar to those contained in previous books, concerning the immense afflictions that were about being imposed upon the Jews and Israelites, who had by frequent idolatries been contaminated. This book is written in the style of lamentation, is slightly figurative, and very little prophetical. It professes to speak of no occurrence, except what was expected to befall the Jewish nation and cities connected therewith.* It refers to the vast amount of evil and wretchedness that was continually pressing more and more upon the Jews and the house of Israel. I discover no principles or figures as contained in this book that will admit of a useful application.

I proceed, then, to the book entitled NAHUM, which succeeds.

* The prophecy recorded in chap. iv. 1–4, concerning what should happen in the latter days, appears to be extracted, almost word for word, from Isaiah ii. 2–4. It is for this reason, I suppose, that the author *appears* not to consider this prophecy as *belonging* to the book of Micah.

The foreboding calamities of the times were also the subject of this writer's meditations. He speaks very briefly concerning the things upon which he felt impressed to prophesy. His book, as it now stands, relates particularly to the evils that were coming upon Nineveh, which city appeared to him to be under the direct curse of an exasperated and revengeful Deity.

Next comes the book of HABAKKUK. This writer spoke concerning previous and present abominations that pervaded the Jewish nation, even to an adulteration of their temple and forms of worship, which idolatrous corruptions seemed to his mind to be the very stepping-stones to destruction. He recapitulated in substance the sayings of other writers concerning the destruction that was to be experienced by the Jewish nation, and concerning an ultimate amelioration. Yet in this book, as in previous ones, I perceive no allusion to a period when would live the great Reformer: but the book is confined, like former ones, to allusions to events and circumstances occurring within the limits of that exciting era.

Then follows the book of ZEPHANIAH. The style of this book is more symbolical, and it contains some severe denunciations against prophets and priests who prophesied untruly, and who had defiled their sanctuaries of devotion. In Zephaniah's visions there are some indefinite allusions to a period when happiness would again bless the Jews, and when the house of Israel and the Lord's house would be cleansed, and the latter rendered once more pure and suitable to receive a congregation of worshippers. But I discover no allusion to the period when the kingdom of Christ should be established on earth, and when the Tree of Righteousness should bloom with beauty and send forth a fragrance of harmony and happiness. But the same reflections concerning the Jews and their unhappy condition that are found in previous records, are presented also in this book, though they are expressed in different language. There are, however, some pleasing and beautifully-expressed sentences in this book, which may be read with profit, though they are not altogether worthy of being made the basis of a long theological discourse. For they refer to then-existing circumstances, and it would be an act of injustice to make them refer to anything different.

The following book is entitled HAGGAI. This is composed mainly of admonitions and remarks concerning the rebuilding of the temple after the Jews had returned from Babylonish bondage, and is of no importance.

§ 127. But I am impressed to speak of the following book, entitled ZECHARIAH, with more caution and gentleness, because of the author's very beautiful and truthful vision concerning Him who was to come. It appears that Zechariah was generally beloved because of his amiable character and superior judgment. He nevertheless had all his feelings and affections involved in the sufferings of his countrymen. He records his prophetical reflections with great warmth of feeling, and displays peculiar force in his expressions. He appears to have written under the influence of a sanguine spirit, characterized by a peculiar positiveness and determination, the same being modified by a kind and affectionate disposition. He also relates a variety of visions; but these are of a local nature, though they are of such a character that they can be applied to more than the then-existing circumstances.

About one third of this book is closely connected with the subjects dwelt upon in previous ones; and the other two thirds are devoted to meditation, and to prophetical allusion concerning the birth of Jesus, which pure and perfect personage was ultimately to arise among the Jewish nation, but whose teachings would be applied and fulfilled only in subsequent generations, even near the present time. I would refer the reader to the sixth chapter and twelfth verse, wherein are recorded some brief thoughts concerning him and this era. I would also refer to the ninth chapter, ninth and tenth verses, which intimate quite as strongly the ultimate relief of the Jews, Gentiles, and all the inhabitants of the earth, from ignorance, mental slavery, and physical disunity.

It would be well for those who have speculated upon the subject, to very cautiously read, and reflect upon, the expression here made use of, to represent Jesus and his social and spiritual government. He is here called "THE BRANCH"—which is indeed one of the most perfect and truthful expressions contained in the Primitive History.

Many theologians have conceived, from observing superficially other isolated passages in the Bible, that Jesus was a being expressly destined and created for the purpose of redeeming the race from a fallen and degenerate condition. Others have supposed that he came merely to establish a connexion between the spiritual nature of man and the Divine Mind, and thus to serve as a medium through which spirits from this rudimental sphere might approach the presence of Him who made from internal Essence, the Universe. Others have supposed that he was a material organization capable of receiving the Divine Mind itself, and that as such he came to reconcile and elevate the spiritual nature of man to a degree whereby perpetual communion with holiness and righteousness might be established.

The first opinion is in a measure true. He *was* a destined medium and agent to unfold a higher degree of perfection than had been before possessed by man; but, for this purpose, he was created, as all the human family are created, by the workings of the laws and elements of Nature. But the supposition that he came to redeem the world of mankind from a fallen condition is exceedingly contrary, both to the laws of Nature and the teachings of the Primitive History, and is derogatory to the unspeakable perfection of that ESSENCE which has breathed life and animation throughout space. By the word *redemption*, the mind is instantly led to conceive of something being *lost*, or *forfeited*. I am impressed that nothing has been forfeited as pertaining to the spiritual nature of man, so as in the least degree to require a supernatural restoration to a position which man once occupied. If mankind had *once been* socially united by an understanding of the laws which breathe unity, harmony, and consequent happiness, then would they, by means of that knowledge, have perpetuated that unity through all generations down to the present day. But mankind have not pre-occupied the position they now sustain: and therefore the race has *not* fallen and degenerated, but was merely misdirected in youth, and now only requires gentleness of instruction, and the attainment of a pure and useful knowledge, to effect its elevation. Therefore the opinion is without foundation, that the race was once pure, perfect, and united, and that it afterward degenerated, because man partook a little of the fruit of the tree of Knowledge. Nor is the opinion any more true that a being was expressly designed and adapted to destroy the deleterious effects of this transgression, and to restore mankind to the position they once sustained.

The *second* opinion, namely, that JESUS is a medium through which mankind may ultimately receive forgiveness, and be admitted to higher spheres, is also unprofitable to entertain. We can not conceive of any work planned and formed by Divine Love and Wisdom, being so incomplete as to lose all connexion with the law of progressive development.

The *third* opinion is exceedingly derogatory to the character of the Divine Mind, and absolutely charges him with a want of foreknowledge and predetermnination, when his living energies were engaged in creating and organizing the Univercœlum. For the supposition that he ever instituted laws *(which are the very elements of his Will,* and which are as unchangeable as his Divine Essence), and afterward found himself incompetent to carry them out, and to perfect the System he had erected—is a supposition exceedingly unrighteous, and altogether opposed to his celestial dignity; and therefore it should be discarded and never more promulgated to the children of men.

But Zechariah has spoken the truth, and calls him a BRANCH—that is, of the Great Tree, whose Body is composed of the whole world of Mankind. He is a Branch of the great Creation, and a putting-forth and development of its interior qualities. And what the world should be thankful for and delighted in, is, that this Branch has produced such delicious fruit. It does not follow that this Branch originated and controlled the Great Tree of Human Existence, but it was produced from the qualities contained in the germ of the world, which were absorbed by the roots of this Great Tree, and thus the latter became developed through all the successive stages of its growth, until it became prepared to unfold a BRANCH which would bloom with the immortal fragrance of interior purity and exterior gentleness. And this Branch is JESUS, the elements of whose soul breathed peace on earth and good-will to men.

This, then, is the Branch alluded to with so much feeling and elevation of thought in the book of Zechariah. And this should be considered the most truthful and significant expression that can be applied to the great moral Reformer.

§ 127. Succeeding Zechariah is the book of MALACHI. In this is contained some superior prophecy concerning this Branch, which was unfolded upon the Tree of Mankind, whose roots extend through all lower creations down to the incomprehensible Vortex from which Love and Wisdom perpetually flow. This great Branch is by Malachi called "THE SUN OF RIGHTEOUSNESS;" and truly might have been called the flower of material and spiritual perfection that would bloom with healing qualities, the application of which would exalt and make happy the whole Body of Mankind.

Such expressions found in this book as "The day cometh that shall burn as an oven," &c., are ambiguous comparisons designed to typify the great calamity that was to befall the Jewish nation at the destruction of Jerusalem. These very severe and indefinite denunciations have conveyed to the world many unprofitable impressions; for they have been interpreted in a most unrighteous manner. The expressions—"The day of the Lord"—"the visitation of the Lord" —"the day of judgment"—"the vengeance," and the "consuming fire of the Lord," and many similar ones—were used by ancient writers, and especially the writers of the manuscripts now composing the Bible, in a very unguarded and indefinite manner. The Jews had been so long in bondage, and had experienced so many devastating invasions, that they were unable any more to repose confidence in their own power of ever procuring relief. So they fled for refuge to the God of Abraham, Isaac, and Jacob, who, they believed, possessed sufficient power and spirit of retaliation to revenge them of their enemies. Hence occur those frequent expressions throughout the Old Testament, and especially in various passages in Malachi.

Malachi intimates that one was to be created who would be king over all the nations, and thus would relieve the then-enslaved inhabitants from their extreme suffering and wretchedness. Him he calls Elijah—who has been supposed to represent the great Reformer of whom I have spoken. I discover no use in this application, nor do I discover any such interior meaning in the passage.

I forego, then, all further comment upon the books of the Old Testament. I have noticed particularly all prophetical allusions to the birth and teachings of Jesus, and shown that they were all general and anticipatory, but not particular, isolated, or circumstantial. To have made them so would have been beyond the reach of prophetic powers.

It is well to remark, also, that all intimations of the coming of the Messiah were suggestions developed from the then-depressed situation of the various nations of the earth. And it was in order to console minds laboring under the prevailing affliction that this event was generally appealed to: and the prospect in some measure restored confidence and energy, and inspired their minds with hope and brilliant anticipations. Aside from this, the writers of the Old Testament professed mostly to relate mere historical truths; and many of their expressions and illustrations are strictly mythological, being derived, as has been shown, from prior and early-imbibed theological opinions. We have seen also that many books in the Old Testament are absolutely useless, because they rather promulgate immoral and unrighteous principles than that purity and celestial refinement which would naturally be expected as coming from the Divine Mind. In some books, however, there are very many beautiful conceptions —figures that admit of literal or spiritual correspondences, in the language of which the ancient inhabitants spoke of themselves and all things created. To this style of communication they became universally habituated; and they would express all their thoughts in an allegorical manner, always relating the *representative* as though it were true, instead of the thing or thought represented.

If, however, all the sayings in the Old Testament were clothed in a spiritual interpretation, it would not be of any possible use to the world, inasmuch as the world needs new and elevating instructions which will produce corresponding results, as affecting their physical and spiritual relations. A spiritual interpretation of these sayings would be positively useless, because it would be incapable of a profitable application. The Bible, thus robed, would not supply the physical requirements of the human race, neither would it soothe the affliction, of the suffering, nor be fit food for the widow or the fatherless. Nor would it reform the arbitrary and unholy governments that now exist in various portions of the earth. It could not wipe tears from off all faces, nor banish pain and sorrow from the earth; nor could it produce a social resurrection, the superior results of which would be spiritual happiness and exaltation.

Moreover, a *literal* interpretation of all the sayings of the Old Testament, for the purpose of collecting materials to sustain a very unrighteous theology, would not have any tendency to produce the good results which are called for from every department of the civilized and uncivilized world. Yet the voices and supplications of Nature can not be hushed, until the things called for are given in abundance; and Nature, dwelling within living forms, speaks, and loudly calls for amelioration from ignorance, vice, imbecility, and every species of social iniquity, transgression, and disorganization. She has unfolded her choicest qualities in some noble forms of the human family, which breathe the very elements of charity and philanthropy. They exercise a benevolence unbounded—an affection and sympathy comprehending the many requirements of all who suffer in pain and poverty.

As the Old Testament, then, pretends only to be a history of circumstances and events of the ages in which it was written, and as the men called prophets pretended to nothing more than expressing hope and anticipation of relief, some of which expressions can be distinctly applied to the life and character of Jesus; and as the books have been collected and arranged by the agency of interested compilers; and as the fixing of the chronology, the positions of the books, and the division of the same into chapters and verses, have all been merely the work of those who were commanded by rulers to collect and arrange them; and as they can not, though generally true, essentially benefit the race, in any particular, it would be well to consider the Primitive History *in its primitive meaning*, and thus let it repose. Mankind should forsake all dogmatism — all sectarianism — all mythology — all unrighteousness — and become at once associated branches of the great Tree of Righteousness. Then the whole world of mankind may fully experience the ennobling consequences arising from a proper development of their inherent qualities. Then, indeed, will the earth bring forth her choicest beauties; and then will man be competent to appreciate the excellency of her productions, and thus BE HAPPY.

---

§ 129. AMONG the Hindoo and other eastern tribes, the *Shaster* is supposed to be of divine origin. They consequently venerate its contents, strictly adhere to its teachings, and endeavor, by all kinds of persuasion, to inspire faith in the minds of those who disbelieve, and also to spread widely its doctrines and precepts. They entertain the highest respect for the writers of their religious book, and believe that they were inspired by good spirits to communicate such a divine revelation. They suppose that the world refuses to accept it because the world is alienated from the favor of their deities, and therefore is not permitted to enter into the enjoyment of their holy religion, which they venerate with the highest devotion.

Such also is the case with the Persians with reference to their religious book; with the Mohammedans, and with the portions of the civilized world who have received, and reposed confidence in, the superficial interpretation of the Primitive History. All sects that base their origin upon things contained in this history, suppose that the reason why all are not as they are, is, because *they* have ascended to a higher degree of knowledge, and, therefore, are permitted to enjoy these divine teachings, exclusively, while others are groping in darkness of the most degrading character, unstrengthened and unassisted by that Mind who created them and the Universe. All sects see the superiority of their own religious possessions, and suppose that their light so far transcends that of all others, as to render the latter absolute darkness. It has been, therefore, most seriously believed and promulgated by the adherents of every sect and system of religion, that the reason why all are not as *they* are, is, because all besides themselves are under the indignation of that Mind who instituted their own peculiar sect or religion.

It is improper, therefore, as is manifest from these considerations, to regard believers in the Primitive History with any more esteem and affection than those who seriously believe the Shaster, the Koran, or the Zend-Avesta, for all are alike devoted to the faith early impressed upon their minds, and therefore are alike subjects of custom, education, and misdirection.

I now proceed to a consideration of many principles and sayings recorded in the New Testament which have been most unjustly interpreted, and the interpretations of which are sowing the seeds of error and sectarian dissension throughout the civilized and uncivilized portions of the earth.

The first opinion that is well to investigate is, that the New Testament was suggested by the Old—that the prophets foresaw and prophesied of it, and that it came to do away with the old law, and to establish a new one in its stead.

In searching among the writings of the Old Testament, there will not be found one slight intimation in favor of this idea. The prophets nowhere speak of a new law that was to be thus written and placed before the world, and by which mankind were to be universally directed. They nowhere intimate that such a thing was ever intended, or that it would be of the least possible use to subsequent generations upon whose amelioration from bondage of a social and mental nature they so feelingly and explicitly prophesied. When they alluded to the dawnings of a new era, and the establishment of the spiritual Zion upon whose summit would bloom the Tree of Righteousness, they in no case intimated that this would be a result caused by any such written record as the New Testament.

Moreover, it is neither correct nor profitable for mankind to believe that the Divine Mind ever instituted laws that he subsequently repealed. There exists no evidence to convince the discerning mind that a single law which once controlled and actuated Nature, has ever been repealed or in any way changed: but there exists universal and unequivocal testimony, both in the general manifestations of Nature, and in the united experience of all mankind, that no established law, physical or mental, has ever changed in the least possible particular. It would be as consistent and as righteous to believe that the Divine mind had created *physical* laws to govern generations past, that he afterward discovered to be incapable of performing all he at first intended, and that he therefore annihilated them, and created new ones to govern the same beings. It would be as proper to suppose that the physiological laws actuating and governing man's physical constitution, are now entirely different from those controlling the forms of previous generations — that the law governing digestion was originally gross and imperfect, while food corresponded thereunto; and that now the same law is changed to an exquisite degree of delicacy to perform the same office, because food is differently compounded and transmitted to the stomach. If these things had ever happened, they would present unequivocal demonstration that a law once instituted by the Divine Mind, can be changed, and a new and different one occupy its position to perform the same office.

Therefore the belief that the law given by Moses to govern the Israelites was of divine origin, and was to be to them a constant and unfailing code of government, and that afterward this law was repealed and annihilated to give place to a new and different combination of actuating principles — is a belief in that which is contradictory of the celestial purity of that Divine Creator, who, like his laws, is unchangeable. Nothing is more unrighteous than limiting the extent of divine knowledge, and circumscribing the movements of Him who communicates life and animation to the whole Universe.

Moreover, if the laws instituted by Moses had been of celestial origin, then their *effects* would have absolutely corresponded. It is well to inquire of those who are familiar with the early ecclesiastical history of the world, whether such effects were universally experienced and manifested? If those laws originated in the Vortex from which Nature sprang, then their effects would have been in accordance with the divinity of the *Cause*, even as Nature unequivocally shows to be the case with herself. Again, if those laws were of *human* and *imperfect* origin, then their effects would manifest imperfection. It is well to inquire of those who reflect, whether this is not according to the unvariable experience of all who are governed by arbitrary and human laws?

The proposition, therefore, that the code of laws contained in the Old Testament was instituted by the Lord, and that, being no longer useful, it suggested the establishment of new laws, which are given in the New Testament, is founded only upon a metaphysical speculation upon the relation which these Testaments sustain to each other, and upon a superficial apprehension of their teachings. Furthermore, the *partial knowledge* relative to the teachings of the Bible is very much against the soundness of the proposition under review. For while theologians have defended the doctrine of the Divine origin of the primitive code of laws, they have at the same time limited the application of those laws to the favored nations of the Jews and the Israelites, while at the same time the great majority of the inhabitants of the earth were influenced and governed by an entirely different set of principles. An admission of these views would circumscribe the Love and Wisdom of the Divine Mind to a very narrow sphere; while on the contrary, *Nature* positively forbids such teachings and such a belief.

Many have supposed that these arbitrary laws and customs were established by the Divine Mind among those only who were capable of receiving their teachings and obeying their requirements, while all the Asiatic world (which contained over two hundred millions of the earth's population) were left in ignorance and imbecility, and were therefore excluded from the Divine favor. But it is manifest to every person of discernment, that any system of worship producing such effects, and being enjoyed with such marked exclusiveness, must have originated in the *human* and not in the *Divine* Mind. Those who enjoy such supposed celestial privileges, believe that it is because of partiality to them in the Divine favor, that they are thus enlightened and blest. It is plain that if these laws came to man from the Deity, they would flow directly among those who need instruction, and therefore the portion of the world that are not enlightened would soon become the receptacles of wisdom and Divine government, the results of which would correspond in their purity and perfection.

Neither is it righteous to believe that the Deity would breathe forth thoughts to a select number on earth, with the intention that those thoughts should be universally believed and made useful, and meanwhile leave their distribution to be governed by the ten thousand contingencies controlling all circumstantial things, and which, though Man may *generally*, he can not *individually* control. Nor is it right to believe that any system of Divine teaching can exist in one land, and be entirely unknown and unenjoyed in another; or that if it ever extends to other lands, it will depend for its dissemination upon paper, accuracy of printing, prudence of men, well-constructed ships, favorable weather, or upon any contingencies which are capable of preventing any artificially-embodied teachings from extending any further than to the small portion of the earth's inhabitants among whom they may now exist. Those who have an exalted conception of the Divine character and government, repose confidence only in that which is beyond the influence of contingencies or circumstances, and which even the constitution of Nature can not oppose or reject. And such believe that all laws emanating from the Divine Creator are such as comprehend all living intelligences, such as know no bounds and manifest no exclusiveness in their application, but breathe a universal security and Divine benevolence.

---

§ 130. Again, it has been supposed that the Primitive History is divinely originated, and is the centre of all moral and righteous truth, to which even Reason — the pure promptings of the judgment — Nature, and all things, should be considered as subordinate; and that the truth therein contained is not universally taught and believed, because the greater portion of the world is yet in ignorance. This supposition is also founded upon a want of due confidence in the potency of *Truth*. For any law, substance, or organization, that is divinely originated, will be the same under all circumstances and conditions, and also will be manifested alike, universally. Remember the earth revolved, though the whole world of mankind was at the same time in ignorance of the fact. But with the same propriety might it be said that the earth revolved not until man ascended to a proper degree of mental refinement to receive this truth, as that any other truths have been concealed in the same way for want of mental capacity to receive them.

It is useful to remark, also, that the productions of the vegetable and animal kingdoms are constant and unfailing, and are not affected by the mental convictions of man in the least particular. Nor has one physiological law been arrested in its operation by a universal ignorance of its nature and mode of action. For the Laws governing the Solar System, developing the vegetable and animal kingdoms, and perpetuating physiological operations in the human constitution, are Divine and Eternal, not affected by belief or disbelief; and thus they proclaim the universal and immutable principles emanating from the bosom of the unchangeable Creator. If any system of religion has the *same* Origin with these laws, then will its effects be as pure, as unfailing, and as universal.

All arbitrary laws that ever existed upon the earth originated in the human mind. And I do not exclude the laws of the Hindoos derived from the Shaster, the laws of the Mohammedans derived from the Koran, the laws of the Medes and Persians derived from the Zend Avesta, or the laws of Moses derived from the Primitive History. Nor is it proper to exclude any of the diversified modifications of these existing in any other portions of the earth: because their influence is partial, and their tendency is to restrict the teachings of the Universal Law as displayed in Nature and in man, and they are therefore unholy, imperfect, and positively unprofitable.

From these considerations it becomes equally just to suppose that all religions and superficial systems of worship have originated also in the human mind. And I do not exclude the system of the Chinese, of the Hindoos, of the Mohammedans, of the Persians, of the Jews, or of any who derive all their distinctive impressions from the teachings of the Primitive History. Any belief that has a tendency to destroy the natural benevolence of a noble mind, or to restrict its movements and circumscribe its sympathies and affections; or any belief which infringes upon the high moral susceptibilities of mankind, and compels man to forsake the pure and divine promptings of Nature, or those manifestations of the Divine Mind, which are *general* and *unrestricted* — is evidently demoralizing, retarding to mental and spiritual progress, and tends to generate sectarianism and unrighteousness, and is indeed not worthy of the most contracted place in the human affections, or among the approved tenets of the judgment.

Those who have speculated upon the imaginary relation which the teachings of the Old Testament sustain to those of the New, should reflect seriously upon all the grounds upon which this speculation is founded. They should also consider that if the Bible is of celestial origin, its *effects* would have been pure and celestial. And if it is of *human* origin, its effects must have been, and will continue to be, in exact correspondence. Let these reflections always constitute a step to be taken before the affections are bestowed upon any system, and before the judgment assents to the truth or falsity of any production.

It will be seen from past investigations that the Old Testament is without a single intimation concerning the production and revealments of the New; that the prophets never intimated that such a book would be written, or once mentioned the name of Jesus, or referred to the account of him which would be given to the world in the New Testament. Nor is there any allusion to the proposition urged by theologians, that the law of Moses, given by the Lord of Abraham, Isaac, and Jacob, was to govern the children of Israel only until a new law and a different set of principles were given to take its place.

This, therefore, is the inevitable and legitimate conclusion of these investigations: that the Divine Mind never institutes a law in one age, to be superseded in another, and by a different law; that Nature everywhere proclaims and demonstrates this truth, and that even the Bible makes no pretensions to the contrary. The prevailing opinion, therefore, must have arisen from a misdirection of the human mind by early impressions and education, and from misinterpretations and falsifications of the Primitive History.

---

§ 131. The first book of the New Testament professes to be *according to*, though not *written by*, MATTHEW. This fact, however, involves no useful consideration, though in connexion therewith it may be stated that the sayings of Matthew were subsequently transposed and modified materially by revisers and compilers.

This book commences with a genealogical history of the succeeding generations from Abraham to the birth of JESUS. It then proceeds in a very serious and unsophisticated manner to relate the birth of Jesus. I am not impressed to enter into particulars in relating the history, or in quoting the account; but it is necessary only to consider the internal manifestations of truth in speaking of the things here related.

It is well to refer to Ecclesiasticus for a proper and truthful declaration concerning the importance of *dreams*.* And with this on the mind, it is well to observe that Joseph is said to have received instruction while *in a dream*, from an angel, concerning the holy and immaculate conception — which surprised Joseph, because it was opposed to his experience. And he was also directed in the same manner in his future movements. If Joseph had presented his own testimony that he had had this influx of Divine instruction, then it would be more proper for confidence to be placed in the relation.

* Ecclesiasticus xxxiv. 1–7.

But the book was not written until long after this alleged occurrence, and after the death of Jesus.

Moreover, it is not proper to believe that a *dream* would have been the only medium of the declaration of such a wonderful and incomprehensible occurrence. If the Divine Mind had intended to produce a conviction in the world that this child was of his Spirit, some more grand and noble manifestations would have occurred — such as would have been convincing from their very nature — such as would have been lofty, sublime, and magnificent, becoming the character of the Omnipotent Parent. The whole world would have received a thrill of conviction — and of such a nature, too, that the *judgment* would approve, and Nature everywhere sanction. Instead of this being the case in the instance before us, a portion of the world is led to believe that a violation of physiological law must have occurred, and that the reproductive principles established in Nature were entirely set aside: moreover, such believe that the conception was produced and determined by an invisible and unknown Cause.

And thus the occurrence is called a *miracle*, because of the strange and incomprehensible causes and violations that were engaged in its accomplishment.* Mankind believe this because it is related in the first book of the New Testament, and because it has been believed by their forefathers and confirmed by commentators. And it is at the present time immersed into the hereditary affections of men, but is not in the least degree sanctioned by a well constituted and developed judgment. It is a speculative hypothesis, but not a well-grounded conviction.

Philosophical researchers and investigators do not believe in any law as governing Nature, the planetary system, or the Universe, because their *forefathers* believed it, but because their *judgments* are convinced, and Nature incessantly exhibits demonstration of the truth of the conviction. If this were the case with theological investigators, then would hereditary affection for peculiar modes of faith be banished, and the judgment would receive and cherish only that of which all things around and above contribute evidence.

It is not necessary to appeal to the united experience of mankind to prove that such a preternatural conception is not true: it is only necessary to contemplate upon the celestial majesty of the Divine Mind, and upon his unchangeable laws, to know that he would *never*

---

* The author remarked incidentally in this connexion that the "virgin" simply meant *young woman* in the language of these writings.

be engaged in such a positive transgression of his own nature and dignity, or condescend to produce such a trivial evidence of his Divine purpose and of the superior character of his Son.

The prevalent ideas concerning this conception can not possibly be received by *every* mind; and it must be plain to all who possess any high degree of spiritual discernment, that whatever opinion can not enter the universal mind, and be sanctioned by the sublime faculty of Reason, must be an untruth.

The human mind will admit all things that agree with its nature, and are congenial to its requirements. But no man (mark the assertion) ever *really believed* the miraculous conception as related in the first book of the New Testament. But mankind have cherished the opinion, not from a conviction of *judgment*, but merely from an *affection for hereditary impressions*. Thus faith in this idea has never ascended the throne of Reason: and when the reasoning faculties turn their attention to the faith of the *affections*, they inevitably discover an unreal and imaginary belief, and retreat from the view as by a positive repulsion. The faculty of Reason is a flower of the Spirit: it blooms, and its fragrance is liberty and knowledge. But the *affections* flow merely from sensation, upon which is impressed hereditary faith. This faith exists only as an unreal direction of the desires and affections; and from the workings of these, some are led to *believe* that the *judgments* are convinced. This is only supporting faith by faith, and endeavoring to deceive the judgment. It is standing in awe, fearing that Reason may break her fetters, discover the deception, and discard all hereditary belief for ever.

The proposition should be well considered, That no *judgment* ever has, or ever can be, convinced of the truth of the miraculous conception. And this is presumptive evidence upon which to predicate the conclusion that the idea in question is untrue. For the reasoning faculty is unfolded as a result of an immutable law, a law that is pure and divine. Consequently, the judgment — the reason — the intellect of man — must be correspondingly divine; and therefore whatever *it* can not sanction, the Divine Mind never created.

The account given of the birth of Jesus by Matthew does not indicate any intention on the part of Joseph and Mary to have it understood and believed that he was the legitimate Son of the Deity, thus deposited and developed in a material form, as is claimed by theologians. If this account of the birth was to be the basis upon which all evidence should rest, of the Divine incarnation, then would Joseph have proclaimed these facts in a tangible form to the world, as also would Mary have proclaimed her absolute knowledge of the same; and this would have established the truth in the minds of many who dwelt within the neighborhood where the occurrence took place. This knowledge would not have been withholden from the world for the space of many months, while the actual indication of the conception existed, during which time thousands of testimonies would have transpired to produce universal conviction and knowledge.

§ 132. Matthew, after having related the account as he received it traditionally, closes by saying—"And all this was done that the prophecy of Esaias might be fulfilled, saying, 'A virgin shall conceive and bear a son.'" This passage is entirely disconnected from the subject on which Matthew was speaking, and can not possibly be made to represent an intention on the part of Isaiah to prophecy concerning this circumstance, nor as in any way affirming its truth, although the occurrence is said to be a fulfilment of the prophecy.

Again, such a Divine manifestation of original design, would not have been inculcated by an appeal to such superficial evidence as proving a foreknowledge of the occurrence, or as demonstrating its accomplishment. This quotation is entirely derived from the seventh chapter and fourteenth verse of Isaiah, and is used for a purpose for which it was manifestly not designed. It is well to understand the origin of this expression in Isaiah, and thus to see how utterly disconnected the passage is with the circumstance related by Matthew. After the death of Solomon, the Jewish nation became divided into two kingdoms or monarchies. The kingdom of Juda possessed Jerusalem as its centre and capital, and at the time this passage was written, Ahaz was their king. The other nation was called the kingdom of Israel, whose capital was in Samaria, and Pekah was at this time their king. The nation of Juda followed the line of David, but the nation of Israel that of Saul. At this time, also, Resin was the king of Syria. Pekah and Resin fought many battles against each other, each, meanwhile, entertaining hostile intentions toward Ahaz and his kingdom, which was then at peace. Subsequently, Resin, king of Syria, and Pekah, king of Israel, joined their armies and marched into the kingdom of Juda, against Ahaz. Isaiah (according to previous delineation) was generally beloved because of his strong social affections, and for the abundant sympathy which he ever manifested toward those who were under trials and afflictions, of whom he was a general consoler. Being a resident of the city of Jerusalem, and possessing much popularity, he was requested by King Ahaz to come and prophesy concerning the result of his anticipated contention with the two kingdoms that were then against him. After having some conversation with Isaiah, he called for a *sign* as evidence of the truth of Isaiah's prophecy; to which the latter said, " Behold, a virgin *is** with child, and beareth a son. Butter and honey shall he eat, and before he shall know to refuse the evil and choose the good, these kingdoms shall be relieved of both their kings."

According to biblical chronology it was over seven hundred years after this prophecy that the birth of Christ related by Matthew took place. But, as has been shown by previous remarks, the signifier must precede the thing signified, or else there is no signification. Therefore, if Isaiah had reference to the birth of Christ, then the *sign* was no evidence nor signification to Ahaz, inasmuch as it happened *after* the thing to be signified. It is plain that Isaiah had no such reference; and it is not right to look upon such *superficial* evidence as sustaining that which has been supposed by commentators to be of *divine* origin and design. When Isaiah prophesied concerning the establishment of the kingdom of peace, and the growth of the Tree of Righteousness, he employed *general* and *unlimited* expressions. He presented no sign, with the exception of those signs existing in the tendency of things, and in the nature of his interior promptings and intuitions.

Nothing could be so much against the character and dignity of any individual as such unjust and unrighteous accounts as are given concerning the birth and life of Jesus. Such things as are related are indeed derogatory to the purity and refinement of the character of this personage, in the minds of those who reflect understandingly. The account also derogates from the character of the Divine Mind, and removes from him his celestial dignity.

Matthew proceeds to relate an account concerning a star that was seen in the east by the wise men who came from the east to Jerusalem; and these were instructed by Herod to go and search out the residence of the child, that he, with them, might go and worship him. He relates that they followed the star, which was a silent indicator of the place where the child was.

* The speaker *incidentally* remarked, in conversation, that the *present tense* was employed by Isaiah.

It is well to remark, that it is not easy to behold a star in the daytime, nor is it probable that any solar system could be so disconcerted, or its movements so deranged, as that a star belonging to it could perform the office of a messenger. This account, however, is only related as a traditional impression received by Matthew.

After the wise men found the child, they presented beautiful gifts of gold, myrrh, and frankincense, and departed, by interior direction, to another portion of the land that they might not be compelled to inform Herod of the child's locality.

Again, it is said that Joseph *dreamed*, and by impressions thus received, was led to depart, with his wife and child, into Egypt. It is well, however, to remark, that Herod's proclamation to put to death all the male children, was generally circulated before Joseph departed into Egypt; and it does not evince much capacity of discernment for a man under any perilous circumstances, to rest when in danger until prompted by a *dream* to escape.

They departed into Egypt, and remained there until the death of Herod. This Matthew endeavors to confirm by quoting a passage from the eleventh chapter of Hosea and first verse. It is only necessary to read the passage quoted to discover its non-allusion to that to which it is here applied, and the uselessness of the application. It will be seen that the chronology of Matthew, and his account given of the death of Herod, contradict entirely the record of the same circumstance in the book of Luke. For Luke in the third chapter and twenty-third verse, says that "Jesus began to be about thirty years of age" before he began to preach, "being as was supposed the son of Joseph;" and afterward, viz., in the thirteenth chapter and thirty-first verse, he relates that one came to Jesus and said, "Get thee out and depart hence, for Herod will kill thee." The language which follows is exceedingly unlike the kind spirit of Jesus. He is represented as calling Herod a fox, and sending a message which could not have been prompted by his refined soul. Thus, Luke represents Jesus as being thirty years of age before he began to preach, and that at *that* time Herod sought his life: while Matthew relates that Herod died before he returned from Egypt. This discrepancy has been overcome by commentators, by referring Luke's account to a king who succeeded Herod, of the same name. But evidence of the independent origin of the two accounts is not derived from any reliable profane or ecclesiastical history, inasmuch as these manuscripts were uncollected and uncompiled for more than three hundred years after the birth and life of Jesus.

§ 133. Matthew then proceeds to speak of the prophecy in the book of Hosea, eleventh chapter, first verse, which says, "out of Egypt have I called my Son." This passage has no signification except in connexion with the verses preceding and following it.

Then, again, in connexion with the account of Herod's putting to death all the male children, he quotes from the thirty-first chapter of Jeremiah and fifteenth verse, which says: "In Rama a voice was heard, weeping and lamentation, Rachel weeping for her children, and would not be comforted, because they were not." It will be remembered that Jeremiah was a pathetic describer of suffering, and a sympathizer with those who were of his brethren and nation, and also that he himself suffered many afflictions, of which his lamentations evidently bear testimony. This passage is derived from one of his pathetic strains while meditating upon a subject sustaining no connexion whatever with the destruction of the children by Herod.

Then, again, Matthew speaks in connexion with the return of Joseph from Egypt, and his going to the city of Nazareth, saying that this was done "that it might be fulfilled which was spoken by the prophet, He shall be called a Nazarene." (Matt. ii. 23.) At the time this passage was recorded, this expression existed in one book of the Psalms, but this was subsequently voted uncanonical; and hence at the present time there is no such book in the Bible.

Further on (chap. viii. 16, 17), there is a quotation from the prophecies of Isaiah, fifty-third chapter, fourth verse, which Matthew cites in connexion with the healing of the sick and casting out of devils, saying that "himself took our infirmities and bore our sicknesses." This is in no way applicable to the doings of Jesus in casting out devils and healing the sick; for notwithstanding Isaiah mentions no name, his remarks are distinctly and *only* applicable to the sufferings and afflictions of one Jeremiah, who lived at the time this was written.*
Although the allusion is indefinite and obscure, yet it is decidedly to him that the passage alludes. It could not have applied to Jesus or his kind and gentle treatment of the sick and diseased; for he neither

---

* In answer to a question, the clairvoyant informed us that this Jeremiah was a friend and associate of Isaiah, was a man of very amiable disposition, and a general sympathizer with human suffering — but still, from various causes, was subjected to persecutions and afflictions.

took upon himself their infirmities nor bore their sicknesses, but was merely active in *relieving* persons of those afflictions which neither they, himself, nor any other person afterward, possessed.

Matthew also quotes a prophecy as referring to Christ's dwelling in Capernaum.* This, again, upon examination, appears to bear no distinct evidence of being intended for the purpose for which it is employed by Matthew.

Again, Matthew relates that Peter drew his sword and cut off an ear of one of the high-priest's followers. He was commanded to desist from any defence, and permit the enemies of Jesus to proceed in their own way, that another prophecy in the Scriptures might be fulfilled (Matt. xxvi. 51, 56). But the verification is not discoverable in any prophecy, when the same is duly analyzed. Neither is it just to associate the deeds of charity, purity, and benevolence, performed by Peter, with such an act as is here ascribed to him; for Peter was a much-engaged disciple of the great Reformer. Swords, and their use, have no possible connexion with charity, purity, and righteousness.

Again: a quotation from Zechariah (xi. 12, 13) is made to refer to the thirty pieces of silver with which a potter's-field was bought for the burial of strangers (Matt. xxvii. 5, 9). This, however, is not the intention of the original text, where the whole account is distinctly given as having no reference to a potter's-field, but merely to a *potter*: while Matthew makes the account affirm the thirty pieces of silver in possession of Judas to have been expended for a *potter's-field*.

He also (chap. xxi. 1–5) relates the account of Jesus riding into Jerusalem upon an ass as fulfilling another prophecy (in Zechariah ix. 9). Commentators have supposed that this was an act evincing the gentleness and humility of the character of Jesus. But there exists no manifest reason for this conclusion, inasmuch as asses were the animals usually employed for such purposes, and camels and dromedaries were engaged in more oppressive labors.

Then, again, he quotes (chap. xxvii. 35) from the prophecies (Ps. xxii. 18) in speaking of the casting of lots for the garments of Jesus, in order to determine to whom they should belong. This can not sustain or confirm this prophecy; neither can the allusion or the quotation be of any use in proving prior knowledge of the occurrence:

---

* Matthew iv. 15, 16, as taken from Isaiah ix. 1, 2.

for the casting of lots for garments in similar cases was a universal custom of those days.

In all, Matthew makes twelve quotations from the prophecies of the Old Testament, each of which is as disconnected from the subject to elucidate which it was quoted, as the birth of Christ was disconnected from the fact that the kingdom of Ahaz should not be invaded or overthrown. These are collateral and abstract sentences contained in various books of the Old Testament, from which, if disconnected, they have no signification. And it must be indeed unrighteous for any history, record, or system, to urge such superficial and evanescent evidences to sustain it. And nothing can convey stronger and more unequivocal evidence against any system, history, or alleged occurrence, than the discovery that it is sustained by a number of superficial and merely-apparent proofs, all of which, when analyzed, are not worthy the serious reflection of any mind, to say nothing of the character of that Divine Being who rules omnipotent in higher spheres. I find no allusion in the Old Testament to any isolated circumstance that happened at the birth or during the life of Jesus. And even if those passages quoted by Matthew appear in their *form of expression* applicable to any circumstance that did occur, this does not prove that they are divine or genuine. For these occurrences recorded by Matthew were minor and isolated circumstances, having no connexion with general law, and could not therefore have been truthfully foretold by any person receiving interior or divine instruction. To understand the force and application of former remarks upon the probabilities of truthful prophecy, it would be well to compare the superficial quotations made by Matthew, with the explanation which has been given of the nature and province of all prophecy or interior instruction.

§ 134. Having briefly spoken concerning the superficial evidences accumulated by Matthew to verify his traditional history, I will now proceed to speak of the origin of many important doctrines, at least esteemed as such by theologians, as derived from the book of Matthew. This book contains many sayings which it is righteous and profitable to analyze and explain, these holding, as they do, a close relation to real, transpiring facts, from which the materials of the record have been superficially collected.

Matthew proceeds to relate, in a promiscuously historical manner, the selection of the apostles who were to follow Jesus and assist his workings, and also to promulgate his existence, character, and teachings, to various nations of the earth. He also gives an account concerning the sermon that was preached upon the mount, the influence it had upon the auditors, the observations which the multitude made upon its prominent features, and concerning the principles therein inculcated. He also relates the prophecy of Jesus concerning the destruction of Jerusalem, and the end of that era, age, world, or dispensation. On the question as to the origin and truth of these relations, I am not at the present time intending to speak; but the object is to analyze some of the most prominent theological speculations that have been based upon this merely-historical narrative of Matthew.

The first of these is the opinion concerning the use and intention of the birth and teachings of CHRIST. It has been supposed that he was a designed instrument, possessing in spirit the Divine qualities of the Creator, to redeem the race from a low degree of physical wretchedness and spiritual death, so that they might thus be restored to a position they once occupied, and become subjects of the favor and goodness of the Divine Mind.

This speculation is founded upon the assumption that man at one time was pure and unsophisticated, and far more advanced in physical and intellectual attainment, than at the present period. It is plain that *this* is founded upon a very equivocal and unwarrantable basis, because it is strictly mythological — an opinion that arose from the early conception of the origin of evil. It was entirely imaginary, and was handed down through each succeeding generation, undergoing successive modifications, until it was historically introduced into the Old Testament, from which it has been extensively disseminated by theologians. Moreover, the belief in such a defect in the human race — in such an absolute retrogression — is a virtual denial of the superior harmony of Creation, and of the perfection and the universal knowledge of the Divine Cause; and the Deity is thereby charged with a want of Wisdom — with an incompetency to produce an *Effect* (which is the Universe) corresponding to himself, who is the *Cause*. From this, it is made unequivocally evident that this speculation concerning the design of Christ's advent is only attributable to the fertile imaginations of those who confined their spiritual and natural observations to the superficial inconsistencies consequent on human existence.

Again, it is supposed that Jesus came to inform the race of principles never before taught, by and from which mankind might be restored to primitive innocence and spiritual perfection. This is a proposition equally unfounded: for it can not be proved from his teachings, or from any ecclesiastical history, that any principles were by him promulgated that had not an existence in the minds of many enlightened men in previous ages. Furthermore, this is giving him power to create that which could not be created, and of unfolding that which had no connexion with the nature and constitution of man, nor even with the pre-knowledge of the Great Positive Mind. If he came to teach that the germ of which was never before deposited in the human mind, then would his teachings have been unprofitable and beyond the possibility of any human practice. If they were *new*— disconnected from the teachings of *Nature*—then would man be incapable of conceiving of their importance, because they would have *no affinity* with any principles dwelling in his constitution.

Again: it is supposed that he came to be and act as a mediator between the Divine Mind and his children. That is, to be a creator of a mutual affinity, such as might join together the universal creations and their Creator! to form a connexion between Cause and Effect, so that a relation might exist between them which never had before existed! If he was designed as a mediator, then he was entirely incapable of performing the office for which he was set apart. For how is it possible for a medium to be added to any *already-united* system, the relations of which are the relations of Cause and Effect? This proposition is also superficially founded; and its tendency is to destroy in the mind the order and uniformity of the vast creations of the Universe, ALL of which sprang spontaneously from an inconceivable VORTEX by the impulse of an ETERNAL CAUSE.

The belief that Christ was to be a medium, by and through which man might ultimately ascend to higher spheres, is a belief which is most unrighteous, and has a tendency to create hostility, exclusive sectarianism, and presumptive arrogance. It elevates one person above another, and tends to establish exclusive privileges. It tends to impress deeply upon the uninformed of mankind that they are by nature exceedingly sinful, depraved, and despised of Him who is called their Creator. It breathes envy, bigotry, and superstition, into the heart of man, into the bosom of society, and almost causes the human judgment to sanction the same. It is a belief that depreciates the constitution of Nature, of man, and of his spiritual principles, together with that CAUSE who breathed them all into being. It is indeed a belief unworthy the human affections; it is too unholy to be entertained even by the uncivilized of the earth; it should be banished from the world for ever, because it is destructive to a proper knowledge of the cause of human existence, of the characteristics of man, of his spiritual possessions, and of his immortal destination.

§ 135. Again: it is supposed that Jesus came to bring life and immortality to light; and that by revealing these to man, and employing means to produce conviction of their truth, the race became instructed, and thus knew of spiritual life and an immortal existence. This proposition can not be legitimately derived from the New Testament; for there it stands as a mere incidental and impassioned remark, and not as designating an important feature in the nature of Christ's mission. If the revealment of this truth was the intention, and Christ was the means employed for that purpose, then the means has been inadequate to the end; for life and immortality are neither demonstrated, nor clearly taught in any of the books, either of the New or Old Testament. A conviction of life and immortality flows only from a knowledge of the nature and constitution of matter, and of the Divine Essence which animates it and all forms in being: also from the spontaneous teachings of the Spirit, and the corresponding sanctions of Nature, of the Divine Mind, and of the immutable principles which control and make of the Universe a perfect and harmonious Whole. He did not unfold the knowledge of these things; and therefore it can not be truthfully said that he was designed to bring life and immortality to light. Besides this, the doctrine of immortality and a belief in spiritual life existed in the world long before either the New or the Old Testament was written.

Then it might be argued that he came to *confirm* and *develop* that which had already been implanted in the human mind. Even this can not be true: for he neither confirmed nor developed the previous convictions of men on this subject: nor have the teachings of any portion of the Bible done this; but instead thereof they have, as interpreted, drawn a darkening mantle between the natural yearnings of the spirit and the blooming beauty of the celestial home. The Bible has even *darkened* the pathway that once was illumined by the spiritual promptings of mankind. It has obstructed the progress of physical and spiritual development, and has therefore operated *against* its *alleged* design, which was to inform man of the relations of his present existence, and to illustrate and demonstrate future and immortal life. It has failed to do this, and hence the proposition under review is more a child of the imagination than of the properly-unfolded human spirit.

Again: it is supposed that Christ was designed as a medium by and through whom man might escape eternal condemnation. This is, indeed, an opinion not transcending the theology of the early inhabitants. And what is more notorious still, is, that it is believed, and flourishes to the greatest extent, where folly, ignorance, and superstition, exist in abundance. It is no less notorious that as the human mind discards preconceived opinions, and becomes intelligent, this horrible and unrighteous dogma recedes; and it is as far from an enlightened judgment, as intelligence is from ignorance. It originated in darkness — it develops darkness — and is itself so exceedingly dark, that it can not approach the serene and brilliant light that surrounds the throne of an enlightened reason. Men have been led to believe in the existence of an ocean of unceasing flame, where one wave of fire succeeds another, sustained by the fuel of discarded and condemned human spirits, whose sufferings would add to the glory and majesty of the Divine Mind, who, with all complacency, receives the perfumes thereof, as the fragrance from an open flower! By him this burning abyss is thought to have been created; and that from him also proceed the fiery darts aimed by the omnipotent vengeance, of dark and *terrible* damnation. Indeed, it is supposed that he is the great *Fire Kindler*, and that he fans the flames by his own breath, and consumes innumerable spirits of his own creation, in the bosom of that terrible gulf, that has so *divinely* and so *properly* originated!

There is no truth, nor can it be said that there is one particle of pure thought, in the proposition that Christ came to pay a debt that mankind contracted. If this were true, then even the fiery gulf supposed to have been created, would be ultimately robbed of its possessions; and thus the Creator would be involved in the charge of instituting that which is absolutely useless, and, consequently, in the charge of absolute imperfection. As this popular and imaginative belief originated in the very bosom of darkness, ignorance, and imbecility, it is not proper to dwell upon its hideousness and absurdity, because it will die in the habitation of its birth, and thus be sacrificed on the altar of pure Reason and Intelligence.

Christ, in foretelling the destruction of Jerusalem, according to the record of Matthew, made use of many metaphorical illustrations and expressions to elucidate the subject on which he was prophesying. He makes use of heathen parables and fearful illustrations, because these were in use, and his hearers could comprehend their meaning. This is conclusive evidence that his auditors were not far beyond the superstitious theology of previous and long-forgotten ages. He makes use of the terms "hell," "angels," "darkness," "weeping and gnashing of teeth," "ye cursed," "the undying worm," "the fire that is not quenched," and in connexion with punishment, uses the word "for ever," "everlasting," etc. These were customary phrases, and were sometimes applied to the great abyss of which the Sun was a representative. At other times they were applied to darkness, death, grave, pain, wretchedness, and a valley near Jerusalem which was used emblematically to represent filth, loathsomeness, disease, perpetual pain, death, and evil spirits or actions. The term *sheol* was synonymous, originally, with the first of these expressions; and *hades* is a Greek term of the same signification. *Gehenna* is an entirely insignificant term, and is a total corruption of two disconnected words. It is derived from *Gai*, the name of the valley near Jerusalem, and *Hinnom*, its owner. Thus joined, it forms in the Greek, *gehenna*; and it is, therefore, a word whose origin is as corrupt as the valley which suggested it, and as that imaginary abyss (hell) to which it is applied at the present day.

Those who urge the *antiquity* of a belief in hell in proof of its sacredness and truth, should pause one moment and reflect, that the further research is made into the depths of antiquity, the deeper and darker grows the folly, ignorance, superstition, and imbecility, of the human mind as then existing. And it may well be said that this doctrine is of so great an age, that it defies all skepticism on that score, and all investigation as to its origin. It is not in the least degree surprising, that such a doctrine should be of so early a birth, inasmuch as all the most repulsive superstitions originated about the same time, and have existed from the remotest periods of national antiquity. More developed and consistent views, which originated only in the pure teachings of the judgment, are not regarded with the same veneration, nor as being equally sacred, because they have so *recently* commenced their destructive work against all long-established superstitions and crude theological systems.

Christ, then, in dealing so extensively in oriental allegories, and the customary expressions of those days, has been understood as teaching this doctrine; and it is supposed that the inculcation of this constituted a part of his peculiar mission to mankind. Notwithstanding the terms which he used were *originally* applied to an actual abyss of burning flame, and are in some instances thus applied in the Bible, the doctrine is as false as the superstition of generations past. Indeed it is so obviously and absolutely inconsistent, that the enlightened judgment can scarcely conceive of so gross a belief having an actual existence.

Here, then, is another theological proposition based upon mere imagination, and for which there is no rational foundation.

§ 136. Theologians are in the habit of manufacturing most ingenious and cunningly-devised creeds, and of claiming them to be founded on the Bible. These are put forth to the world, accompanied with most severe and imperative demands that they should be *believed*. To enforce these demands, theologians will quote a passage from the New Testament which says: "He that believeth and is baptized, shall be saved; but he that believeth not, shall be damned." This policy somewhat resembles that of Matthew, who labored to confirm the truthfulness of his record by quoting promiscuously from the prophecies.

People of many nations will bow in silence when their potentate exclaims, "I am your king." Others will tremble when their king exclaims, "You shall be beheaded." The Medes and Persians shudder when recurrence is made to the immutable laws and requirements derived from the Zend Avesta. The Chinese are in a similar state of fear, bondage, and depression. The Hindoos will fall and worship the Shaster, and will greatly tremble as the Brahmin points to it, and then to a flash of vivid lightning, in enforcing faith and submission. And what is still more to be regretted is, that the whole Christian world can be made to tremble, and to discard the dictates of their judgment, and almost to renounce proprietorship over their own persons, when the theological teacher points to the Bible and exclaims, "*He that believeth not shall be damned!*" It is to be deeply lamented, even unto tears, that a portion of the world should be thus called *Christianized*, while public teachers are examples of folly, ignorance, and fanaticism, unworthy of an existence in the nineteenth century.

Thus an evanescent and unreal theology is in the world, because men have been so situated and influenced as to become superficial expounders and commentators. These men are indeed most unjustly called theologians; for it is absolutely demonstrated that the Universe or Nature, is the Great Revelation of the Divine Mind, and is the universal and eternal Expounder, Commentator, and Preacher. In order that a man may be properly termed a theologian, he should take his text in the universal book of Nature; and his sanctuary should be the expanded earth, and the unfolded heavens.

From the foregoing considerations, it is made evident that not one of these propositions concerning the mission of Christ, can possibly have the least foundation in truth. The universal testimonies of Nature and her laws, justify any strength of assertion to this effect.

Again: it is said that Christ had a *Divine commission*, to prove and establish which, he performed many incomprehensible *miracles*. How such an opinion can be derived from the literal teachings of the New Testament, it is impossible to conceive; for although Matthew and the apostles seriously believed in the miracles, they have not in all their writings intimated that these were designed as a confirmation of Christ's mission, nor do they represent him as ever making any such a declaration.

Matthew relates some miracles that were performed by Christ after descending from the mount, and while travelling through various portions of the land. It is well to mark the reading of those records. Those miracles would apparently never have been performed, had not Christ been earnestly solicited by those desiring relief and assistance. He is represented as rewarding their faith and confidence in him by complying with their desires. But if the miracles had ever been designed as a means by which the exalted character of his mission might be demonstrated, then would they have been performed under different circumstances, and at other times besides when he was prompted by his own sympathy for the suffering, and by their earnest solicitations for relief.

So far, then, biblical interpretation has transcended the meaning of the expressions interpreted, and is therefore void of all proper and truthful suggestion, and has its foundation only in imagination and misconception.

Again: it is said that no system of religion is sustained by miracles, with the exception of that found in the Bible. This is not true. Mohammed, who wrote the Koran, appeals to the authority of miracles to establish a belief in his revelation—miracles, too, which he says he himself performed. He says that he was transfigured, and thus passed through ninety heavens in one night—had a long conversation with the Deity, and returned again to the earth early on the subsequent morning! Surely, a greater miracle than this has never been recorded. Zoroaster also constantly appealed to the marvellous faculty of the human mind for credence in relation to his very strange and miraculous conversation with the gods. Moreover, the doctrines of miracles, like the doctrine of endless suffering and condemnation, can boast of a very early origin; and hence the claims of theologians, as based upon this ground, are worthy of at least as much veneration, because of their antiquated birth.

Again: it is said that miracles were not only intended to demonstrate and establish the Divine commission of Jesus, but also to establish incontrovertibly the Christian system of theology, and that his mission and the Bible were established by *supernatural* evidences and manifestations. Thus the miracles are considered works accomplished by supernatural potency. It is perfectly clear that nothing *is*, and nothing *can be*, but the Divine Mind, which is the *Cause*, and the Universe, which is the *Effect*. Cause and Effect thus *uniting* and *harmonizing* in one sole System, it follows that whatever occurs in any of the innumerable departments of the Universe, *must* occur because it is caused by a *natural instigation*. Nothing, therefore, can occur in the vast empire of universal creation opposed to, or transcending, the principles of Nature. All things, then, whether organized or unorganized, developed or undeveloped, must be strictly and unequivocally NATURAL. If anything, therefore, *transcends* Nature or the natural movements of the Universe, it must be an effect of absolutely *nothing*. The term *supernatural*, then, indicating something *above* Nature, is a solecism; and nothing is more distinct than the untruth of the theological proposition that miracles were accomplished by *supernatural* power: for that is clearly teaching that they originated from *nothing*, and consequently never existed. It is indeed remarkable that any system of religion could have been so effectually established by manifestations in evidence of its truth, caused by an Omnipotent NOTHING! On the other hand, it would indeed be a miracle if such systems of *belief* did *not* exist where folly and ignorance universally prevail, and where have existed circumstances favorable to the development of so many superstitious ideas.

§ 137. Again, it is alleged that the apostles were selected to witness these miraculous displays, and to communicate the facts to the world. This, it is supposed, they would truthfully do, because they were good and disinterested men. This is a proposition scarcely worthy of comment. If these apostles were chosen, did they not become at once deeply interested? And if they were such good and righteous men as they are represented to have been, would they not have been so pure and harmless in disposition as not to carry with them *swords?* for it is plain to every mind that *swords* and *goodness* have not a very *close* affinity. And what prevented Peter, when he drew his sword and cut off an *ear* of the servant of the high-priest, from cutting off his *head* also, is not clearly explained. It is plain that whatever spirit prompted the first act, could have severed the head with as little compunction.

If the apostles were chosen to communicate the knowledge of those miracles and the teachings of Christ to the world, would they not have drawn up a voluminous account of the miracles performed, such as would have flowed through all the channels of the Christian dispensation? And would not this account stand at the present day as a monumental evidence of a Divine intention as connected with the display; of the absolute truth of the Christian religion, and also of the unequivocal knowledge of those who were eye-witnesses of the things related? Instead of this, they make no announcement of any such intention of Christ, or of any such conviction in their own minds. In their writings in the New Testament, they relate the miracles as being acts merely incidental to their journeyings; and those performed by Christ were not regarded by any of the apostles, nor by Christ himself, in any other light than as promiscuous and incidental occurrences of his life.

Matthew was certainly not capable of being an eye-witness to those miraculous works of which he speaks, because he was an officer under the Roman government many years after the death of Jesus, and did not become an apostle until he was greatly advanced in life. He then only wrote a few accounts, and at last died a martyr in Persia. Ecclesiastical historians have striven to make it appear that he wrote the first chapters in the book ascribed to him; but they have failed, merely because *it is not true.* Besides this, no information is given of Matthew by any historian who lived in those days, because he deserted the Jewish and adopted the Christian religion in the latter part of his life, and did not become in any degree popular, except from the fact that he suffered martyrdom under the government of Persia.

Then the proposition under review can not be proved, either from ecclesiastical or profane history. Besides, this proposition was never taught by Jesus, scarcely intimated by the apostles, and entirely disbelieved by the whole Jewish nation, who were in a condition to be eye-witnesses of the occurrences; and if these had been convincing, they would have been convinced.

Again: it is said that as the miracles were designed to confirm and establish the Christian religion, and as they really were performed and actually witnessed eighteen hundred years ago, it is absurd and even unrighteous to entertain a suspicion concerning their original intention or actual occurrence. This proposition bears no evidence of consistency, inasmuch as it arbitrarily demands *universal faith*. It is impossible for the divine principle of reason to be convinced of anything without a positive knowledge of some foundation whereon its truth may rest. Faith may exist as an evanescent conviction of the *affections*; but the *judgment* knows of no faith, no belief, but that which flows from the basis of absolute and unequivocal knowledge. Then in order to justify the demand for universal faith in this proposition, equal evidence must be presented to every mind, in every age: for otherwise mankind can not be convinced.

But the proposition as it stands is equivalent to saying, that, as the sun gave forth its light, heat, and fertilizing atmosphere, six thousand years ago — at which time it ceased to shine; and as those who were then living recorded that occurrence, together with a description of all the fertility produced by the sun's congenial influence; therefore man must *believe* that it once shone; and then to him the productions of the earth will continue the same. This would be as consistent as to demand faith of the human mind in a thing or occurrence which all probabilities and possibilities, and the universal testimonies of Nature, are against. It would be like calling upon man to enjoy the light and heat of the sun *now*, because it was enjoyed six thousand years ago; or to believe that the earth continues to be fertile, because it was so when blessed by the smiles of the sun. Belief in the miracles must cease with the cessation of the evidence — the same as the earth would be rendered barren should the sun cease to shine. An approval of the proposition under contemplation would be as impossible to the enlightened judgment (because of the universal evidence against it) as it would be to believe that the sun had been arrested in its course, while Divine harmony continues to pervade, and join inseparably, all created things.

§ 138. The miracles as recorded in the New Testament are of such a nature as only to create *fear* and *marvellousness* in the minds of those who might witness them, and also in the minds of those who hear or read the accounts of them. They are not represented in a manner becoming the object for which they are supposed to have been intended, and are entirely void of all that high and celestial dignity which they would naturally be expected to possess if they were of Divine origin. Nothing can be more unjust than to interpret those relations in the New Testament as having an important bearing upon the question as to the truth or falsity of Christ's Messiahship; for they are entirely destitute of those high and exalted manifestations which are constantly and unvaryingly displayed in the mighty architecture of the Universe. There exists in them no grand and elevated principles — no intrinsic beauty or excellency which can or will have any tendency to benefit or reorganize Mankind. It is well to inquire what possible good can arise from a little experiment like that of turning water into wine, or from any of similar nature? Besides this, all who are acquainted with the chemical relations of substances, and the laws of their combination, will at once conceive that such an occurrence would be entirely opposed to those laws, and could not, therefore, have taken place.

Another account is related of two men " possessed of devils" presenting themselves to Jesus for relief. The devils are represented as at that moment beseeching Christ to let them depart from the human form, and enter into a herd of swine at a short distance from them. Jesus is represented as granting their solicitation; and at once they left the persons and entered into the swine — which, being exceedingly deranged by this very unjust intrusion, ran over a steep place, and were destroyed. It appears from this, that man in that instance was but little superior in his nature and organization to these animals whose lives were destroyed: for the " devils" would not have desired to change their habitation thus *immediately* and *directly* from the forms of the men to the forms of the swine, had not some close *relation* existed between the two. And there could not possibly have been instituted a better and wiser plan to accomplish the destruction of a multitude of such annoying and intrusive devils than the plan here carried into execution. For there exists no account whether they evacuated the interior of the swine on their way down the precipice to the water, or whether they, with the swine, most effectually " perished." Certainly no one will presume to say that this is not one of the most *useful* and *important* miracles that is recorded in the New Testament.

Further, this wonderful performance astonished and excited the inhabitants of the place to such a degree, that they are represented as persuading Jesus to depart out of their coast. Indeed, nothing can be more just and natural than this; for what man or community would not apprehend a great deal of injury and injustice from the existence of a person among them so effectually engaged in destroying their herds? It is a most happy reflection that this is a mere record of Matthew, but was not an actual occurrence.

The character and tendency of the miracles related prohibit completely the possibility of their Divine intention as apprehended by theologians, because they were exceedingly limited, and their use was confined exclusively to the persons receiving such medical assistance as they afforded. Such deeds of charity, sympathy, and benevolence, are to be admired in the character of any person who ever has lived or ever will live on earth; but further than this, they are of no importance, and demand no veneration nor approbation. For they are simply the good and just deeds which may be performed by any person who is *naturally* qualified for their accomplishment.

But there has arisen a vast amount of misapprehension concerning these miracles, from the *style* of the written record. Matthew, and all the other apostles, record the cause and effect as occurring in rapid succession — almost simultaneously. Such expressions frequently occur as — "He laid his hands upon him, and he was healed." So in all the cases mentioned of palsy, lameness, blindness, deafness, and other physical infirmities, cured by Jesus, the effect is related as though it followed the cause *immediately*. All who are acquainted with physiological principles, and with the calm, gentle, and energetic movements of the human organization, are persuaded — even positively convinced — that no cause can be brought to act so as to produce health as an *immediate* result, in case of any established disease. Therefore, notwithstanding the things recorded *were* performed, they were effected by causes agreeing with the nature of the human system; and the re-establishment of health, which actually occurred, was effected *gradually*, and by means adapted to the temperament of the individual, and the nature of the disease.

But Matthew and others have conveyed a wrong impression by relating those circumstances in such an unqualified manner. Their form of expression was similar to saying, " The sun retired behind the western hills, and all was involved in darkness ;" or, " One applied such a medicine, and was cured ;" or, " I deposited a germ in the earth, and behold this beautiful tree !" or, " We sowed the seed, and we gathered the harvest." This would be leaving, as Matthew did, the intermediate period between cause and effect entirely unnoticed, and recording the occurrence in *general* terms, and in a comprehensive manner ; and the same style of narrative is frequently exemplified in the writings of the apostles. I do not make this remark to relieve those passages of their inconsistency (though the writers of them evidently believed as they wrote), but merely for the purpose of revealing the cause and origin of those expressions.

If thousands of such experiments were performed as the casting out of devils, or transforming water into wine, or destroying the lives of a number of undeserving swine, or the withering of a verdant figtree — what possible use — what grand design — what celestial result would be accomplished ? Would not such means be altogether inadequate to the fulfilment of the end for which they are supposed to have been originally designed ? Are they not useless and insignificant manifestations, such as have a tendency to corrupt a just faith in the workings of the Great Divine Mind ? Are they not, indeed, most unworthy the dignity of any *human* being, to say nothing of the GREAT CAUSE, which is the very Essence of Infinite Perfection ? Have they any tendency to extirpate evil from the earth ? It is distinctly evident that the race of mankind were not benefited when they were performed, nor prevented from subsequently becoming most unrighteously disorganized. And have not the very existence of those accounts caused war, persecution, martyrdom, and death ? Have they not divided nation from nation, by establishing an antagonism in those personal and national interests which should unite them as a brotherhood ? Nay, has not even the whole Christian world, so called, been divided, and each person drawn the sword of sectarian hostility against another ? Are these celestial effects, indicating that the cause was divine intention, and born from the bosom of celestial Perfection ? If such is the cause, do the effects correspond ? If these things were designed to produce conviction of the Messiahship of Christ, could it have been possible for the efforts of Divine Wisdom and Power to be thus completely deranged and baffled ? And if they were designed to convince mankind, why does skepticism go on increasing as knowledge advances ?

It is distinctly clear, that they have produced precisely the effects which might naturally have been expected from their operation upon the minds of the superstitious and uneducated generation which so earnestly believed them. They were written under the promptings of misguided judgment; and having thus originated, their effects have fully corresponded in every generation, even to the unfolding and ripening of the human mind in the nineteenth century.

The theological propositions, founded upon the supposed performance of supernatural miracles, are so completely transparent, that the discerning mind can not fail to see their utter nothingness. And though volume after volume has been written to elucidate these opinions metaphysically, I am constrained to leave them all unnoticed, because they appear to me as the shadows, and not the substance of things.

§ 139. I now proceed to an investigation of the fundamental and essential principles of what is claimed to be a pure and celestial theology, or, rather, of the four pillars upon which the theological superstructure is sustained. And I would bespeak particular attention to this attack, because it may be that it will demolish the whole system, and leave nothing of it but a mass of disgusting rubbish. The first point is "Original Sin;" the second, "the Atonement;" the third, "Faith;" and the fourth, "Regeneration."

1st. *Original Sin.* To dissect this proposition in all its numerous forms and modifications, would be to interfere with that which is not capable, because of its unsoundness, of receiving any interference. But there is one principle involved in the subject, by which the human mind has been most unjustly perverted, and this principle demands a brief notice. It represents man as being originally pure as to his physical and spiritual nature, even as a flower from the bud of the divine creation; and that he possessed nearly all the characteristics of a celestial being, pure, spotless, unsophisticated. While thus existing, temptations were placed before him, of so captivating a nature that he was unable to resist them. Oh, how unjust, to charge the Divine Mind with creating man, and endowing him with all the attributes of purity and goodness, and at the same time withholding from him a competency to resist temptation! How unholy to accuse him of constituting man a perfect being, and at the same time instituting a most destructive plot to injure him for life, and perhaps for ever! a plot, too, which would implicate an unborn race for thousands of years!

Original sin, then, is based upon this grand but most unrighteous impeachment of the Wisdom and Love of the Creator. It assumes that man was tempted, that he yielded, and that spiritual death ensued; a death so terrible in its influence, that an unborn and innocent creation were necessarily involved in its inconceivable horrors! Nay more, it disconnects the whole world of mankind from any spiritual communication with that Holy Essence which breathed them into being — even totally banishes them from all parental favor, and presses them to the very brink of an awful burning gulf! Still more horrible, it teaches that millions on millions are, owing to this *divine* curse, destined to writhe in the waves of darkness — in the bosom of a burning abyss, whose dissolving fires were blown into a flame by the very breath of — *Divine Love!*

Thus, according to the doctrine under review, an innocent man, who had no experience — who was pure and undefiled — came under the wrath and curse of that Being whose very essence is Love, Wisdom, and celestial Perfection. In this his posterity are also unavoidably implicated, and thus are charged with a debt which they had no agency in contracting, and which was incurred before they were born! Here is a most unjust and impious charge; and the proposition involving it is too corrupt and vitiating to the moral sensibilities of men, to have an existence even in the darkest recess of a distorted imagination.

This great debt, caused by spiritual death, the whole race is said to owe to Him who spoke, and they lived! The *Divine Mind* is said to have assumed the *human form*, in which he calls himself *the Son*, for the purpose of relieving the race of this debt, which he himself created — by living on earth, suffering all descriptions of persecution, and at last dying an ignominious death! He himself thus suffers innocently to remove effects that must have originated in his own *Infinite Wisdom!* And this is called "THE ATONEMENT." All this is equivalent to saying that the Creator instituted a celestial plan to deceive and implicate mankind, of which he subsequently repented, and could not annihilate its awful consequences without his Son — even *himself* — dying the death of a persecuted martyr! Nature, retain thy complacency! Continue to unfold thy charms! Perpetuate thy undying beauty and grandeur, even though man in his audacious folly, has clothed thee in a mantle of darkness, terrible as the vengeance of an exasperated Deity!

Ye theologians, behold now your speculations! Your " original sin," is discovered to be a repulsive blasphemy; and your "atonement" to be the very climax of a deranged imagination, and one that is of the most unrighteous and immoral character. The first is diametrically opposed to all distributive justice—annihilates all conception of wisdom—banishes from the soul of man all appreciation of celestial Love—dissipates all thirst for knowledge and progress—and shuts the very portals of reason by the hand of omnipotent vengeance, and by pointing to a fount of infernal fires! More terrible darkness—a more soul-revolting conception—a more wretched display of human folly, could not possibly occur in any of the wide fields and spheres of creation. The *second* proposition involves a charge of injustice unworthy the deeds of and character of a heathen potentate. Its tendency is to generate absolute immorality in the world, and so far it is absolutely a curse to man. But its deleterious power is limited, for it can not arrest the sublime workings of established and immutable LAWS.

The third essential element in the received theology, is called *Faith*. This, like many other alleged Christian virtues, is not capable of manifesting itself, nor is it even known to be existing until its possessor verbally makes the fact known to the world. It is like many Christian principles, so called, that are never manifested by deeds or proper actions, but are only known to exist when the world is *told* of them.

FAITH—what is it? Certainly it is a conviction of the judgment, resulting from appropriate and adequate evidence. Then it is an effect derived from knowledge. It is therefore void of all merit or demerit, inasmuch as it is a natural consequence of known facts, and not a voluntary acquirement of the mind. Is it proper to call upon man to believe an inconsistency in order that he may escape an irretrievable condemnation? This, indeed, is the most unnatural demand that folly can possibly urge. Is a man to be approbated because he has faith in the existence of any external things received through the channels of the senses? Is it to be considered a *merit* for a man to believe that the sun shines, and that the earth is rendered fertile thereby? or that the earth, together with the whole solar system, revolves? Is faith to be considered a *merit*, when it is a result of a conviction of the judgment? It is plain, then, that the common religious requirement of faith is unjust, untrue, *immoral* —because it is opposed to all laws of causation, and all teachings of the interior and external world.

The fourth point is *Regeneration*. This is founded upon the assumption of *degeneration*, and therefore the doctrine is only an evanescent and unreal effect, proceeding from a cause equally unreal and unsubstantial. Regeneration is considered as an effect resulting from *faith;* the latter results from — it is impossible to tell *what!* And it is entirely useless to dwell upon a term containing no interior meaning, and which has generated, and will continue to do the same unless abandoned, every species of superstition and unrighteous thoughts.

Such, then, are the substantial and inherent elements which constitute and sustain the great theological superstructure. Their qualities are impure, their composition is decayed, they are performing the work of their own destruction; and behold the temple falls: and who shall stand, subsequent generations will testify.

§ 140. No class or series of expressions have been associated in the enfeebled mind of man with more fear and depressing dread, than some of those said to have been used by Christ while preaching and prophesying. It has been a source of wonder and extreme perplexity that a being represented as possessing so much spiritual refinement and brotherly kindness, should have employed such violent and unkind terms in speaking of those who were merely opposed to the doctrines he promulgated! For it is plain to every pure, benevolent, and philanthropic mind, that the mental constitution of that person must be impure indeed, who could look abroad upon the face of creation and mark the weakness of erring humanity, and then say to his own brethren — " Ye serpents, ye generation of vipers;" or, " Ye scribes and Pharisees — hypocrites!" for these were merely misdirected brethren, whose condition of mind was not caused by themselves, but by inferior and unpropitious circumstances. The well-informed mind is personally conscious that the causes of evil lie not IN man, but ABOUT him; and this knowledge at once creates a universal forgiveness, and forbids the application of any harsh terms to a brother — much more to a brotherhood. Persons who are not acquainted with the cause of moral evil, are in the habit of accusing each other falsely, and applying to each other terms no less unjust than such as, " Ye serpents, ye generation of vipers! how can ye escape the damnation of hell?" Surely a more unrighteous sentence could not proceed from an ignorant devotee of the Juggernaut!

If it is said that these expressions as ascribed to Christ have an *interior signification* which is not discoverable upon the surface, then still more should the language be discarded: for it no longer answers the purpose for which it was designed. If the expressions have a meaning which is not perceptible, then should they not be uttered, because they are, to say the least, entirely useless.

Perhaps no terms have oppressed the mind with more gloom and dread than the terms "hell-fire," "everlasting fire prepared for the devil and his angels," "weeping, wailing, and gnashing of teeth," &c. It will be remembered that it is the *expression*, and not the *meaning*, which terrifies the weak and uninformed mind: for *sheol* being a Hebrew word, has no specific application, but was used promiscuously among the early inhabitants in application to almost anything they disliked. And *hades* is a Greek word applied in the same way. And as *gehenna* is a Greek word derived from two Hebrew expressions, it can not be truthfully said that either of these words is worthy of the least regard, much less that they should be productive of fear, and thus circumscribe the movements and lofty aspirations of the human spirit. I am deeply impressed, and that, too, by an influx of superior information, that if these remarks will assist the efforts of others to rend the dark curtain of superficiality from off the windows of the soul, one great and glorious achievement will be accomplished, and light will illuminate the spiritual possessions of every human form.

A most remarkable and conspicuous personage, who may be considered as an inmate of this theological temple, I have not as yet specifically noticed. I allude to the being called THE DEVIL. This potent personage has been as active in establishing his portion of the kingdom as any influence which we have as yet considered. But it is well to analyze the term "devil," so that we may arrive at a more familiar acquaintance with his origin and disposition. This term is synonymous with *satan*, which latter is derived from *shaitan*. This originally signified almost *nothing*, but was generally used in a loose and unguarded manner, meaning spritely, godly man, deified spirit, disease, monomania, evil-doer, &c. All of these significations are comprehended in various expressions in the Bible, such as satan, death, devil, &c. But even in the Bible, *devil* signifies evil, wickedness, abomination. And when this evil deity is represented as "going up and down the earth," or "going about like a roaring lion seeking whom he may devour," the word "devil" is nothing more than a figurative personification of *evil*. As a proof of this, every discerning person can see that he creates the most tumult and disturbance where ignorance and superstition abound to the greatest extent.

It is well known to biblical commentators, or at least to those who have investigated the early application of terms, that the ancient magicians deified an Evil Principle, and that their theology was systematized by Zoroaster, who possessed all the materials existing prior to his life, from which he erected his supernatural revelation. As the word *shaitan* meant only a *little* more than nothing, certainly the deified imaginary evil principle to which it is *now* applied can not mean a *great deal* more.

But the terms "hell," "devil," "satan," &c., have created more fear and superstitious apprehension than any others contained in the whole Primitive History. But as has been shown, they were intended to express only that which the uncultivated inhabitants of the earth created by false conceptions of the manifestations of Nature, and of the character and attributes of man. Therefore they should be regarded with at least as much respect as any oriental, poetical *mythos*, merely because of the imaginative and marvellous conceptions which they exemplify.

While I am speaking thus, I feel a constant and insuppressible yearning for the elevation of every mind to that degree of mental discernment in which these things which I relate might be equally known to them, and equally discarded by them. This would be a benefit to man, because he would then be restored to communion with the sublime teachings of his nature within, and of Nature without, the happy results of which would not only be experienced in the present, but more perfectly in *higher* spheres.

It is also supposed by the majority of mankind, especially by those acquainted with the teachings of the Old and New Testaments, that the *resurrection* and *general judgment* were never presented to the world before the life and disclosures of Jesus; and that the "golden rule" was then for the first time promulgated by Jesus, and was never conceived of or expressed by any *previous* mind. That is not true. It is well known to some who have explored the pages of antiquity, that CONFUCIUS, the Chinese philosopher, expressed the golden rule nearly six hundred years before Christ lived — about which time ZOROASTER also flourished, who succeeded in establishing throughout the whole eastern world the doctrine of a physical resurrection and general judgment. Zoroaster even *prophesied*, with a great deal of perspicuity, ingenuity, and truthfulness. Notwithstanding his conceptions of a general resurrection and judgment were derived from the many conceptions of earlier ages, they are presented in a more systematic and rational form than those which are contained in the New Testament, and which the apostles endeavored to promulgate on the authority of the teachings and martyrdom of Christ.

§ 141. Matthew, after having related the prophecy of Jesus concerning the destruction of Jerusalem, and many other promiscuous sayings, closes by giving a description of the trials, sufferings, condemnation, and crucifixion of Christ, who was a person of remarkable excellence in all his physical and spiritual possessions. But as I shall speak concerning this subject hereafter, I dismiss it for the present, and proceed to notice some remarks of Matthew upon this very unjust crucifixion.

He relates that Christ was exceedingly disliked by the Jewish nation, and that he was accused, arrested, and conveyed to the presence of Pontius Pilate—who was not over-anxious to condemn, but was compelled by the vociferous multitude to yield his assent and seal the condemnation. After this, a cross was prepared, which Jesus was enforced to carry, and which he did with a great deal of gentleness and humiliation, until he arrived at the spot where his noble and dignified person was to be sacrificed. They placed a crown of thorns upon his head, and gave him impure and bitter drink to quench his thirst; and what is still more to be lamented is, that they nailed him to the cross, and then perforated his body with their spears, that his sufferings might be increased, and their exasperation gratified! He is represented to have had but a few followers, and these came and wept beneath his body.

After he was taken from the cross and deposited in the sepulchre, before whose mouth a stone was placed, he is represented as being guarded for three days, and then coming forth and appearing to three of his disciples. After this, he was seen, it is said, by upward of five hundred souls; and not long afterward he ascended amid the clouds and disappeared, to occupy a position as Judge on high.

This, as it will be remembered, is recorded by Matthew, Mark, Luke, and John. The record is not a demonstration of its actual occurrence, although those who wrote were pure and undesigning men, whose testimonies are worthy of the highest respect and consideration. I will explain hereafter how this opinion was created, the causes engaged in producing it, and why these persons wrote with so much pure simplicity. But at present I am only investigating the theological speculations based upon these records.

This martyrdom of Jesus is called the "Vicarious Atonement;" that is, his suffering for the sins of the world—suffering an innocent and ignominious death for that which his death could not alter, and that which the Divine Creator is represented as having instituted! Why should the Jews be persecuted for crucifying Jesus, if indeed it was originally designed that the latter should thus suffer for the redemption of mankind? The merit did not consist in his death independently, because he would not have been persecuted nor put to death had not the Jews performed that office. Then why not say that the Jews were essential means employed in the accomplishment of this vicarious atonement? and why should the whole be ascribed to the object sacrificed? The Jews, however, are charged with exceeding cruelty, injustice, and unholy persecution. They are accused in every possible way, and with a degree of virulence which is much against their accusers; but how could they be guilty when they were made agents of the Divine Mind to fulfil one of his original designs? Then the Jews should receive a great share of the adoration and praise: for it was by them that this great end was accomplished, and not so much by the sacrifice or vicarious atonement, which was merely the *effect* of their united efforts. Why, then, place merit, adoration, and praise, where they do not belong?—for it is manifestly unjust to adore and venerate an *effect* more than its *cause*.

But the death of Christ had no possible connexion with the sins of the world, nor with the cause of sin. Sin, indeed, in the common acceptation of that term, does not really exist; but what is called sin is merely a *misdirection* of man's physical and spiritual powers, which generates unhappy consequences. The death of no being will extirpate these evil consequences. Nothing short of a general knowledge of the *causes* of these evils, and of the general capabilities of mankind, will restore permanent harmony and happiness to the race. Nor is it possible for any principles involved in the idea of a vicarious atonement, to produce the work of general reorganization; but a *rejection* of this doctrine will be one of the mightiest steps toward ultimate amelioration and consequent happiness.

Further: there is no law governing any composition, that will admit of its ascension above the forms of Nature, before *each part* of that composition becomes fitted for ascension. Then the body of a person can not be made to ascend while the law of association exists and governs Nature universally. Nevertheless, it has been supposed that the composition constituting the body of Christ might have undergone a process of *refinement* suitable to render an ascension possible. But then it must have become completely *intangible*, and could not have been seen by those who were present at the ascension. But this supposition is not founded upon a knowledge of general laws, or of their unvarying effects as manifested in every department of Nature. Such an ascension would indeed have been impossible: because there could not have been such an accelerated process of refinement as to perfect any composition in the space of three days.

Moreover, the term *anastasis*, rendered *resurrection* in the New Testament, does not originally express any such an ascension. It there signifies a rising up, an elevation, a progressive reform, a resurrection, a gradual and steady improvement. It may be added that the doctrine of a general resurrection is founded only upon the supposition that the Bible teaches it, which it can not be proved to do; nor is there any such meaning attached to the original expression *anastasis*. It is well to remark, however, that Paul, who philosophized upon the subject, really believed in a general, corporeal resurrection. Still, all his expressions, as well as those of the other writers, will admit of a different signification; for terms have become greatly modified since language has become so copious and superfluous, and therefore what they mean *now* is not always what they meant originally.

Then, again, Matthew relates a most marvellous phenomenon concerning the temple being rent, the earth quaking, graves opening, and their tenants being quickened into life, and appearing unto many in the city. (Matt. xxvii. 51-53.) This would not have been believed for one moment, had it been related in any portion of the Zend Avesta—although there are more remarkable things therein recorded than this. When such things are presented for credence, it is always proper to reflect upon the probable *origin* of such relations—their *use*, if *true*, and then to inquire whether they are susceptible of an *application*. If these questions were urged with reference to this account, its truth or untruth would not be regarded as of any importance; for it is manifestly a confusion of the order of Nature, and void of all practical utility.

As to a day of general Judgment, not much comment is required; for it is neither taught in the Scriptures, nor believed by any biblical investigator of a superiorly-enlightened mind. A remark heretofore made, will answer instead of a protracted argument: "Whatever the judgment can not sanction, the Divine Mind never created."

§ 142. As the book of Matthew comprehends all that is related in the succeeding books, I have given attention to its contents to the exclusion, as yet, of all the collateral evidences found in the other books for or against the propositions touched upon and analyzed. But I will proceed to a general reflection upon each of these books, in the order in which they are placed, speaking also of their origin and prominent principles. Before doing so, however, I will state a few facts in the history of Matthew.

Matthew became an officer under the Roman government some time previous to the death of Christ, in which occupation he continued for a long period, even until old age, at which time Paul, Dionysius, and others, were preaching the important doctrines of Christ. Matthew deserted the Jewish and embraced the Christian religion, not long after Paul's conversion, and he then soon began to write concerning the things heard and seen as appertaining to Christ and his teachings. It will be seen by a review of his book, that he apparently grouped the sayings of Christ, not in the order in which they occurred, but merely as they were presented to his mind; for, in many places, he evidently comprehends in one sentence an historical account of the miracles and sayings of Jesus which seemingly occupied many months. Besides this, his manuscripts have never been known to the world. The only remains of them are contained in a *Greek* manuscript. But they were, as commentators admit, originally written in *Hebrew*, and for the express use of some Jewish converts. There evidently existed no intention on his part, nor on the part of those who transcribed his writings, to ever have them merged into a canonical book. Certainly he was never directed by Christ to write and present this manuscript to the world for this purpose. Nor can it be proved that he ever had such an intention himself, either from the nature of his record, or from the very unsatisfactory manner in which the same has been compiled, received as canonical, and voted as the first book of the New Testament. Nothing could be more proper than the *title* of this book, which designates it as "according to," though not as written by, Matthew. They who prefixed this title were themselves doubtful as to its origin. Ecclesiastical history proves that its chronology is discrepant with that of the preceding and subsequent writings; and very many even admit that the first two chapters are exceedingly doubtful, while none are very anxious to vouch for their truth.

After Matthew had written a few manuscripts, he was captured by two officers of the Persian customs, carried to the governor, pronounced guilty of heterodoxy, and was condemned, and died a martyr.

Some wise men have written profound criticisms upon the contents of the Old and New Testaments, and seem to have mistaken evidence to be against, rather than in favor of, the writings of the apostles; especially where unguarded expressions occur, or quotations from the Old Testament, or historical relations which do in reality oppose the records of other writers. The book of Mark contains many things that are discrepant with the contents of the book of Matthew. But this is no evidence that they intended imposition upon the world. Nor is it in any respect against the moral purity and rectitude of their historical writings; but it rather manifests a pure design in giving to the world that which they seriously believed, and which was equally believed by others. It proves that there existed no designing plot—no collusion, whereby all things therein related might be joined and confirmed in such a manner as to exclude the possibility of detection and exposure. It proves, also, that they wrote merely from an influx of external impressions; and the reflux of these gave rise to the manuscripts of the New Testament. It proves, also, that they wrote with an entire unacquaintance with each other's private opinions or concurrent views; and that they wrote free from any intention except that of presenting a pure and truthful account.

§ 143. The book of MARK commences unlike that of Matthew; for, instead of introducing a genealogy, it begins by quoting from the book of Malachi, third chapter and first verse, a prophecy concerning one who would (and did) come to prepare the way for the introduction of the teachings of Christ to the world. It will be seen, by reading the quotation in Malachi, that it is in the first person, and has no connexion whatever with the future. But the expression is applicable to the fact that John preached and prepared the way for the introduction of the gospel. Considered as a *prophecy*, however, the expression is not applicable.

This book contains fewer references to the prophecies than Matthew, and is confined particularly to a comprehensive relation of many things which are also recorded in Matthew, and with a very little dissimilarity. Mark makes mention of the colt on which Jesus rode to Jerusalem, adding to the account, what Matthew did not mention, that it was a colt " upon whose back man never before sat," with the exception of this slight variation, which was supposed to make the occurrence nearer a miracle than the simple relation of Matthew, the two accounts coincide. He mentions, also, the casting of lots, to ascertain who should possess the garments of Jesus. This, also, is related differently from what we find it in Matthew. For Matthew, in connexion, makes a quotation, which he appears to have considered as a confirmation of the idea concerning the preknowledge of the early writers. Such quotations consist of incidental expressions occurring in the Old Testament, having in all cases a connexion with the historical events or circumstances referred to in those books.

Mark then proceeds to quote from the fifty-third chapter of Isaiah, the words, " And he was numbered with the transgressors." This he applies to the crucifixion of Christ with the two thieves. It is well to remember, again, that it was the *expression* which they quoted, and that in order to relate the circumstance in the language of others, instead of employing their own — the same as one at the present day would quote from the poetical, theological, or philosophical productions of any previous writer, when passages are found which are applicable, in order to embody or confirm his own reasonings or impressions. If Mark and the other New Testament writers had used the phrase, " that the expression might be verified," instead of, " that the prophecy might be fulfilled," the reader would not be led to believe so many unwarrantable ideas concerning the foreknowledge of those prophets.

The expression that occurs in Isaiah, " He shall be numbered with the transgressors," applies only to, and was originally intended to represent, the sufferings and trials of Jeremiah.* For although he was a very affectionate and amiable man, and was generally beloved, he was nevertheless numbered with the transgressors many times, and was thus as often despised. It is true that Isaiah mentions no name, but a careful reading will decide that the allusion was to something of this kind, though made in an indefinite and obscure manner.

* See note on page 498.

The book of Mark contains no distinct doctrines that are not contained in Matthew. It is written in a more condensed and perspicuous manner than the book of Matthew. It is generally regarded favorably for its brevity and plainness of historical and biographical details.

The writer closes the book by relating a command given to the apostles to go forth into all the world and preach the Gospel; and, according to what follows, their testimony was to be offered to the world on terms most severe and absolute. It does not seem possible that any being possessing a very high degree of spiritual knowledge, could have uttered such a sentence as, "He that believeth not shall be damned." This declaration is contrary to the teachings of all laws of cause and effect. He who believes any principle, faith, or philosophy, must believe it as the result of a deep and immovable conviction of the judgment. Certainly the mere fact of the *apostles preaching* could not have been sufficient to produce such a faith as was demanded. Faith could not be expected when there did not exist sufficient cause to produce it.

Again: the *reward* for faith was to be a salvation — a saving, perhaps, from sin, from skepticism, from destruction by moral or physical death, or from an abode of suffering and wretchedness. Neither of these is distinctly mentioned; but whether it was to be a salvation from one or all of these calamities, it would be well to inquire, How is it possible for faith, by any natural process, to produce such an effect as is herein stated? The effect of faith is merely a tranquillity of mind, from which flow bright hopes and anticipations. Therefore faith can not save from sin, or pain, or wretchedness, or moral or spiritual death. For the world to be saved from such direful evils, the laws of society and the arbitrary governments of nations must be changed, so as to coincide with the principles of Nature, with the constitution of man, and with all his physical and spiritual requirements.

The blessings that would follow such an harmonious organization of Mankind could not properly be considered as a reward or effect of faith; because faith is merely an involuntary assent of the judgment, and produces that calmness and tranquillity of mind which constitute happiness. This happiness is confined to the mind whose judgment is thus decided, and it is not capable of being communicated to another, nor can it even supply the physical or spiritual necessities of its possessor. How, then, can salvation be a result of *faith?* And what can be more unjust than the severity and positiveness of that declaration which says, "He that believeth not shall be damned"? A man can not believe or disbelieve *at will*. He can not control the convictions of his own judgment, but is obliged to submit to be controlled. He can no more have faith upon any subject at will, than he can, by the exercise of will, have a warm or cold feeling, or a love or hatred, or a delight or displeasure. How unjust is it, then, to call upon man to do that which is so entirely beyond his power! It would be as proper and consistent to cast a man upon a burning pile, and bid him live, under the penalty of being for ever damned if he did not comply; or to cast a man into the waters of a foaming ocean, and bid him preserve his existence, while at the same time all means of salvation are beyond his reach; or to place a man under the keen-edged guillotine, and, at the moment appointed for the severing instrument to drop, to exclaim — "Resist and prevent the blow, or you shall be for ever lost in the depths of a burning abyss!" Any being who would do these things would be called by the world a tyrant, a heathen, a being not worthy of the human form or of its sublime possessions.

Listen, then, ye who admire the sentiment expressed in the book of Mark, while I inquire, "How can the least degree of justice exist in the absoluteness of that demand which attaches the penalty of damnation to the non-performance of that which is beyond the powers of man's nature to accomplish?" If, then, this expression was ever uttered by Christ, it bears all the marks of cruelty and heathenish unrighteousness. This is no less the case if it proceeded from the mouth of any other being. But I am happy to relate that although this is in the book of Mark, it was not uttered in the preaching of Jesus.

§ 144. The next passage states a number of evidences to be manifested by those who truly believed. It reads as follows: "And these signs shall follow them that believe: In my name shall they cast out devils; they shall speak with new tongues; they shall take up serpents without harm; and if they drink any deadly thing, it shall not hurt them; they shall lay hands on the sick, and they shall recover." This is one of the most unfortunate passages that could possibly occur for theologians and the followers of their philosophy and teachings. It can not be truly said that *any* possess the power of casting out devils, in the sense in which the phrase is here used.

If the passage had said, "They shall cast *in* devils" (or *evils*), then would it have been verified throughout the whole heathen and Christian world; for nothing is clearer than that the very believers and promulgators of this system of theology have cast evils, or devils, into the bosom of man, and into the heart of society, to an extent that is beyond estimation. Believers, then, cast devils IN, not OUT, by preaching the doctrines *supposed* to have been taught by Christ. But it can not be said with the same degree of truth that they ever succeeded in effectually banishing one devil, or evil, from the world.

The sentence which immediately follows has been fully verified, viz.: "They shall speak with new tongues." It has appeared in the course of past investigations, that theologians (at least many of them) do frequently employ words in which neither they nor any other person can discover the least particle of signification. Therefore they truly speak in new tongues. For the terms "satan," "hell," "reward," "punishment," "involuntary," "supernatural," "disinterested," &c., are terms which express as near the shadow of no substance as it is possible for the mind to conceive. And I do not hesitate to venture any strength of assertion that these terms, with a vast number of others, are significant of no *real* thought, and are incapable of being applied to any *real* principle, phenomenon, or development, in any department of Nature or the Universe. Any person, then, entertaining the least particle of doubt concerning the truthfulness of the above sentence from Mark, should reflect on these things, and banish all doubt immediately; for it is evident that these theologians do speak in new tongues, inasmuch as they are scarcely comprehended either by themselves or any other being.

I can not let this opportunity pass without observing some late developments among the followers of new faiths. These have occurred within the last century, and therefore no particular historical detail is required. So I proceed to mention the performances of the sect known as the MORMONS. The founder of this sect presented to the world, not only his own testimony, but that of many others, in relation to his and their religious faith and miraculous performances. They professed to heal the sick by the "laying-on of hands," to cast out devils, and to converse in unknown tongues. They can produce evidence of an artificial character of these things, and of their actual occurrence. But there exists no interior evidence, probability, or use, in any such performances, and therefore they should not receive the credence of any rational mind. One thing, however, in evidence of the possession of the right faith, they could produce in abundance; and that is, they could converse in unknown tongues. Strictly true is this statement, for some of the dissenters from that faith do not hesitate to acknowledge that they could and did converse in a language unknown either to *themselves* or to *anybody else!* The followers of ANN LEE, also, whose history is well known, make the same pretensions, and produce the same evidence; and their dissenters make, without hesitation, precisely the same acknowledgment.

Therefore beware of superficial testimony, external appearances, visible, tangible, sensual evidences, because such are invariably liable to deceive, and are oftentimes unrighteous. Beware, too, of the character of every external testimony. Search well the cause of its existence. Reflect well upon the external means employed to produce credence in respect to any phenomenon — any marvellous circumstance — any miraculous development, either in Nature or in man, and also upon the uses made of such; because there exists a strong probability that there are latent intentions connected with such evidences that constitute the very elements of deception.

§ 145. Many in past ages believed that the *elephant* was a prodigy or miracle of Nature. Some of the ancients supposed that he was not only the result of a miraculous conception of Nature, but that he possessed a *spirit*, and reasoning powers, equal if not superior to those possessed by man. Besides this, his social habits were believed by some to be established, directed, and controlled, by spirits of the mountains, forests, and other places, which they frequented. The ancients had also an opinion that spirits communed with elephants, and instigated their thoughts; and that spirits, ghosts, witches, angels, devils, and many similar personages, existed in great abundance. Is there not testimony in favor of the most marvellous transactions of angels, devils, ghosts, witches, and other active, invisible beings? — testimonies, too, of the most unexceptionable character?

There are also *now* persons who believe that man is in constant communion with spirits, either of a good or evil character; the first being the cause of all good thoughts, and the latter of all evil ones. They also believe that men possess the power to move toward the gulf of evil, or the throne of goodness. This power is termed "*free will.*" They thus make man an independent and self-existent creature, and endeavor to impress upon his mind that if he is sinful, it is the result merely of his will, or his affection for evil; a quality which he need not possess if he desires to be free from it. Moreover, it is said that he can approach the throne or sphere of celestial goodness by the same exercise of his own will-power. Such an attribute would give man unlimited control over the laws, forces, and actuating principles, of the Universe. It would make him possess the requisite power to resist all temptation, and all influences of eternal laws. It would give him power to command, and teach him that he existed uncommanded. It would give him power to control, while he is not at all capable of being controlled, influenced, or actuated!

But it may be said that he has "free will" only in a *qualified sense*. But the very moment a qualification is needed, the doctrine is proved to be unsound, and man's power is shown to be limited. If he can not under all circumstances and conditions resist being influenced or actuated, then the philosophy under notice is not true; because the fact of man's being once influenced, establishes the truth that he is actuated by adequate forces, and governed throughout eternity by immutable laws.

Others believe that man may reproduce in himself the power of working miracles, and say they have succeeded in presenting a demonstration. Others at the present day believe that man possesses no spiritual principle which will retain its identity after the physical dissolution. These reason deductively, but not analytically; hence the conclusion is illegitimate and unsound. And there are existing innumerable sects, entertaining as many different opinions; and each sect is anxious to sustain its own particular creed.

The followers of Ann Lee seriously believe and teach that select persons among them commune with the spirits that inhabit celestial spheres. They frequently induce, by excitement, a cataleptic condition of the body, and then are said to be in heaven, walking among and conversing with the angels. And when they return to outward consciousness, they relate these marvellous peregrinations with all the seriousness and solemnity of truth—because they believe them. Surely, then, miracles exist in our midst, of the same character as those which are mentioned in the book of Mark as following all true believers.

Is it not as reasonable to esteem heathen, ancient, Chinese, Persianic, or Mohammedan credulity, as the credulity of those who implicitly believe and teach the doctrines of the Primitive History? Is it not just to regard the Mormon and Shaker evidences and credulity that exist in our midst, with the same degree of veneration as the things merely related in the books of the New Testament, and believed by many in the world? Certainly *modern* credulity is as much to be respected as *ancient*. Then why *confine* belief, when external evidences of *true faiths* exist about and among us in abundance?

The sentence which follows the last one commented upon, refers to the handling of serpents without harm. Unfortunately, there exists much *actual danger* in this experiment; and hence it is not so frequently attempted as the former ones. There exists evidence that more men who have possessed *scarcely any* faith, have handled serpents with perfect safety, than there have been persons who have performed the same things among those possessing faith sufficiently powerful almost to remove a *light* mountain.

Furthermore, it is said, " They shall drink any deadly thing without injury." It is strange how *deadly* things can be drunk without injuring *life!* It is unnecessary to speak of the action of the human system in repulsing or yielding to that which is opposed to its nature or composition. Poison can be taken into the system in *minute portions* without injury; but if too great a portion is taken, it is incapable of assimilating with the elements of the body, and thus constitutes a violation (though not a suspension) of natural law, the inevitable result of which would be a cessation of life. A true believer, then, may take a *small* portion without receiving harm; but then this would not be taking a *deadly* thing in the sense implied in the passage. Besides this, an *unbeliever* could, without injury, take the same quantity. But it is plain that the handling of serpents and the drinking of poison is an experiment that is rather *too personal* to be often attempted.

Alas for theologians, and those who think they are unerring believers! for the evidences which they can produce are so few and so intangible, that the human mind is incapable of discerning their existence. Remember these *external* evidences are not to be in any case relied upon as proving *anything* to which they are applied. If what I reveal requires external testimony to prove its truth, then indeed its truth might with propriety be doubted. But if, while it possesses the external clothing of sensuous and superficial testimony, it sinks deep into the recesses of the judgment, even to the interior of the human spirit, and there receives a response, its truth is at once placed beyond doubt, and is established to a demonstration. In this manner should all things be tested; and then truth, goodness, and tranquillity, will be the legitimate consequences.

With these remarks, I leave the contents of the book of Mark, to speak of the writer personally. His name was JOHN MARK. He was born and brought up, and resided through his life, in the city of Jerusalem. He lived at the time John the Baptist and Jesus were preaching. He was a believer, and felt anxious to have the new faith promulgated and believed; but he can not be properly termed an apostle. He had a small family, and was pleasantly situated, both as to the capacity of his residence and his financial affairs. He was accustomed to keep open his house as a place of entertainment and resort for Jesus and the apostles; and this continued during the whole public life of Jesus, and especially from about the time he began to preach until his crucifixion. After this event, John Mark compiled some of the remarks of Jesus, and some impressions concerning him, from a few registered notes which he had kept, into the form of a manuscript, which he designed and intended only for the reading of some converts, mainly from paganism.

But it should be remembered that manuscripts written in those days, upon bark or some similar substance, were never copied as writings are copied in modern days. So he alone possessed this record, and it was scarcely read or known to be existing by any other persons than those for whom it was immediately designed, until a long period after his death. And what right Constantine and the bishops assembled at Nice and Laodicea had to vote the book of Mark as canonical, is not very easily explained; inasmuch as many similar manuscripts and epistles were rejected and burned according to the decision of their misdirected judgments. Mark never intimated that he desired or intended that the world at the nineteenth century should read his registered historical impressions; nor was he ever directed by Jesus to even write or publish them. Whence, then, this superstitious veneration for that which was never intended by those whom you love most, even Jesus and the apostles, to be thus superstitiously believed and sanctified by subsequent generations?

§ 146. I now proceed to a brief consideration of the book of LUKE, which follows:—

LUKE was a very candid, worthy, and well-instructed author. His writings manifest a great deal of perspicuity, candor, and intended truthfulness. He is serious in every respect, and worthy of the deepest regard; and confidence should not be withholden from his historical relations. He prefaced his remarks with a very clear and lucid description of the character of his impressions concerning Jesus and the apostles, speaking particularly of the *source* of the information from which he wrote. He intimates that he penned that which himself and many others "most surely believed." He attaches no inspiration to his knowledge. He courts the favor of no person. He does not claim to be believed because he writes; but his whole introduction displays a beautiful simplicity and candor which can not fail to commend the author to respect and esteem. And what is still more remarkable is, that he discards that which is claimed for him by commentators, and all who profess to believe that he, in common with his associate writers, was supernaturally inspired. How unrighteous, how injurious to the race it is, for men to claim for the Bible that fear, that superstitious and unreal veneration, which the Bible does not demand for itself!

Some may consider these sayings as derogatory to the holy purity of the Bible, especially to that purity which interpreters attach to it, but which can not be found in that book. But instead of *opposing* I am *defending* the writers of the New and Old Testament against the superstitious falsifications that are imposed upon their writings by those who profess to be their expounders. I feel impressed to say that the Bible, like all other books, should be respected for *the intrinsic worth* and *truthfulness* which may characterize it; but for *no other reason*. Moreover, in speaking of superstitious and false interpretations, I refer to the fact that it is taught with a great deal of sanctimoniousness, that its contents are an influx from the Divine Mind into the minds of those who wrote it. I am distinctly impressed with the conviction that no book, or any other superficia production of man, can legitimately and truthfully claim such inspiration. For nothing can be of divine origin which is not inseparably connected with, and incessantly developed by, the laws, qualities, and principles, contained in the great Tree of universal causation. And I have shown that that which man creates or invents merely by his evanescent imagination, can not be anything more than a mass of imperfection. Thus those books may contain truth, yet no book is worthy the veneration which the Mohammedan pays to the KORAN, the Brahmin to the SHASTER, the Persian to the ZEND AVESTA, or the Christian to the BIBLE.

I have made these remarks with distinctness, so that there may be no misapprehension, concerning that of which I am impressed to speak, and that there may not exist any obscurity or discrepancy in the minds of those who seriously reflect, who candidly investigate, and who fear not to read, untrammelled by sectarian prejudice.

The book of Luke is very free from quotations from the prophecies. Those, however, that are made, are similar to those which I have previously noticed. This book advances no particular doctrine which in any way needs an explanation or comment. Nor do I discover that its teachings are in any particular different from those of the previous books, with the exception of some new parabolical illustrations, some change in the expression, and also in the grouping of the historical accounts of the life, preaching, and crucifixion of Jesus. And those things which are in it advanced, have been, in a general manner, commented upon in reviewing the several propositions, derived from the book of Matthew. So I will conclude all reflections on this book, and offer a few remarks concerning its author.

Luke also was of Jewish birth—was educated in the Jewish religion, and in this continued nearly to the time of Paul's conversion from the Jewish to the Christian religion. Luke in his early life learned a trade, which was the custom among the Jewish people, whether the parents of the young were or were not wealthy. He succeeded eminently in his profession, which was that of an *artist*, He is said to have painted the first portrait of Christ, which is to be seen at the present day in the Roman Academy of Design. After Luke embraced the Christian religion, he was a constant co-worker with many of the apostles and believers in various portions of the eastern world. He obtained his information principally from communications received from those who were eye-witnesses of the things related concerning Jesus. He wrote not from actual knowledge, but from that which he received from others. One of his particular friends was THEOPHILUS, whom he felt very anxious to convince of the truth of Christianity. To him he wrote this gospel and the Acts of the Apostles; and these books were written for no other purpose than to produce a conviction in the mind of his friend, corresponding to that in his own. And it is well to inquire on what authority were these writings voted canonical, when, at the same time, many as worthy manuscripts were deprived of their existence. Meanwhile, consider, reader, that Luke intended merely to convince *his friend* by writing and transmitting his thoughts in a connected manner, and had no design that the whole world should be taught to believe that of which he desired only to convince Theophilus. It may be that he *desired* that such might be the case, because all who are firmly convinced of any faith, desire to have it become universal. But one thing is absolutely certain : he neither pretended to inspiration nor even anticipated being classed as he has been, in a standard cyclopedia of theology. Nor did he even once intimate that he entertained any thought as to the distinction which his writings have subsequently received.

Luke also wrote concerning the origin of the Ephesian church; how it was established; what teachings and ceremonies were adopted, and how he and the brethren of the church exulted, and congratulated each other, in the possession of their new faith. His books are full of information, and they demand respect and approbation for their simplicity and fluency of expression — at least as much respect as the writings of any other good and worthy man.

§ 147. I next proceed to the book of JOHN. This book displays great warmth of feeling, affection, and social and religious attachment. It manifests a great deal of veneration, and aspiring and noble sentiment; and these characterized the life, disposition, and spiritual constitution of its author. Its contents are mostly a repetition of things recorded in the former books; and it contains but few appeals to promiscuous expressions among the prophecies. It establishes no proposition that differs from those heretofore noticed, and hence needs no further comment.

I can not, however, very well avoid one remark upon a casual and unguarded sentence at the close of this book, in which John expresses the supposition, that if all the things which Christ performed were written, "even the world itself could not contain the books that would be written." Notwithstanding there were thousands of things said and done by Jesus which neither John nor any other writer recorded, it is plain to every mind that if those things were written, the world *would* hold them. This is an evidence of John's unbounded and sanguine love for the faith which he had embraced. And even a *little* exaggeration on the part of the apostles, in writing their impressions, forbids at once the possibility of their minds being under the controlling influence of inspiration from the Divine Mind. Whatever is divine — strictly of celestial birth — must bear *unexceptionable* evidence of its holy origin.

JOHN was born, and resided the greater portion of his life, in Ephesus. His early religious impressions were few; and when these things were presented to his mind, he exercised a great deal of judgment and reflection upon their merits, and afterward adopted and promulgated them with a great deal of sanguine confidence and energy. His manuscripts, like Mark's, were a long time concealed from public observation, but were subsequently translated into the Hebrew language, were sanctioned by the council of Nice, sealed as canonical by Constantine, and thus were presented to the world as constituting the fourth book of the New Testament.

The fifth book, which follows, entitled "ACTS OF THE APOSTLES," is an historical commentary and registral production of LUKE. It contains only a record of circumstances, experiences, travels, discussions, and vicissitudes, of the apostles; an account of the formation and establishment of the church; and descriptions of the unity, peace, quietness, and brotherly love, which prevailed among the believers. It does not contain any principles requiring comment or elucidation. And inasmuch as it is a book of historical information, it claims for itself only this character. If any other claims are set up as to its origin, contents, or importance, then these claims are unwarrantable; and Luke, its writer, completely overthrows them. It certainly contains many beautiful and forcible expressions of sentiments, but no new principles; and hence I pass on to the consideration of the following books.

§ 148. I come now to reflect upon the birth, life, preachings, experience, disposition, and death, of a very highly-educated and much-beloved writer. Indeed, I can not resist the attraction toward so worthy a mind—one possessing so much purity of soul and so much lofty magnanimity.

Before I speak of his many friendly epistles to associated brethren and established churches in various portions of the east, I will dwell upon his birth, life, disposition, and experiences.

Ecclesiastical historians have collected some very truthful information concerning the birth and life of PAUL; and to their historical accounts much credit should be given. PAUL was born in Tarsus. He dwelt during the early portion of his life in the city of Rome, and was there much esteemed as a highly-talented and respectable citizen. After receiving a very superior education through various means of instruction, he subjected himself to a long and protracted course of studies under the guidance and instruction of Gamaliel in

Jerusalem. Gamaliel was a professor of ancient literature, natural philosophy, and traditional science, and was recognised as a superior teacher of the various languages. He was a Jewish rabbin. From him Paul received many doctrines and religious hypotheses, which afterward in a measure gave direction to his religious meditations and writings. After Paul had completed his education, he was truly an enlightened man, so far as a knowledge of external science and philosophy is worthy to be termed enlightenment.

He was also familiar with the Grecian poets and philosophers, and from them received much of his sublime thought and rational philosophy. Indeed, this is plain from a part of his writings contained in the New Testament; for many of his expressions as connected with his moral philosophy, evince a striking similarity of views and style to those of the Grecian poets and metaphysicians.

PAUL cultivated many useful social accomplishments. His social life was of an exceedingly complex character, for it was extensively interwoven with various experiences both of a pleasing and disappointing nature. These were of such a character as tended constantly to modify and develop in him new traits of mental constitution. He, like Luke, learned a very useful trade, namely, that of *tent-making*, which he subsequently discovered to be of great advantage and importance to him. Being a Roman citizen for a great portion of his life, his character, religion, philosophy, and deportment, were very much like those with whom he familiarly associated; and therefore he can not be said to have possessed a predisposition to become what he subsequently did become. Nor can it be said that he required a spiritual influx of superior truths to write his moral philosophy; for he was superiorly enlightened in all important branches of knowledge, such as the arts, science, logic, metaphysics, and physical and religious philosophy. But this much can be said—and the assertion is fully attested by his own productions—that he was a most pure, worthy, benevolent, and devotional man, characterized by all those superior qualifications that are required to constitute a truly great and good mind.

During the time that Jesus lived, and while his doctrines were being disseminated, Paul was a most violent opposer, and unqualifiedly rejected and despised the doctrines that he afterward so rapturously embraced. This opposition continued for many years after the death of Christ, during which period he embraced the Pharisaical philosophy, which contained some truth, though that truth was entirely concealed by a superabundance of error arising merely from external, material observation. And after Paul joined this sect, he assumed the position of commander, at the head of a band or army composed of the same sect, and marched against and persecuted the Christian believers to an unjust and unwarrantable extent. Thus was he employed for a long period. He manifested in all cases the most violent and sanguinary intentions against the Christians. All his movements were characterized by a great degree of firmness, and an eager and positive determination to have his own opinions and principles prevail.

It is related that while on his way to Damascus, he experienced a sudden change in his actuating motives and intentions; and this occurrence has been related in such a manner as to convey the impression that it proceeded from a miraculous or supernatural interposition of the Divine Mind. I am fully aware of the circumstance, and also why such an ocular impression was received; and an acquaintance with the fact as it occurred dissipates immediately all superstitious ideas of a miraculous interposition.

From this period, the faculties of Paul took a different direction, and he became devoted to the Christian religion; the consequence of which was a violent denouncement of the doctrines and persecutions of his past life. Thus were displayed the extremes in the workings of a nervous-sanguine temperament: for he then rejected the Pharisaical and exerted his powers to sustain the Christian religion, with the same degree of ardor and positiveness that he had before manifested in defence of the Pharisaical religion against the Christian.

He now devoted his life and talents to the promulgation of the gospel. In this he was employed for thirty years, during which time he travelled and preached in Arabia, Greece, Asia Minor, and on many islands of the Mediterranean. He was active in establishing societies and religious associations, in order to bring more closely together those who believed the new faith, so that they might congregate and worship in accordance with the doctrines which they had embraced. In this work he manifested much zeal, devotion, and activity. He likewise adopted the custom of epistolary correspondence, which had previously been introduced by other converts and apostles. His epistles were generally directed to the prominent members of the churches, and were also addressed indirectly to the whole congregation in each vicinity where he had labored to deposite a germ of Christianity. Hence, some of those epistles were preserved, collected, compiled, and immersed into the New Testament, in the following order :—

1. *Paul's Epistle to the Romans.*— This was addressed to the Roman church or congregation that had associated to enjoy the faith which both he and they had embraced. 2. *Paul's Epistles to the Corinthians*, or to the congregation of associated brethren in the faith at Corinth. 3. *Paul's Epistle to the Galatians;* being a letter of exhortation, expressive of friendship and brotherly kindness, to the worshipping brethren in the church of Galatia. 4. *Paul's Epistle to the Ephesians;* being a kind and friendly letter to those who had embraced the faith, and who desired the encouragement and approbation of Paul, at Ephesus. 5. *Paul's Epistle to the Philippians;* being a kind letter of encouragement and congratulation to the church of Philippi on the possession of their new faith. 6. *Paul's Epistle to the Colossians ;* which is a letter expressing spiritual sympathy and congeniality of affection for the brethren in Colosse, together with earnest desires for the success of the gospel among them. 7. Two of the many epistles written by *Paul to the Thessalonians;* consisting of prayerful and devout exhortations, and expressions of approbation, sympathy, affection, and love, to the whole congregation of worshippers at Thessalonica. 8. Paul's epistles to his much-admired friend TIMOTHY, who was a private correspondent and a general co-worker with Paul. This Timothy sustained an office in the church modernly called *deacon*, and in this capacity presented Paul's much-admired advice to the congregation of which he was a member. 9. Paul's epistle to TITUS, who was in a similar office, and who was equally beloved as a brother and correspondent, by Paul. 10. *Paul's Epistle to the Hebrews;* in which he expresses all his devotional sympathy for the doctrines cherished in his memory, and also manifests all that loving-kindness and perseverance which characterized all his efforts in the propagation and establishment of the Christian faith.

§ 149. Thus Paul's letters occupy and compose a large portion of the New Testament. On investigation of these letters, it appears plain that they never were intended or expected by Paul to be universally read. Not only is the internal evidence sufficient to warrant this conclusion, but the historical evidence is such as entirely to demonstrate its truth. What I mean by the internal evidence or signification of written thoughts, is that connected with the *source* or *origin* from which they sprang—the basis upon which the *thought* or the *element* of the expression reposes.

Some suppose that an interior meaning is discoverable in every expression in the Bible; but that this can be perceived only by those who have a high degree of spiritual discernment—while others, whose knowledge is confined to the sphere of sensuous observation and impression, are constantly interpreting the contents of the Bible in a gross and literal manner. Giving to any book or its contents a "spiritual signification," is not to unfold an interior origin or cause of the ideas expressed; but it is merely setting aside its literal signification, and clothing its teachings with a spiritual garment. This is manifestly covering or concealing expressions, which are sometimes loose, unguarded, and even unighteous and insignificant, with a brilliant external and ornamental garment. But it is distinctly clear that in order to search into the *interior* or *germ* of a thought, the mind must become acquainted with the *causes* engaged in developing that germ into the form of a written expression. And it is absolutely impossible to give a *real* signification to expressions the *soul* or *cause* of which originated merely in the theology and mythology of an age when misdirection and unreasonable hallucination had possession, to a great extent, of the mind of every human being.

Language may and has changed. When the inhabitants of early ages used the terms Mercury, Venus, Mars, Jupiter, Saturn, Juno, Pallas, &c., their thoughts became directly associated with various gods that were supposed to be existing in the invisible world, the history of whom they had preserved in hieroglyphics. But *now* when these terms are used, the mind does not revert to these heathen deities, but becomes directly associated with the various planets and asteroids of our solar system. Thus it is that language has, in its application, become exceedingly changed. Therefore, what Matthew, Mark, Luke, John, Christ, Paul, or any of the writers of the Bible, have written, may have signified at that time what at the present day can not be understood by the same terms. Inasmuch, then, as the application of many terms has ceased to be as it was in former ages, whatever signification may *now*, by conventional usage, be given to terms employed by oriental writers, can not possibly change the positive fact that their writings were conceived and brought forth amid various causes which it is necessary to *analyze* and *comprehend,* before there can be such a thing as understanding what the germ, soul, or element of any expression, would indicate as its real and original signification.

I am particularly desirous of being apprehended aright in speaking of this important distinction between the *interior signification* of a term or expression, and that *spiritual application* which has been *called* an interior meaning. In order to be distinctly understood, I again repeat that no mind can search into and analyze the interior meaning or origin of words or expressions, without arriving irresistibly at the conclusion which has been heretofore attained — that the contents of the Bible, like those of all other books, have originated among a number of productive causes, all of which must be taken into consideration before any validity or importance can be attached to the records therein contained. No analytical mind can by any possible means arrive at conclusions contrary to those which are here established. And be it further understood that I stay not on terms, or on the thousands of sermons and commentaries that have grown out of a supposed hidden signification of expressions in the Bible. For to dwell upon these would be only to analyze the shadows, the intangible unrealities, which consist of the innumerable interpretations of the Bible — which latter is *assumed* to be what it does not *itself profess* to be, and what it in reality is not, and never was. Know, then, reader, that I am analyzing, dissecting, and investigating the *germ* of all these superfluous productions. And this is the result of the strict and severe analysis: that the elements and qualities contained in the Bible, or the germ of this great theological tree, are positively impure, and unworthy of the interpretations and veneration which they have received in the form of the book to which they have given origin. And this book can not by any possible means be proved to contain those pure and celestial qualities that dwell in Divine Love and Wisdom, which constitute the GERM, the *development* of which is a grand, sublime, and harmonious Universe, of which Man is a branch and a perfect representative. As this latter, therefore, constitutes the true theology, certainly a theology can not be *unlike* it and at the same time true.

These considerations (the truth of which certainly can not be disproved without *some* investigation) show that it is impossible to give an interior signification of a *spiritual* character to that which does not already contain a Divine and celestial element. Hence the doctrine which I discover in the world as resulting from a spiritual commentation upon the Bible, is *not* a revealment or development of the interior possessions of that book, but only a new and attractive garment in which the whole confused collection of matter is concealed from the mind, both of the casual and the reflective reader. This much, however, may be said for the consolation of him who reads understandingly, and with the yearnings of a philanthropic bosom: that Reason and Wisdom, like the sun, will shine and bring forth all desirable and congenial results, when the clouds of obstruction and misconception are dissipated for ever!

§ 150. In the ten books or epistles of PAUL, I discover no distinct doctrine that I have not in a general way noticed and commented upon in previous remarks. My object at present is to make it clear to the mind of the reader that Paul was a good man — worthy of great esteem and confidence, and that he embraced his faith, and wrote concerning it, as any other man would have done, who felt convinced that the faith which he had adopted ought to be extensively believed.

PAUL is the only writer in the whole Bible who attempts to prove his faith by an appeal to *Nature*. His philosophy was evidently impressed upon his mind prior to his embracing Christianity; and he appealed to external and visible manifestations to illustrate or demonstrate his peculiar doctrines. These he presented to the brethren with whom he familiarly and frequently corresponded. But he never wrote a system of moral philosophy to be taught and believed by subsequent generations of the earth; and that he did, there exists no evidence in his epistolary correspondence.

The doctrine of the resurrection — of a literal rising of the natural body — is supposed by some to be positively taught and clearly demonstrated by Paul. This, however, is not true, though the form of expression evinces a belief in such a doctrine. Thus he says, "We are sown in a natural body, and raised in a spiritual body; we are sown in dishonor, and raised in glory." (1 Cor. xv.) It is clear, from these expressions, that Paul uses the terms *natural* and *spiritual, dishonor* and *glory*, in contradistinction to each other; so that the superior would be rendered more beautiful by being placed in contrast with the inferior. Thus his thoughts were elevated by a high degree of hope and anticipation. But it will be admitted by those who carefully reflect upon the preceding remarks, that these illustrations and appeals to natural phenomena by Paul, are of a very superficial character; for although we are, in one sense, sown in a natural and raised in a spiritual body, these terms are more an expression of the *act* than of the *principle* of a resurrection. So, also, being sown in dishonor and raised in glory, represents the external phenomenon of death, and the elevation of the real, or internal man, to a higher sphere. It was but the *fact* that he related, not the interior moving and productive principles which effect the rising, refinement, *anastasis*, or resurrection. Therefore, I say, Paul's external philosophy of the resurrection possesses none of that elaborateness, or of those appeals to the laws governing Nature and man, which would be necessary to satisfy any rational mind of the reality of a future or interior existence.

Again: Paul was given to great internal meditation, especially so far as his peculiar temperament and disposition would admit. At times his cogitations were of a very instructive and useful character. But he sometimes became confused in endeavoring to make a distinction between the intrusions of the outer world upon the senses, affections, and passions, and the promptings and monitions of the internal sense of purity, justice, refinement, and righteousness. Hence he says, "While I would do good, evil is present with me." When forced to this exclamation, he was endeavoring to distinguish the characters and causes of the two suggestive influences, the one to evil and the other to good. Theological speculators have derived from this and similar expressions of Paul, a smoothly-woven theory, that a pervading evil spirit, or his agents, are incessantly affecting man's internal purity through the outer; and that the good is preserved by the Divine Mind; and proceeding upon this hypothesis, they say that man should distinguish the good from the evil—the broad road which leads to a burning abyss of everlasting destruction, from the narrow path leading as far from that dreadful abode as one extremity of the Universe can be from another. Thus they throw the responsibility upon, and accuse man, of immorality, and at the same time teach him that ten thousand influences are actuating and even *controlling* him, either for good or for evil. It is plain that such not only misunderstand the writings and teachings of Paul, but are exceedingly uninformed as to the nature, constitution, and characteristics of mankind.

PAUL, after having preached for thirty years, and consoling himself on the reflection that he had declared the whole gospel without reservation, was captured, brought before a Roman consul, and at length before Festus; who, being moved by Paul's eloquence, absolved him from the charge brought against him. Paul, however, having appealed to Cæsar, was sent to Rome, where he finally died, a martyr to Christianity.

Following the epistles of Paul, are the similar letters of JAMES, PETER, JOHN, and JUDE. The contents of these are very similar to the letters of Paul, pertaining, as they do, to the establishing of the same general principles in the minds of the persons and congregations to whom they were respectively addressed. They introduce no new principle which requires comment; and their teachings have no important bearing upon the proposition advanced in or derived from the preceding books.

---

§ 151. After these epistles, follows the APOCALYPSE or REVELATION OF ST. JOHN. The contents of this book have appeared to all commentators as being completely enigmatical, beyond the possibility of receiving a useful application, and so exceedingly indefinite and obscure as almost to defy any attempt at analysis. It bears truly every mark of a *revelation;* nor can this fact be doubted when it is carefully read and as carefully reflected upon. Its prominent features are obscurity, ambiguity, and all kinds of fantastic and figurative expression. Nevertheless, some of its figures are well applied, though their application is scarcely discoverable. Indeed, nothing can be more obscure than this revelation; for its contents defy interpretation, though they at the same time severely demand the most unreserved faith. The book even forbids the erasure or interpolation of a single sentence, under the most imperative command, for a disobedience of which condemnation is denounced. Such a demand of itself removes from it all that celestial purity which should be expected to characterize a spiritual influx of heavenly truth; for the demand is strictly dogmatical, and unjustly imperative. This book ends the New Testament.

It should be remarked that the books of James and Jude have been received with a great deal of doubt as to their authenticity, by those who have ventured to inquire into the origin of the manuscripts. Moreover, let it be remembered that they, together with the Revelation of St. John, were not received into the New Testament as pure and canonical until nearly three hundred years after the council of Nice. The Apocalypse, and the books of James and Jude, together with the second chapter of the second epistle of Peter, were voted pure and canonical in the year 633, at the council of Toledo; when they, in their seventeenth canon, decided unanimously that the Revelation was written by John, and that the books of James and John should be compiled and immersed into the New Testament, and stamped with the holy seal, and considered the *Word of God!*

It would indeed have been fortunate for many a profound theologian, had this council, like the councils of Nice and Laodicea, rejected this book as not being the word of God; for then much time and noble talent would very probably have been expended on something that would have been of use and importance in the way of ameliorating the condition of a suffering and ignorant humanity. Inasmuch, however, as the Apocalypse was decided to be the word of God in 633, it is proper to institute a few considerations concerning its teachings, and enigmatical, fantastical, and spiritual contents.

It is a truth worthy of notice, that many things therein contained are susceptible of being verified by appealing to the actual appearances and manifestations of the interior* or spiritual world. Panoramas and dissolving representations such as this book presents may be observed in the spirit-world by spirits whose internal perception is not opened, and when their exteriors are clothed by an aerial mantle of imagination. Such are witnessed in what may be termed a transition state between the external and internal spheres of the spiritual constitution.

For a very truthful solution of the many grand displays of phantasm recorded in the Apocalypse, and conveying an impression of their being real, I would refer the reader to a well-written Latin production of EMANUEL SWEDENBORG, entitled "*Apocalypsis Revelata;*" also to another by the same author, appertaining to the same subject, and entitled "*Apocalypsis Explicata*" — which will clearly elucidate his views of the use and application of this book. I would again, however, guard the reader against the danger of misconception while reading the works referred to. For it is distinctly clear that their author was in the same general condition, both physically and mentally, with the writer of the Apocalypse. It will be seen that he verifies their general contents by appeals to spiritual disclosures and manifestations occurring in an intermediate or transition state

---

* By the "interior world," the lecturer said he intended here to represent that which is invisible — rather above but not perceptible to the natural senses; but not the second sphere of human existence in its real state.

between the rudimental and the spiritual spheres. By this I would be understood that both writers had a perception of that which was between the real and the unreal. I may remark, however, that the author of the "*Apocalypsis Revelata*" was *at times* in a condition of spiritual elevation which enabled him to arrive accurately at the most important truths as pertaining to the spiritual states, or the spheres of the inner world. But it is proper to state distinctly that the conclusions at which he at such times arrives, though true, are not the legitimate results of his philosophy. It appears that his mind received its direction from an impression originally received concerning an interior signification of the Word, or Bible. The result of this was to lead his mind into a correspondential mode of philosophizing concerning the thoughts, desires, passions, affections, and the states of the judgments of men, considering these as being represented by various species of animals, vegetables, and even minerals. According to his philosophy, the animal kingdom was merely a transcript or universal representation of the various thoughts, desires, passions, and judgments of mankind. He applies this mode of philosophizing in interpreting the contents of the Old and New Testaments, and represents the figures therein contained as holding an inseparable connexion with, and as corresponding to, the various truths in the exterior as well as to those in the interior world. He teaches that in the spiritual world, in like manner, exist representatives, both such as are and such as are not within the power of infernal spirits to render apparently real and substantial to the uninitiated and uninformed spirits.

Thus his mind flowed from the Bible into the natural world, not for the purpose of testing its truth by instituting a disinterested inquiry into the teachings of Nature, but more for the purpose of interpreting physical or external manifestations in such a way as to make the Bible and Nature mutually confirm each other. Then, in like manner, his mind flowed from the Word or Bible into the spiritual or interior world, where the same direction of mind produced a desire to make each manifestation accord with his prepossessions in favor of the Bible as being the great Centre and Fount of Truth. Thus he made the Word, or Bible, the focus or centre of Divine truth, to which the teachings of Nature should be considered as subordinate; and he supposed that her productions were nothing more than particular correspondences, or rather were verifications of the truth of the Bible — and likewise representatives of the thoughts and spiritual characteristics of man. So, according to him, the material world is only a reflection, a microcosm, a representation of the Bible, of its truths, and of the interior or spiritual world. And while the natural world should be considered as below, inferior, and subordinate to the Bible, the spirit-world should be considered as no more than a response to this biblical philosophy. Thus he joins the natural and spiritual world, by making "the Word" the fulcrum, the mediator, the centre and source, from which proceeds all the natural and spiritual knowledge worthy of being attained, and to which the two worlds converge: so that around the Bible the whole natural and spiritual world may be said to revolve.

I shall have occasion hereafter to recur to the main spiritual teachings of this author, which in their prominent features are substantially true, though they need the same kind of interpretation to make them correspond with the mighty movements of the universal principle of the Divine Mind, which he has given to the Bible, Nature, and the spirit-world.

---

§ 152. I have already related the manner in which those three books in the New Testament were decided as canonical, and as being the word of God. In connexion with what I have said on this subject I would ask, "Why were they not as much the word of God as other manuscripts of a similar character — and why were they not received as canonical in the year 325, when assembled the council of two thousand ferocious and exasperated bishops?" Let it also be remembered in connexion with this important inquiry, that the bishops were so much interested in having their peculiar theological opinions prevail, as to come near having a general quarrel; and over fifteen hundred of them were as a consequence disqualified from having a vote! Only a few more than three hundred, together with Constantine, at last remained!

I would now propose another question, to which I am not anxious to receive a personal answer, but I desire that the answer should be fully and truthfully presented to the world: "Why were not those fifteen hundred bishops who were discarded, as well qualified to decide which books were the word of God, as those who remained? For those who *did* vote were under the imperative command of Constantine — at least not to transgress the rules of the council. Did justice prevail when foul fanaticism, folly, and unrighteousness, took possession of the minds of those bishops?"

Also remember, reader, that when you read the encyclopædia of religious knowledge called *the Bible*, you are merely reading a book pronounced the word of God by three hundred exasperated bishops, and sealed by their emperor Constantine! Moreover, reflect that nearly as many manuscripts as are now embodied in the Old Testament, suffered *martyrdom!* And why, or how, or by whose imperative command, shall we believe that those which *are saved* are the word of God, any more than those which were destroyed?

I will close these comments upon the books of the Bible by presenting a few considerations that should govern every mind in its love for the many truths, and its dislike for the many falsities, that exist in the world. When I was first impressed to reveal my convictions concerning the Primitive History, I was led to consider this one important query: "What is the *use* that such a book may subserve in accomplishing the end for which mankind were created? Suppose that every sentence, for instance, in *the Apocalypse*, is true, and can be verified in the third sphere of spiritual existence, what possible *use* or *benefit* can be derived from truths that are *only* truths in spheres beyond the comprehension of any human being on earth?" I am distinctly impressed that the sayings of the Apocalypse, and also that the sayings of many men at the present day, may be verified, and can be proved true. That, however, is not conclusive evidence that even those who uttered these sayings were *themselves* conscious of their truth, or of their susceptibility of being verified in higher degrees of development. Then all minds should be influenced by the inquiry, "What possible good can a revelation of any kind do for mankind in their rudimental sphere, when the principles presented in such revelation are beyond the possibility of human practice? The truth or falsity of the contents of the Apocalypse can not in the least particular accelerate the movements of mankind toward the goal of social happiness, or the elevation of the spiritual constitutions of men to a high degree of refinement and knowledge. Anything that has not a use of a practical nature, is not worth the room it occupies in the world; for all such things are productions of the misconceptions of men, and are thus unreal as well as impracticable. Therefore the *importance* of a truth should be determined by the inquiry as to its *use*, and by its capability of a beneficial application.

---

§ 153. In conclusion to my previous remarks on the contents and teachings of the Primitive History, I discover a use in inserting some important synthetical remarks, commending the same to universal thought and consideration.

1. As to the origin of the conceptions of Adam and Eve, the Garden of Eden, the Fall of Man, and Original Sin. The first intimation of these conceptions, I find in my impressions concerning the early inhabitants of the earth. They were not believed or imbibed to a great extent until several generations after the tradition was fully established. It continued to be a tradition for several ages, without any particular modification, until finally it became a part of the religion of the Hindoos, and especially of the Persians, who wrote the same, and preserved it in manuscript. It was scarcely taught or believed among the Jews until those Persian manuscripts were translated into Hebrew, during their captivity at Babylon. After this it was considered as an *allegory*, and much venerated by the Jews and others, as being a symbolical representation of something substantially true: but what its meaning was, they knew not. Still, the *antiquity* of the tradition sacredized it in their minds; and hence it is presented in the book of Genesis. Since its introduction into this book, it has been interpreted, and clothed with all the seriousness and veneration which should properly be connected with the beauties of Nature, with man, and with heaven. Since that period, successive modifications of this supposed divine relation have so far concealed its original simplicity from mankind generally, that they are incapable, through fear, dread, and prejudice, of instituting a proper investigation respecting its real merits. Thus it is entirely within the power of those who present it to the world for credence, and is entirely removed from the mass of mankind.

2. The conception of an evil spirit or devil, may also be traced to the interior history of mankind. At first it was called "*breath*," and was attributed to the heat and light of the sun. This continued to be believed in various forms by each subsequent generation, until it was systematized as I have related, when it received the name of *Siva*. This was promoted by the magi of Persia to the office of a deified principle of evil, and was elevated by Zoroaster to a position as high, as great, and as mighty, as the Creator, at which time it was named *Ahriman*. It was not believed by the early Christian writers to be anything more than an influx of evil, or of a spirit of wickedness; which was similar to the belief of mankind in the early ages. And when the early Christians used the term *Satan*, they used it unguardedly, and not as signifying any definite and established principle of being. The same thing was also named *Shaitan*, which is rendered "satan," "devil," "darkness," "evil," and by similar

indefinite terms, meaning in no case an evil being or fallen angel, but representing that only which interfered with their peace and tranquillity of mind.

3. The conception of a *hell* originated among the inhabitants of central America, and became established by a very ingenious and enlightened chieftain. The tradition of this ultimately run into the Jewish nation, and was strongly entertained by various sects among them, though by others as strenuously discarded, until the meaning of the original term was changed from that of a local, burning abyss, to a condition of darkness, the grave, sepulchre, death, and similar things, which are expressed by the Hebrew word *sheol*, and by the Greek words *hades* and *gehenna*. These terms bore a synonymous signification, but all of them were employed in the sacred writings of the Jews in a metaphorical manner, as signifying no more than the terms previously mentioned. In no case are those words in the Bible significant of a fount of evil, sin, or burning, such as has been supposed to be meant by the word "hell." This word itself, in its strictest sense, signifies concealment, invisible, darkness, under ground, abyss, sepulchre, and all things that are opposed to the light of investigation.

4. The doctrine of a *General Resurrection and Judgment*, was believed among various sects of the Jews and Persians, over fifteen hundred years before Christ lived, and was firmly established all over the eastern world by Zoroaster, the Persian Bible-maker, six hundred years before Christ began to preach. In the New Testament, these doctrines of Zoroaster are used in a symbolical manner, by Christ and others, to represent states of mind, and various other things, in order that his hearers, and the eastern world generally, might understand the teachings presented. A general resurrection and judgment is not taught *in one page* of the Bible; and even if it were, that fact would not be proof of its truth, so long as *Nature* continues to exist and to unfold and manifest her immutable laws.

5. The conception of *Prophecy* existed among the Egyptians and eastern tribes, many centuries before either the Old or New Testament had an existence; and then the word *prophecy* did not necessarily, as it does not even in the Bible, imply the announcement of a future occurrence, or the revealment of anything foreseen by those impressed to speak or write, and which afterward was fulfilled. In this sense the word "prophecy" does not occur in the Bible. It was then used in the sense of terms modernly employed, such as, to "speak," "relate," or to express one's opinion; and the phrase,

"prophesy unto us," simply meant, "let us hear your reasons"— "what is your mind?"—"express your thoughts freely," &c. Hence 1 Samuel, x. 5, speaks of a company of prophets who "prophesied" on various musical instruments; "prophesying" meaning, in this instance, as in all others, nothing more than a delivery or announcement of any thought, sound, action, or a relation of any traditional occurrence. In modern days, commentators have supposed that the term *prophecy* was employed to express knowledge (derived from inspiration) of some great occurrence to transpire in future. Hence they have changed the term from its original meaning to a signification which it never was intended to bear. When the writers of the New Testament quote from the writings of the Old, they merely appeal to expressions which seem applicable to the occurrence which they are recording, in the same way as an author at the present day would quote a sentence from Homer, Cicero, Xenophon, Confucius, Pope, or any poetical or theological writer, using language which seemed to correspond to or verify the thoughts which he might be expressing. Therefore I positively affirm, without going into the details of evidence, that the term *prophecy*, in its original meaning, applies only to the mere act of expressing or announcing thoughts; and in no case was it used to represent a preknowledge of a future occurrence.

6. The term *Atonement* is entirely a manufactured expression, having no connexion with the pure and reforming principles of Jesus, or of any other good and philanthrophic being. It is impossible for any mind to conceive of any propriety in its present application.

7. The words "*Faith*" and "*Regeneration*" are words suggested by tenets previously and unwarrantably assumed. Hence they apply only to a system of man's invention, but not to the grand constitution of a Divine creation, of which man is a flower and a perfected organization.

---

§ 154. Thus I discover that the opinions in the world concerning Adam and Eve, the garden of Eden, the fall of man, the devil, hell, and many such subjects referred to in the Bible, are more or less mythological and parabolical, and were traditional among the eastern inhabitants until they became introduced, in a very modified form, into the writings of the Primitive History, where they are now supposed by many good, but misdirected and uneducated minds, to be the revealed thoughts of that Great Divine Essence, whose very life animates man and Nature, and makes of all things one grand, sublime, and harmonious System! So also I discover that the opinions concerning a general resurrection and judgment are likewise mythological in the strictest possible sense — containing not the least particle of useful or substantial truth, and hence they can have no tendency to elevate and purify the race.

The original conception of the *Trinity* arose from the three supposed beings called Parama, Vishnu, and Siva, which are no more nor less than what are named by some theologians "Father," "Son," and "Spirit." This trinity was not established in the world until the Egyptian priests of the Sun, and the Persian magi, promoted the three beings to a higher degree of potency than they originally possessed; and the conception was grasped by Zoroaster, who immediately converted them into three united beings, equal and infinite in power, and the same in essence and constitution. Subsequently, these were introduced into the sacred writings of the Jews, or the Bible, more as symbolic representatives than as real doctrines to be taught and believed. But the Athanasian creed erected of them three infinite Gods, equal to those of Zoroaster. In this they are termed "Father, Son, and Holy Ghost;" and it is said that the Father is infinite — the Son is infinite — the Holy Ghost is infinite: yet these are not *three*, but ONE. But in the first place, persons who are acquainted with arithmetical calculation will perceive that this is a violation of all numerical rules: for *three* can in no case be made to count *one*, nor can *one* ever be made to equal *three*. Therefore the creed in this particular must transcend all *ordinary* minds!

It may be further remarked that *three Infinites* can not possibly exist, because ONE INFINITE comprehends the Whole. And if one being is greater than another, then the creed must be false — however such a conclusion may interfere with the tranquillity of those who at present repose confidence in its truth.

The doctrine of the trinity was thus derived from the early conception of three original beings that were supposed to have been engaged in creating the earth and man — the earth being supposed in those days to be the centre of the whole Universe. And as I clearly perceive the origin of this doctrine, I hesitate not to declare that it is strictly a *mythos*; and it is rendered no more sacred or worthy of veneration because the original fantastic conception has in modern days been so beautifully sublimated.

Furthermore, I am happy to be in a condition to know that whatever things in the Bible are not historical, are, with few exceptions, entirely allegorical and mythological, and are not worth the time that has been employed in their investigation by so vast a number of good and righteous theologians who might have been much better employed, and thus have merited and received the thanks and approbation of an improved and benefited race.

I descend not into details to collect external proofs of the seemingly mere assertions that have been made; for this would not comport with the use and object of these revealments concerning the laws and requirements of Nature. But be it distinctly understood that I am impressed to maintain the responsibility of the statements herein presented; and at a future period I shall descend into the minutiæ of the various subjects generalized in this book, for the sole purpose of giving forth an incontestable encyclopædia in which every unreal and erroneous conception may be exhibited in its proper light, and in which may be established every important truth that is not at the present day known or comprehended by the generality of mankind.*

* Several times during the period in which this book was in process of dictation, the author incidentally remarked in substance, that inasmuch as this work was merely intended to establish *general principles*, it would be inappropriate to enter into minutiæ; for that would not only be to swell this volume to an unreasonable size, but to divert the mind of readers from great, leading, and essential points, by a multiplicity of particulars which, whether true or untrue, can be of little consequence, until the *great general* Truths are properly established, which constitute the *Foundation* of all particulars, and the *Basis* of all true reasoning. It will be observed that in the foregoing pages, the author promises a revealment or discussion of the particulars of several things, which, after all, are not subsequently mentioned *in this book*. His prophetic impressions taught him that he was to be the instrument of revealing to the world the things referred to; but according to explanations which he has given in foregoing pages, such impressions take no cognizance of *times* or *circumstances*. He did not, therefore, know what *specific points* in his proposed revelation were to be embodied in this book, and what were to be reserved for *another*, until this book was completed. He does not even profess to know *how soon* the next book will be given: but says he knows that he will be impressed to commence it at the proper time, and that it will be before the world as soon as it is needed. He has promised us in the next book a more thorough and minute discussion of all the important subjects introduced in this, particularly of the subjects of cosmogony, geology, archæology, ethnology, language, mythology, hagiography, theology, and the spiritual spheres. The structure of the Universe, for instance, will be more particularly unfolded to the mental view, and calculations in regard to distances, magnitudes, numbers, periods, &c., will be introduced. Also the laws of nebulous agglomeration and planetary motion will be more thoroughly explained; the inhabitants of the planets of our Solar System, with their institutions and customs, will be more minutely described; and other subjects will in like manner be enlarged upon. Also the details of the new Social System proposed in the *third part* of this book (and which is the grand object of the whole work), will then be given, and all further necessary rules will

§ 155. In concluding my remarks upon the Bible, I will speak historically concerning its *origin and formation*. Let it first be observed that a great deal of veneration is attached to the *word* BIBLE —more, indeed, than should be attached to a large portion of its contents. The word *bible* signifies merely *a book*. It is derived from the Greek *biblos*, which signifies the soft bark of a tree upon which the ancients wrote their thoughts. To this was subsequently prefixed the word "*holy*," which term was employed by the Jews to express *excellence*. Thus the terms "Holy Bible" might be rendered "*excellent soft bark;*" and then the world would understand their original signification.

The books that compose the Old Testament were originally manuscripts written by various Jewish and Egyptian authors. Each book bears the name of its writer, with the exception of the books of Genesis, Kings, Chronicles, Jonah, and a portion of the Psalms. These were originally written on soft bark, palm-tree leaves, soft and impressible stones, and various compositions, among which were those of which the Egyptians made their hieroglyphical figures and cornice work, such as were displayed in the interior of their temples and of the temple of Solomon. There were very many more manuscripts written than are preserved, or than those of which any knowledge is to be had at the present day. The manuscripts composing the New Testament were produced and preserved in a similar manner, and the whole of them were collected about three hundred years after Christ lived.

There was, however, before Christ, a council of Jewish rabbins, by whom it was decided that all manuscripts of a sacred and traditional character that might be found in possession of any nation, should be immediately collected. At that time the interest taken in manuscripts of a sacred character was such as has never met with a parallel, excepting at one subsequent period, when there existed an actual mania upon the same subject, and which period has been distinguished by some writers as the age of *bibliomania*. The Jews succeeded in collecting a vast number of writings, which they preserved for several centuries. To these was superadded a collection of about fifty gospels, or books relative to Christ and the apostles, together with other historical and sacred records. Some of these are now found in the New Testament. They were thus preserved

be laid down, the observance of which will insure the permanent establishment of the kingdom of heaven upon earth.

until the year 325, when at the command of Constantine two thousand and forty-eight bishops assembled at Nice.

It is well to remark in this connexion, that these bishops were nothing more than *organized human beings*, nor were they sufficiently refined to merit many very high encomiums. After they had assembled, they were so violent and vociferous, that had it not been for the emperor's presence, they would have engaged in open battle. For each one had prejudices so strong in favor of certain· peculiar doctrines, and all were so anxious to have their pre-convictions prevail, that justice and purity were entirely excluded from their proceedings, and were as far from their deliberations as mythology is from the truths of the Divine Mind. Constantine was obliged to disqualify *seventeen hundred and thirty* from having a voice in deciding which books were and which were not the word of God : and only *three hundred and eighteen* were left. These decided that the books which composed the Bible as subsequently known, were the word of God. Several books, however, have since that time been rejected. Out of fifty gospels then extant, they decided that those only of Matthew, Mark, Luke, and John, were worthy of being preserved ; while they *rejected entirely* the books of James, Jude, and the Apocalypse. After this decision, Constantine arose and solemnly declared that the same should be considered as sanctioned by the Divine Will ; and that the books thus fixed upon should thereafter be implicitly believed as the word of God. Those manuscripts that were rejected (among which were three well-written gospels) were committed to the flames.

In this general condition the Bible remained until the year 633. During the interval there were frequent councils called, which frequently annulled the decisions of each other—each establishing new propositions and passing new rules to be observed until the assemblage of another council. Thus were produced, from time to time, modifications in *the form* of the Bible, as well as in the number of books that were to be considered as composing it.

At the council of Toledo, in the year 633, the books of James, Jude, and the Revelation of St. John, were received into the canon. Then the Old and New Testaments were established in nearly the same form in which they exist at the present day. They continued, however, for many centuries unread and unknown by the mass of mankind ; and it was not until the fourteenth century that the first English version was made. During the intermediate period, portions of the Bible were copied into the German, Danish, and Saxon languages. A thousand years elapsed after the council of Nice, before the Bible became much known; and probably it would have sunk into oblivion had not the art of printing been established in the fourteenth and fifteenth centuries. This at once afforded a means by which those who were anxious for its circulation, and to have its doctrines prevail, could accomplish their desires.

It is well known, however, that the priests of the Roman Catholic church held this, what may be properly called "excellent soft bark," in their personal possession, and were very actively engaged in promulgating its teachings to the world, many of them seriously believing these to be inspired. They believed that they themselves were the designed apostles of this great faith; and they taught their followers to consider them as the instruments to perpetuate apostolic power, prophetic wisdom, and heavenly teaching. Hence they claimed the power to cure diseased persons, and to be authorized to make believers, if not by preaching, yet by the sword, the stake, the rack, or in a more honorable way, by their sacred inquisitions! Thus these doctrines continued to prevail until a Reformer arose.

And I would here remark, that had the pope been disposed to grant this Reformer one simple request, the Reformation would not have proceeded far, or interfered to any extent with the sacredness of Catholicism. But by the occurrence of a simple circumstance, this dissenter or protestant was raised up, who succeeded in establishing his cause by a peculiar decision of character, and perseverance, arising more from wrath and indignation than from a solemn conviction of the justice of the work in which he was engaged. Thus arose the first Reformer, who openly protested against the iniquities of the then-prevailing system of religion.

After him sprang up another, who differed slightly from the faith and creed of the former, and interpreted, according to his conceptions of truth, the teachings of the admitted sacred oracles. He also succeeded in establishing *his* beloved faith, which in some respects is true, especially in those relating to the knowledge and wisdom of the Divine Mind, to his original design, and to predestination. But that he was mistaken on some points is clear to every enlightened mind.

Thus LUTHER and CALVIN embraced doctrines essentially different from the religion so long established, so tenaciously believed, and so ingeniously promulgated by the Catholic priests. Since the time of Luther and Calvin, many very important modifications have been made in Christian opinions, rules, customs, ordinances, ceremonies, and ecclesiastical organization, and these have most effectually operated in destroying the harmony and peace of mankind, and in casting a shroud of sectarianism over the world that is almost the last indication of the death and burial of rational intelligence! The whole world, physically, morally, and spiritually, appears to me at this moment as being immersed in the dark and turbid waters of sectarianism, into which the light of reason and of divine truth scarcely casts one relieving ray! The whole is gloomy, desolate, and uncongenial! Man, it is true, is the lord of creation, the flower of Nature; but alas, how poorly he sustains his position, and how humiliating to reflect upon the present state of his mental possessions!

§ 156. Thus, reader, you are believing a book voted as being the word of God by three hundred and eighteen bishops, and sealed as true by the emperor Constantine! You understand, now, the origin and formation of what is called the "*Holy Bible*," which means *excellent soft bark*. You understand, now, how that which can boast of antiquity, can assume the ground of being sacred, and how, being defended by a multitude of interested promulgators, it can defy the yearnings of your thoughts to be free, and set at naught all your attempts at investigation. You will now be able to bear it in mind, that the *Hindoo* has a Bible which he venerates as much as you do yours. So also has the *Mohammedan*, and the *Persian*. Each equally impelled by prejudice and hereditary affection, will inquire, "If you deprive us of our Bible, what shall we have in its stead?" Beloved reader, there is a Book in which beauties and divine truths are inexhaustible; a Book filled with texts that no Egyptian, Jewish, Persian, or Hindoo priest or theologian can counterfeit; a Book which can not be concealed—whose teachings can not be misapprehended, and whose results will be purity, virtue, morality, and celestial righteousness; a Book from which the whole world may derive indestructible consolation, and learn of that Divine Essence which is the Cause and Parent of human existence. It will at the same time unfold the unspeakable grandeur of your *celestial* habitations, each of which will be only a sphere or step in the grand and magnificent gallery that leads to the Flower of celestial Beauty, whose fragrance is the perfection of an unchangeable Universe. Will you ask, then, reader, what will be given you instead of a material book, composed of paper and impressed with type, when a UNIVERSE is open to the researches of your aspiring mind? Certainly nothing can be more unreasonable than the superstitious claims that are in the world for the teachings of a simple *book*, that can be altered in a thousand ways in going through the operations of a press! But there exists a BOOK that teaches purity, morality, and immortality, and demonstrates the loveliness of the GREAT CREATOR—a Book, too, that is as indestructible and unvarying as the constitution and divine qualities of NATURE.

I have but a few more remarks to offer concerning the Bible, and these are as follows: It does not teach that pure morality which belongs to the nature of man, and which will result from a superior condition of the race. From this remark must be excepted a few incidental expressions said to have been used by JESUS—such as "the Golden Rule,"—which was comprehensively taught six hundred years before, by CONFUCIUS, the Chinese philosopher. Again: it does not prove *immortality;* neither does it teach the mighty truths contained in the successive spheres or degrees of future existence. Nor does it even present any substantial proof of the transition from this rudimental condition, to a higher degree of material and physical organization; or in other words, it does not demonstrate a resurrection to a future life. Nor does it present one proper conception of the constitution, character, greatness, omnipotence, and majesty of the Divine Mind. Nor does it do justice to his works, except in those meditations upon which I have heretofore commented. Nor does it contain one substantial proof of an unvarying law upon which to found a hope of ever being regenerated, or of ascending to a sphere of more perfect and harmonious existence. Nor does it teach that holy virtue, morality, and refinement, which should receive the name of religion.

This term *religion*, however, is quite inexpressive, and needs, in order to be understood, a brief definition. The term *ligo* is a Latin word, signifying *to tie* or *bind*. *Re*-ligo is to *re*-tie or bind over again, and make still stronger. The *n* being attached, forms the word *religion*, which means to bind and rebind, and make secure. It is well to say that, understood in this sense, it has performed its office most effectually. For the term "religion," indeed, implies little more than being sacredly bound to *sectarianism*. The word as used by commentators is very potent, and very expressive; and it may be seen by these remarks that it is *very applicable*.

Thus the "Primitive History" is useful as a history of mythology, ancient theology, false and imaginary deities — as containing accounts of wars, pestilences, persecutions, desolations of cities, false prophesyings, long and tedious expeditions, most unjust assassinations, murders, adulteries, abominations, trials, afflictions, imagination, phantasm, rebellion; as presenting information concerning oriental customs, expressions, ordinances, prejudices, religious wars, martyrdoms, and all kinds of injustice, immorality, and unrighteousness. Viewed in the light of a *history*, I say, its writers should be respected, and its contents preserved. But as a *theological* book it should not be read; for it contains no absolute doctrine — and all those doctrines which are supposed to be taught therein, are merely the false interpretations given of it by various commentators in all ages since the book was compiled for the exclusive use of the adherents of Catholicism. From *falsifications* I would rescue its teachings. I therefore say, the book is good as a *history*, and would not have done the least harm in the world, had not forced interpretations been given of its contents, and had not claims been preferred in its behalf to a sacredness which it does not claim for itself, and, as I can positively say, which it does not inherently possess.

But the objection may arise, that some tribes and nations of the earth know nothing of this book, and yet they are miserable, ignorant, and wretched, in the extreme. The answer to this will be hereafter given and comprehended in the third part, or the Application, of this portion of the work.

§ 157. I NOW proceed to give a true history of JESUS, from his birth to his death, and to state the causes of so many unjust sayings contained in the New Testament concerning him and others.

In Nazareth in Galilee, there dwelt a family but little known to the world, or to the inhabitants of the town in which they resided. The father, whose name was JOSEPH, was a very active and industrious mechanic. He was a carver and sculptor, and was frequently engaged in various branches of carpentry. His associate, MARY, was a very gentle and kindly-disposed woman. They lived generally unknown, because of their domestic retirement, and love of the quietude pervading an undisturbed and happy home. They neither possessed an affection for literature, nor for the study of any science or philosophy that was then cultivated among the inhabitants, as derived from the Grecians and other enlightened nations. It was in this family that that little personage, about whose birth, life, and death, so many marvellous accounts have been written, was born.

Not long after his birth, Joseph and his wife were disinherited from the house they occupied, because of an unfavorable report that became extant, through the agency of some designing and evil-disposed persons. Before they left the house, however, Joseph dreamed that it was proper for him and his family to journey into Egypt.

Previous to this journey, a necessary circumstance compelled Mary to lay her child in a manger, in which place, as I am distinctly impressed, he lay not over forty minutes. Joseph, not knowing what else to do, obeyed the suggestion of his impressive dream, and departed into Egypt. They were not long there before a suitable relief was procured for them, which induced their return, and established them again comfortably in their previous habitation.

It is well that all should bear in mind that dreams were supposed in those days to be something more than the workings of the elements and imaginations of the mind, and the suggestions, especially, of those dreams which were highly impressive, were obeyed as a voice from an angel of the Divine Mind.

This much is related in the New Testament, in a truthful manner; and the account there given is correct, with the exception of the interpretation that was given to these simple occurrences, by people generally, and especially by the writers of this history.

But the New Testament leaves two chasms in the life of Christ, which are of great importance, inasmuch as they are periods in human life that as much as any other require attention. Matthew and others speak of his birth, and then are silent until they introduce him into the presence of learned doctors and philosophers, in the temple. And no account is given of him after this, again, until he became thirty years of age; and then he is said to have begun his preaching. It is plain, that from birth to the age of twelve years, and also from the age of twelve to thirty, many most important occurrences might have transpired, of which the world, through these sacred historians, have not the least intimation.

After Joseph returned with his family, all his secular and domestic affairs were rendered agreeable and easy; and he was likewise restored to the bosom of society, and was beloved as a worthy citizen. No particular impression existed among the inhabitants concerning their young and beautiful son, with the exception that he was generally admired for the perfect symmetry of his form and cerebral structure. I am presented with no such an occurrence as the command related by Matthew to have been issued by Herod. But as I proceed, the origin of this account will distinctly appear. The child was named JESUS — which was a name occasionally occurring, but seldom admired, because of its association in the mind with the supposed spirit of an Egyptian deity, much worshipped by the priests of the Sun, and spoken of in various portions of the second book of Kings. His physical constitution was beautifully proportioned, and he possessed a corresponding beauty of the mental faculties.

His general organization was indeed remarkable, inasmuch as he possessed combined the perfection of physical beauty, mental powers, and refined accomplishments. He was generally beloved during his youth, for his great powers of discernment, his thirst after knowledge, and his disposition to inquire into the causes of mental phenomena, of the conditions of society, and of the visible manifestations of Nature. He was also much beloved for his pure natural sympathy for all who were suffering afflictions either of a physical or mental character. His benevolence and love toward all without distinction; his constant yearning for the companionship of those who were considered good and righteous; his marked respect and affection for those who were much older than himself; his constant visits to those who required relief from their afflictions; and his kind words of consolation to those who were depressed either by disease or unhappy social circumstances — all contributed to render him an object of general love and attachment. These were the peculiarities which distinguished him from all other persons then living.

It is true that at the age of twelve years he was admitted to the presence of the learned doctors. There he manifested some of his powers of discernment, interior and natural philosophy, unsophisticated love, simplicity of expression, kindness of disposition, and universal sympathy and benevolence. These he displayed with all the naturalness and spontaneousness resulting from the promptings of an uncorrupted and purely-organized spiritual principle. He answered their pertinent interrogations with great benignity, promptitude, and freedom of conception and expression. What most astonished the doctors was the demonstration of his philosophical conceptions and mathematical powers — all of which were blended into a perfect system by the pervading element of his mind, which was LOVE.

§ 158. I would have the reader understand the reason why these things were to be expected from, and were manifested by, him. I have related that Jesus was perfectly constituted, both as to his physical and spiritual organization. This being the case, his mental faculties were early developed to a degree even transcending the capacities of those philosophers in whose presence he showed forth his wonderful mental qualifications. Even at the present time there is a youth whose mind is in a similar manner prematurely developed, especially his faculties of perception and causality, and his powers of mathematical calculation. He is in one of the eastern states — and is already surprising the learned doctors and philosophers by his astronomical and mathematical powers. Frequently there are persons who have one or more of the mental faculties fully developed while they are as yet in a youthful state. Many also have the power of perceiving material substances or colors, or reading, without employing the natural organs of vision. Others are capable of having the interior faculties of their minds opened by being thrown into an abnormal condition, which relieves the mind of much of its burdensome obstruction, and renders it suitable for the influx of superior knowledge. This fact is at the present day arresting the attention of many observing doctors and philosophers of the land.

Jesus while in youth, and especially at the age of twelve, possessed all those superior qualifications which many scarcely possess when their interiors are expanded by the modern discovery of manipulations. Hence I discover that he became noted, because of his superior and highly-refined powers of discernment, together with his gentleness, kindness, and sweetness of disposition.

After he had manifested his marvellous powers to the learned doctors in this instance, he courted no longer their presence, and lived principally among his brethren, spending a large portion of his time in the visitation of the diseased, depressed, disconsolate, and suffering inhabitants in various portions of the land. He seemed to possess an intuitive knowledge of the medicinal properties of plants, of mineral and animal substances — of their use, and of the proper time and manner of their application in the curing of various diseases. This qualification, however, he acquired during the period which elapsed from the age of fifteen to thirty-three. He also possessed a great *physical soothing power* over the disordered or disconcerted forces of the human system. This was because of his superior physical endowments. Hence it is related in various places in the New Testament, that he laid his hands upon persons, and they were cured. When relieving the palsy, he is reported as having said, " Thy faith hath cured thee : rise, take up thy bed, and walk." Also he is said to have laid wet sand or clay upon tne eyes of the blind, and thus to have restored sight. And in various other instances he is represented as having made use of *physical means* to produce the cures which are by his biographers and others insignificantly termed "*miracles.*"

The reason is clear why those sacred historians employed expressions so mysterious and ambiguous—expressions which often did violence to the human judgment by conveying ideas which reason can never sanction. It was the general impression, after he became so noted for his many benevolent and charitable deeds, that he must either be actuated by the Spirit of the God of Abraham, Isaac, and Jacob, or by the Evil One whom their imaginations had promoted to an equal degree of almightiness. Finally, it became so general a belief that he was actuated by the *first*, that they designated him by the title of " the Son of God." Then the ignorant and uninformed bowed with a trembling veneration at the mere mention of the name of " JESUS, the Son of God," although many of them had never beheld him.

The inhabitants in those days were greatly inclined to extremes of faith and incredulity. If any particular theory, principle, or philosophy, were presented for their consideration, they were accustomed to embrace or combat it violently. Thus it was that most of the Jews *despised* Jesus, while others *worshipped him*, and believed all the marvels that had been related of him. It is well to remark that Jesus never professed to be what they make him to say he was. He was a kind, amiable, and unassuming being, discarded by many because of his superior and benevolent traits, and as much beloved by those whom he immediately benefited by the smiles of his loving-kindness and by his soothing power.

He often during his youth, and also after ascending to manhood, preached for the purpose of consoling and instructing multitudes of those who were depressed in spirit, and unfortunately situated in the world. One of those beautiful lessons of consolation and exhortation is recorded in the fifth, sixth, and seventh chapters of Matthew— where, with all the simplicity of a confiding disposition, he consoles the multitude by saying, " Happy are they that mourn, for they shall be comforted ; happy are the poor in spirit, for they shall see God ; happy are the peace-makers, for theirs is the kingdom of heaven ;"

and in like manner he proceeds with his expressions of kindness and of all those sentiments that might be expected from the workings of such a well-constituted mind. In his preaching he employed the terms that were then in use, and he professed to be nothing more than a teacher of pure and unadultered love, and also a general sympathizer with all who needed relief, consolation, and sympathy.

I am exceedingly attracted by the purity of his life, disposition, teachings, and spirit of reform. He saw distinctly, and realized fully, the unhappy situation of his fellow-men; and he yearned for the time to come when there would be a new heaven and a new earth, wherein might dwell righteousness. He was anxious for the prevalence of a general harmony of interests and action, such as would join in one the whole race of mankind. He desired that prudence and industry should so reign throughout this material sphere, as that the desert might blossom as the rose, and the wilderness bloom with a smiling, inviting beauty. Thus he delighted to contemplate the establishment of the spiritual Zion — the great Temple of Knowledge and Righteousness so feelingly spoken of, and so earnestly desired by, that good and worthy writer, ISAIAH. Such are the yearnings of all naturally-philanthropic bosoms. Such are the aspirations of those exalted minds who behold the human race as a Whole, and in their superior benevolence cherish no selfishness or pride.

§ 159. Thus Jesus lived, doing good to those who came and required assistance, exhorting those who were uneducated, and preaching to multitudes — *not* in the temple or the synagogue, because those places were *too pure* for his deeds and his philosophy — but on the mountain and by the wayside; thus lifting up his voice in what has before been termed "the sanctuary of the expanded earth and the unfolded heavens." He taught thus because he felt it an imperative duty devolving upon him to instruct the ignorant, and to deposite if possible that pure spirit of reform in the social world that might result in establishing the beauties of the spiritual Zion, and in perfecting the qualities of the Tree of Righteousness. He felt prompted to preach, what had been before conceived, that men should do unto others as they would have others do unto them; and he desired that the simple, good, and tranquillizing influence of this principle might be deposited and developed in the bosom of every human form. He desired that the day of righteousness should be ushered in, when there would be no more pain, sorrow, or crying, for the old things would all have been passed away, and all things would have become new. And in the accomplishment of his desires, sin would be destroyed, together with that which hath the power of sin, that is darkness, ignorance, folly, imagination, imbecility, and every species of sectarianism and unholy philosophy.

JESUS continued to obey those beneficent monitions of his mind (which were to cure the diseased, to visit the fatherless and widows in their afflictions, and to preach peace on earth and good-will to men) until prejudice became so strong against him, that he was unable to proceed any further in his career of purity and benevolence. He was censured by various learned, and, as they were thought to be, very *great*, theologians, and was persecuted to a great extent by the multitudes, who were exasperated from the workings of religious prejudice against him. So he was captured, brought before a council of judicature, who were all disposed to condemn him without a hearing, for disturbance of the peace, for interference with their long-cherished religious faiths, their social organization, their modes of worship, their rites and ceremonies, their long and loud prayers to Him whom they supposed to be the Lord of Abraham, Isaac, and Jacob, for blasphemy, and for doing deeds that were good on the sabbath-day. All these and many similar accusations were brought against him; and they exhibited a spirit of persecution that will be ere long fully exemplified in this nineteenth century. On these accusations they condemned him to die the death of a martyr! And as was the custom in cases of similar accusations in those days, they crucified him, two others sharing the same fate with him. During the infliction of this most unjust penalty, the Jews manifested the same spirit of sectarian vengeance, and the same desire for the destruction of all invasive philanthropy and purity of principle, that will ere long be exhibited again. Thus will be demonstrated the existence of precisely the same spirit as that which characterized the Jews of old, and the influence of this will clothe the rising and unborn generation in the armor of prejudice, hostility, and fanaticism!

Thus JESUS was a good man, a noble and unparalleled Moral Reformer, considering him as disconnected from all those unjust things that are in the New Testament recorded of him. He did not profess to be the Son of God in any other sense than that of a branch, as all are, of the great Tree of universal and eternal Causation. He did not profess to be directed and impelled by any other spirit than that of Divine love, the germ of which dwells in every other being undeveloped. And to this principle, as existing in others, he appealed so feelingly, in order that its qualities might be unfolded, and that they might advance to the degree of refinement in love and wisdom then occupied by himself. He was, then, A TYPE OF A PERFECT MAN, both in physical and spiritual qualifications. But those representations which make him more than this, I discover are all *untrue*, and express that only which was professed *for*, but never *by* him.

Thus, then, he died a martyr to the principles of truth, reason, and virtue. So likewise did Matthew, Paul, and others. And it is lamentable to reflect that the world has been guilty of such flagrant injustice that even many in subsequent generations have been subjected to the torturing rack, to the stake, and to the dissolving flames! Men have even rushed to the field of battle, and there, impelled by envy and sectarian prejudice, they have poured out each other's life's blood, thereby causing Nature to blush for shame for the degradation of her children! Brethren have joined in open hostility, actuated by no other cause than the terrible and fiery elements of sectarian envy, prejudice, and local affection! How fearful, indeed, is the gloom of the dark thought, that man has died a martyr to the natural promptings of the spirit within, and to the principles of virtue, morality, and love!

I behold Jesus, then, as a great and good Reformer; as connected with no marvellous or mysterious aristocracy, but as being born of lowly parents, and fostered in the bosom of their domestic habitation; as possessing intelligence to a surpassing degree; as manifesting unbounded love, benevolence, and sympathy; as healing the sick, restoring the blind, curing the lame, and visiting the disconsolate in their afflictions; as preaching love, morality, peace on earth and good will to men; as instructing the multitudes in the paths of pleasantness and peace; and as loving all and disliking none. I behold him as being condemned, nailed to the cross, and dying a martyr to the cause of love, wisdom, and virtue! Such is one of the parts in the great monument which an ignorant and misdirected world have erected to their own shame and folly!

§ 160. I now proceed to account for the origin of those unjust statements in relation to him recorded in the New Testament.

First, however, it is proper to introduce some considerations concerning the habits, customs, laws, ordinances, and states of society then existing: for it must be plain to every mind that language and forms of expression are governed by the general habits, ordinances, and circumstances of any nation or society, and that the former are changed to correspond with the changes of the latter.

It was a custom in those days to obey the main suggestions of any impressive dream, with great carefulness. Dreams were considered, among all classes, as an inflowing of the thoughts of angels or invisible beings, who were monitors and prompters to those who dwelt on the earth. Hence they believed that dreams were induced and designed by God for the purpose of having men obey his will. Of these things I have spoken in different places before: still, I would refer the reader to the older manuscripts of the Bible as containing many illustrations upon this point. Besides this, it was the custom to write or express a figure, parable, or representative, as being *itself* true, instead of the *thought* which suggested the figure or representative to the mind.

Moreover, it was a rule in those days, especially among the Jews and Samaritans, always to admit a proposition or statement when the same appeared to be demonstrated by appeals to a number of incidental and known facts; and if any different account or proposition were presented by a different person, it would be rejected without investigation. For a proof of this I would refer the reader to a very valuable work written by Plutarch, in which he says, that if any person presents a proposition contradicted by another, the first should in all cases be considered as true and valid, and the latter rejected, because it was not the first presented for consideration. This, Plutarch says, was the rule recognised by the Stoics, whenever they were called upon to investigate conflicting accounts or propositions. It is well to add, that this is precisely the course pursued by many at the present day. They assume and believe that their *first impressions*, or *hereditary opinions*, are true, and reject all *new ones, unheard;* at the same time making their previous opinions the standard by which all subsequent propositions should be tested. So it is scarcely necessary to refer to early historians for the truth of this relation, when the same is fully verified in every department of the theological, scientific, and philosophical world at the present day.

Another custom was to consider the universally-prevailing impression concerning any person or thing, as being created and sanctioned by the will of the Deity. This belief at once unchained their marvellousness and credulity for an unlimited exercise upon any subject which appeared thus fully sanctioned; and such they felt it their duty to venerate and promulgate without restriction.

It was also a prevailing belief in those days, especially among the lower classes, that the earth was the centre of the Universe, and that the stars, moon, and sun, were necessary appendages to the earth, and that no other earth was in existence besides this. On this ground they accounted for so much attention, prompting, and guidance, as they supposed to be bestowed upon them by the Deity; for they supposed that he invisibly occupied a position in the firmament for the purpose of guiding them into all proper ways, whether such appertained to peace or to war.

Moreover, there were many sects existing in those days, each of which was distinguished by some peculiarity, either as to speech, garments, habits of living, or some other mark, which served in all cases to designate them, and to establish their exclusiveness. The Druids* were known by their peculiar simplicity of dress, and by their holding their meetings in sequestered places. The worshippers of the Sun, and typifyers of the tower of Babel and of the temple of Solomon, distinguished themselves by wearing garments that were indicative of the degree of masonry or of mechanical perfection to which each had arrived. The Samaritans were distinguished by the length of their beards, and the style of wearing their hair, and also by their peculiar religious sentiments. The Jews were distinguished by their countenances, their dress, and by the mark of the covenant, called the circumcision. Thus exclusive classes were established; and each nation, and especially the Jews, earnestly desired to be considered as the favorites of God — the latter class claiming to be the descendants of Abraham, Isaac, and Jacob, in proof of which circumcision was presented. They also desired to monopolize the general favors supposed to be directly transferred from God to mankind on earth.

Such was the condition of things when Jesus was born; and the same continued during his life, and for many generations after his death. And it was owing in a measure to the customs of society — the rules and ordinances of nations, and the modes and habits of thinking, that so many very mysterious, unjust, and unreasonable things were believed, propagated, and written, concerning Jesus, and his peculiar manifestations of physical energy in the healing the diseased, and

* The lecturer incidentally remarked, that these were of the same stock with the Druids of Gaul and Britain.

also concerning his superior love and wisdom which were expressed with so much gentleness, kindness, and humiliation. I am exceedingly desirous to impress on the reader's mind the importance of these considerations, inasmuch as they constitute the key by which may be unlocked the great mystery so long clothing the birth, life, and death of Jesus.

§ 161. A long time elapsed after Jesus became noted for his moral teachings and benevolent acts, before any inquiries were instituted concerning the peculiarities of his birth and early life, or concerning the circumstances attending the same. It is well to say, that the chief inquiries, and the collection of facts, relative to the birth, life, and deeds of Jesus, were not made *until many years after his death*. Therefore the *general impressions* of his early followers were assumed *as a basis* whereon his subsequent historians and followers predicated their faith and doctrine. The unfavorable report concerning Joseph and Mary, heretofore mentioned, gave rise to the first impression as to the illegitimacy of Jesus. It was in consequence of this report that Joseph was disinherited for a season; but after the report subsided, he returned to his former home, and all the previous impressions, were obliterated entirely, and no more was thought upon the subject.

When the first inquiries were made concerning the birth of Jesus, the conclusion, as derived from superficial testimony, was as follows: That Jesus, doing good, performing many cures, and manifesting great powers of intellect, must necessarily be supposed to be the Son of the Good Spirit, or God. In confirmation of this, proof was supposed to exist in the report referred to; and Mary, the mother of Jesus, was supposed to have conceived, in her virginity, by the breathing influence of the Holy Ghost. And it was known that Joseph had a dream which caused his departure into Egypt; and this was believed to be angelic instruction. Jesus, it was thought, could not have been so perfect as he was, without having an origin unlike that of others. And as he had manifested brotherly-kindness, and accomplished benevolent acts, this was deemed conclusive evidence that his origin must have been *pure*. The conclusion, then, was irresistible, that Jesus was begotten of the Holy Spirit, and born of the Virgin Mary, and therefore was the Son of God. And they supposed that he was named Jesus because he was sent to save his people from their sins. All these things were retrospectively viewed by the generation succeeding the death of Jesus, and were considered undeniable evidences of his miraculous conception, of his immaculate purity, and that he must have been the Son of God. All this was in perfect harmony with their prepossessions of mind.

Here the New Testament leaves the history of Jesus until he arrives at the age of twelve years. But surely some things must have been said to have occurred as connected with his life during this period. But the accounts which were collected seemed too crude and imperfect to receive a canonical sanction; and they were hence rejected on account of their inconsistency and the unsound manner in which they were recorded. Some of the rejected books are still in existence, and are full of marvellous relations concerning the childhood of Jesus, and the peculiarities which distinguished his whole life. Some of these stories are not worthy a moment's consideration, inasmuch as they are derived from the marvellous and exaggerated impressions hereditarily received by the persons who wrote them. Among other things, it is related that while Jesus was a little boy, and associated with other children, the stars were seen to follow his course, while his companions were not in the least thus honored; and that the moon appeared to trace and retrace her steps, following the various movements of the boy Jesus: also that a peculiar illumination was visible on his countenance, which would blind the eyes of those near him: also that while a very little boy, he would with other boys approach the streams, and of the moistened clay make birds and other small forms; and it is related that those which were made by the other boys would remain inanimate, while those formed by Jesus would be immediately animated and transformed into beautiful birds! It is also related that seeds which were deposited in the earth by his hand would germinate and grow up in the space of thirty hours to full maturity. Much is also said concerning many visions and dreams that he had, all of which tended to confirm the opinion that he was the Son of God.

The account concerning Jesus being introduced among the learned doctors is strictly true, but it was not written until after his death. All the things accomplished by him which are called *miracles*, were related as such mainly by those who received the traditions from those who were the immediate followers and companions of Jesus. It was a general belief that he was the person whom many of the earlier historians and prophets foretold. Hence, in various instances, quotations are made from their writings which seemed to have an immediate bearing upon, or connexion with, the things they had heard concerning the birth, life, and deeds of Jesus.

The writers of the books in the New Testament could not resist the conviction that Christ was thus miraculously born; and that inasmuch as he accomplished so many miracles, discoursed so eloquently, harmed no one, but did good to all, and died ignominiously for his cause, he must have been the Son of God — the application of this title being in accordance with the general mode of expression and belief. They likewise cherished the conviction that he must have been foreseen by the prophets of previous generations. Hence by research among their writings, passages were found which seemingly had a connexion with the prominent circumstances in the life of Christ, which they were recording. Therefore they made those quotations with a serious conviction that they had immediate reference to the things which they were employed in relating.

§ 162. The history of the deeds accomplished by Jesus from the age of twelve to thirty, was registered promiscuously in various books, some of which are now called the Apocrypha of the New Testament. These relate more miraculous manifestations of the physical and mental powers of Jesus than are recorded in the New Testament. Yet they were written more from hearsay than from actual knowledge. And I am impressed to say that the account of *the ascension* was also transmitted by others to those who wrote it, with the exception of one account preserved on bark, and said to have been written by Mark, who was present as an eye-witness of the occurrence. For be it remembered that the art of writing was then understood only by a very few, and that paper, ink, and the art of printing, were to them unknown. Hence the accounts impressed on bark and other substances would in some instances remain untranscribed for one, two, or three centuries. Some of these were preserved until a species of paper was invented upon which their contents were transcribed. Very few persons were able to write; while the vast multitude were only capable of conveying their thoughts verbally: and the constant verbal delivery of these accounts subjected them to constant modifications. Yet from impressions thus traditionally transmitted, the subsequent writers produced those records of which the world is in possession at the present day.

Still more emphatically am I impressed to say that the birth of Christ as related, the correspondingly-inconsistent stories of his youth, the accounts of the instantaneous cures effected by him, the pretensions that are made in his behalf in respect to his mediatorship, and of his being in a superior sense the Son of the Deity — and also the account of his literal ascension — are all strictly the traditional impressions imbibed and written of him, none of which are true as they are related. It is impossible to be in communion with, and possess a knowledge of, the unerring and unchangeable principles of the Divine Mind, and at the same time admit the truth of these traditional records. And it is given me to know that he who believes fully in their truth is not in communion with the laws, purposes, and Essence of the Great Positive Mind. But he who is interiorly enlightened concerning these, hesitates not to declare, from a serious conviction of the judgment, that such things *can not* be true; for their very nature precludes their possibility.

While I am thus compelled to speak, I am none the less conscious of having myself supposed these things to be true, and of having believed them with a vast degree of veneration, while my mind, like others, was trammelled by sensuous opinions and philosophy. Yet now, having the external senses closed, and the perceptive powers of the internal opened, I am acquainted with those things which in outward life appeared unaccountable mysteries. These historical accounts, concerning which I in common with others have had mysterious impressions, now appear entirely transparent, even to their origin, and their confirmation in the minds of mankind. And I now rejoice to know that this superficial theology has not the least connexion with the Divine Essence, or Great Creative Cause, with his laws, or with the great system of material and spiritual worlds. And the belief in these things forms no part of the theology which every department of Nature and the Universe unequivocally demonstrates and establishes.

Now my affections are directed entirely by that wisdom which discards a theology so impure and superficial. Yet when I return again to the exterior world, and know things only by sensuous impressions, then also will my affections return and control my superficial wisdom; and these affections will at once connect me again with all those superficial views, theories, and philosophies, that at this present moment occupy no tangible position in my conceptions of the structure of the Universe, or of the character of the Great Positive Mind. Hence, while I am in this condition, I am knowledging that which is opposed to the present affections of men, in the departments of theology and philosophy. But it is nevertheless proper—

nay, it is an imperative duty — for me to develop that which I now perceive is seriously interfering with all social happiness and mental progression. Let it be, then, the serious effort of all vigorous minds, to learn soon to modify their affections for supposed truths, so that their *reason*, and not their *prejudices*, may in all cases be the governing principle of their minds. These developments will then lose their apparent irreverence, and become at once a vehicle to convey to the judgment truth and wisdom. I will have occasion to speak on this point again, when treating on the physical and spiritual constitution of man; but at the present time it is necessary still further to confine the attention to those things heretofore investigated.

§ 163. The men who are called *prophets* were reformers and philosophers in respect to subjects appertaining to the sufferings of humanity. Hence, while situated among those sufferings, they consoled themselves and others by endeavoring to forget the past, or by considering it as an index to a new and more desirable era. Their writings, then, are prophetical on the same principle that all inductive reasonings are; and on this principle they anticipated a day of human industry, of righteousness, and of general knowledge. And as they were subject to the tyranny of despotic rulers, their minds sought refuge in the hope that a new king of the Jews would appear, whose reign would give them relief, and change their physical condition. Hence the king of the Jews of whom they spoke, and whose generation Isaiah indulged great hope of beholding, was exemplified in the great Reformer, JESUS. But they saw him not, nor the distinct *period* of the amelioration; but they were interiorly enlightened sufficiently to recognise the progress of those laws which would as a necessary consequence usher in the King or Reformer whom they contemplated, and the era which they so ardently desired. Christ, then, in the New Testament, is called " the King of the Jews;" but the latter believed not that he was their predicted king. Yet the writers of the New Testament supposed that Christ should be thus designated and promoted, because no other being had ever lived among them who had displayed all those righteous qualities and those manifestations of supreme love that in any way corresponded to the predictions or impressions of the earlier generations.

Understand, then, that the New Testament was written in such a manner as to convey the impression that Jesus was the being actually foreseen by previous writers — in confirmation of which the words of those writers are quoted. Meanwhile remember that the men called prophets knew not of *the* person, nor *the* period, but knew of *a* person and *a* period, which, according to the progress of all things, must inevitably be ushered in. And distinctly does it appear that JESUS possessed those reforming characteristics which constituted him A PERFECT MAN; and that he well represents the King or Reformer spoken of by the prophets as being the Tree of Righteousness, and the founder of the Spiritual Zion. But the era when were to be developed those principles which he exemplified, was not when he lived, but is to be in future. And only can this occur when society has attained to that perfect symmetry of form and structure which was exemplified in the body of Jesus, as then alone will the spiritual possessions thereof be correspondingly perfect.

According to the custom of those days, Jesus spoke parables, which appeared to have allusion to occurrences thereafter to take place in a manner corresponding to the *letter* of the parables. The prediction recorded in Matthew concerning the destruction of Jerusalem and the temple, contains many ambiguous expressions and illustrations. These clothe the prophecy in a very mysterious garment, which to the general mind is rendered the more so because it is recorded in the *New Testament*. The parables of the sheep and goats, the rich man and the poor one, the gehenna of fire, &c., are all related as being spoken by Jesus to represent literal occurrences as affecting man in the material and spiritual world. And they do convey this impression, merely because they are expressed in a style as if the parable or illustration was itself the actual occurrence referred to. This was a customary mode of representing an occurrence or discoursing upon any principle in those days.

But this much is clear, that no good and well-informed mind will ever draw lines of demarcation between any human beings. Therefore it is doing great injustice to the loving-kindness and unbounded sympathy of Jesus, to believe that he employed such expressions intending them to be literally understood; for, as has been before stated, he was one of those well-developed beings whose sympathy and benevolence gushed forth spontaneously, and flowed irrespectively throughout every recess of human existence.

Herein, again, is the test of knowledge and righteousness: He who is ignorant, and whose sympathies are contracted by prejudice; whose benevolence is circumscribed by the circle occupied by any sect or institution; whose feelings, being perverted by local affection and prejudice, are unmoved by the calls of mankind for amelioration — will fix the line of eternal distinction between mankind, and presumptuously calls one class " the wicked," " the sinful," " the abandoned," and the other " the righteous," " the children of God," " the elect." All but the latter class he will call hypocrites, deceivers, and all kinds of unholy names, which naturally are conceived by an ignorant and misdirected mind.

But he whose movements in the world of thought are unrestricted; whose sympathy flows to all, without distinction, excited by a knowledge of human weakness and misdirection ; whose feelings and affections are but gushing aspirations for universal peace and industry; whose energies of soul are concentrated upon the great era of physical and mental freedom and exaltation — he it is that is truly and purely enlightened. Such a one knows no aristocracy, no distinction, no condemnation as a punishment, no bliss as a reward; but recognises the truth, that all causes do inevitably produce corresponding effects. Therefore he makes no distinction except that which *Nature* establishes by her laws of association. The mind which recognises all these things is the highest development of Nature, and should be admired because of its purity and unsophistication. Then, I'say, if Jesus, from a conviction of his judgment, made any actual distinction, such as the language attributed to him would indicate if literally understood, he must be numbered with the ignorant and uneducated, who occupy no very high position in the sphere of thought and wisdom. On the other hand, if he uttered not those expressions which are ascribed to him, except for the purpose of *illustration*, then he may have been that pure and truly enlightened being whom the world at the present day is striving to know, to appreciate, and to follow.

§ 164. To speak still more plainly : All impure, ignorant, and improperly-instructed minds, can, without hesitation, condemn a portion of the race, and presume to stigmatize them as Pharisees, hypocrites, evil-doers, and workers of unrighteousness. But that mind which is pure, and properly educated in the ways of wisdom, can only recognise mankind as a Brotherhood; and he will consider their imperfections as owing only to the misdirection of their physical and mental powers. A knowledge of this truth breathes a universal sympathy and forgiveness; and the mind possessing it can not but recognise the principle of doing good unto all, and loving one another. Whoever says, then, that Jesus ever used such expressions in a literal sense, as is generally taught by theologians, virtually charges him with being an impure and unrighteous man. But he who believes not these things, may consistently admit Jesus to have been a good man, and a natural philanthropist.

I discover, however, that these things were not recorded until sometime after the death of Jesus, and then were written according to the traditional accounts received by the writers; and they were expressed in a manner corresponding to the customs, beliefs, and modes of expression, prevalent in those days. I perceive it is proper to affirm, that this language was employed by Jesus to convey his conceptions in a style suitable to be understood by the multitudes who listened to his preaching. The language presents no particular principles capable of being applied to the world at the present day. And it would indeed be a mark of wisdom, and a good sign of a mental resurrection from ignorance and superstition, if theologians and commentators would discard all further effort to draw instruction from those illustrations that were only useful nearly two thousand years ago.

In respect to the origin of the account concerning the ascension of Jesus, it is at the present time not important that I should enter into particulars; especially as former comments lead to a solution of this question, and also exclude the possibility of such an actual occurrence. I will refer, however, for a detailed consideration of these and kindred subjects, to a work that will hereafter be given, as devoted to a discussion of minor and general opinions and principles.

Here, then, follows a summary of that which has already been related concerning Jesus: The account given of his birth sprang from an unfavorable report in the neighborhood where Jesus was born, concerning his illegitimacy. This is its *origin;* but the *style* in which it is recorded, is a creation that arose from those general impressions concerning him entertained by those who wrote. The alleged prophecies concerning him, quoted from the Old Testament, were not originally intended to be thus applied; but they were cited by the biographers of Jesus because they had a seeming appositeness to some of the circumstances of his life. They were suggested to the writers of the New Testament as having an allusion to Christ, because they believed that past and present revealments formed one perfect system of inspiration and theology, as derived from the Divine Being. This was merely a conviction of their minds caused by the seeming evidence afforded by every external, superficial, and traditional indication. The accounts given of miracles also derived their character from the customary use of language in those days, which was to associate cause and effect in one sentence, without alluding to the intermediate period which elapsed between the application and the result. Of this, also, I have spoken before.

Those passages which speak of Jesus as being the Son of God, and of his making those vast distinctions between men, are merely expressions employed by those who wrote their convictions concerning him, and are worthy of no more attention than may arise from the fact that they embody the opinions of men who lived many hundred years ago.

Moreover, it becomes necessary to mark the very great injustice that such accounts do to the character and life of Christ. It is certainly doing no good to any being to claim for him an illegitimate or supernatural origin. Nor does it do any credit to his character to relate the many inconsistent things that are reported concerning his youth, his deeds, his preaching, and his death. Besides, it is absolutely inconsistent with the high moral sensibilities of an enlightened judgment, to clothe the life and preachings of Jesus with the things that are now known to be believed only by those who are ignorant, misdirected, or prejudiced.

A belief of many things related of Jesus, not only does injustice to his birth, life, wisdom, and benevolence, but it removes the Great Moving Principle of the Universe from his exalted position to a grade only worthy of an ignorant and capricious potentate. It depreciates the character of the Divine Mind, by making him institute a system of theology merely to change that which he himself created imperfect in the beginning of human existence. It makes the Universe an inconsistent, disorganized, and unholy mass of creations. It destroys the harmony of the Divine Plans, by teaching that the Deity has interfered with his established laws, instituting new ones to destroy those which he previously established.

It likewise teaches that the Divine Mind and his Son have both failed to accomplish the End to attain which they are represented as having made active efforts. For the "miraculous conception" can never be believed so long as Nature continues her unvarying manifestations; and this doctrine can never be of the least possible use in effecting a physical or mental elevation of the race. It rather has a *contrary* tendency, inasmuch as it inspires feeble minds with awe, fear, and superstition. And if the "miracles" were intended to prove the divine power of Christ, and to establish a divine theology in the world, then have they proved ineffectual; because in the enlightened mind they neither establish a belief in a Divine power as possessed by Christ, nor convey any conviction in favor of what is supposed to be the true theology. And if Christ was what they represented him to be, and if all the contents of the New Testament are true, the miracles can not make them more so. On the other hand, if they are *not* true, no miracles nor anything else can ever make them true. And, moreover, if all those things related of him are literally true, then he is proved to have been an impure and undeveloped being, even from his birth upward. Moreover, if they are true, that which I am now saying can not possibly affect their intrinsic truthfulness.

This much, however, it is well to know: that that which Reason and Nature sanction, should be believed in preference to that which is contradictory of all known laws, and is incompatible with the harmony which pervades the Universe. Therefore it would be doing Christ injustice to believe concerning him all that is related in the New Testament. Yet those who wrote these things were perfectly honest, and were impelled only by a sense of duty and zeal to write their serious convictions, and present them to those who wished to know what they believed, and from what source sprang their convictions. But there is no evidence connected with the origin of these records to justify the belief that they were ever intended for universal reading and comment.

§ 165. There exists no history or account of the birth and teachings of Jesus corresponding to that which is recorded in the New Testament, with the exception of the account in Josephus; and that occupies no conspicuous position, but is merely recorded as a passing remark of no very great importance. Some have supposed that this passage is an interpolation. I do not discover that this supposition is true; for the record is genuine, although not contained in some of the early versions of Josephus. Yet it is clear that this historian attached no such importance to the life and character of Christ as was attached thereunto by those who wrote the gospels. It is reasonable to suppose that if the birth and life of Christ had been of such a supernatural character, more historians would have received conviction accordingly, and would have devoted considerable portions of their writings to a relation of his miraculous manifestations, setting forth the importance of his birth, death, and resurrection. But as no more historians devoted themselves to this work, the conclusion inevitably follows that few, if any, firmly believed these things, except those who wrote the primitive manuscripts of the New Testament; and that the latter believed because they received a mass of apparent evidence which no others were in a situation to receive.

The object of speaking concerning these things is to free the minds of men from all superstitious prejudice as connected with a belief in the same, which prejudice has a tendency to retard the physical and spiritual development of mankind. Society can not be reorganized in harmony with the laws and requirements of Nature, until all obstacles are removed which obstruct the unfoldings of the general mind, and stand in the way of universal action: and this superstitious belief in an unreal theology is one of those obstacles that are to be of all others the most dreaded and the most repulsed from the bosom of mankind. Such obstacles can be removed only by cautiously revealing the *causes* engaged in their creation; and a knowledge of these will cause the mind to repulse and discard their effects as these are existing at the present time in every portion of the world.

Therefore I have descended to the causes that were engaged in creating the book that is now called *the Bible;* and a knowledge of these removes at once all that superstition concerning it, and all those ideas of its supernaturalness, that have preserved it in the bosom of fanaticism from the period of its origin to the present day. The effects of these causes have been folly, ignorance, prejudice, bigotry, superstition, injustice, wretchedness, immorality, and aristocratic distinctions, among the various nations of the earth. Now he who can sympathize with these *effects*, may still continue to cherish their parent *causes;* but he who feels an inward repulsion at the very thought of their existence, will most certainly display his nobleness of mind in discarding for ever those unholy causes which produced them, as well as the effects themselves, and begin to live a new life in the physical and mental world, and thus be fitted to ascend to the highest point in the second sphere of knowledge and understanding.

Still nothing should be venerated more than the beautiful and truthful prophetic meditations of the early writers concerning a universal deliverance from tyranny, bondage, and wretchedness. And the many useful and beautiful moral precepts contained in the New

Testament, as spoken by Jesus, demand equal reverence. All such moral teachings should be regarded with deep veneration, especially when that veneration is an offspring of the judgment, and not of the affections; for the affections are not the developed principles, but merely the elements of the judgment.

And it will be perceived that the nobleness of those early writers, and the superior physical and mental endowments of Jesus, are still preserved as a source of instruction, and that they even shine forth with a brilliancy they never have before displayed, because they have been so much obscured beneath a heterogeneous mass of unjust and useless materials. And what has been preserved of their characters and teachings is capable of being applied to the great subject of Moral Reform, which is only to be affected by first reforming the physical and social conditions of men. The beauty of their lives and characters, the perseverance which distinguished their efforts, and their adherence to the principles of virtue, goodness, and righteousness, even unto martyrdom — all stand forth as conspicuous examples by which all men may profit.

And let it be known that JESUS was the greatest of them all in this great field of labor — in this great vineyard of natural (not *un*natural) culture. He possessed pre-eminently those ennobling attributes which are worthy a living imitation in the lives and deeds of all men. I therefore place Jesus and these early writers or prophets in the same category with those worthy and noble philanthropists who have lived since their time, and those who still live to adorn the world. They were general sympathizers with the afflictions of men, general actors for the public good, general relievers of the widows and fatherless, general preachers of the great principles controlling the Universe and Man with an unerring government, and general relievers of despondency and mental wretchedness, by unfolding to the minds of men the great and glorious era when would exist universal peace, industry, and righteousness.

And it is an honor to the human race to become now acquainted with the pure characters of former days, as disconnected from all the extraneous obscurities that have shut out their real characters from the mental perceptions of the world. It is an honor now to know and appreciate the trueness, goodness, brotherly-kindness, and benevolence of JESUS, as disconnected from all the falsifications heretofore obscuring his intrinsic physical and spiritual qualifications.

Thus I close all reflections on the character and application of the principles of the early writers, and of JESUS, until the delivery of the third part of this work.

---

§ 166. THE foregoing considerations in reference to theology, and the misconceptions that exist in the world, have so far advanced the subject as to render necessary, as next in order, some reflections upon many revelations that have been made in past ages, by various persons who were qualified for the inflowing and the outward expression of truths. In all ages of the world, revelations of various degrees of importance have been made, though in many instances the world knew it not. I discover that more have been given than are recorded in the Bible; and some of these, too, were of the most important and instructive nature: although in the Bible are contained many that have scarcely ever been excelled in any previous or subsequent age.

It is proper for every mind to venerate revelations of every kind, in proportion to their congeniality with the uniform teachings of Nature, and the highest sanctions of a well-constituted judgment. And in connexion with this remark, I would again enforce the absolute importance of not bestowing veneration upon any revealments that are to be found in the Bible, more than upon those found among the productions of other writers.

The most useful revelations contained in the Bible are those given by David, Isaiah, Jeremiah, Zechariah, Malachi, and Jesus. ISAIAH'S mind was so expanded, that a knowledge of ultimate alleviation from physical and social wretchedness flowed into it with a natural ease, with which also he expressed the same to the world. But as the application of his revelations will be made in the sequel, it is unnecessary at present to dwell upon them. He should, however, be recognised in this place as one of those spiritually-enlightened men whose teachings to the social world have not as yet been appreciated or justly interpreted.

And DAVID, too, instituted prophetical meditations that are worthy of the deepest attention and the highest respect. And JEREMIAH, and likewise ZECHARIAH, revealed many things pertaining to the same social resurrection, and to the grand and sublime results in the *moral* world as flowing so naturally and spontaneously from the harmony and unity of action that will ultimately pervade the whole *physical* world. And MALACHI also spoke briefly, yet truthfully, concerning the great and glorious era yet unrealized by the inhabitants of the earth, but which, according to progressive law, may be had in bright anticipation.

It is well to remark, in order to prevent misunderstanding, that I use the terms *revelation* and *development* as *synonymous;* for a revelation is nothing more than an outward development of truths flowing into the mind.

No being ever existed before JESUS, who possessed the same degree of spiritual elevation and refinement: for he possessed the highest development of the physical and mental powers. And it is plain that no being ever revealed so much pure and substantial truth so capable of receiving an immediate and useful application. His mind, as I have before intimated, was properly constituted for the inflowing of truths, both from the natural and spiritual world. Therefore his superior judgment taught him to reveal only useful and natural truths, relating to the social conditions and material constitutions of men. For, as has been shown, he taught not the doctrine of immortality, but only incidentally made mention of that truth when endeavoring to inspire the human mind with hope and confidence. Jesus is to be more respected and appreciated, and his principles more practised, than they have as yet been. The beauty of his natural principles have never as yet been duly recognised, because they have not escaped the darkening influence of theological interpretations. And I feel it proper to affirm that the beauty of his life and character never has been nor never will be known, and fully exemplified in the lives of men, until all speculation, both of a psychological and theological nature, as connected therewith, is abandoned. For the more this is persisted in, the further his life, character, and principles, become removed from the understanding and practice of mankind. The distinction must be made between natural truth and spiritual imagination, before there can exist universal peace on earth and good-will to men. If no more were revealed by Jesus than *this* consummation, the high illumination of his mind would be sufficiently demonstrated; because he spoke not of that which *was,* but of that which shall be *yet* in future.

The use, therefore, of his principles, has not been comprehended by those who profess to have the most knowledge of their utility and application. And it now becomes important that men should discard previous interpretations of his teachings, and press onward to the consummation, when their truth will be triumphantly demonstrated. I recognise the revelations made by JESUS as more useful, more truthful, and more natural, than any of those who have presented different or higher truths to the world. What I mean by higher truths is, such as are involved in many of those metaphorical allusions in the Apocalypse—which are incapable of benefiting the world of mankind, though they are susceptible of being fully verified in the third sphere of spiritual habitation. Notwithstanding their truth, they are impracticable, and therefore they demand not that attention and veneration which have been given them by many erudite commentators. It has been proved that the Apocalypse contains no principles that are intimately connected with any other revelation, with the exception of that made by Emanuel Swedenborg.

§ 167. Many revelations have been made by persons among the Chinese, Hindoos, and Persians. CONFUCIUS revealed many moral principles which have not an equal in any revealment except that of Jesus. Also BRAMA revealed many interior truths that have not as yet been, but *will* be, verified, both in the social and spirit world. Many truths are obtained even unconsciously to the person who receives them, by implication, induction, and progressive thought. And in like manner do men sometimes become *subjects* or *agents* to reveal truths altogether unknown and unbelieved by themselves, but which are, nevertheless, in subsequent ages, discovered to be truths of the most astounding character and the greatest intrinsic worth. Thus it was with ZOROASTER—who revealed and taught to the whole eastern world, that sin would ultimately be abolished, and everlasting righteousness brought in; and that then the Deity (Ormuzd) would rejoice with joy unspeakable for ever and ever. Never was a greater truth proclaimed to the inhabitants of the earth: and for the accomplishment of the end which it contemplates, the most active efforts should be employed. Yet this is not venerated, merely because it was presented by *Zoroaster*—he being, notwithstanding, an *agent* or *subject* by and through which this most important revelation was made.

Also MOHAMMED declared many spiritual truths—truths that have been verified by psychological research, and also by the spiritual developments of Swedenborg. Yet, again, these truths are not revered, merely because the revelation has proceeded from Mohammed, and because hereditary impression and education preclude all affection from the truths and their revealer.

A few centuries ago, many physical truths were revealed by GALEN — truths, too, that are susceptible of the most useful application. These relate to the *trinity of principles* or *substances* as forming any one compound or organization. This trinity is discoverable in every department of Nature and the Universe. This does not, however, in any way demonstrate the supposed *spiritual* Trinity that has been so seriously defended, so ably discussed, and so reverentially cherished. Galen, then, revealed that which no other physician or physical researcher ever did; and he is worthy of being classed with those revelators who occupy the highest position in the departments of useful and natural truths.

I find also many important discoveries and revelations among the *Germans* — owing very much to their peculiar habits of thinking, and of investigating all seen and unseen laws and operations of Nature; and among them have been persons whose interior perceptions were so unfolded as to enable them to recognise the reality of the spirit world, and its close connexion with this rudimental sphere. One should be noticed particularly, because her mind was in a condition occupied by all at the period of death or transformation. She is known as the SEERESS OF PREVORST — and has revealed many truths concerning the connexion between the natural and spiritual world, and between the soul and the body; and concerning the powers of spiritual perception, and the medium by which the spirit is united with the form. These things are too important to escape the attention of any inquiring mind; for they manifestly involve evidences such as mankind at present need to satisfy them of the powers of the soul, and of other physiological truths.

MARTIN LUTHER likewise revealed some truths that are very useful, practical, and important. Yet error preponderates in his productions, and these, therefore, are not worthy of so high a degree of attention and esteem. His mind, like that of CALVIN, was changed by a very sudden conception that what he was educated to believe was not all true. This conception at once inspired new faculties of the soul, and the whole resulted in the development of many truths, which, though mingled with errors, deserve the title of *revelations*.

§ 168. The *French* have also produced unfolded minds, whose revelations demand equal attention and respect. The system of

Nature and philosophy of human social existence and harmony, by BARON D'HOLBACH, is a production worthy of attention and respect, because of its beauty of expression, sublimity of sentiment, and expansiveness of philosophy. And I hesitate not to affirm, that he is the author of many revelations too capable of a beneficial application to be ever lost or forgotten. His conceptions, however, are not *all* true, nor are his conclusions all perfectly legitimate as deduced from the basis assumed, which *is* true. Hence his production contains a mixture of error and truth. Yet the truth preponderates; and this should, therefore, be recognised, appreciated, and duly acknowledged.

France has produced many very learned men in the *superficial* attainments of life. And their philosophies are not of the purest and highest order, merely because they partake so much of the *external* and *sensuous* in their processes of investigation. Such a mode of investigation is not to any great extent calculated to unfold those *moral* truths and progressive principles that will harmonize the human family, and unfold the beauties of the spirit world.

There is one, however, whose teachings I can not fail to recognise as the most useful, most truthful, and most exceedingly sublime, even as seeking a level with, and being confirmed by, the teachings of Jesus. This is the great and noble Reformer, CHARLES FOURIER —whose capacity of soul and extent of revelation have not as yet been perceived to any great extent by mankind. His mind was superiorly constituted and developed; for a proof of which, see his unparalleled disclosures concerning the unspeakable harmony that pervades the Universe, and concerning the reciprocal action of all bodies, which, to express it in his own language, "breathe a melody of harmonious sounds, like an instrument well tuned, and every note touched in unity by wisdom." And, says he, the harmony of the Universe is developed and displayed in the planetary system; for each planet occupies a position, and plays a part in the great system of united action, as the notes of a well-tuned instrument. And as a tune can not be played unless each note is properly adjusted, and occupies a position in reference to the rest suitable to produce harmony and melody, when a tune is thus played, the Universe is at the same time represented.

Then he proceeds to reveal the all-important truth, that as *harmony* exists among all the bodies of the Universe, so can it prevail among, and join inseparably, the inhabitants of the earth. And he proceeds to assure the world, by mathematical demonstration, that every note exists in this animated sphere; and that each note needs only to be properly placed, in order that the whole race may, like a perfectly-tuned instrument, move in harmony, melody, happiness, and unity of action.

Behold, mankind, these sublime and eternal truths crushed and almost entombed in the dark mass of prevailing ignorance, prejudice, and fanaticism! Hear ye not, when a noble and expansive mind, like that of CHARLES FOURIER, demonstrates the interior truth, even to your *senses*, that the world of mankind is composed of the requisite notes to play a perfect tune of peace and harmony? And observe how gently, seriously, and cautiously, he informs the world that these notes can only be properly placed by following the light of wisdom and knowledge!

He also mathematically analyzes the developments of each planet in our solar system, and proves that the mental advancement of the inhabitants of each must necessarily constitute such a Brotherhood and such an association of congenial parts as to render the whole an harmonious existence, such as he expended his powers to have accomplished on earth. And I have the means of knowing that his general conceptions were strictly true as regards the inhabitants of the planets belonging to our solar system. And it becomes me in justice to sanction and confirm that which he proved true by the dissimilar process of mathematical induction. I therefore affirm that his statements concerning the harmony and unity existing among the inhabitants of the planets, as to their social condition and mental culture, are decidedly and unequivocally *true* — being in no essential particular discrepant with those things which I have revealed concerning the world, Nature, and the Universe.

I am drawn to that person whose whole physical and spiritual powers were devoted to the great work of moral reform. Such was CHARLES FOURIER: and those things which he revealed are capable of being applied in improving the social condition of man, and their truth will be demonstrated in the moral consequences of the perfect restitution to peace, harmony, and pure principles, for which he labored.

Concerning this very noble personage, and his philosophy, more will hereafter be related, especially when the principles of his microcosmogony make their appearance prominently in the third part, or application, of this work.

§ 169. I am also impressed to recognise the important revelations made by and through EMANUEL SWEDENBORG, the Swedish philosopher and psychologist.

His mind possessed many superior endowments, and he presented to the world many pure and healthy principles. Some of his revealments, however, will be capable of an application only when the race advances to a high degree of social and mental refinement. His mind was interiorly expanded, which fact enabled him to receive and express many interior truths connected both with the material and spiritual world.

I discover more practical utility in his scientific and philosophical revealments than in any other of his productions. No work should be more esteemed and generally read than a book written by him entitled "*The Economy of the Animal Kingdom*," in two volumes. The first volume presents a close and severe analytical investigation of the three functions performed by all animated bodies; in which he develops that order of "end, cause, and effect," which are alike observable in all portions of the creations of the Divine Mind. He plainly reveals that the *end*, or ultimate design, is the primary cause of all movement. A knowledge of the *end* prompts and procures the *means*, which are the *secondary* causes: and the action of these produce the *effects*, which are the ends predetermined to be accomplished. The *end* or object to be accomplished is in every instance the creator of the causes and effects that are instituted—or of the means and effects combined as one in accomplishing that which was the *original cause* of the institution of both. This much is clearly revealed in the first part of his work; and is true, useful, and will be acknowledged and applied to the necessities of human existence.

The second part is devoted to a consideration of the three functions of the animal kingdom—their interior, mediatorial, and exterior qualities, as performing their respective offices and manifesting their peculiar spiritual forces, with a mutual dependence upon each other. Indeed, his revealments concerning the *beginnings* of power in the human system are beyond all general comprehension at the present day. He discourses deeply upon the cortical composition of the brain, describing the glands or "little hearts" (as he calls them), as constituting the cause of all motion or spiritual exercise in the material form, and describes how they expand and contract like the movements of the chest and heart. And he demonstrates the reciprocity of the systolic and diastolic motions of the cortical glands of the brain, and that they are the beginnings and causes of all corresponding movements belonging to the animal economy.

The last portion of this valuable work is devoted to some very rational and truthful intimations of a psychological character, and concerning the powers of the human soul. It contains a very clear and lucid explanation of the distinction between the nature and powers of the soul and spirit as connected with the human form; and it likewise exhibits a very gentle emergement from the material into the spiritual sphere of thought and investigation.

I am led also to notice a still higher spiritual development of the same kind which is presented in the latter portion of his "Animal Kingdom:" and that is found in his production entitled "*True Worship and Love of God.*" Nothing can evince more substantial purity of meditations and superior conceptions of the mind than this very impressive and well-constructed work. It flowed, as it were, spontaneously from his high reverence for those unspeaking truths contained in the animal creations. And this work is indeed a revealment much to be read, appreciated, and practised.

After the period which was occupied in writing these works, his mind became exceedingly exalted, and all its powers of conception were absorbed completely in the phenomena and truths of the spirit-world. The truths that he thus reveals concerning these things are in very many particulars susceptible of benefiting the human race — though this can not be said of every general feature of his psychological system. He revealed those spiritual truths that will be verified in subsequent lectures: but only in a general and correspondential manner. For I now discover that many of his interior disclosures are not in the least particular comprehended even by those who at the present time are most actively engaged in their advocacy. And I am impressed to say that if, instead of conveying the idea that he unfolded the spiritual and interior teachings of the *Bible*, he had said that he unfolded the spiritual and interior teachings of *Nature*, the world would sooner have approached his sphere of reason and knowledge: because then the connexion would have been more distinctly observed between the material and spiritual world. But I am not able to discover any such interior meaning in any portion of the contents of the Word as he represents. And if objection is made to any of these sayings, as based upon the want of interior perception which may here seem to be acknowledged, I would request the reader to reconsider the explanation I have given of the interior qualities of the Bible. If, however, the objection be persisted in, I refer for future demonstration to the ENCYCLOPÆDIA that will succeed this book.

I am much drawn to the pure, gigantic, and powerfully-intellectual spirit of SWEDENBORG. His philosophical revelations are of vast importance, because of their truth; and his spiritual and psychological revelations are also *qualifiedly* true, and are susceptible of being verified in the spiritual spheres, and will be in the disclosures soon to follow.

I recognise, however, too much profuseness of expression — too much repetition of correspondences and established principles — in various portions of his works. There is too much intensity of ardor, and too much obscurity, ambiguity, and spiritually-inflated conception, in his psychological works, for them to be of any particular utility to the social world at the present time. But a proper and abundant supply of the social requirements of mankind will so elevate their moral and spiritual perceptions, that they will readily discover the signification of his spiritual teachings, which at present, to the mass of mankind, seem like the wildest hallucinations of a misdirected and inflated mind. Then in view of these considerations, it is impossible to conceive of the practical utility of his spiritual revelations to the disordered world at this present time. The fact that they are not capable of being comprehended is at least presumptive evidence that they are not such truths as are at present required to benefit the social world.

Therefore I observe this gigantic mind as in its conceptions transcending completely the ordinary powers, even of all *interiorly* enlightened men, and consequently as being removed from the natural into spiritual spheres. Hence some of his mighty revelations will only be known to be true when man ascends to a higher degree of wisdom and knowledge. And as these things are so, I notice those things only in his revelations that are adapted to the wants of the social world, in order that mankind may be, as Fourier has expressed it, organized according to the melodious, harmonious reciprocations of a Brotherhood.

§ 170. Many revelations have been made in previous ages, which I can not now stop to notice. And all these are in a greater or less degree important and profitable as contributing to the general stock of wisdom that mankind require.

It is proper, however, to briefly reflect upon the revelations of

Plato concerning the spiritual identity of man, and a future life: It can not be doubted, when his whole philosophy is taken into consideration, that he revealed some very important laws in Nature, and many psychological truths. These, however, were much obscured by the mingling of external and internal evidences: the first being mostly the developments of circumstances, and the latter the unvarying movements presented in all parts of Nature that he investigated. His mind was much clouded and his perceptions much darkened by a vast number of hereditary impressions. Yet his psychological revealments make their appearance even through the many superficial evidences which he accumulates in their favor.

Also those things unfolded by the interior reflections of Xenophon possess a high degree of beauty, truth, and profitableness. No mind ever was more deeply impressed with the truths of immortality than his, because his convictions proceeded from the gushing aspirations of the living principle within. And his philosophy contains more substantial reasons for this doctrine than are to be found in any portion of the Old or New Testament. His writings are therefore useful and important to the world, because of their many truthful intimations, these suggesting higher truths.

In the revealments of Socrates I do not discover so much *interior* perception of principles, but more comprehensiveness in the observance of *superficial* evidences; and the ideas deduced from these are in many instances true, though illegitimate.

Cicero was also a defender of those unvarying principles that govern the Universe, a consciousness of the truth of which compelled him to discard all superficial theories that then pervaded the general mind, in the form of a mythological theology. And he, like the former writers, should be very deeply esteemed and appreciated for his pure and important revealments, of which confirmation may be derived from the interior perceptions of every enlightened judgment.

I discover a harmony in the revelations of each age, from the first decided conception and expression of truth, to the unfoldings of the present generation. I discover, however, that each revelator has presented truth in proportion to the favorable situations in which his mind was placed, and the favorable developments to which it attained. Yet that truth which is discoverable among the writings of each, is confirmed with great simplicity in the moral and social teachings of Jesus, and in the corresponding teachings of Charles Fourier, who systematized those pure principles in order that they might be reduced to practice, and thus produce a moral renovation of the race.

Then, again, I discover the more superficial modifications of these principles in the writings of SWEDENBORG, who proceeds to the interior, not so much of *principles*, as of their detailed parts. Thus in his writings are set forth the innumerable ramifications, both of things and principles belonging to the natural world, and of the corresponding literal possessions of the spirit-world. And as I have stated, I do not discover sufficient distinctness or naturalness in the writings of this philosopher to render them susceptible of a practical application to the social requirements of the human race. It is no more than just in all such instances to enforce the question, "Of what possible use can any revelation be, that can neither be understood nor applied?" A revelation developing no practical principles existing in the natural world as adapted to social life, can not be of any possible utility to the social or moral world.

From these considerations, the object of glancing at the writings of each philosopher becomes apparent. It is to point out the good and practical parts of each, that they may be preserved for future application; and if these are duly distinguished and preserved, all the unreal and excrescent parts of each revelation and philosophy will at once be disregarded, because of their non-importance.

Since the existence of those men, many new and dissimilar theories, hypotheses, and revelations, have made their appearance, both in the scientific and theological world. These have been of such a nature as to disunite the modes of natural and social life from the moral principles of man. This fact, again, demonstrates the nonutility of such revelations, inasmuch as they are destructive to the social harmony of mankind, and to that pure morality which is inseparably connected therewith.

Again: Any theory or hypothesis having a tendency to disunite the material from the spiritual, or the social from the moral, or to disunite in any way the human race, is entirely unprofitable, and should be for ever discarded. For it is made plain from past investigations, that a perfect morality can not be developed, unless the rudimental and social condition of the race is first made suitable for its spontaneous development. It is, therefore, absolutely useless to promulgate theological systems of morality, when the causes relating to such are in direct opposition to the required result. Then, in order to benefit the world, instead of being engaged in psychological investigations, men should turn their attention immediately to the establishing of those superior conditions in the social world, the effects of which will greatly transcend their present anticipations. It is clear to every mind, that the latter must be accomplished before the moral results so much admired can, as a consequence, be permanently obtained. In other words, the social and natural must be superiorly situated and organized, before the moral and spiritual elements of man can possibly be developed to a proper degree. The many revelations that are now existing in the scientific and theological departments, are of minor importance compared to the great and essential principles which must be discovered and acknowledged before that social and moral condition of the race can be attained for which all should strive.

It is proper to understand that the influx of principles into the mind of a person or persons, is a result of the peculiar constitution and development of such minds; and not that revelations of any character proceed *directly* from a Divine Source. Therefore, he whose mind is unfolded, or whose spiritual perceptions are extended to a higher sphere of knowledge, comprehends more than ordinary minds, because he perceives that which exists below his exalted sphere of investigation. Such see, also, that which would be of use and importance to the world, and reveal it in order that it may be applied. Thus *every* mind conceives and expresses truth in proportion to its degree of development, or of spiritual elevation. Then such revelations as the Apocalypse and those contained in many other portions of the New Testament, together with many portions of Swedenborg's writings, can not, though true, be of any possible use to mankind in their natural state. Whether they are or are not true, therefore, they are unimportant. Hence it is proper for every theologian and commentator, before devoting much time to such, to inquire their *use*, even admitting them to be of the purest origin and the highest truth.

There are many worthy persons who have distinguished themselves in various departments of thought, whom I am obliged to leave unnoticed, for the reason that their cogitations are subordinate to the object of these present considerations. I am impressed to say, however, that those who have been active in unfolding the teachings of others will be specifically noticed hereafter.

§ 171. THESE revealments having proceeded thus far, a different though connected subject may now be introduced. I have descended into the interior history of mankind, discovered the origin of social disunity, false impressions, unreal theology and consequent mythology, and have specifically considered the successive modifications of each, until the whole presents itself to the generations of the present century. I have spoken of man, physically and mentally, only as it was necessary in order to elucidate the many causes of conditions existing in the world. I have not spoken particularly of the physical production and constitution of man, nor of those peculiar elements, qualities, and essential principles, that elevate him above the animal creation, and that constitute and characterize that animated principle known as the *Soul, Spirit*, or *Mind*. I find it necessary to generalize these, in order to establish the connexion between Nature, with its various lower forms, and Man, and between man and the higher spheres. An inseparable unity and reciprocation of action must be discovered and established between these, and then the whole social world may hereafter become a true representative of the grand and harmonious movements of Nature and the Universe.

I have ascended, then, to the important question, *What is Man* MATERIALLY? And the answer is, He is the wisdom, head, and King of all animated forms.—He is a perfection of matter.*

I proceed to prove this proposition by descending to the interior forms and substances that constitute the rudiments of all organic beings, and tracing them connectedly until they ascend and become perfected in the human organization.†

The first forms or particles that made their appearance after the condensation of the matter composing the earth, were those constituting the *mineral kingdom*. This is composed of particles of matter

---

* The word "*perfection*" is here used in the absolute sense, though relatively.

† NOTE BY THE AUTHOR. For a demonstration of the things I now relate, reference is made to the truths established in the department of *geology*, upon which subject I have more minutely treated. And herein is developed the use of the truths revealed in the geological portions of this work; for they are now applied as a means by which my present revealments may be elucidated and demonstrated as true. I will also institute illustrations and comparisons of a very familiar nature, in order that the main principles to be presented may be easily conceived and comprehended. It will be seen, also, that the following sustains a close relation to the scientific parts of this work; and they will mutually explain and confirm each other. I would, therefore, have the reader's memory duly impressed with the previous philosophical investigations, so that he may perceive the connexion, and readily apprehend the things now to follow.

in their *rudimental* forms. These are angular, amorpho-angular, and multi-angular. These forms, when associated, compose the various mineral bodies in the earth. The first of these particles are the most perfectly angular; the ascending forms are the amorpho-angular, and the perfect forms among these are the multi-angular. The first is the parent and measure of the second, and *this* again is the beginning of the third, which completes a trinity and also pervades the lower forms. Thus the second and third forms are each higher degrees of development from the first. The highest proceed from the lowest, and, when developed, pervade and comprehend the whole body, which thus forms a mineral compound.

Then, again, *Series* are established by the successive unfoldings of forms. These series are strata of associated particles, such as are exemplified in the strata of the earth, and of various bodies which possess successive coatings, all of which are necessary to form one body, substance, or compound. These series are *three;* and these characterize the various compounds in the mineral kingdom.

Then, again, *Series* develop *Degrees*. These are the successive states of purity of particles, and of their approach to perfection, both in form, series, and association. The highest degree in the mineral kingdom approaches, and inseparably flows into, the vegetable kingdom. For the highest degree of mineral substance exemplifies both the lower particles of its own nature, and the first particles of the successive compound, which is the vegetable creation. The highest *form*, also, in the mineral, which is the multi-angular, flows directly into, and becomes the origin, parent, and measure of the first forms in, the vegetable kingdom. So also do the highest *Series* flow into the vegetable formation, through the degrees of association determined by the ascending forms, the sequence of series, and the unfolding of the same.

So the forms in the mineral world are of three degrees of development. Thus they form one compound—which develops series, associations, and degrees, all of which are necessary to establish the various mineral bodies, to designate their degree of refinement, and to determine with what order of particles or elements they are capable of being assimilated. The forms, series, and degrees in the mineral world, are thus developed in the most perfect harmony. The highest of each in all cases pervade the lower; and at the same time they become the parent and measure of the rudimental productions in the vegetable world.

In the vegetable compounds there exist *circular* forms — which are the unfolded forms of the perfected angular. Then the rudimental circular develops diameters, and ascending circulars which very slightly approach the *spiral*. Thus three different forms are also discoverable in the vegetable world: that is, the perfected angular (or multi-angular); the first circular, which develops diameters; and both of these ascend toward, and very slightly represent, the *spiral* forms, which flow directly into the animal world. In the vegetable creation also are the three *Series*, or the three degrees of perfection in forms. These Series also represent the Degrees that are unfolded by the ascending series of forms that flow from the parent or measure consisting of the lower forms. Meanwhile, they make a perfect compound, the whole of which forms the Vegetable Creation.

The highest form, which is the ascending circular, becomes the connecting form between the vegetable and animal; and in the latter it becomes the perfect *spiral*. Also the highest *Degrees* of vegetable compounds become the first degrees of animal organization. And each series and association of forms, in like manner progressively ascends to the first series and degrees of the animal forms; and all pass into, and become the germ, parent, measure, and substance of, the whole Animal World. The *first* forms discovered in the animal are the *spiral* or progressive particles which develop the reciprocal motions of the whole frame. The *second* forms are the unfolded spiral, which are the *spiritual* forms or active particles that become the receptacles of all progressive movement. The *highest* forms in the animal creation are the perfected spiritual — which join the animal compound to the material organization of Man.

Here, then, the spiritual forms introduce the particles to compose the organization of Man — which, when perfected, develops the *highest* or *celestial* forms in matter. Thus the perfect *spiritual* become the *first celestial* forms, the perfection of which establishes the human organization. What I mean by *celestial* forms are those particles of matter that contain in themselves perfected every species of form in the subordinate kingdoms, and meanwhile become the receptacles of all degrees of spiritual life, which are not only contained in, but are developed by them, in such a perfect and corresponding manner that all the lower forms in the animal, vegetable, and mineral worlds, are by them governed, mirrored, and vividly represented.

Then, again, the highest *series* or *strata* of forms in the animal world, flow directly into the rudimental forms of mankind. These establish the various *series*, *strata*, or *associations*, of the human family. Also the highest *degree* in the animal, by which I mean the most perfect structure, not only typifies, but becomes the parent, measure, and germ, of the Human World.

§ 172. Thus in Man are these lower forms fully developed and perfected: for in him are the spiritual, the perfect spiritual, and the celestial forms of the particles of matter. The celestial are the highest and most minute particles in the human organization — such as exist in the lower kingdoms only in an *imperfect* and *undeveloped* state.

Man also possesses the three *degrees* of the ascended forms. These degrees establish and preserve the individuality of every Form in the human world; while at the same time every Form develops in perfect harmony, series, degrees, associations, and representations, which are in every particular in the most perfect unity, harmony, and mutual dependence upon each other.

It will be seen by this that the *angular* particles of matter develop the *circular* — which in their turn unfold rectilinear planes, diameters, axes, and poles — all of which are imperfectly discovered in the *Vegetable World*.

Then, again, the progressive *circular* forms unfold and become the *spiral*, which is a more important stage in the process of progressive development. The spiral contains the circular and all its properties; and all these are discoverable in the Animal World. Then, again, the successive spiral forms unfold the *spiritual* — which latter, in like manner, unfold the *celestial* or *perfect* forms of rudimental matter. Thus the *angular* develops the *circular*, this the *spiral*, this the *spiritual*, and this the *celestial* — all of which are contained in the perfect Forms of the Human World.

From this it is seen that the *angular* is the parent of all higher forms, and contains them all undeveloped: while the *highest* when developed pervades all the lower forms, and unites them as one perfect Whole. Therefore the celestial forms of matter which compose the human organization are the *flower* of the germinal form, or seed, which is the *angular*. For the seed of all material compounds is involved in the lowest stage of matter, which germinates and produces the *Mineral World*. This, again, adds to the body of the great Tree of Creation, whose next stage of development is in the form of the *Vegetable World*. The next expansion of the body of this great Tree develops the *Animal World*. It now puts forth branches, which bud, and the flower is the *Human World*. Thus it is that the material Tree of Causation has successively yielded new forms, which correspond in every general feature to germ, body, branches, buds, and blossoms.

It is made evident from these considerations, that matter is the same in every department of the Universe — but that it forms dissimilar organizations only as it, in various degrees of development, becomes differently combined. I find, then, that all things are constituted of the same materials, but that these are combined in different forms and proportions. Thus are developed successively, uniformly, and progressively, Forms, Series, and Degrees; and these are all necessary in order that each compound and each animated organization may perform the office of an organ to transfer that which is below it to a higher degree of material association. It is by this diversity of forms that the various Degrees of creation are rendered perfect, reciprocal, and harmonious.

The dissimilar combinations of matter, then, are the designed means by which all the various forms may, in series and degrees, be progressively developed. And the moment such development is completed, a combined Form of the same, capable of preserving its identity, is at once established, as is also its absolute dependence upon the lower forms for its existence.

Thus Man is the highest and most perfect combination of organized matter. He therefore exercises an unlimited proprietorship over all below his exalted position, and is the governor, director, and lord of all subordinate creations. He in this sense pervades all below him. At the same time he is dependent upon the perfect fulfilment of every office which is sustained by the subordinate kingdoms; and without them and their perpetual contributions, he could not possibly exist. Man, then, is not only the *highest* form, but comprehends likewise the *lowest;* and without the lowest, the highest could not be. He therefore should practically acknowledge his dependence accordingly; and in properly doing this, he would so perfect his wisdom as that he might be truly the director, governor, and lord of all things.

The mineral, vegetable, and animal compounds, all enter into the composition of the human form — though these are essentially modified in the process, according to the law of progression. And man is thus a representative of all subordinate forms; for in him their properties and essential principles exist, but are developed and modified in a manner dissimilar to their original state. He is, therefore a perfect *microcosm*—and is the perfection of all material compounds.

The *mineral* formation is to the great Form or structure of Nature, what the *bone* is to the human organization—a *basis* or *frame* upon which the superstructure may rest and be perfected. The forms in the *vegetable* kingdom are to Nature, what the *absorbing vessels* are to the human body; that is, receptacles for the influx, and organs for the reflux, of circulating and ascending particles. The forms in the *animal* kingdom are to Nature, what the *visceral* system is to the human body; that is, organs by and through which rudimental particles may be secreted, decomposed, recombined, and sublimated:—and they are thus necessary parts to perform the various functions of one harmonious Structure. *Man* is to Nature, what the *head* is to man; that is, a throne from which proceeds wisdom, power, direction, government, and distributive justice, to all the lower, useful, and subordinate departments of the same perfect Whole.

§ 173. It is seen from these considerations, that a *trinity* consisting of three degrees of forms, is existing in one substance, the same being necessary to constitute such substance a perfect creation. Let it be duly impressed, that every form in the mineral, vegetable, and animal world, is determined and established by the peculiar forms of the atoms or particles of matter which enter into and compose such. It is to this specificness of atomic forms that the mineral, vegetable, animal, and human worlds, owe their respective existences. For if particles of matter did not become in form essentially modified, by uniform ascension through successive series and degrees of development, these various worlds of creation could not possibly be unfolded. Let this, then, be the standard formula exhibiting the relative degrees of perfection in matter, in order that the mind may conceive of the relation that exists between the lowest and the highest developments of Nature. And by knowing this much, the first principles involved in the material creation of Man, are clearly impressed upon the understanding; and from this the mind will be led to higher and corresponding degrees of the same species of knowledge.

A trinity exists in every substance, and in every possible manner, both as to forms, series, and degrees, and their relations to subsequent creations. First, in the mineral world there exist *interior, mediatorial,* and *exterior* forms: that is, the *lower, transition,* and *perfected* bodies or particles of matter. The lowest contains the highest; and until the highest is developed, a mineral compound is not formed. But when the highest is perfectly unfolded, it forms the seal and crown, and is the governing property which forms of the whole a perfect composition.

Then there are *Series,* and these are three in number. The first series comprehends the lower angular forms, until they progressively change and flow into the transition or mediatorial forms. Then the second series in like manner comprehends these intermediate forms, until they flow into the highest or multi-angulars. The third series comprehends these higher forms, and also pervades and acts on the lower forms, and unites the whole as one compound. Then in like manner do the lower forms and lower series form one *degree,* or decided part—which also explains the second degree, which comprehends the second form and second series. And the third degree, which is the highest of the mineral kingdom, includes the third form and third series. The degrees in every department of Nature determine the states of perfection which are exemplified in exterior and manifest forms. By presenting the descriptions in this form, the mind is enabled to perceive the *rationale* of the whole subject. As it is in the Mineral World, so it is in every possible particular with the Vegetable and Animal Worlds.

To render the subject still more familiar, I will explain it differently. The *interior* or *first* form is the *soul* or moving principle of the compound, containing in itself all the forms and properties displayed in the higher degrees of the same substance. The *mediatorial* form is a connecting link between the soul and the exterior form, which is the perfected body. Thus the *exterior* is the perfectly manifest form, displaying minutely the qualities that were contained undeveloped in the *first* or *rudimental* forms, which now are known to be the creator of the external. Thus a *perfect Whole* is formed, composed of Soul and Body.

When ascending to the vegetable world, we find the same forms, series, and degrees, unfolded and manifested in a most perfectly-corresponding manner. And again, were it not for a change in the forms of the particles of matter, the vegetable creation could not be, because it would not have had a uniformly-actuating creator, such as is the mineral world with its present laws.

In ascending to the animal kingdom, we find new external forms presenting similar varieties to those in the mineral kingdom. And in the animal are not only manifested new *forms*, but new *series* and *degrees*. Again: the animal world could not have existed had not the vegetable world ascended to such a degree of perfection as to become the creator and measure of a higher development.

Thus it is that the mineral kingdom when perfected becomes the soul, measure, and creator, of the vegetable; and this latter, when perfected, becomes the parent, soul, and creator, of the animal. So likewise does the animal become the soul, measure, and creator, of the human organization.

It is now made clear that the form, size, and symmetry, of the specific creations of each kingdom, including Man, are determined only by the perfection of prior creations on which they are dependent. And it is from the lower, inferior, gross, and unseemly forms, that the human organization has been established, with all its beauty, symmetry, and perfection of constitution. I desire to call special attention to this fact, as it shows that the mind can only know of perfection by viewing forms, series of forms, and degrees of these, *comparatively*—these pervading alike the lower and higher departments of animated Nature.

Thus we have an irresistible demonstration that the lowest form is the interior or soul, parent, and measure, of all higher forms, even to the perfect and symmetrical organization of Man; and that *he* is the grand effect or ultimate design of Nature. This is manifest from the fact that all forms flow progressively into, and are comprehended by, the human organization. This makes man the *flower* of creation, possessing all the essences, properties, and characteristics, of the lower creations, while these at the same time contribute to his necessities, and he insensibly performs a similar office toward them.

Again: the *angular* forms correspond to the mineral; the *circular* forms correspond to the *vegetable;* the *spiral* forms correspond to and represent the *animal* world; and the *spiritual* and *celestial* forms typify and correspond to the *human world*—while *it* in return, typifies, represents, and corresponds to, every subordinate form in this whole rudimental sphere of successive developments.

Again: the mineral world is the *interior*, the vegetable world is the *mediatorial*, and the animal world is the *perfect Body*, of the whole system of creation. That is, the mineral is the *soul* or *creator* from which flows spontaneously the *transition* link, which is the vegetable; and this flows onward to the completion of the *perfect Body*, which is the whole animal kingdom.

Thus it is made manifest that the three degrees of creation (which are the Mineral, Vegetable, and Animal) flow into, and as it were spontaneously unfold, the whole *human* creation; and that the three are necessary in order to unfold a complete and symmetrical organization. And this is the great Head, Flower, and lord of creation, and is called MAN.

§ 174. A Trinity is now unfolded in every department of Nature: for it is discovered in the form of particles, in the series or associations of these, and in the degree of each form and series; and all may be discovered in any established, organized substance. This truth is also exemplified in the three great worlds of formation, viz., the mineral, vegetable, and animal kingdoms. For these, when generally comprehended, form a perfect Trinity; and all are engaged in the development of Man.

It is, however, proper to introduce a few more illustrations. The first of these is to be found in the Key, and is established in the subsequent scientific considerations: and that is, "The *interior* is the real reality, and the productive cause of all external effects." And here this proposition is demonstrated even beyond the possibility of a doubt or refutation. For now we discover that the interior and real cause of the mineral, vegetable, and animal creations, is found only in the rudimental forms or first particles in each specific degree of formation and development. Hence it is impossible to discover the causes of visible effects in as visible a manner as the effects themselves are manifested. But in order to understand the nature and cause of effects, the substance constituting the effect must be *analyzed*, and its actuating principle discovered. In no other way can there be any absolute knowledge obtained concerning the nature and cause of any of the effects made manifest to the natural senses in the outer world.

The bones in the human system correspond in their functions to the *mineral* structure. The secreting and absorbing vessels of the human body correspond to, and perform a similar office with, the *vegetable* structure. The viscera or internal organs of the human body perform an office analogous to that of the *animal* structure in the outer world, in relation to the great System of divine organizations. The head, or seat of government belonging to the human system, corresponds in the office it performs, to the *human* creation in its connexion with the whole Body of animated Nature. In other words, the mineral, vegetable, and animal degrees of creation, compose *one perfect human Form.* For they are situated harmoniously one with reference to another, and so connectedly that they perform all the functions, possess all the parts, display all the distributive justice and harmony, develop all the reciprocal motions, exemplify all the symmetry of, and finally absolutely represent and correspond to, the *human* organization. There is more sublimity in this view of the great actuating, governing, and productive forms in Nature, than can be possibly perceived in any superficial system that now prevails in the world.

I have proved that man possesses a form so beautful in symmetry and perfect in constitution merely because all subordinate forms of particles of matter have progressively ascended to, and finally developed, the form of the human being. And I have proved also that *series* or *associations* of forms likewise spontaneously unfold all the innumerable parts displayed in the constitution of Man ; and likewise that *degrees* of forms, or of perfection in substances, have in a corresponding manner created and developed *Man.* Then in view of all this, I repeat the question, " What is man materially?"—and I affirm the answer, that " he is the *perfection of matter*, the *flower of creation*, and the *lord over all animated things.*"

From the unvarying teachings of these truths, it is proved that Man is a united Whole—a congregation of perfected forms that exist in the material world. By this I mean, that all the lower and inferior forms of the particles of matter have, by progressive degrees of ascension, passed into the human organization. And, as has been stated, the most perfect forms in the atomic universe are the *celestial.* These are the last forms of rudimental matter—because another change would immerse them into another sphere of material existence and composition. For a proof of these things, I would request the reflecting mind to reconsider the interior and external forms that now exist upon the earth, the highest of which is Man.

It is seen from this, that if matter in a rudimental state proceeded any higher than the celestial forms, which constitute the *human* form, *new* forms would inevitably be developed, even *above* man, and would be existing as organized beings. But as there are no organized beings higher than man in the rudimental state, this amounts to no less than a demonstration that there are no higher forms than the *celestial*, in the rudimental world.* And as composed of them, man stands as a representative, correspondent, and governor of all material things.

This much is, then, established — That Man is the perfection of all forms, and degrees of these : and that they all have ascended in a uniform and progressive manner, to the *human* form, which is the grand result of all the subordinate creations.

Again : the mineral world is like a *stomach*, whose office it is to receive, digest, and transfer particles from the still more imperfect substances of the earth. The mineral kingdom, then, as soon as established, commenced its work of unceasing activity. It is a receptacle for the influx of particles still inferior, and is an agent to modify and transfer them, by a process of refluxation, into the form of the first particles capable of associating with the vegetable world. This, in its turn, performs the same office, receiving particles into its composition, modifying them by its own qualities and properties, and transferring them to the animal world. This in like manner, digests, recombines, and prepares substances to enter into the *human* world. Then *this* world comprehends all the lower departments of creation, and is a receptacle for the influx of the essences and properties of all subordinate organizations. It is likewise a *microcosm* of the whole united energies and creations of Nature. Meanwhile, it stands as an indestructible representative of the original intention of the Divine Mind, by which unchangeable laws were instituted to govern materials, with a view to the production of this end. Thus Law and Matter have accomplished the first end for which they were inseparably created.

Further : the various kingdoms and forms in this rudimental sphere, are all organs for the purpose of transferring, advancing, perfecting, and sublimating all particles in the lower forms of matter, so that they may all conjoin in harmony, and produce Man. Still further : the subordinate kingdoms are forms indispensable for the purpose of communicating a proper energy and quality to each particle of matter, in order to render it suitable to associate and assimilate with the human form. All particles must be modified, recomposed,

---

* I am directed to say, that the terms " angular," " circular," " spiral," &c., are employed *comparatively*, owing to the imperfection of language; and that for distinction, the same classifications might be made of the various forms *above* those belonging to the rudimental world.

and brought to a proper degree of perfection, or else the human form could not receive nourishment from, and be sustained by, the lower forms in Nature. This, again, is proof that man is a perfection of matter in all its forms and degrees of sublimation, and that he is the great Flower of the living Germ of this rudimental sphere, and is a centre to and from which flow spontaneously favors, from and to all the lower forms.

Herein are displayed the order, harmony, and perfection of the movements of Nature, even to such a degree of beauty and grandeur as the human mind is incapable of comprehending by exterior sight. But man can do this when the more interior qualities of his mind are opened. Thus it is again proved, that man is a *perfect organization* of all the atomic forms in Nature and the Universe.*

---

§ 175. It is now made distinctly clear, that Man *materially* is the lord and governor of animated Nature. And this being clearly established, the all-important and as yet undecided question next comes up, *What is man spiritually?*

I answer: *He is the perfection of Motion*, or of the *first great moving Principle of the Universe.* In other words, *He is the Wisdom of Love.*

I have hitherto considered Nature and her forms and developments, only in a *physical* point of view, and have not associated with them the moving or living Soul that actuates each particle in all its progressive movements toward perfection. But now we come directly to a consideration of those life-giving principles that are the souls of every form in being.

We begin, then, at the germ of all life, or the rudiments of Motion. Motion flows into every particle of primeval matter, creates an incessant activity, generates new qualities, tendencies, and spheres of association, and finally enters into, and becomes the living Soul of the whole Mineral World.

Motion primarily was in form, *angular;* that is, it displayed eccentric variations, passing from one extreme to another in an impulsive and unorganized manner. Its irregularities were very inconsistent with a uniform order, but still it displayed all the active properties that could then by any possible means be developed. Motion had not suitable forms to unfold more perfect living principles: neither

---

* That is, the *material* Universe.

had the forms of matter *motion* to give them new characters and new tendencies to refinement.

The *second* form of Motion was similar to the angular forms in matter which have been termed *mediatorial*. Motion likewise ascended to the multi-angular; and this constituted Motion the perfect Soul of the mineral kingdom.

Motion, like the particles of matter, has series of forms, and degrees of forms and series — all of which are displayed in the atomic constitution of substances. After Motion had thus ascended to one perfect degree, it began to unfold new powers, forces, tendencies, and actuating laws. That is, it unfolded the *circular* motion — which passed through all the degrees of this form until it became the *perfect circular* — during which time it developed diameters, axes, poles, rectilinear movements, and centripetal and centrifugal forces. Having all these attributes, Motion, in the three united degrees of this form, became a new principle, which was *Life*: and this is the Soul of the *Vegetable* World.

Life, therefore, is a development of Motion. This life, which is now exemplified in the vegetable creation, proceeded from the *circular* into the *spiral* form. And after it had ascended through all the modifications of this form, it developed a *new* tendency — a new principle — and one which was differently manifested. This was *Sensation*; and this is the Soul of the *Animal* World.

It is thus made clear that Motion was only organized as such after it had fully developed the properties of the Mineral Kingdom; and then it became the abiding soul and actuating principle of this kingdom. So likewise Motion passed through the successive stages of the *circular* form; and until it became perfected in this peculiar form, it could not have developed that essential principle which became the Soul of the *Vegetable* Creation. So likewise did Life, thus established, ascend through all of *its* subsequent forms, which were the *spiral*, and unfold that new principle of life and energy, which is Sensation, and which became the Soul and moving principle of the Animal World. And it is made also clear that Motion, Life, and Sensation, which form one, as included in the latter, progressed to the *spiritual*, and through this into the *perfect* spiritual, which is the *celestial* form. Sensation, becoming thus perfected, constitutes the Soul of Man, which is Intelligence.

Thus Motion contained *in germ* all the essential parts and forms, which, when ascended and perfected, constitute the Soul of the *Hu-*

man World, which is the Wisdom and Intelligence of this whole rudimental system of creations. Thus Motion is the Soul of the Mineral World, Life is the Soul of the Vegetable World, Sensation is the Soul of the Animal World, and Intelligence is the Soul of the Human World.

---

§ 176. It would be well for the reader to keep in memory the remarks concerning the external forms of matter, in order that he may recognise the relation that exists between the moving principles of each form, and understand how they determine and confirm one another's individual existence. It has been shown that Motion is only established as such, in an order which is indestructible, after it has passed through all the innumerable forms in the angular developments of matter. For when Motion and Matter ascend alike to a degree that confirms their organized existence, and can not ascend any higher without changing completely their mode of existence and order of form — it is then that Matter and Motion become perfectly and indestructibly organized, never to change their rudimental structure and power of external development. Let it be deeply impressed that Motion becomes a perfectly-organized and individualized principle, when Matter has assumed a form of existence from which it is never known to change: and this is fully exemplified in the Mineral World. Then it is that Motion becomes the undying Soul of this mineral structure. Though continually changing the elements of its being, it never changes in its essential constitution.

So when *Life* has become similarly established, it has likewise become an indestructible organization. And Life is developed only as the particles of matter correspondingly ascend to, and fully develop, the vegetable structure. Then it is that Life is established as Life, for ever. It undergoes no constitutional change, but preserves its identity throughout all time.

And *Sensation* is only known as such after Life has ascended through all the successive forms in the animal world to the highest of them; and when this is accomplished, Sensation becomes also an unvarying and unchangeable principle. It assumes an identity which it for ever preserves. And then Sensation becomes the immortal Soul of the animal structure.

Intelligence, in like manner, becomes such only after Sensation has ascended through all the forms in the *Human* World to the highest type and most perfect organization; and then it becomes an organized and immortal principle. It assumes an identity which can not be destroyed, and it continues thus for ever. Then it is that Intelligence becomes the unchangeable Soul of the *Human* structure.

After Motion has ascended to Intelligence, Intelligence comprehends all the subordinate degrees of the same living principle. It pervades alike all the interior moving principles that actuate all forms of matter in their various degrees of activity, force, refinement, and animation. Intelligence, therefore, is the perfection of the principle of Motion: and this answers the question, " What is man *spiritually ?*"

Motion is the Germ, Life the Body, Sensation the Branches, and Intelligence the Flower. Or, Motion is the parent and soul of Life; Life is the parent, measure, and creator, of Sensation; and Sensation is the parent and creator of Intelligence. Thus each one becomes the creator of another. In other words, from the interior possessions of Motion is unfolded Life; and from *its* interior properties is unfolded Sensation; and out of *its* inconceivable attributes flows spontaneously the perfection of all the rest, which is *Intelligence.*

Again: Motion corresponds to the Mineral; Life corresponds to the Vegetable; Sensation corresponds to the Animal; and Intelligence corresponds to the *Human World.* Once more: the rudiments of Motion, which are eccentric movements, are the *interior;* the transition or more uniform movements are the *mediatorial;* and the exterior or perfect movement is the Form or Body. This completes the organization; and this constitutes of the whole a principle of undying Motion. The rudimental circular is the interior; the transition is the mediatorial or ascending movement; and the exterior is the Body, which confirms of Motion a principle of undying Life. So are the interior, mediatorial, and exterior movements, discovered in the organized form of Sensation; and likewise are they discoverable in that individualized principle of man which is termed *Intelligence.*

To speak in more general terms, the spirit of man is constructed as follows: The interior or Soul is Motion; the transition or mediatorial is Life; the exterior is the perfect Body, which is Sensation; the elements of the *whole* of these combined, constitute the spiritual form of man, which is Intelligence. And as the subordinate developments of these principles are not known to change in the least possible particular, this is conclusive evidence that the highest of them all, which is the spiritual form of Man, can not possibly change its essential constitution, or lose its absolute identity.

§ 177. The all-important truth to be established in the mind is, that the interior essence is the soul and creator of all external forms, which forms determine and demonstrate the mode of such soul's existence. The form which every particle of matter assumes, is that created and determined by the peculiar essence which is latent in the particle itself. A knowledge of this truth conveys to the mind a perfect conception of the interior, creative Cause of all things, and its attributes as displayed and developed in its external form. *Motion* being the first all-pervading principle, as derived from the Great Positive Mind, becomes the creator of all rudimental and elementary substances. Therefore Motion is the principle which gives to the mineral compounds their peculiar form, texture, and mode of existence.

Motion thus develops material forms, which are merely the effect of the essence, and its use in relation to higher degrees of its own constitution. *Forms*, then, are the *mode* by which Motion in the lowest degrees of Nature comes in contact, and forms a relation with, the higher degrees of external development. In like manner *Life* is the essence, soul, and creator, of the whole vegetable formation; and this displays the use of Life, and manifests its relation to the lower and higher degrees of organic structure. So *Sensation* is the soul, essence, and creator, of the Animal World; and in, by, and through this, all the qualities and essential attributes of its *interior* are made manifest to the *outer* world. Moroever, it here establishes a relation to the lower and the higher structures of the same combinations of matter. So Motion, Life, and Sensation, as three, flow into, and become *one* established essence and creator, of and by which the *human organization* is developed and perfected. And the highest attribute of this form is Intelligence; and this was contained in, and is unfolded from, the germinal properties that exist in the peculiar essence from which the whole human structure is developed as a perfect Form. Thus all things are unfolded to the outer world by the incessant activity of the qualities, attributes, and unchangeable tendencies of the internal essence or soul, which is the interior or life of all external and material existences.

I perceive that metaphysicians and theologians have confined their attention to, and based their theories upon, the superficial manifestations of the human mind; and thereby they have unavoidably misconceived the true relation which exists between the interior or prompting cause, and the form through, by, and upon which, the effects of the human mind become visible. They have in almost every instance confounded the effect and cause, and have as often misconceived the *real* cause, upon a knowledge of which must rest the soundness of all metaphysical and psychological theories. No one among such investigators has been able to demonstrate the existence of the soul or essence of the human form as disconnected from the form itself. All philosophy that directs the attention to the external *only*, takes from the human mind those evidences that are necessary to direct the enlightened perception to a more interior understanding of the *real essence*, which unfolds itself to the outer world, in the shape of the human structure.

Motion, being the soul of the Mineral World, becomes, as has been related, an established an unchangeable principle as confined in a specific manner to that mode of external existence. By this I would be understood to mean that the *whole mineral creation* is the external mode and form by which Motion exists, and is manifested to the outer world. Motion being the creative principle, unfolds the essence in a material Body, which Body is composed of innumerable and dissimilar combinations of atoms, all of which enter into the whole constitution with inconceivable varieties of affinities or affections, one particle for another. Meanwhile it renders the whole structure suitable to develop, and communicate its interior possessions to, as many analogous forms in the higher plane of creation. It is well to keep in mind that I am speaking of the *whole* mineral world as *one Body*, whose soul is *Motion*, or that incessant and invisible principle whose attributes are only known by effects perceptible in the physical constitution of Nature. The first unfolded attribute of Motion is discoverable in the first degree of mineral forms.

Then, in like manner, *Life* is an essence that unfolds to the outer world *its* inner possessions; and this unfolding is the whole Vegetable Creation — the *whole* being as one perfect Form. Understand, then, that all knowledge which can be obtained of the interior qualities of Life, is only to be derived from its outward mode of existence. For as Life is the soul and creator of the whole vegetable Form, so this Form becomes the *mode* of the material existence of Life. The innumerable varieties of form that constitute the vegetable kingdom are only the successive degrees of modified development—each form at the same time being elaborated as an outward existence by the interior energies and promptings of the essence of Life. This whole vegetable world, as a perfect form, is, then, a material mode of the existence of Life; for by this mode of material development, Life can communicate its unfolded possessions to higher degrees of matter, which become the receptacles of, and at once determine, a new mode of existence, for a new element of life, which is *Sensation.*

Keeping in mind, then, the uniform developments from the inner to the outer world, a knowledge is received concerning the corresponding development of the animal world. For as by understanding one particle of matter, with all its properties, tendencies, and capabilities, a corresponding knowledge is obtained concerning the structure of the whole Universe—so by understanding the mode of the existence of Life, an understanding is at once established concerning the higher degrees and similar modes of existence, as determined by *their* Soul or essence. And as by knowing the measurement of *one inch*, a rule is obtained by which may be measured the length and breadth of all material existence—so it is equally plain that if the existence of Life and Sensation is understood, the same laws and principles which govern these will introduce the mind into higher degrees and planes of corresponding exterior development.

The mode by which *Sensation* exists in its relation to the outer world, consists only in the structure of the whole animal creation. The mode by which Motion, Life, and Sensation, exist as one united essence and Soul in its relation to the material world, consists only in the perfect structure of the *human organization.* Then it is not the *body,* the *form,* the *material,* that develops and organizes the *spiritual* principles: for if this were true, then indeed the human mind could not sustain its identity as disconnected from the instrument by which it was developed. This would likewise be unfailingly true of all material organizations and their living principles.

§ 178. The mineral, vegetable, and animal worlds, bodies, or forms of existence, each have as their essence, a *general,* living Soul, which unitedly appertains to the whole Body, and only exists in the outer world as the Body is unfolded. Hence when I say that Motion became an organized Soul, or an unchangeable principle, I have reference to its connexion with the whole Body or Form of the mineral world. So also with the vegetable and animal worlds. Not that each individual form in the vegetable and animal structure has a distinct, organized, and immortal soul, but that the whole of each kingdom, as a Body, has for its Soul the prompting essence, the one of *Life*, and the other of *Sensation*.

But the *human* world constitutes a degree of material existence exceedingly superior to the lower forms which each general living soul has developed. And it is in the human world that Motion, Life, and Sensation, become united and perfected as one living, organized essence — an *individualized Soul*, by and from which every human form is created. Each *individual* human structure also possesses an organized soul, composed of the subordinate attributes existing in the lower planes of material forms. Therefore this essence unfolds and displays its interior qualities in the human form, which is Man. Thus the exterior form of man is the perfect representative of the peculiar constitution and qualities of his spiritual essence or soul. In other words, it is an exact correspondent of all the tendencies, attributes, qualities, and possessions of his interior soul, essence, and creator.

The truth of this principle is manifested in every department of the material Universe, and especially in the various departments of material life. The *mineral* Body or world, displays the perfect complexion of its prompting essence. The *vegetable* displays, corresponds to, and represents, the character and quality of *its* Soul, which is *Life*. So with the whole animal Form; and so it is with Man. The *interior* or inner essence, in every instance, and without variation, is the soul, substance, creator, and cause, of all *effects*, which are the forms visible in the outer world. The external evidence of this truth consists in the appearances of all external forms; in the relations which they sustain to one another; in their invariable manifestations and developments, and in that general relation which they all sustain to the great structure of the material Universe.

The evidences of Motion are in the mineral compounds of the earth; for by and through them, Motion is represented and made manifest to the outer world. Yet Motion is not an organized Principle in every *individual* compound; for the *individuals* are imperfect in their structure, and mode of existence. But Motion is a living principle and actuating cause to the *whole plane* of mineral creation, because the whole united forms a *perfect Body* — though an imperfect one in its relation to higher combinations of matter. The evidence of *Life* is in the external structure of the vegetable world: yet Life is not a perfected and organized soul in *individual* forms composing the *great* Form, because these invariably display *imperfection*. But when considering the *whole* structure of the vegetable creation, we have displayed one *perfect* Form, which is the evidence that Life is the cause and actuating principle; and of this, the *whole* is a perfect external representation. The evidence of *Sensation* is confined to, and discoverable only in, the vast Form of animal existence. Yet an individualized existence of this principle is not established by the perfectness of any isolated organization; for all such display the most eccentric and irregular forms, inclinations, and habits. But when observing the *whole* animal world, as united, we behold a *perfect* Form — which is an evidence of the perfect structure of the principle of *Sensation:* for by it the external is developed.

But when we ascend to the *Human* World, the evidence which conveys to the mind a corresponding though indefinite perception concerning the interior and creative essence, is essentially changed: because every individual human form, is of itself a *perfect organization*, not in the least particular transcended by any other forms — but instead thereof, consists of a combination of all the lower and subordinate material forms and structures in Nature. And as each human form is thus a congregation of all subordinate ones, so each becomes a perfect organization of the material Universe, a receptacle of the lower degrees of matter, and a *microcosm* in which the Universe is seen in miniature. Thus the human form is a perfect representation of all material existences. And it is a reflection, fulfilment, and demonstration of the ultimate design of the Divine Mind, which was conceived and established in the depths of that inconceivable Vortex from which incessantly flows an infinity of perfected things.

Here, then, is the *sensuous* evidence that the human form is a form determined by a corresponding creative essence, which is man's organized and immortal soul. Not only in viewing the whole Human World as *one* Form, is Intelligence discovered as an interior quality and essence, but in every *individual* structure are all the required qualities to demonstrate an absolute individualization of the interior, creative essence. The whole Human Form or World, is of itself the *perfect* creation of Nature. This can not be said of the *subordinate* kingdoms. Moreover, a *single* human form is a *perfect* organization, representative, and reflection, of all the lower compounds in Nature. And thus man is the perfect *flower*, being progressively developed from all the lower parts of the same great Tree of ceaseless causation. Herein, then, lies the *external* evidence that man possesses an actuating and organized essence which no other form possesses. And this will continue to retain its individuality, because it is the *perfect* form and *perfect* soul of all the lower degrees of Motion, Life, and Sensation, *these* being only the *elements* of the germ which, when perfected, flow into and form one perfect and indestructible Whole, which is the soul or spiritual essence of man.

§ 179. As has been stated, if the human form were the instrument by and through which the mind is created, then it would be impossible for the mind to exist as disconnected from the form which produced it. The opinion that the mind is thus produced, has for a long time prevailed in the world, because *sensuous observation* has been made the basis of metaphysical speculation. But those who have believed thus have been misimpressed; and it is owing to such a conviction that too little belief has been entertained concerning the spiritual identity of man when the form is no more. Such impressions have resulted from deep investigation, but from that investigation which is confined to the superficial evidences of the laws of Nature and of Man. Another class has, by a superficial interpretation of theological writings, believed more strongly in the identity of the spirit of man, after the body is by it rejected, than their premises have warranted. All this is consequent of the uninstructed state of the mind, and of the direction of its faculties more in favor of those things which are imaginary than of those which are real.

But instead of the body creating and developing the spirit, the spirit is *first* organized, individualized, and potentialized. From it is unfolded the outer, or the organization. The latter thus becomes an instrument by and through which the interior principle or form, communicates with the material world. Therefore, the body is only a mode, a form, by and through which the spirit or essence displays itself to the outer world. Thus it is that the body is in constant subordination. While the spirit enfolds itself in a material form, it likewise exerts the most absolute power over every portion of its outward form, and is perpetually distributing motion, life, and sensation, throughout all the avenues and recesses of the same.

Motion is the lowest and first attribute of the human soul. This has flown through all the kingdoms uniformly, up to and into the human form; and there, as a subordinate element of the spirit, it performs all the corresponding motions that are displayed in the human body. *Life* is a higher element of the spirit, and in like manner communicates to its outer form all the incessant and reciprocal motions to which every minute particle of the body is subjected, and in which are manifested precision and perfection of action not discoverable in any other material constitution. *Sensation* also flows spontaneously out of Life, as Life does out of *Motion*. This is a still higher element of the spirit. It exists upon the external surfaces of the visceral and muscular systems, and pervades the serous surfaces of every organ throughout the whole body; and it serves as the mediator to connect the material form to material and foreign substances. Likewise it serves as a lever upon which the spirit acts to produce its various manifestations to the outer world. In other words, Sensation being the highest of the subordinate elements of the spirit, becomes the connecting link between the material and spiritual constitution. For were it not for a conscious, pervading medium that penetrates alike every particle of the human form, the spiritual organization could not by any possible means sustain a connexion with a material constitution, like the body of man.

Thus it is made manifest why Sensation is the highest Soul of the *subordinate* kingdoms: for by sensation the spirit is connected with the inanimate particles of matter, which constitute its body and its external form. Sensation is the universal medium between spirit and matter: and matter would display no motion, no life, no sensation, were it not for the indestructible and ascending elements of which the individualized spirit of man is an ultimate result.

Thus *Motion* animates the Mineral World, in which it creates, determines, and manifests, its own material mode of existence. So Life is the creator and animator of the Vegetable, and Sensation is the creator and animator of the Animal World: and all of these combined and perfected, develop Intelligence; and this, as the soul, the essence, the creator, of Man, animates the whole Human World.

Here, then, is the demonstration that essence determines, and unfolds itself into, its material form; and this displays the use and end for which the form is created. And inasmuch as essence is the parent and animator of material organizations, it therefore follows that each body is an external representation of its interior essence and creating cause. Man, then, in his material or outward form, is a perfect representation of the essence, quality, and individual structure of the spirit within. Thus the body is merely a coating, a garment, a sheathing of the spiritual principle, whereby the latter is enabled to communicate with all material things within its plane of existence, and meanwhile is the unchangeable type of the great End determined upon by the Divine Mind.

So the spirit, or soul, or essence, which are here considered as one, is not dependent upon the physical organization for its identity and existence. But the *body* is *subordinate* to the spirit, and is dependent for its motion, life, energies, animation, and even for its existence, upon the immortal spirit within, whose continuous identity is determined by eternal law, according to which matter in all cases stands only as its representative and external development.

---

§ 180. *Form*, then, is the only external mode by which *all* essences exist, and is the state which they assume in reference to all material things. The most delicate plant puts forth its tendrils, fibres, and finely-interwoven substances, only by virtue of the essence which develops itself from the inner to the outer world in that form. And the rose, with all its beauty, delicacy, and fragrance, is a perfect representative of the interior essence that developed it. All such forms, however complicated and varied in appearance they may be, manifest only the essential qualities of their own creative soul. The outer, in every instance, is a perfect type, image, and correspondent, of the inner, from which it proceeded. The most delicate *animal* form is also a representation of its interior, living essence and actuating principle: and the most gigantic animal form is only a higher degree of development and a higher representative of corresponding qualities which are *its* soul and creator.

Yet the whole animal, vegetable, and mineral worlds, are as *one* Form to the body of Man; for they collectively only possess what the human organization individually is composed of. Thus it is that the human form is the perfection of *all* forms. And as this is established, it is made equally clear that *its* soul or essence is a corresponding structure, of which the *exterior* is the manifest mode of being, and the exact representative.

And it is necessary that it should be well understood and borne in mind that *form* is not the creator of life, or of its attributes, but that the form, in *every* department of Nature, is the *exterior mode* of every living soul's existence. But in neither of the *lower* kingdoms have the forms an organized principle of interior life *individually*, but they have *collectively*, as constituting one perfect plane of form and creation. The *human* form *has* an organized principle *individually*, because every human organization is a congregation of all subordinate forms and substances in matter, and is likewise an indestructible representation of all. Thus the human body is a *Universe*, subsisting and existing upon all lower forms of organic life, and is of itself a *whole creation*, in and by which the labors of Nature, and the ultimate design of the Great Eternal Cause, are typified and absolutely fulfilled. And the human form is of all this a clear and living demonstration.

The *use* of every organized substance is displayed in its external relations to all inferior and superior constitutions of matter; and it depends upon them for its existence and its capacity to fulfil the use and accomplish the end for which it was designed. Forms of all series and classifications contain in themselves evidences of their use to the material world; and they also determine the specific degrees of uniform and ceaseless progression. A series of forms is merely a congregation of organic beings of one type, from the lowest form through the successive modifications, to the highest; all of which compose one full and decided degree of organization.

The uses of all things to the outer world are discoverable only in the inseparable relations which they sustain to all things, and in the offices which they are incessantly fulfilling. Thus there is a use in the mineral, vegetable, and animal creations; and their external modes of existence demonstrate their offices, and also prove that they are indispensable developments for the purpose of unfolding and perfecting the *human* form. This latter is to all of them a seal, crown, and throne of power; and it is a centre around which the whole creations of Nature revolve in their ascending progress.

Three distinct uses are discoverable in the forms in the outer world. Their *first* and subordinate use is to establish the mode in and by which all essence may exist, and preserve its identity of unceasing life and energy: also to constitute of the material world a grand, perfect, and harmonious System, the whole of which is an exterior demonstration of the interior harmony contained in all essential elements of Divine Love, Divine Life, and Divine Wisdom.

The *second* use consists in the fact that each form is a recipient for the influx of inferior particles of matter, for the recombination of these, and for the effluxation of the same into the first degree of higher forms. So each form in each kingdom of creation is a polygastric composition that subserves the purpose of receiving, digesting, and transferring particles, to become the constituents of higher organizations. Every form is of itself a perfect stomach, and every particle that flows into established forms in Nature, assumes the likeness and qualities of the form which thus receives it. Therefore every particle of matter proceeds by and through the medium of forms in Nature, to the highest degree of organic matter, by an unceasing gyration. And every change of form in matter is to the outer world *death* or disorganization: for death is nothing more than a change of any organized form or composition, as to its mode of existence. But speaking in relation to the whole System of organized creation, a death of form or principle can not possibly occur: for a change in the form of matter is neither death nor annihilation, but is only an ascension and recombination, and consequently a new organization, such as can only be constituted of the ascending forms in Nature.

Therefore the use of forms in their *second* degree of external being, is to convey the inferior particles of matter, constituting their own and lower compositions, to higher planes of organic development. Forms, in every case, are *mediums* of communication between the lower degrees of matter and the highest organization in Nature, which is *Man*. And forming, as they do, this medium, they constitute of the whole system of the outer world an harmonious and inseparable creation, all parts of which are mutually dependent upon each other.

The *third* use of forms is discoverable in their perpetual tendency to perfect and sublimate all inflowing particles of matter. All forms, then, are the established organs by which gross and inferior particles are purified and refined, in order that they may become suitable to enter into, and create and sustain, the highest form of matter, which is Man. Thus the mineral assists to perfect particles by which the vegetable is created, sustained, developed, and perfected. So also the latter, in its turn, purifies and recombines atoms of matter, which thus become unsuited to remain in the vegetable world, and ascend immediately to the *animal* creation, which is thus produced, sustained, and perfected. So with the whole animal plane of creation: this in like manner performs *its* specific office, rendering particles of matter suitable to enter into, and to compose, the *human organization*. Then the latter Form comprehends and subsists upon them all, receiving constantly into its composition the particles of purified and refined matter that flow through all the subordinate forms up to itself.

Another department of this use in animated forms is, that they establish a perfect principle of affinity, of affection, of association, of reciprocation, of harmony, and unity of action, and display an inseparable relation to each other, all of which united binds together the whole system of Nature as one grand and stupendous *Whole.*

---

§ 181. Thus it is made manifest that all material things are forms, each of which is merely an external mode by which its interior essence establishes a communication between itself and the outer world, the form being only a medium of communication between the inner and the outer. Nature, then, is composed of these innumerable combinations of matter, and is a manifest type of the whole Universe. The Great Positive Mind is the Interior and Divine Essence — is the creative Cause of all external effects. The Great Divine Mind is a SOUL, existing as a perfect organization of essential properties, essences, and attributes; and the *Mode* by which this Essence or Soul exists, is the Form or outward development of the whole UNIVERCŒLUM. The Divine Essence being the *Soul*, the Univercœlum is the *Body*. Moreover, the latter is a perfect representative, or, in other words, is a bold and clear expression of the interior possessions of the Divine Mind. The Universe is the Mode by which the Divine Essence exists: and the latter could not exist as an Organization without being made perfect by a corresponding exterior Form, such as is displayed in the mighty, grand, and inexpressibly-harmonious Universe.

Thus it is that *form* is the express image of its interior or first principle of life and being. And the use of everything is determined by the specificness of its own interior possessions, and especially by its relation in form, in series, and in degrees of perfection, to all other living essences in Nature and the Universe.

It is on the same principle that the *human* form is an express likeness of the quality of its interior soul. And it has been absolutely demonstrated that man *materially* is a perfection of all matter in Nature, and that man *spiritually* is a perfection of all Motion. Therefore man as a whole, constitutes a complete system of organized *spirit* and *matter;* and thus it is that the spiritual principle of man is individualized, and is expressed by the human form, to the outer world. And thus likewise is the *body* unfolded by the specific and potential essence of its interior soul. Man is above all forms in being, and all congregations of forms; for he is the point, centre, and goal, to which all other forms flow and are perfected, refined, and made useful to the whole constitution of Nature and the Universe.

Meanwhile man in reality is *invisible* to the material senses; but all that sensuous observers know of man is derived only from his *exterior representative* and express likeness, which is the outward form that his inward being assumes.

From these considerations it is made clear that every human form possesses an organized interior principle by which the exterior is determined and developed. And as the body performs its use considered as a medium by which the inner man communicates with the *outer* world, so does the inner principle perform a use in establishing a connexion with the *interior* world. So the human body individualizes the spirit in its relation to the outer world, while the spirit now connected with the body determines the perpetuity and identical existence of the spirit in its connexion with the inner world, the *spiritual* form being also an expression of *its* interior soul. Thus it is that the soul is a prior organization; and when unfolding itself to the outer world, it only assumes a coating, a body, a form, suited to its existence in this rudimental sphere of material and spiritual creation.

As everything is constantly assuming *form*, which is an express likeness of its interior cause, so the soul is constantly evolving *thoughts*, which are suggested by influences proceeding from the outer, or from the promptings of its own internal principles: and the thought is the *form* of these suggestions. The forms of thoughts are *words*—these always being the express likeness of the thought evolved. Not that any form in being, especially the *human* form, is an exact expression in *aspect* or *feature*, of the form and constitution of its soul—but the general form is always the express image of the soul that produced it. The *aspect* or *features* of a form are not the form itself; but these are the collateral appendages, which of themselves are no decided expression, only as they are animated and configurated by the active suggestions of the spirit within. But what is well to understand is, that the exterior form of man is the express representation of its productive essence, the soul. Hence form is not the *shape* or *aspect* of any substance whose general form is uniformly manifested. For while form is the mode by which essence exists, and is the *type* of the essence, the *aspect*, *shape*, and *features* of the form, are merely the external *particulars* of the established structure, and are in no case decidedly expressive of the image of the interior essence.

§ 182. We have now ascended in these psychological researches to a consideration of the specific attributes of the soul of man, their relations to each other, and their modes of manifestation from the inner to the outer world. For the question is now fully and irrefutably answered, What is man spiritually? Likewise it is proved, that the soul of man is a decided and established organization, preserving its identity by virtue of the peculiar character of its own constitution, and by the absence of all affinities which could absorb it in anything else. It has been made clear that every soul is differently constructed, this being manifest from the varieties and peculiarities of the human species. Every soul is thus individually organized, and can not by any possible means become blended or inter-associated with others in such a way as that the soul's individual existence would be annihilated or immersed in the great ocean of moving and intangible substances. The law of *association* determines the perpetuity of every soul's identity, in both the material and spiritual world: for being in constitution dissimilar to each other and to all things, they can not become annihilated or disorganized.

The law of eternal progression also governs the constant development of all forms, both of a material and spiritual nature. And from the tendencies of this law flow all affinities, affections, relations, forms, and degrees of refinement. So each law develops forces and tendencies corresponding to the peculiarities of the forms that need to be actuated and governed unchangeably. Then it is proved that the soul of man (which is himself), with its form (which is its body), is an organized essence, such as can not be annihilated or lost as to its identity. For the dissimilarity of men not only establishes their identity in respect to the *outer*, but also in respect to the *inner*. And being thus differently combined, they can not associate with each other in such a manner as to become individually lost in a general commingling mass: but each, according to the law of eternal association, must necessarily preserve his own identity. And men will approach each other's spheres only as they are mutually congenial on the outer, in all worlds of spiritual existence, as well as in the physical world.

Everything is developed in Order and Form, and all things united form one mighty external expression of Infinite Wisdom, one of the essential attributes of the Divine Mind. Everything is actuated primarily by Light and Life; which are also an outward expression of Divine Thought, or of that potential essence which is

Love. Thus Light and Life are Love, and Order and Form are Wisdom.

These considerations, I repeat, advance the subject to another train of thought, which is to be confined exclusively to the human soul itself. And it will be found that the previous revealments contain within themselves latent arguments whose strength and tendency are not as yet perceived.

It has been said that *sensation* is the highest subordinate element of the soul, and hence becomes the medium of communication between the soul and the form, and through the form, with the material world. This truth is fully exemplified in the animal creation; for the highest element of their constitution is this principle or medium of sensation. Thus all animals are governed according to the promptings of Nature; that is, they have suggestions from the outer only, which they invariably obey. All their movements are strictly *mechanical*, being in every instance created by outward influences which affect the *sensation*. This being affected, creates *inclination;* and this operates upon the *will* to accomplish its gratification. The animal, however, possesses a decided *will*, which serves as a moderator, and acts very much upon, and modifies the, external suggestions that are presented for gratification: and this will, combined with their mechanical ingenuity displayed in escaping danger and in procuring gratification, has been termed *instinct*, and sometimes absolute wisdom. The animal, however, has no mental possessions sufficient of themselves to be a governor; for all the causes of movement, ingenuity, experience, instinct, and wisdom, perceptible in animals, are situated on, and proceed from, the *outer*. They are influences that operate upon the sensation, and thus create a desire for gratification: and this desire may be called the ruling love of animals. For whatever they desire or choose to indulge in, is such only as gratifies the element of *sensation*, which is the actuating soul and prompter of all their external movements.

The *vegetable* possesses *motion* and *life*. Thus its particles are constantly changing, and the whole structure is constantly passing through various stages of development. But the animal possesses motion, life, and sensation, combined. Motion governs the constant action of the constituent particles of its body: life is displayed in the energy and animation of the form; and sensation is the soul or moving principle by which it is made to act, and from which are evolved all inclinations and desires. Motion can exist where life and sensation do not; but life can not exist where motion is not, nor can sensation exist where life and motion are absent. This makes it clear that one is unfolded from the other; and sensation, being the highest of them all, and connected with the human soul, forms the actuating principle of the animal, and establishes a perfect adaptation between its organization, with its ruling loves and passions, and all things in which it habitually indulges.

As sensation is the highest property of the animal's spiritual essence, it becomes the lowest of the spiritual essence of man. Thus, as has been related, it establishes a communication between the inner principle of man and external Nature. Hence, I say, sensation is the lowest element of the human soul, and is the animating principle which flows spontaneously from the animal into the human form.

---

§ 183. It now becomes necessary to classify the parts of the soul, in order to conceive of the relation which they sustain to each other, and of the three great essential parts, which correspond to *end, cause,* and *effect.* The end or ultimate design in prospect, is always the *cause,* which cause institutes an *effect;* and both of these are engaged in accomplishing the *end.*

I discover, then, that the soul is composed of three distinct parts; and these are LOVE, WILL, and WISDOM.

LOVE is the first or rudimental element of the human soul. It is that liquid, mingling, delicate, inexpressible element which is felt in the depths of every human spirit, because it is its germinal essence.

WILL is a living force which serves as the connecting medium between Love and Wisdom, being subject to the influence and suggestions of each. It is the innate consciousness of energy, or force; and it has been supposed to be an absolutely-independent element of the mind, beyond the possibility of being influenced by external captivations.

WISDOM is the perfection of Love. It is the sealing element of the human soul; it is the establishment of the soul's perfect constitution. Wisdom flows from love, is directed by experience, modified by will, and rendered perfect by knowledge. Wisdom is the thinking principle, the faculty that cogitates, investigates, searches, and explores, the fields of terrestrial and celestial existence. It is the faculty that analyzes, calculates, and imperatively commands obedience from all the subordinate possessions of Will and Love.

These three parts of the human soul, then, being designated, I will descend into some considerations relative to their mode of manifestation through the body in the outer world, in order that the great question respecting the powers and actuating principles of the human soul may become settled, and equally comprehended by all.

Love being the first element, or the essence of the soul, is accordingly imperfect, unguided, and, like the lower forms in Nature, is developed *angularly*. It is the parent of eccentricity, impulse, fantasy, imagination, and inflated conceptions of all things invisible, intangible, and unreal. Also Love is the element of tenderness, kindness, affection, attachment, and of all kinds of pure and unsophisticated sentiments, such as gush spontaneously from the depths of the soul, and are expressed in music, in language, in paintings, in foliage, in embroidery, and in all the indescribable beauties that line the vaulted chambers of the expanded heavens. Love is the element that conceives of all loveliness, of gentleness, of sweetness, of fragrance, and of beauty, in all their various modes of exterior manifestation.

Love gives rise to an affection for *other forms*, or *for mankind generally*. To gratify this affection, men form societies, associations, communities, brotherhoods, sects, and congregations, as these are exemplified in the outer world.

Love also manifests itself in *conjugal attachment;* which is outwardly expressed in individual association and matrimony. And this same love is modified into a love for mankind generally: and this begets families, sects, and associations.

Love has also an affection for *music.* This is outwardly expressed even in the confusion of sounds that are invented by the uncultivated inhabitants of the earth, and which they endeavor to express by employing instruments of the most imperfect and discordant character. The sounds created are always in accordance with the wisdom of this love; and thus, on the other hand, this insuppressible affection for musical harmony has also led to the invention of delicate and finely-constructed instruments, by which it expresses itself outwardly in the most delicate and harmonious sounds, which have a corresponding influence upon the thoughts and conceptions of the soul.

Love involves an affection for the *beautiful*. This is expressed in the outer world by the construction of forms of the most perfect symmetry, and by ideal embodiments of what is angelic and celestial: also by beautiful expressions, or superior combinations of words expressive of the eloquence of the soul, and likewise of the inward conceptions of the beautiful. Statuary and symmetrical forms of every variety are constructed; mansions, edifices, and temples, are erected according to the most perfect conceptions of the grand, the beautiful, and the magnificent. Gardens of shrubbery and flowers are planned according to a conception of perfect order and beauty. —And all of these are but expressions of love as it assumes this specific direction.

Love has also an affection for the *invisible* and the *sublime*—the outward expressions of which are the many ideal conceptions that clothe themselves in words, and which also infuse into all the other affections an element of chastity, refinement, and amiability. This affection of the love imparts grace, ease, and elegance, to every external expression of the other affections of love.

Love has an affection for *self*—which is expressed by the ingenious, secretive, and unrighteous plans that are invented for purposes of self-emolument; by the many disturbances that occur in society; by the destruction of life; by the employment of deceptive expressions; and by all those unreal and unsanctified forms and corrupt inventions, which, through the misdirection of this affection, prevail throughout the whole human brotherhood.

Love involves the affection of *unbounded benevolence*. This is openly expressed by the formation of societies and institutions, and by all those great and mighty movements that are so much admired by all expanded minds, for their tendency to an amelioration of the condition of mankind, and to the ultimate establishment of distributive justice and universal righteousness.

Love has an affection for the *just*. This is openly expressed by all the conscientious relations that exist between man and man, and by those exchanges which are just and reciprocal. This love is the love of the moral, of the holy, and of the righteous. It is the love which conceives of all Divine perfection, and which creates all yearnings for purity, refinement, and distributive goodness. It is that which breathes an affection for all that is of the Divine Mind, and for all those exalted and moral sentiments which constitute the highest attributes of man.

Another affection of love gives rise to *hope*. This clothes itself in an aerial garment of contemplation, anticipation, and expectation, of all that which is desired by the other affections of love.

Love also embraces an affection for the food which enters into man's material form. This love expresses itself outwardly in procuring and delicately combining food, and committing it to the stomach. It leads to the cultivation of those portions of the vegetable and animal kingdoms which contribute most to its gratification. It leads also to a great variety of preparations of food, and it is constantly expressing itself by imparting delicious flavors to the vegetable and animal substances that are agreeable to its desires and suitable to the requirements of the human body.

Thus it is seen that Love, as the germ of the human soul, has various modes of manifestation; and these consist in the external and ingenious inventions and structures that are existing in the world. A more definite understanding will hereafter be obtained concerning Love, when I proceed to consider the modifying tendency of Wisdom, which is the proper controlling influence of all the affections embraced in the love-principle.

---

§ 184. From the faculty of Love, as the basis of the soul, flows the faculty of WILL. This then becomes the mediatorial faculty of the human mind, and is the means employed by Love to accomplish whatever end it desires. Herein are made plain the three moving principles engaged in accomplishing any end conceived of and desired. Love perceives and conceives that which is congenial to its affections. The *end* to be attained is the *cause* of Love's prompting the Will to act upon the body in order to accomplish it. In other words, *Will* is employed as a *means* by Love to attain the end for which it has an affection.

Will in all cases is subject to the promptings of the element of Love, and its acts in all cases originate in the suggestions thence derived. Will is the faculty employed to move the body in the performance of any external work for the accomplishment of which the Love has conceived an affection. Love conceives of the end or object which would be suited to its affection, and gratifying to its desires; and the perception of this is the primary cause of the Love's prompting the Will to act for its accomplishment. The Will, however, is a living force, a perfect faculty, and a decided portion of the soul. By its inherent possessions and influence, the body is made to move; and all the changing attitudes of the latter are the exterior forms and projections of the faculty of Will. In other words, Will evolves thoughts, as they are suggested by the workings of Love and

Love's affections; and these thoughts of the Will are expressed in manifest forms to the outer world—that is, in the assumed appearances and movements of the body, and in all external actions that are put forth by it. All these are the exterior forms of the thoughts evolved by Will. The latter being a means employed by Love to institute, construct, or create, any form for which the Love has conceived an affection, it is therefore a mediator and means by which all motion, all construction, and all exterior manifestations, are produced.

Will has no independent action, and can not institute a movement of itself: but it moves only as it is excited and prompted by the Love. *Love*, therefore, is the *primary cause* of external action; and *Will* is the *effect* produced: and the effects of this, again, are the exterior things which it accomplishes. In other words, Will is employed by Love to develop externally the expression of its own thoughts.

If a man has in view the construction of a beautiful edifice, the exterior and interior portions of which are perfectly defined in the mind, it is because he has first conceived of the *uses* which the edifice with its various portions may fulfil. And as it is the *use* that plans and arranges the whole construction, it may be said that the plan of the edifice, as to proposed form and appearance, precisely corresponds to, and represents, the *use*, the conception of which was the cause of the plan's being instituted.

Again, it may be said that the use to which the edifice is adapted corresponds precisely to the form of his affections, or the prompting desires of his love. Having the use and plan properly impressed upon the mind, his love for the attainment of the end prompts the Will to action, which implicitly obeys, and external movements are at once instituted for the construction and completion of the edifice. Then the edifice in its parts also corresponds to the isolated movements of the Will among the materials which are adapted to its structure, and which serve to form the perfect Whole.

As the *use* perceived, suggested the form and structure of the building, so the building corresponds to the *use* to which it is adapted; and the building and its use connectedly represent the affection or conception of the Love. Thus the Love has openly expressed its thought; and this expression consists in the edifice which has been erected. It is thus seen that the *cause* of the building is involved in the *use* to which it is adapted. This operates upon the

Love; and this, again, prompts the Will: and thus the end is accomplished.

§ 185. The *third* faculty of the soul is evolved from Will and Love, and is the highest and most perfect one; and this joins and pervades the others, so that the three form a perfect Whole. This faculty is WISDOM.

The office of Wisdom is to listen silently to the suggestions of Love and Will, and to modify these according to reason, form, order, and perfect harmony. Love without Will would be eccentric, impulsive, disorderly, and confused, even to such an extent that the whole system of Nature would be nothing more than a vast congregation of disorganized forms. Everything would be misplaced, misformed, misconstructed, and rendered useless to the requirements of man. But Love being modified by Will, becomes at once limited as to its circle of movement, and confined in its conceptions to a definite sphere. Yet Love and Will would both be eccentric and ungoverned in their movements among material things, were it not for the presence of *Wisdom*, which presides over and directs them both. Wisdom is contained in the germ of the soul, which is Love — is developed in the body, which is Will — and perfected in the flower, which is *itself*. Wisdom, then, pervades, directs, modifies, and governs them all, because it is the crowning faculty of the soul, and the most perfect of all its attributes.

Will, then, is the perfection of Love, and hence receives, contains, and continually manifests, all the qualities, thoughts, affections, and desires of Love. And Wisdom is the perfect form of them both, because Wisdom is an ultimate progression of them; and it is a representation of all their latent qualities and unexpressed affections. Wisdom is that faculty of the soul which gives order and form to all things in the outer world; and Love gives to order and form light, life, taste, grace, and elegance. And Will is the executive faculty between Wisdom and Love, and obeys perpetually the suggestions of Love as these are sanctioned by Wisdom.

The eccentricity of Love and Will is very much modified by the pervading and controlling influence of Wisdom, which becomes their director, governor, and lord. Were it not for Wisdom, order, form, and adaptation, would not be known, either in the natural or artificial world. So, then, the outward form of Wisdom is the perfect order and uniformity displayed in the outer world. The perfect form of Love is the use for which all external things are designed and adapted. Love is also expressed in the life, grace, and elegance, which render every exterior form lovely and admirable.

Thus it is seen that Wisdom is the great head and flower of the human soul, and that it is perpetually engaged in the evolution of thoughts which clothe themselves in material things in the outer world. The more Wisdom is permitted to act, the more its sphere of action is extended, and the more will the natural and artificial world display beauty, order, and harmony. But the more it is restricted in its action, and the less its teachings are heeded, the more will Nature and the artificial creations of man become a disorganized and useless system, instead of displaying peace, order, beauty, and universal reciprocation. Love is only the *life* of things; Will is the means employed to obtain a desired end; but Wisdom is the order, beauty, harmony, and perfection of them all.

The Great Divine Mind, in essence, is Love: this is the light and life of the Universe. The Universe itself is the *Body* of Love, and its perfect Form. But Wisdom is the highest attribute, and the great ultimate of eternal Design. And Wisdom gives to Light and Life a Body — and to this Body, Order and Form. The whole is rendered thereby an harmonious System, each outward form being a perfect representative of its creative cause.

The following, then, are the three Parts of the great and universal System: The Divine Mind, or Love, which is the Soul; the Universe, which is the Form, Means, Mediator, and Body; and *Spirit*, which is the Order, the Form, the Wisdom, and the GRAND DESIGN of the whole System of the Univercœlum. The *End* primarily designed to be accomplished was *the individualization of the human spirit;* and for the attainment of this, Cause and Effect were brought into requisition. The Divine Mind is the Cause, the Universe is the Effect, and Spirit is the ultimate Design. The truth of this is demonstrated in every department of this terrestrial sphere, and is particularly exemplified in the nature and developments of the human soul, which are in exact correspondence with the great System of the Universe. Everything is perpetually displaying, in its inward and outward movements, End, Cause, and Effect; and Light and Life are Love, and Order and Form are Wisdom.*

---

* It may be well here to remark, once for all, upon these expressions, that "Light and Life" mean simply the *conception* of the end desired, and the *activity* which ensues as tending toward its accomplishment. The two combined constitute the prin-

It is highly necessary, then, that the human mind should comprehend the great truth that nothing exists in the outer world except as it is produced and developed by an interior essence, and that of this essence the *exterior* is the perfect representative. Among all the various arts and sciences that now exist in the world, may be found demonstrations of this truth, and also of its vast importance. Forms do not exist with the mechanic or with the artist, merely as productions of the outer combinations of matter; but every form invented by man is a precise representative of the interior thought which is the *cause* of its creation. Every form is such as corresponds to the inward suggestion of Love, and is created by the living effort of Will, and modified and rendered perfect by the admonitions and directions of Wisdom.

§ 186. Metaphysicians have devoted much time to discussing questions concerning the innate consciousness of the soul, "free will," "necessity," and the nature and relations of the faculties. The faculties thought to compose the various portions of the soul, have been minutely classified under the general divisions of propensities, sentiments, and intellectual faculties. The first of these are represented as relating to self and to things in the outer world; the second as giving rise to moral conceptions and the sense of justice; and the third as comprising the powers of reason, analysis, and investigation. Many such classifiers have given to the soul the faculty of absolute *free will*, or a power to act or not to act in any specified manner, uninfluenced by any interior or external thing. They have also given to the soul innate faculties perpetually disposed to wickedness and abomination, delighting to indulge in every species of evil and licentiousness, thirsting to injure mankind, to destroy life, and seeking, by a sacrifice of all moral principles, one's own emolument. Meanwhile, such metaphysicians have believed the human mind to be possessed of absolute independence as to its powers of action, and have disconnected it from the influence of every material thing.

I now discover *why* all these opinions have arisen, and why they have become embodied in all the philosophical and metaphysical

ciple of Love, which is nothing more than an operative *attraction* toward an end or object first definitely conceived in the mind. "Order and Form" mean the perfect organization and arrangement: and as *Wisdom* alone can prescribe a consistent organization and arrangement, and such as would be permanently gratifying to the Love, so the Order and Form displayed when the organization and arrangement are completed, are considered as a perfect *embodiment* or *expression* of Wisdom.

systems which most prevail. It is because the mind can not *analyze and comprehend itself.* I moreover discover that the soul has no such inherent propensities and desires for evil and unrighteousness — that it has no desire to injure, or to dissemble, or to be deceptive. Moreover, I discover that it has no absolute independence, and that all those metaphysical theories are decidedly untrue — merely because they have sprung from the superficial conceptions of the mind, and not from a knowledge of its interior and divine essence. It is given me to know that the human soul is, in a low degree, an express image and likeness of the Great Positive Mind, and that it is an offspring of the incessant and successive developments of those mighty attributes which, connectedly, are the cause of ALL THINGS.

The cause of these metaphysical misconceptions, I repeat, lies in the fact that no substance, or compound, or mind, possesses within itself the power of self-investigation. The *germ* can not understand its own qualities, but the perfect *development* can ; because it is a higher and unfolded state of the qualities of the germ, and is thereby enabled to comprehend all below its exalted state of being. So the human mind can comprehend all that is *below* it, but can not either comprehend *itself* or any *higher* degrees or spheres of animation. And thus, were it not that I am permitted to occupy a higher sphere of thought and observation, the soul would also appear to *me* as an indefinite and ambiguous consciousness which is neither to be comprehended as embracing any form, order, or substance, tangible to the senses.

Man, when investigating the faculties, propensities, and tendencies, of the soul, inquires *outwardly* — and thus the evidence on which legitimate conclusions might be based necessarily escapes his attention. This evidence would otherwise gush from the promptings of his own *interior self*, and proclaim truthful conclusions and their demonstration. Herein, then, is found the reason why man has not as yet understood his own nature and composition. The reason why all these evil propensities have been attributed to man as inherent in the nature of his soul, is, that men have confined themselves to the outer plane of observation, and have there beheld the fantastic misdirections of the human love — of love unguided and unmodified by the admonitions of *Wisdom.* They judge merely from the *externals* or *clothings* of things, and from these accuse the affections of the soul of being degenerated, degraded, and absolutely evil. By beholding the inconsistent movements of men, the mind conceives at once of the misdirection of Love and Will, and of their misapplication as respects the individual and general benefit of the race. And in order to create harmony in all things, and beauty and utility in all external forms, it is necessary to inform and develop the human *Wisdom;* and this will immediately dissipate all confusion and disorder in the outer world, and make all things useful, harmonious, and reciprocal.

---

§ 187. Remember that the outer forms will correspond to the condition of the interior man. Remember, too, that *Wisdom* is the grand faculty of the human soul, and that it must occupy a position commanding and pre-eminent. It should exert an influence over all the subordinate faculties and affections of the soul, and they should (and *will* ultimately) bow in obedience to its mandates.

Wisdom is the lord of creation: for by it the fields of the vegetable kingdom are rendered fertile and useful, and the forms in the animal world are made to fulfil the office for which they were designed, and to benefit and administer to the happiness of the human race. By it Love is directed, and all its affections are modified and rendered useful. By it the various objects that are created by Love, are all adapted to uses and made beneficial to mankind.

Love enjoys intercourse with the outer world by and through the medium of sensation. Were it not for this latter, commerce would not exist; for it is by this only that the human soul can sympathize with things on the outer, and conceive of uses adapted to its nature and constitution; and it is by this that the soul is enabled to enjoy the incessant inflowings of the elements of all material things. It is by this medium that Love breathes forth an affection for external things; and it is by this that the inner and the outer are enabled to associate with each other. Therefore, by Wisdom should Love be directed; and notwithstanding its conceptions and affections are ambiguous, eccentric, and imaginative, a well-developed Wisdom never permits an action of the Will before those affections are essentially modified, according to principles of utility.

Will is likewise under the the potential direction of Wisdom. Whenever the faculty of Will is instigated by Love to perform an external act, Wisdom perceives the suggestion, conceives of its use, and directs the Will-force to its accomplishment. Will is sometimes actuated by Love alone; and this is when the faculty of Wisdom is undeveloped — and then the exterior manifestations of Will are impulsive, unreasonable, and often injurious to the well-being of man. When Will is thus acted on, the consequences are injurious to the general harmony and required unity of all things. A knowledge of this fact shows the importance of a universal elevation of the human mind, and of its being properly instructed concerning its own interior nature, and also concerning its relation to the outer world. It shows that the form or body should be superiorly situated in order to cause a proper development of the intellect; and this can only be accomplished by following the dictates of a well-constituted and well-developed Wisdom.

The cause of disunity in the actions, feelings, and affections, of men, is to be found in the uneducated condition and misdirection of the faculties of the human soul, and not in their innate depravity, or tendency to sin. The cause of every species of licentiousness and immorality, and of the unrestrained action of what are now called the baser passions of the soul, is found only in the ignorance, folly, and imbecility, of minds unguided by the faculty of Wisdom. Then, again, it is clear that these things would not exist were the human race spiritually elevated, and their faculties so expanded as that nothing would exist but the perfect Order and Form of Wisdom. This would (and *will*) be universal harmony, distributive justice, equal love to the neighbor, and brotherly kindness and charity. Let every one, then, desist from proclaiming metaphysical hypotheses derogatory to the innate divineness of the human soul, and rise to the plane of interior and natural thought — and then let all their external movements correspond, not to the hereditary affections and belief of the Love, but to the unrestricted sanctions of a well-instructed and well-developed Wisdom.

Here, then, is the reason why men have so long adhered to the imaginative beliefs of their *Love*, and not listened to the spontaneous teachings of their *judgment*. Hereditary opinions of every kind are merely the early impressions made upon the Love. But men who discard all hereditary affection for thought are those in whom is developed the highest faculty of the soul, which is Wisdom. From this they receive and impart instruction; by it all their external movements are governed; and all their constructions and inventions, which are prompted by the Love, are by it made perfect in Order and Form.

§ 188. Men in general believe that they have power to act independently of all influences, either from interior promptings or the suggestions of the outer world. Of the truth of this they suppose they have an internal consciousness—feeling, as they do, a sense of a self-existent power to move according to a desire of the *Will*, which appears to be born of and governed by itself. The reason of this conviction is plain : No man has the power within himself to perceive the relation and connexion existing between each portion of the soul ; and therefore all the conceptions which man can have of himself internal are only shadowy, intangible, and unsatisfactory. He feels a conviction that he exists and moves independently of every other tangible form, and uninfluenced by any apparent cause. He feels that he has the power to do or *not* to do anything which presents itself to the mind. He feels that he possesses strength and independence to receive or reject, to act or not to act; and he has been taught to believe that he is a "*free agent*," unacted on, uninfluenced, ungoverned, and unrestrained, in any of his actions.

The cause of this inward conviction lies in the individual workings of the three parts of the soul, which are Love, Will, and Wisdom. It has been shown that Love prompts action, both from its own interior workings and also by its desires excited by material things holding a close relation to the sensation of the body. Love is thus the primary cause of all action, of all will, and of all thought, in the human soul. The transition of thought from Love to Will is imperceptible ; and at the moment thought arouses the Will to volition, a man feels conscious that he has power to withstand the impulse, and remain unmoved. This conviction is truthful ; but this does not establish the independence of the will-force of the soul : for Will in all cases is a passive faculty, never acting unless prompted by foreign influences or interior causes.

Furthermore, a man can not be conscious of the transition of thought from the faculty of Will to Wisdom ; and the moment this latter faculty is brought into requisition, he apparently experiences an additional strength, and the conviction of an independent power of action. The reason of this is equally plain : the will-force seldom acts without first receiving approbation from the faculty of Wisdom ; and the hesitation which occurs in the mind between the periods of the suggestion of Love and the sanction of the Wisdom, impresses the conviction upon the mind that there is a choice or independence of action residing within the Will itself. Man feels an impulse to move, but hesitates; and this is an indication of the workings and deliberations of the Wisdom. And when *it* sanctions, the mind feels consciously impelled onward; and the person manifests great force and firmness, and presses forward with an innate conviction of prudence, justice, and truth, and thus feels an interior approbation. This always occurs with minds well constituted and superiorly developed.

But the Wisdom itself is not a faculty self-instructed and uninfluenced by interior or external things; for the judgment is developed by interior and outward experience, from which it learns policy, prudence, order, harmony, and propriety, as to its movements in reference to its associate faculties, and its interior direction in respect to outward action.

When the Will is impressed with an irresistible impulse from the Love, it sometimes acts without consulting or listening to the admonitions of the Wisdom. When this is the case, a man feels an innate consciousness of violation, and an unnerving sense of impropriety and injustice. He experiences an inward conviction of guilt, and of ingratitude to the silent but constant promptings of the Wisdom. And the internal condemnation which he feels results from the disapprobations of the judgment; and the workings of a violated conscience are expressed in the configurations of the countenance.

Thus it is seen that the Will is a passive faculty, subject to the command and action of the Love and Wisdom. There exists a perpetual strife between the suggestions of the Love and the approbations of the judgment. This would not exist if men would turn their attention to the cultivation of their interior faculties, so that they might recognise the great principles of the Universe, and thus learn to live in their external sphere of movement in a correspondingly-harmonious manner. Then the judgment would always be the supreme and governing faculty among the other departments of the human soul; and then would all things in the outer world precisely correspond to its dictates. When Wisdom assumes an immoveable position on the throne of the interior world or the soul, then will all other faculties, as *subjects*, be influenced, directed, and governed with a righteous government.

Thus the conviction of the soul's independence arises from an insufficient development of the faculty of Wisdom, from the misdirection of all the faculties, and especially from the very superficial modes of educating them which prevail.

Will, I repeat, is a passive faculty. It is, however, not only the *receptacle* of thought, but a faculty of thought itself; and it is also a medium of communication between the Love and Wisdom. Hence it is that when thoughts are evolved from the will-force, man feels that he has an independence of action and a " free will" uninfluenced. I say it is when the *thoughts* are evolved from the Will, and not when the Will prompts the system to outward movement, that a man conceives of the freedom of his own Will. For when volition is produced, the *judgment* takes cognizance of the operations of the Will.

Then, again, a man sometimes feels a conviction of " free will" when his *judgment* evolves the thought, and while the Will is engaged in perpetual volition.

The combinations of the soul are of themselves an enigma beyond the possibility of any mind to solve. And it is the evanescentness of the action of each faculty that gives rise to the interior conviction of " free will." Another cause of this conviction is that man does not individualize the specific promptings and suggestions of the internal. He therefore becomes confused in the general evolution of thought, and rushes to erroneous conclusions, and adopts unsound principles of metaphysical speculation.

And man is incessantly subject to the suggestions of Love and the promptings of thoughts which the judgment disapproves. Thus he feels a constant antagonism within his own being; that is, between the lower affections and desires of Love, and the approbations of the Wisdom. Meanwhile Will, as the mediator between the two other faculties, is passive. A man may feel impressed to act in a given way, yet he obeys not the impulse, and says, " I will not, until my mind is convinced of the propriety of so doing." This certainly is a most truthful acknowledgment of absolute dependence, and is an expression flowing from an undecided judgment. Man always makes himself, or the pronoun I, the *subject* of action, or the acted on, whenever the judgment directs or approves an external action. In the expression, " I will not act until my judgment approves the action," the pronoun I represents the Will or passive faculty; while the terms " my judgment" represent the higher faculty, which is the Wisdom. And as the Wisdom is dependent for its judgment, its development, or its capabilities of discernment, upon the character of the thoughts within, and the influences and experiences without, it can not be truthfully said that *this* possesses an independent power of commanding action, which could with any propriety be termed "free will."

Hence the idea of the existence of "free will" proceeds from an indistinct consciousness that pervades the whole workings of the soul. The belief arises also from a confounding of the actions of the individual faculties, without perceiving the relations which they sustain to outward things, to the forms which they inhabit, or to one another. Hence there exists no law, principle, or fact, which affords of this belief the least particle of proof.

It has been said by some metaphysicians, and especially by Locke and Plato, that the "free will" of man is proved by his superiority over all the other forms in Nature; that the animal is governed by an instinctive impulse, and by influences that proceed from surrounding things — while Man is prompted to act, and is at liberty to positively refuse. Thus it is said that he moves under a manifest freedom of the will.

The discerning mind will perceive instantly that this indicates a very superficial view of the *cause* of action in the animal and human form; and the hypothesis is assumed without analyzing the individual faculties of the human soul, and their specific modes of action. Man is only an elevated form among all the forms in Nature; and from the variety of which he is a part, the whole is made a complete system, in which may be observed series, degrees, and states of progression, both as relate to the essence and the form, or the soul and the body. But there exists no proof in the perceptible superiority of man over the lower creations that he possesses an independent power of action, while all other things in the Universe are inseparably and unchangeably united.

It certainly is evident that there is a *species* of independence possessed by every particle of matter in existence; and that consists only in the fact that forms have an individual being. In this sense the term independence can be applied to all things. But speaking in reference to the whole System of divine creation, it can not be said that there is any such thing as absolute independence; for all things are but *parts* of one stupendous Whole — and from this is demonstrated the unity and dependence of all things.

The numerous classifications that have been made of the phrenic development of the soul, have no direct bearing upon the principles herein advanced, inasmuch as they are founded upon the anatomical constitution of the brain, and are therefore *external*, and not decidedly connected with any of the real-realities of the *interior* or thinking principle.

§ 189. I next proceed to consider the spiritual and material SENSES, and their relations to the outer world. But I discover that two have been given to man which he does not possess except in a qualified sense, and then only as branches of others.

FEELING (or *touch*) is a distinct sense, and sustains a close relation to the faculty of Love.

HEARING, or the sense of external sound, is also a distinct sense, and is conjoined with the united action of Love and Will, and especially with the Will, for it is by this faculty that this sense is rendered a delicate medium of communication between the inner and outer world.

The sense of SEEING is related to the faculty of Wisdom; and hence it is subject to the Will. Seeing is always an act of the Will, approved or permitted by the Wisdom; for a person may or may not employ his organ of vision to behold material things.

But HEARING is a sense related to Love and Will; and hence Will has no power to prevent the inflowing vibrations of sound. And *Touch* is a sense related to Love alone, and is a connecting link between the human faculties and the instincts of the animal creation. Hence it is that the Will and Love have no power over it, and can not govern the sensation produced by it, or modify the intrusions of external things upon its susceptibility.

Two other senses have been recognised as belonging to man, and these are *Taste* and *Smell*. But this classification can not be true; for taste and smell are confined to the sense of Touch, and their organs are only avenues through which peculiar *sensations* are received. *Smelling* is subject neither to the judgment nor to the Will; nor is the sense of *Taste;* for each of them, unlike the others, is subject to be acted on, but has not power to resist external invasions.

It can be proved that the sense of *Hearing* depends upon the medium of Touch only *primarily*, for its power of communicating sound to the internal, and that the details of its action, and its effects upon the internal, are for the most part governed by the influence of the Will and Wisdom. That is, sound is governed not so much by the structure of the ear, as by the operation of the Will and Wisdom upon it. Thus sound is rendered by the judgment, gentle, congenial, or repulsive; and that too by calling into action of the will-force. I say, then, that this can be proved; and this will establish the position of this sense between that of Touch and Vision: for Hearing is a mediatorial sense.

Man, then, has three distinct senses:—the subordinate or suggestive sense, which is *Touch;* the passive or modifying sense, which is *Hearing;* and the superior or protective sense, which is above and over them all, and this is *Seeing.* *Seeing* is related especially to the Wisdom; and both are watchful and careful to protect all the subordinate possessions of the interior and exterior form. Hearing is a medium sense, related to the Will and Love, and is passive. Therefore it is subject to receive all sounds created or courted by love, and to admit them into the interior, according to the modifying tendency of the Wisdom. And Touch is the germinal or rudimental sense, subject to the suggestions of Love, and the influence of outer things upon the body.

It is now made manifest why man's external form corresponds to and represents his interior being. For it is now perceived that there is a trinity in everything, and that there is a perfect likeness between the external form of man and the form and structure of the soul. The soul of man is thus proved to be a tangible reality; for it has been made distinctly clear, even to the sensuous observer, that *forms* are created and determined only by their *essence.* This all-important truth applies to man and to the whole Universe. To behold the soul or spirit of man, then, observe his material mode of being. Meanwhile consider that the *real* man is the *internal*, this only animating the material form, in order that it may perfect its constitution and preserve its identity, and also establish an inseparable connexion between the material and spiritual world.*

---

* It may not be improper to note a phenomenon which here occurred. Having spoken for about three hours, and the fatigue incident to the protracted sitting posture of those present having become somewhat severe, the lecturer paused and remarked to his magnetizer as follows: "I perceive that I shall now have to be absent (that is, from the body) about six or seven minutes, during which time the scribe and others of you may relieve your muscles by taking exercise." He then assumed his usual inclined position, and remained rigid and statue-like, breathing very slightly, for about seven minutes, at the end of which period he returned with rather unusual muscular convulsions, and under mental emotions which he could not entirely suppress. Said he, "I see I have but little more to say before speaking of a totally different and altogether higher subject; and as my impressions flow easily, I will now proceed to give all that will precede the revelations on the spiritual spheres." He

§ 190. From past considerations it is made clear that *man materially is a perfection of all Matter in Nature;* and that *man spiritually is a perfection of all Motion in the Universe*, or of the First Great Principle of Motion, which is the Divine Mind, whose Essence is Love : and that man spiritually is constituted of the wisdom of Love. It has also been shown that every form is unfolded by progressive stages from the lower particles of matter to the perfect symmetry of the material organization of man; and that the form or essence has in like manner advanced through successive degrees of development, to the perfect spiritual organization. Moreover, it has been shown that the exterior or the form is the express likeness of its interior essence, which latter has unfolded itself from the inner to the outer on the principle of *end, cause,* and *effect*.

And I am desirous of enforcing that *great spiritual and eternal truth* which it is necessary for man to know and appreciate before he can know himself and be happy : and that is, *that all manifest substances, forms, compositions — indeed, that* ALL THINGS VISIBLE, *are expressions of an interior productive cause, which is the spiritual essence :* that the Mineral Kingdom is an expression of *Motion*, the Vegetable an expression of *Life*, the Animal an expression of *Sensation*, and that Man is an expression of *Intelligence;* that the planets in our solar system are a perfect expression of the Sun from which they sprang; that the various combined bodies and planetary systems in the Universe are a perfect expression of the Great Sun of the Univercœlum; that the Great Sun is a perfect expression of the SPIRITUAL SUN within it; and that the Spiritual Sun is a perfect expression of the Divine Mind, Love, or Essence. The Spiritual Sun is thus the Centre and Cause of all material things. It is a diverging or radiating Sphere or Atmosphere of the Great Eternal Cause. It is an *aroma* — a garment and a perfect radiation of the more interior Essence, the Divine, Creative Soul.

Behold the truth — that the *material* Universe is a perfect representation of the *spiritual* Universe, in which nothing exists but what is everlasting and infinite; that the whole material System is the Body of the Creative Soul; and that the Spiritual Essence has unfolded and manifested itself in a material Form ! And this Form is the Order and Wisdom of the Divine Mind.

then proceeded to give in a prompt and unhesitating manner all that precedes his remarks on the process of death, the whole duration of the sitting being upward of four hours.

Light and Love constituted the first development of the Spiritual Sun; and that was Light and Life inconceivable — a brilliancy that extended throughout the height, and depth, and length, and breadth of space — that became illuminated space itself; and yet space is not limited, nor could it transcend the expansive illuminations of the Great Spiritual Sun. And when the Universe was completed, Order and Form reigned omnipresent throughout the whole Univercœlum! And such was the grand and stupendous Development of the Great Spiritual Sun — this having developed the Material Sun, and this the expanded Universe!

All things that *man* creates are such as represent his *thoughts*. They are merely the outward expressions of the thoughts of his soul. He creates nothing but what is a living evidence and representation of a thought previously conceived. This truth is useful as a guide to the mind; for now, when the inquiry is made as to what the soul is, where it is, how it exists, and what are the evidences — the *tangible* evidences of its existence — this truth, which is now proved to be a *universal* one, should be recalled to the mind: that all things tangible are in reality the living evidences of the soul within, made manifest to the material senses, and useful to the requirements of the outer world.

Every mind must conceive of the existence of a *Cause* as the parent of any *effects* visible to the senses. And the cause must be admitted as *corresponding* to the effect, or else the effect can not be attributed to *any* producing cause. Hence it follows that all external and visible things are *effects*, prompted, created, and unfolded to the outer world, by a corresponding interior cause; and that the cause must be the *real reality*, or else such tangible effects could not have been produced. So all material things created by man are the *forms of his thoughts;* and these are the offspring of the soul. The form of man is a likeness, a type, a representative of the *cause* or *soul* which animates and unfolds it to the outer world. The outer senses are typical of the inner ones; for they are unfolded from the corresponding parts of the interior essence.

And I feel authorized to affirm, from the nature of my impressions, that if man were differently situated and superiorly educated, he would not be so far removed from the *spiritual world* as he now is in his sphere of thought. And, moreover, he would recognise the proper use of all things, and apply them to his wants, as directed by the governor of all things, which is Wisdom. And he would recognise the relation existing between the natural and the spiritual world; and that, too, without experiencing a metamorphosis or transformation of the real man from the outer to the inner world.

Furthermore, I now discover that man, as to soul and form, becomes individualized in this sphere, and preserves his form henceforward, and knows no change; and that man exists in the other world in a perfect human form, and among as many expressed forms of essence, and as many projections of thought, as are existing in this sphere of being. I discover that the Second Sphere is unfolded from this, the first, and that it is the perfect form of this its parent and creator.

---

§ 191. I would have the reader apprehend the manner in which I employ words to express thought; for it is proper to guard against all obscurity and indefinite and imaginative thoughts. Know, then, that I use the terms "essence," "spirit," "soul," and "interior being," as *synonymous*—signifying the form which animates the body, which body is of it an outward expression. I use the terms "spiritual," "celestial," and "heavenly," as representing distinct degrees of material refinement. I employ language in a *relative* sense, though I intend every expression to be understood in its *absolute* sense, being relative only in reference to the whole System of the Universe, of which this philosophy is intended to be a tangible, verbal expression. In using the terms "*spirit*" and "*soul*," I am adapting myself to the forms of expression imposed on philosophy by speculative minds in order to convey their ideas.

I would, moreover, have all understand that I consider (because I perceive) that all things, whether tangible or intangible, are *material;* that there exists no such thing as "*immaterial*" or "*imponderable*" elements, gases, or pervading mediums; and that there exists no such a thing as *absolute perfection*, save that Divine Essence which is composed of Love and infinite Perfection itself. Therefore, when I speak concerning the spiritual Spheres, I will speak as if all things were visible to the material senses; for they *are* so to the senses unclothed and free from outward obstructions.

I shall preserve a sameness in the mode of expression, and a naturalness in all my descriptions of the things which I shall hereafter know and be enabled to relate. And many things which I have not explained concerning the various manifestations of the soul, will hereafter be spoken of as collateral with the general descriptions. I shall employ the terms "*man*" and "*form*" throughout all the forthcoming relations, in order that there may not exist any confusion in terms; and these I shall use synonymously.

I now perceive the *objections* that will be raised against the preceding relations, and those which are to follow. The first of these is embodied in the question, "What proof have we that this account of the spirit-world is true?" I perceive the answer: and that is, Recognise the unchangeable tendency of the universal laws and principles that govern the whole System of creation; and by them and their unvarying teachings the mind may decide upon the truth or falsity of all assertions beyond the possibility of sensuous demonstration. If they are recognised as *immutable*, then a sameness in their tendency must be manifested in all parts of the general structure of the Universe; and all philosophy that is truthful must correspond thereunto. If they proclaim *universal association*, then the same principle should be considered as holding alike in every department of Nature and the Univercœlum. If they proclaim *universal development*, then the same must inevitably be perpetuated from the lowest point of time to the highest point in eternity. Upon these universal and eternal principles of progression, rests the truth of that which will hereafter be asserted.—And that which has been asserted will, in the main, receive the approbation of the most enlightened judgments, and is analogically demonstrated in the visible fields of creation.

The *second* objection is, " That it is impious, presumptuous, and inconsistent with the nature of things, for any being to pretend to a knowledge of heavenly things. Therefore what is said, must be an ingenious invention, or a systematized fabrication of unreal and chimerical things." This objection flows only from a misdirected and uneducated judgment, and therefore requires the most unbounded forgiveness: for it is plain that no enlightened mind would make an objection based upon such a mere superficial presumption. The evidence that it is *not* a fanciful and ingenious invention is contained in the exterior form of the work, and the irrespective presentation of truth, without courting the prejudices or beliefs that at present prevail in the world. And that it is not imaginary, evidence may be derived from the order of the whole revelation, and from the naturalness of the expressions, of the applications, and of the conclusions, which are irresistible to the higher perceptions of any expanded intellect.

The *third* objection is the most powerful of them all, and is to be feared more than any other enemy, however formidable, that will be arrayed against the truth — and that is, "*I do not believe it.*" This, certainly, is an objection which no argument or reason can reach, because it flows from the depths of ignorance. And to such objectors I would only say, Abandon all such insignificant expressions, or your ignorance will become imbecility; and press onward to attain that degree of knowledge that will enable you to *understand* whether these things are true or chimerical.

I hereafter employ no arguments to prove the things which I relate; but I shall be prompted to employ *illustrations* to make the relations intelligible to the mind in its present plane of thought. With these remarks, then, I am prepared to venture the assertion of truths hereafter without fear as to their rightful apprehension. I will now, therefore, ascend to the *second world* of human existence. Meanwhile, I shall recognise the truthfulness of the saying, that "*Light and Life are Love, and Order and Form are Wisdom;*" that man internally, is constituted of the "*Wisdom of Love;*" and that he is the ultimate design of Nature, of the Universe, and of its Eternal Cause.*

---

§ 192. Thoughts that are associated with the process of dying, and with the state of death, are to some minds dark, doubtful, cheerless,

* After having been in the abnormal state for upward of four hours, and closing his lecture at this place, the author remarked, that he perceived on the mind of one of the witnesses present (Mr. Theron R. Lapham) a desire that he should examine his wife, who was ill (a fact which had not been previously stated). He accordingly passed off, and on returning to outward consciousness he remarked, that it was very singular that all the inflowings of those exalted truths of which he had been speaking had now entirely ceased, and that his perceptions of them now were but little more expansive than they would be if he were in the normal state! This we understood him to attribute to the fact that the spiritual light governed by the associated minds of the second sphere had now ceased to shine upon his understanding to the same degree as while lecturing. He said his mind then rested on altogether a lower plane of thought, and that he was at that moment only qualified for the examination and treatment of the diseased. He then proceeded with the examination of the patient (who was absent), and to give a prescription, the results of which, it is scarcely necessary to say, were precisely accordant with facts, and attended with the relief sought by the patient.

and disconsolating; while to others death seems a welcome state, productive of peace, quietness, blessing, and elevation. It is in a degree terrifying to all, and to many it seems of all things the most to be dreaded and shunned. It is generally feared by the brave and the timid, the wise and the foolish, the old and the young. It is to all a fearful process, rendered much more so by the prospect of a cold and unrelenting grave! This, I perceive, is in consequence of wrongly apprehending the process of dying, and of not knowing the ineffable beauties that surround the living man when it escapes the outer form.

As soon as the human organization is perfected in its form, size, and general developments, and as soon as the period has arrived when the spirit exercises its full control over the body, the process of transformation commences. The change is imperceptible, yet it is incessant and progressive. The body is not dying for a few hours only, but for many years — during which time the faculties and powers of the inner being gradually release their proprietorship over the form, and the soul continues its aspirations toward the higher spheres.

When the form is yet a child, it manifests all the angular, eccentric, and irregular traits of character, inclinations, and movements. When childhood advances to youth, the eccentricity gives way to more uniformity, and then is displayed the circular, in every possible modification of that form. When youth ascends to manhood, the perfect circular and spiral make their appearance, and are uniformly displayed in the inclinations and characteristics of that progressed stage of development. At this period the process of dying or transformation commences. The spirit is continually developing and expanding its faculties, and putting them forth as *feelers* into the higher spheres. The tendencies of the spirit are no more descending, but ascending, and that, too, to an immensity beyond the power of language to express, or the most exalted intellect to comprehend.

And as manhood progresses to old age, the body gradually becomes incapable of performing the office required by the spirit. Hence, when people are aged, their faculties seem buried beneath the wornout and useless materials of the body. They appear weak in intellect, imbecile, and unconsociable to all around them that is youthful, blooming, and seemingly perfected. One faculty after another withdraws from the material form, and their energy, brilliancy, and susceptibility, seem to decline. The body, finally, is almost disconnected from the spirit which gives it animation; and then the body is a dweller in the rudimental sphere, and the spirit is an inhabitant of the inner life, or the spiritual world. And when the moment of dissolution occurs, the *sensation*, or clothing medium of the body, is attracted and absorbed by the spirit, of which it then becomes the *material form*. At this instant the body manifests faint and almost imperceptible movements, as if it were grasping for the life which had fled; and these are contortions of the countenance, spasmodic contractions of the muscles, and seeming efforts of the whole frame to regain its animating soul.

Such are the visible appearances connected with the process of death. But these are deceptive: for the process occurring in the *interior* is far more beautiful than it is possible to describe. When the body contracts its muscles and apparently manifests the most agonizing and writhing efforts, it is merely an open indication of joy unspeakable in the inner being, and of ecstasy unknown to all but itself. When the countenance is contorted, pain is not experienced; but such is an expression of ineffable delight. And when the body gives forth its last possession, a smile is impressed on the countenance, which of itself is an index of the brightness and resplendent beauty that pervade the spirit's home! In the last moments of outer life the spiritual perceptions are greatly expanded and illuminated, and the spirit is thus rendered competent to behold the immense possessions of its second habitation.

It is given me to know these truths by daily experiencing them, and having them verified in the frequent transitions that occur within my being, from the outer to the inner world, or from the lower to the higher spheres. I speak, therefore, from personal experience, which is knowledge fully confirmed by the unvarying sensations and phenomena that occur.

The butterfly escapes its gross and rudimental body, and wings its way to the sunny bower, and is sensible of its new existence. The drop of water that reposes on the earth is rendered invisible by the absorbing invitations of the sun, and ascends to associate with, and repose in, the bosom of the atmosphere. The day that is known by its warmth and illumination, dispenses its blessings to the forms of earth, and sinks into repose in the bosom of the night. Night is, then, an index of a new day, which is first cradled in the horizon, and afterward perfected in its noontide light, beauty, and animation. The flower, being unfolded from the interior by virtue of its own essence and the sun, is variegated in every possible manner, and thus becomes a representative of light and beauty; but having attained its perfection, it soon begins to change its form, its color, and its beauty of external being. Its fragrance goes forth and pervades all congenial and suitable forms, and its beauty is indelibly impressed upon the memory of its beholder and admirer, when the flower itself is no more. The foliage, tinted with the breath of winter, no longer retains its outward beauty: but this is an index of new life and animation, which is perfectly exemplified in the return of foliage in the youthful season. As it is with these, so it is with the spirit. The body dies on the outer, or rather changes its mode of existence, while the spirit ascends to a higher habitation, suited to its nature and requirements. And as it is with these, so it is with me, and the transitions which I continually experience.

The transition of my being from the outer to the inner world is produced by the action of forces contained in another body, upon the similar forces contained in my own material form. The process is that of destroying the sensation of the outer, or rather of changing it to the sensation of the spirit—at which time the medium that connects my body with another is sustained by a mingling of the forces of the two bodies, while the actual sensation leaves the body and becomes the Form of my spirit. This Form, then, is the body which I possess while occupying higher positions in material existence. Inasmuch, then, as the body is thus deserted, I am enabled, by causes unrelated, to behold the possessions of the Second Sphere, and to commune with the knowledge there existing, together with that of earth. This elevation assists me to penetrate with spiritual perception the whole arcana of the various earths in the Universe.

Thus I am constantly experiencing a transition from the outer to the inner sphere of thought, existence, and investigation. This change will be experienced by all, though the means by which it will be accomplished may seem in some instances painful, terrifying, and disconsolating. Death, or the transition so termed, is, however, of all things the most to be admired, and its prospect is the first thing to be cherished and appreciated.

In these relations the inhabitants of the earth may repose confidence; and they should meanwhile strive to have all the faculties and powers of the spirit so developed as to be able to perceive and appreciate the grandeur of that superior existence to which all must inevitably ascend.

§ 193. I now behold the forms of earth and the bodies of men, including my own, in a light and with a degree of perception never before presented. I discover that I can only see the forms by judging what and where they are, by the light of the spirit: for the outer body is beyond my perception, and I only see well-constituted and living spirits. By possessing this perception, I am enabled to commune with all the possessions of this Second Sphere, and now behold the extended fields and living habitations of this elevated existence.

There are to be observed three specific degrees of form and development: the young and unmatured; the advanced stages of these up to the mediatorial degree of manhood; and the highest of them all, which is the perfect form and most highly developed of all the spirits there existing.

I perceive that whenever an *infant* dies on any of the earths, the germ or undeveloped body of its spirit becomes deposited in this Sphere, and is fully unfolded in intellect, and highly enlightened concerning all of its own existence and prior situation. The infant that has had life, and dies in infancy, is, I perceive, in this Sphere, fully developed and perfected. So it is with all uninformed spirits who escape the body on any earth: for each is here educated in the truths and beauties of the whole existence. So it is also with the intelligent and highly cultivated; for they are here more advanced, and occupy a position more elevated and refined.

Moreover, I discover three distinct *societies* or associations of men and females, each occupying a position determined by their degree of cultivation, sympathy for one another, and power of approaching each other's sphere of knowledge and attainment. And what is well to relate is, that each society is encompassed by a peculiar sphere or atmosphere, which is an exhalation from the specific quality of their interior or spiritual characters. Every spirit has a peculiar sphere of its own, and also a general one in which it can with pleasure exist. And spirits know and associate with each other according to the quality of the sphere which is exhaled from their interiors. They associate only as spheres are agreeable, and as they are capable of approaching each other with pleasure.

So it is also with mankind on earth. — They dwell in each other's society only as they can coalesce, and approach each other with pleasure. So also are existing on earth the three specific degrees of development, which are youth, manhood, and mature age. But they are in a rudimental condition, and not situated in order as they are in the Second Sphere.

I perceive that spirits approach each other according to the relative degrees of brilliancy which surrounds and encompasses their forms. Thus association is determined and made perfect by the law of congeniality and affinity, or affection. They have an affection for one another in proportion to the similarity in the degrees of love and purity to which they have attained. Thus are the three states or societies established.

In the *first* society are an immense number of infant and uncultivated spirits, which are in various degrees of advancement and cultivation, according as such have proceeded from the earth. In the *second* group or society, are those who have become highly instructed in the principles and truths of the Divine Mind. And into this society all who die on earth with minds properly unfolded, are immersed, because here they can associate agreeably. In the *third* society I discover spirits of the most enlightened character. The most of them proceed from the planets Jupiter and Saturn, and also from planets in other solar systems. This society is so highly illuminated with wisdom, that it is almost impossible for the spirits of the lower societies to approach it. If they make an effort to enter their midst, this is immediately overcome by the strong repulsion arising from the non-affinity existing between them and their respective spheres.

The atmosphere that flows from and encompasses and protects the first society, is of a mingled and rather unilluminated appearance. Its brilliancy is rather faint in comparison to that of those above it. It appears gloomy, dark, and rather uncongenial, because it is an emanation from uncultivated intellects. Yet there is a purity — an exceeding purity among them, viewed comparatively with that existing on earth.

The *second* society is enveloped with an atmosphere of far more congenial variegations, presenting a resplendent brilliancy which indicates purity and elevation. It appears like the mingling of many colors, such as are not known on earth. And these are all so perfectly conjoined, and are blended together in such harmony, that the whole *aroma* is of itself a representation of purity and refinement. Yet it is a sphere emanating from the whole body of the society, indicating the wisdom of the spirits composing it. Their wisdom consists in a knowledge of truths and principles concerning material and rudimental things; and in them they are highly enlightened. And the inconceivable variety of colors surrounding them arises from their dissimilar stages of intellectual advancement. Yet they are all in the same plane of wisdom, and thus form one society, enveloped by this beautiful and refined atmosphere.

The *third* society is also clothed with an aerial garment, which is a perfect representation of the character and perfection of their interiors. I behold in it all colors, and a variety of reflections proceeding from the subordinate societies; and these reflections render their spiritual emanation so very beautiful that language is inadequate to describe it.

Those of the *first* society are in the plane of natural thought; that is, they are just emerging from the instructions and impressions of earth, into the wisdom of the higher societies.

The *second* society is in the plane or sphere of *causes;* that is, they are just emerging from a superior knowledge of visible effects presented on earth, to a perception of the interior causes of them: and their wisdom extends to the lowest and first cause of all material things. Therefore they have a knowledge of all interior causes, essences, and their modes of external manifestation: but they are not in the possession of superior wisdom concerning the *uses* for which causes and effects were instituted.

The *third* society is in the plane of *effects;* and those composing it have a perception of all ultimate design, and of the universal adaptation of things to each other. Their minds are exceedingly luminous. With their powers of penetration, the externals of things are laid open, and they perceive only the character and quality of the interior. Their vision extends to every recess of their own habitation, and their knowledge comprehends all subordinate material existences. They have a most unlimited presentation of all created things below their elevated position; and their wisdom is light, and love, and brilliancy, and even ecstasy, to a degree that transcends description. With their unfolded spiritual powers, they behold the vast landscapes of the spirit-home, too extensive to be comprehended by men on earth, and too beautiful to be appreciated or enjoyed by them.

The third society are not only in a state of emergement from the plane of causes to that of effects, but also from their sphere to the third world of human existence.

§ 194. And what is well to relate is, that notwithstanding the dissimilitude that exists between the three societies, there is a perfect unity among them, and a mutual dependence one upon another; and there is a continual aspiring affection that gyrates from the infant intellect to the high and superior wisdom of the third society. There is a unity of action, an agreeableness of situation, and a propriety of position, which cause them all to live for one another, like a brotherhood.

And, moreover, it is profitable to remark that each society or group is well situated, well conditioned, and well cultivated, in reference to the specific state which each is compelled to sustain. The situations are perfect in proportion to the degree of wisdom and refinement to which each has attained. The lowest appears inferior in comparison to the higher and superior; though even the first, to man on earth, would appear to be a high state of perfection. By the varieties of condition and development, the societies are made perfect. They are thus as one brotherhood, joined by mutual affections and actions, and perpetuated in goodness by the benign and gentle influences that proceed from the highest society to the lower ones, and from these to it again.

The societies in the Second Sphere are very much to be admired, because of the perfect harmony which pervades them, and the perfect melody and concert of rudimental and perfected knowledge which they manifest. In a corresponding manner does there exist a concert of action, a unity of feeling, and a universal love, one for another.

The inhabitants do not converse *vocally*, but immerse their thoughts into one another by radiating them upon the countenance. And I perceive that thought enters the spirit by a process of *breathing*, or rather it is introduced by influx according to the desires of those conversing. They perceive thought by and through the eyes, inasmuch as *these*, like the general countenance, are an index to the quality and workings of the interior. They seemingly *hear* each other converse; but that is owing to a previous knowledge of sound by which words are distinguished and their meaning apprehended.

They perceive things without them by their sense of *vision*; but they are conscious that it is the *reflection* which they perceive, and not the *substance*. Therefore they exercise *judgment* concerning all they perceive—not judging from sensuous observation, but from the character of the substance observed.

I also discover that spirits in this Sphere approach and associate with each other according to the mutual affinity subsisting between them, even as do the inhabitants of earth; but the difference is in the *mode* of associating. Men on earth associate with one another by the guidance of their gross and rudimental senses, as these are productive of inclination and desire. Instead of this, men associate in this higher Sphere by a knowledge of each other's inherent purity, and the state of each other's affections.

Moreover, I perceive that the *former experience* of every person, both male and female, is treasured up in the memory, from which they can extract representations of that which they previously knew or experienced. Everything appears indelibly impressed upon the memory, and is mirrored forth with a vividness in proportion to the strength of the impression. Therefore whatever thought enters the human mind on earth, becomes a resident in the memory, and is here brought forth with the appearance of newness that makes it both interesting and instructive. Those things experienced which are disagreeable to the memory, are deposited in its depths and concealed from the view of any other being, by the prevalence of those events and experiences which it pleases the mind to remember, and which the mind takes delight in contemplating. Hence it is proper for all men on earth to do and think only that which pleases them most (according to wisdom), and which they would most earnestly desire to remember; and *not* to do those things, or encourage those thoughts, which are opposed to the superior delights of the mind. If this can not be done in the present social and mental condition of the world, then it is proper to *change* those conditions, so that even *this* great good and pleasure may be obtained.

When spirits conversing appeal to each other's memory, the memory mirrors forth a perfect representation of the thing remembered, which is perceived and understood by the conversing spirit. I behold beautiful representations in the memory of those in the higher societies. These representations are of the most exquisite character, because they proceed from the memory of highly-enlightened intellects; and they are therefore delightful, inviting, and instructive.

I perceive that everything in this Sphere is created and manifested only by and through the exercise and direction of *Wisdom*. Hence the perfect order and uniformity that subsist, and the inexpressible happiness that flows as a consequence from such exquisite harmony and unity of action. Everything is appreciated as a blessing conferred upon them by the light and life of Divine Love, and the order and form of Divine Wisdom.

It is pleasing to behold these heavenly societies: for I see them at this moment existing in the most perfect degree of brotherly love, and joined inseparably together by constant ascending and descending affections. How very clear and bright are their countenances and expressions! They are unblemished by artificiality, and unspotted by rudimental and gross intrusions—for they are above and superior to these, and highly developed. The first society is indeed low in comparison to the highest; but the variety and the degrees nevertheless form of the whole a complete brotherhood. The diversity consists in the different degrees of development; and the lowest can not approach the highest, because of the dissimilarity of quality and spheres. But the lowest contains and involves the highest, while the latter in return comprehends and pervades the whole Sphere, manifesting a grace and beauty beyond the power of language to describe. And there exists almost an infinite variety of dispositions, of loves, of affections, and of wisdom, among them; yet each modification of previous conditions of mind is only an ascending degree of refinement toward perfection.

The whole is beautiful—surpassingly beautiful and sublime!—for there exists that continual emanation of love and wisdom from societies and individual forms, displaying a brilliancy of illumination beyond any light or color on earth. It is even so very bright and beautiful that those in the lower societies who approach are almost thrown into ecstasies of delight. They become prostrated, and apparently fall on their faces, because of the beauty and brilliancy of the *aroma* that encompasses the superior societies of the spirit-home.

Thus it is that all preserve an order in their lives and situations; and thus it is that their approach to each other is graduated according to the unfolding of the spiritual senses and faculties to the external. They represent the circular and spiral forms; for there exists among them a uniform and also an ascending movement. And one is continually unfolding the possessions of another, even as from the germ are unfolded the body and the flower. And even as the flower perpetuates the species of the plant, so does the superior society pervade the lower ones, and is constantly introducing them into its own vast possessions; and thus all go onward to a still higher Sphere of spiritual and intellectual elevation.

§ 195. I now proceed to relate the *external* beauties that appertain to this Second Sphere of human existence. For it is necessary that the whole aspect of the spirit-home should be vividly represented to the inhabitants of the earth, so that it may be an inducement for them to advance in their social and spiritual condition.

I behold the *spiritual* Sphere as containing all the beauties of the *natural* Sphere combined and perfected. And in every natural Sphere these beauties are represented, though in the first and rudimental degree; so that every earth is of itself an index and an introduction to the beauty and grandeur that are existing in the Second Sphere. For from the natural the spiritual is unfolded, or made manifest.

The extended surface of this Sphere, I perceive, presents regular and gentle undulations, which render the whole diversified and exceedingly inviting. And very extensive plains are presented, which are clothed with great fertility, and with innumerable varieties of forms such as deck the bosom of the earth when all things are favorable to a thrifty production. In those vast plains is represented the most perfect order. They are gardens, typical of purity, unity, and celestial love. Their diversified paths continually lead to new and instructive portions, all of which are useful as displaying Divine Love and Wisdom, which generate unity and affinity in all created things. All flowers, and even their *leaves*, are observed as so many voices proclaiming the beauty of interior perfection, and the infinite Source from which they sprang. Every plant, flower, bird, and tree, is perceived and appreciated as the express creation of Divine love and Divine action.

And there is a beauty in the external of each created thing, which is of itself an open expression of celestial love and wisdom. The flowers and foliage are of the most variegated appearance; and their variety renders them instructive and impressive, insomuch that they act as enchantments upon the minds of those who behold them, and induce thoughts beautiful, elevating, and edifying. A fragrance perpetually ascends from those vast plains of creation, giving life and brilliancy to the atmosphere, which is thereby rendered suitable to be inhaled as the breath of love and exhaled as the thoughts of wisdom. Every created thing possesses within itself a living love and affection; and this is communicated from one thing to another, all things thus becoming as it were electrified and illuminated. The beauty of one flower is imparted to another, which in its turn communicates an equal bestowment upon others. And thus those plains are a living representation of Divine Love and Wisdom.

There exists among the many inviting things of this Sphere a peculiar blending of inherent affections that different forms possess. This remark applies to all things in the spiritual Spheres. The beginning and ending of things appear not; but their *actual existence* is made manifest with all their living beauties.

Wisdom here existing consists not in words, nor in the depths of the memory; but in the actual manifestation that everything vividly displays. In other words, instruction and admonition are not derived from speech, but from action and representation. And everything here is profitable and practical—nothing is useless or imaginative.

Those of the *first* society dwell much in the delights of these plains and their variegated foliage, from a sense and susceptibility of love, but not with an appreciation of wisdom: and they are thereby instructed, developed, and rendered pure. Herein is displayed a perfect adaptation; for while they are irresistibly drawn to the beauties thus presented, those beauties in return breathe into them the breath of living love, enkindling the flame of perfect wisdom, which then burns to purity. All things are adapted to the necessities of man; and this they feel, both from an inherent consciousness, and also from a living desire to become instructed in the ways of goodness, which are those paths that lead throughout the many portions of this Sphere.

Those of the *second* society enjoy very much the unity displayed among those of the first group, and also the delights courted by the first. Besides this, they are continually investigating, analyzing, exploring, and cultivating, those many things which are within their sphere of comprehension, and thus producing living evidences of their wisdom and united ingenuity.

Those of the *third* society are to the rest ministering angels, directing spirits, and perfect examples of exalted wisdom. By their knowledge the lower societies, and even the spiritual possessions of the whole Sphere, are illuminated and made bright, beautiful, and enchanting.

There are also flowing through these gardens rivers of clear and placid waters; and even in these are exemplified the ceaseless flowings of Love and Wisdom, that are breathed, not only into heaven, but into the Universe, and become the light and life of all created things. The Love of each society, like the still water agitated by a falling pebble, expands and waves throughout all the lower and higher spheres until the wave has almost reached the bounds of space, which is then filled with love. There is no limiting the extension of the wave of water, nor can the unfoldings of love be circumscribed. And as the waters will roll gently against the shore, so Love flows forth and unfolds itself until it becomes merged into Wisdom, which then is rendered surpassingly beautiful, because Love is its creative soul and living principle.

Those rivers are representations of Divine creation. They also represent Life: for as the river flows from the rill, so Life flows from the germ that is deposited deep in the interior of the Universe; and as the rill flows into and becomes an immense ocean, so Life flows into and becomes the animating soul of all things. These rivers are so very clear and translucent, that the brilliancy of the azure heavens is in them vividly reflected. And as night makes the stars appear, so do these waters represent the whole celestial scenery above them.

These rivers flow through *valleys* abounding in the most beautiful and varied creations, and in every species of variegated foliage that also adorns those vast plains; and the whole presents the most exalted representation of life and Wisdom.

I behold, also, *groves* that are of the most charming and enchanting character. It is impossible to behold them without being impressed with new and beautiful thoughts, such as they naturally suggest. In these groves are reposing those who investigate and who love wisdom and the Divine Mind supremely. And those that are in the first society, or in Love only, court the refreshing shades of those groves, and learn with docility and yet with dignity, of the beauties that are around and above them, and are instructed by these beauties' expounders.

§ 196. I perceive that all spirits are engaged in loving their neighbors, and advancing their welfare; and here is good will without distinction. I perceive that spirits are engaged in exploring the fields of Thought, and searching deeply into the *causes* of things; and thus they learn of love and accumulate wisdom. And there is no inertia, no stagnation, but activity and industry are visible in every department of this heavenly Sphere. And it is well to relate that every one is engaged in that for which he has an affection, and there is, therefore, no confusion. Nor are there any disqualifying conditions, but every one is qualified to labor in that for which he has an affection. Affections are varied according to the degrees to which each spirit from the first to the highest society, has advanced in the stages of development. Hence industry is equal, useful, harmonious, and reciprocal; for every one gravitates to the situation which accords with his predisposing desire.

Moreover, I behold here some of the most magnificent creations of Will and Wisdom. It is well to remark, that everything created in this sphere is suggested by Love and perfected by Wisdom — and is, therefore, a living projection from their minds. Things are created by Will; and these I discover are distributed in a uniform manner throughout the plains, valleys, rivers, and groves of the spirit-home. I discover constructions of the most grand and magnificent character, each having a brilliancy and illumination according to the advanced state of the society in which it is found. The first society have creations which are representations of their Love, and Will, and uncultivated Wisdom; and these they behold as representations of their interior thoughts. The creations of the second society display more uniformity, order, and usefulness; and thus they subserve the purposes of the first society and themselves. The third society have splendid constructions, too vast and elegant to describe, and the most ambitious imagination could not transcend them in its conceptions. For they are in reality too perfect and too magnificent to be conceived of by any mind in its rudimentary state of being.

And there exists among them a pervading happiness; a soothing and tranquillizing element of forgiveness and universal love; a cordiality in the bestowment of inherent love upon each other, and a mingling, and yet perfect harmony, of thoughts, all of which it is delightful to contemplate. These manifestations all proclaim the divinity of the life and love that flow into and animate all the heavens.

The waftings of thought from one mind to another, are such as can be felt, and yet no spirit receives thought uncongenial with its quality and being. These waftings are breaths that are inhaled by unfolded spirits willing to receive them. It appears as if thoughts were continually descending into the recesses of less advanced spiritual existence, and also ascending through all the higher Spheres even to the highest, which is the seat and Throne of the Divine Mind.

There are truths here known of the most novel and mysterious character; but these I am not permitted to relate at this time; for they are unimportant to the human race. Yet there is a class of truths which it is profitable to mention — and these are concerning the experiences, opinions, and beliefs, that exist among the inhabitants of this spiritual Sphere.

I perceive that when infants are introduced from the human races into the first society, they are believed to be born among them: for appearances to them are the same as to families in the human race. After the infant is ushered into their midst, they behold and admire it; for it teaches tenderness, kindness, and immaculate purity. Infants, therefore, are caressed, nourished, guided, and admonished by them, according to the high degree of love and wisdom that exists among the various societies. The infant is beheld as constituted only of love, and as possessing inherent qualities that will unfold and lead to perfection. Their whole object is to produce a proper development of the germinal qualities contained in love; and this they do by processes of the most simple and gentle character.

And so it is also with spirits from the human race that are imperfectly developed while in the human body, and with such as have had their faculties and spiritual principles misdirected, obstructed, or disconcerted. Thus, I perceive that imbecile persons, especially if they have become so by accident or disease, are received into this Sphere as *infant* spirits, and are then unfolded and rendered beautiful.

I moreover perceive that those who are interiorly deformed from birth, have no identity, or even birth in the higher Sphere. And so it is with all unorganized bodies; for such are not capable of developing the qualities and faculties of the spirit, and hence do not preserve their identity.

Spirits from the human race who have been from birth dejected and disconsolated, and who have suffered trials and afflictions of the most severe character, are received to the bosom of the first, or second, or third society, with exceeding great joy — so great is the fondness of love for them, and the desire to make them happy. They are received to the bosom of their affection, and to the life of their love, as the mother receives and embraces her child. They are cherished and loved with all the combined affection that dwells in the depths of each spirit. How joyful it is to see those welcomes, and those soothing and tranquillizing affections breathed into that spirit who has suffered trials and afflictions in the human race!

The quality of a spirit is at once perceived, and what is better than all, is, the dwellers in this sphere judge not by external or superficial manifestations, such as passions or impulses of the soul, but by the quality and advanced state of the spirit itself; and it is according to this that they love the spirit introduced into their midst. Yet the strength of their love is in proportion to the capability of the introduced spirit to appreciate and enjoy it. Love is not bestowed too abundantly, nor is any privilege granted which is not useful; but everything of this nature is graduated according to capabilities. Thus it is that " to whom much is given, of him is much required." This is a truth which angels know; and these are the words of superior wisdom.

And what may appear strange is, that often when a spirit leaves the human form, and is introduced into this Sphere, it for a moment can not realize the change, for it is imperceptible. Spirits retain the same bodily form in the spiritual Sphere; and at first they feel as if they were only transferred to a country they knew not. It is, however, not long after the transition before their interior senses are opened; and then they behold and appreciate the change, and the beauties with which they are surrounded. And some spirits appear to wonder that they did not see it before, and that they did not believe it while in the body; for now it appears so tangible, and so perfectly agreeable with the universal teachings of natural law.

Men who have been impressed on earth with certain doctrines concerning the other life, seem to smile at themselves, and marvel because they were so misled, and so easy to be misdirected. Some who have believed in the literal resurrection of the material body, are so ashamed of this conviction that they strive to hide their memory of it from the perception of others. And some strive to modify their previous beliefs so as to make them harmonize with what they now experience and know to be true. And such is the ease with those who have imbibed gross doctrines while on earth, and which are still impressed upon their memory; for immediately after the transition, they recognise the falsity of their previous convictions, and for a little while strive to conceal and modify them. This desire, I discover, continues only for a little season; for being penetrated by the perceptions of others with ease, they are led to discard with pleasure the impressions of the memory, and their hereditary affection for doctrines; and they then become enlightened by the light and love of heaven, and begin their ascending progress toward the higher societies of their new home.

§ 197. The *first* society is in Love, the *second* is in Will, and the *third* is in Wisdom. These societies are composed of families, groups, and associations. And these live in an harmonious manner one with another, displaying perfect order, form, and series of development and position. And all are thus as ONE BROTHERHOOD.

Even *one* of these societies is composed of more individuals than are existing upon all the planets in the solar system, and even upon all the earths belonging to the fifth Circle of Suns. Their numbers transcend computation. And I discover that the first Sphere of spiritual existence is unfolded from the last Sphere of material creation, which is the Circle of Suns above referred to. It appears now a little strange to me that men have not conceived this truth before. But when man is in the human body, with his *material* senses opened, he perceives *material things*, because he is animated from the inner to the *outer* world: but when he escapes the body, at death, though the form is not changed, nor any of its qualities or properties, yet instead of seeing with his *material* he perceives with his *spiritual* senses; and the spirit-world is unfolded to his view. The transition is imperceptible.

I discover that most of the inhabitants of Mercury, Venus, the Earth, and Mars, are dwelling in the first society of the Second Sphere; and that those of the other planets occupy higher positions in the plane of thought and wisdom.

And a holy quietness pervades the whole spirit-world. There is happiness of the most inexpressible character—and ecstasies, and exultations, and glorifications, are continually ascending. There is so much purity and holiness that my mind is scarcely capable of withstanding its moving influence, such as would instantly annihilate all speech. Yet I have now a strength which I have not before known. I can receive the inflowings of these truths, and behold these holy and celestial beauties, without becoming disconcerted or incapable of declaration.

They have a sense of *music*: but it proceeds not from *hearing*, for they *perceive* harmony, and the *soul* of harmony, which *is* music. Such floats along the strata of the atmosphere, and is wafted into the soul as the fragrance of a flower into the senses. I do not *hear* but *see* music. I see it in the united voices of flowers, that speak, yet make no sound—in the shrubbery and foliage that proclaim truths, yet speak not—and in the harmony of each heavenly society: for that harmony is heavenly music. Music is perceived by the unfolded senses, and appreciated by the Wisdom. It is the soul of order, the creator of all celestial harmony and melody. The music thus perceived sinks into the depths of the soul, and unfolds sentiments of which the spirit-home alone is worthy. There is not a labyrinth or avenue of the spirit-land that is not penetrated by the vibrations and silent echoings of this heavenly harmony. There is not a thought concealed in the soul which is not quickened into life and awakened into the act of glorification thereby. There is not a recess in the material or spiritual Universe that is not quickened with life and illuminated with light, even Divine Love; and wherever this exists, music flows and is congenial. Hence everything loves and appreciates music; and this is perfected only in the Second Sphere.

There is a translucent beauty, and glory, and holiness, and happiness, that pervade and quicken into life the spirit-home, that defy all verbal expression. There is such a specificness manifested in all things, and yet such an inseparable unity and brotherly love, as can not be described, but is to be known only when experienced. It is impossible to portray the delights, the ecstasies, and the enchantments, which flow into the mind as it is immersed into this beautiful Sphere of spiritual existence.

I can read from the memory of any spirit, either in the human form or in this spiritual Sphere, with as much ease as one can read from a book. I can converse with the spirits distinctly, and learn from them the peculiar impressions and affections of their souls; and this I can communicate to any person in the human form. But this I am not permitted to do at all times, inasmuch as it would be revealing that which the human race should not know.

One more important truth it is well to relate; and that is, that those who form a mutual attachment while on earth, which is pure and true, continue to preserve an affection for one another throughout the spiritual Spheres. If the attachment is pure, it will be their conjugal affection, of the highest degree of refinement. And if one leaves the form before the other, this will make no difference: for when they are both out of the form, they recognise each other in the same manner as friends do in the human race. And if one has progressed further than the other, the one possessing wisdom will pervade and cultivate the love of the other, until their natures become assimilated, and they become fully suited to associate with one another. All attachments are of the Love; and all love is modified and perfected by Wisdom. Hence, while all conjugal affection on earth is of the Love, all conjugal affection in heaven is of the Wisdom, strengthened and quickened into life by the Love which gave birth to the prior attachment.

And also *little children* are recognised and loved here as they are on earth. Parents who love their children while in the form, continue to love them in this Sphere; and their love is here strengthened by superior wisdom. If a child leave the form while very young, and the parents when aged, the child must of necessity be far advanced, both in its outward size and its inward developments. But when the parents are introduced into the same Sphere, they *know* their child by a peculiar sense of rudimental love — by a relation of a constitutional character which they instantly perceive; and they rush (with wisdom) into each other's embrace.

All are joined according to the purity and realness of their attachment. Degrees of *refinement* do not determine the attachment so much as the *quality* of the spiritual constitution; and this is according to a law pervading all material and spiritual things.

Such is the Second Sphere of human existence; and such substantially are its truths. The relation between it and the earth, and all earths, may be perceived by the similitude of external manifestations, these differing only in degrees of purity and development. And it is proper and advantageous that the human race should know and appreciate these truths, so that they may be induced to press onward and upward in the ascending scale of progress toward the great Fount of Love and Happiness. This is the object of the present relation, and it can not well fail to perform its office: and when this is fulfilled, the race will be elevated to a high degree of social and moral culture, and thus all as one will be holy, happy, and perfect.

§ 198. Inasmuch as on the various earths there are born several millions of spirits in one second of time, from which fact there necessarily occur also as many deaths, so an equal number at every second are being introduced into the spiritual Sphere. And as there is this incessant influx from the natural into the spiritual Sphere, so there is also an equal refluxation from the Second Sphere into the *Third*, which is the *Celestial* Sphere. Thus the movements that are incessantly and imperceptibly going on, are in number beyond the comprehension of any except that mighty Mind who moved, and they all sprang into being!

There is, then, an incessant transition from the *Second* to the

Third Sphere; but the darkness incident thereunto is light, and the death is life inconceivable. Pain is a living index of pleasure, and love is the first indication of superior wisdom. The highly-cultivated spirits of the Second Sphere contemplate this transition with delight that surpasses all human speech. There is no more death to them, for death is life, and this springs up and blooms in the Sphere above, with a brighter beauty and a more lovely wisdom. It is impossible to describe the sensations of delight which exist in the interior of that spirit who lies down to repose in the Second Sphere, to be quickened into newness of life in the first society in the third heavens. They experience ecstasies which none but spirits know; and what is more beautiful than all is, that they govern their delights with the most transcending wisdom. They only migrate from the habitation of the second state, into the more congenial climes of the Sphere above. "The sting of death" is lost in the pleasures of life and beauty, and herein is that passage fully verified which speaks of this consummation.* Such are the views of the spirits in the Second Sphere concerning their flight to higher habitations, which takes place according to the workings of natural law.

In this Sphere I perceive also three distinct societies, and three aromas of the most inexpressible brilliancy: and I perceive that they correspond to perfected Love, to perfected Wisdom, and to celestial purity.

The *first* society is composed of those whose last stage of being was in the third society in the Sphere below. They have Love, Will, and Wisdom, combined, and to a degree of perfection that transcends all human thought. Their love is so pure that there is a visible radiation from their countenances, and a halo of purity surrounding them that possesses inexpressible attractions. Yea, it is like the electric fire: for it is instantaneously communicated from one to another; and thus all send forth smiles of delight, until the whole society is *exceedingly* delighted. It is attractive to behold their perfect Will, or the holy passiveness of that faculty, which is not prompted to an improper act, or to do one thing derogatory to the general welfare. And it is more than beautiful to behold their highly-cultivated Wisdom; for it blooms and sends forth a fragrance that no flower can more than faintly imitate. And this fragrance makes glad every spirit in heaven.

The *second* society are still more advanced, insomuch that they

---

* "Death is swallowed up in victory," &c., 1 Cor. xv. 54-57.

transcend all human description. They are so perfectly conjoined one with another, and their mutual affections are so absorbing and penetrating, that it requires a high degree of discernment to make a distinction between them.

And the *third* society is the highest of the Third Sphere; and they have celestial purity. So exceedingly pure are they that every subordinate spirit is repelled with an innate consciousness of non-association. Their purity gives forth a radiation brighter than the brightest sun. It is even a light of love, of wisdom, and of celestial purity, that gives life to every spirit in the lower societies. They are guardian angels to those below them, to whom they are constantly descending, with no other end in view than to gratify their thirstings for purity, and their desires that are holy and celestial.

I perceive here also those *plains* that are undulated as the gentle waves of the ocean. I perceive a celestial fragrance arising from every flower that blooms in the garden of the living Mind with an immortal beauty. I behold those diversified creations; and each one is as an angel proclaiming immortal truths in the sanctuary of the Divine Mind.

It is well to relate that everything has a *use* and *design*, to which it is with promptness applied: and there are thereby ends of the most inconceivable importance accomplished. These advance the condition and quality of each spirit; and each created thing is only a step to perpetuate infinite progression. Everything is as an act of the Divine Mind, and every representation is as a word fitly spoken. These things are all *perceived* by their expanded powers. Thus it is that *hearing* is transformed into *seeing*, and seeing is correspondingly elevated, and includes all the powers of the other senses combined.

I behold also those *valleys*. Their termination can not be seen, and their excellences can not be appreciated, except by those who dwell among them. Each valley is as a volume whose contents are sublime beyond conception, and each plain is as an unbounded field of knowledge.

And I behold also those very placid *rivers* — whose power of reflection seems only fitted to represent the unspeakable grandeur that pervades the atmosphere of the celestial heaven. A holy pensiveness seems to be manifested by those rivers and the atmosphere; and they seem to welcome and embrace each other. The still waters seem to spring up unto everlasting life; and they seem to play and sport with the brilliant atmosphere, as if there were a mutual and lively sympathy between them.

Again, I see those *groves*—and how they extend to, and line the surfy margin of those living rivers: and their roots and foliage are baptized in them, and purified to the glory of the Infinite Mind. There is a precision in every form, in every bud, and leaf, and flower, that garland and render beautiful those heavenly groves. Indeed, their shade casts a freshness which inspires every living form that reposes therein with vigor and vivacity; and thus are they means employed by the Divine Mind to refine the faculties of his spirit-children, and prepare them for a home in the highest Spheres.

---

§ 199. Inasmuch as the *knowledge* of this Sphere is entirely above the comprehension of the human race, I am not permitted to dwell upon it to any extent. For I perceive that all these relations are only permitted as a means to elevate the inhabitants of the earth, and to purify all their spiritual sentiments. But I now perceive the truth of a passage in the Primitive History, by one of the lovely spirits that dwell in the celestial Sphere, and also its application. For here are beauties innumerable, all of which are means employed by Divine Wisdom to perpetuate infinite progression, and whereby his spirit-children of all earths and all Spheres may dwell in the "Father's house not made with hands, eternal in the heavens." And I perceive that "in the Father's house there are many mansions," all of which are illuminated by Divine Love, animated by perfected spirits, and send forth an expanding brilliancy throughout all space, which is the order, and form, and soul, of Divine Wisdom.

The inhabitants of the Third Sphere impart knowledge and express love to each other, as the sun imparts life and beauty to the forms on earth. And in this Sphere are also imparted a grace, ease, and elegance, that beautify and sublimate every spirit.

It is charming beyond description to behold the stately palms, and how they by every movement proclaim humiliation—and to see with what grace they bow their majestic tops to the breaths of divine Wisdom! And while spirits are seeking repose under their wide-spread branches, they learn a lesson of grace, and meekness, and gentleness, which is indestructible. It is, moreover, enchanting to behold the fertility, so expressive of divine Love, and to perceive the fragrance so typical of celestial purity.

Every spirit has an exhalation or bodily atmosphere which is an exact indication of the quality and purity of its interiors; and thereby are all distinguished. For spheres are of every possible variety of color, according to the qualities of the spirits from which they emanate. Some have mingled colors, and some have only one. And it is also given me to know, that every natural earth, and that every mineral, vegetable, animal, man, and spirit—yea, that every particle of matter in the universe, has a peculiar sphere, by which it may be designated and recognised:—also, that every *spiritual* sphere, from the lowest to the highest, has a spherical emanation that describes its interior. It is surpassingly delightful to see those aromas and haloes of purity that surround every spirit.

So true is it that all things have a *language*, that even the spirits learn as children in a book, from the united voices coming from everything created. The whole forms a Volume whose contents are celestial, and whose philosophy is the Divine Creator's. Every passage which it contains proclaims goodness infinite, and every page unfolds volumes of immense love. The whole Book is an offspring of Wisdom. Yea, it was written in the great temple of Truth, and in the home of many mansions. The spring, the rill, the stream, and the river, are introductions to this great Volume. The groves, ravines, and forests, are margins that cast a reflection on its contents, and speak only of harmony and inherent affection. The valleys, plains, and beautiful gardens, abounding in all the luxuriant and immense creations of the spirit-home, are the impressed words on the leaves of this divine Book. And angels are the recipients of the instruction thereof, through which their interior powers are expanded to the glory of the Divine Mind for ever and ever. They drink at the fount of Wisdom, and walk in the fields and gardens of celestial Love. They are incessantly employed in imparting blessings to those who need, and meanwhile they receive in return the smiles and approbations of a delighted heaven. Yea, in this the angels rejoice, and give forth songs of thanksgiving and praise that ascend through all the Spheres, to be recognised by Him who spake, and all things became alive!

Such are the combined beauties of the Celestial Sphere: but what has been said concerning Nature, Man, the Second Sphere, and the Universe, is as nothing in comparison to that which might be related concerning this *one state* of spiritual existence. We have only as yet entered the *vestibule* that introduces the mind into the great Temple of divine Truth, whose foundation is in the depths of the Universe, whose immensity fills all space, and whose aspiring domes are lost in the heights of infinity! Nay, the heights, and depths, and lengths, and breadths, thereof, can be known only by its Maker and Builder, who is the Living Soul of all things. This Temple has splendor and gorgeous magnificence that no mind can conceive or appreciate save that Divine Architect who fills and animates it by the living fire of his own Love, and beautifies it by the living energies of his own Wisdom!

What has been said concerning the Third Sphere, and all previous ones, is, then, as but one particle compared to that which is, and shall for ever remain, unrelated. Expand the Universe to an extent that will outdo space, and make spheres so numerous as to defy all computation—and yet there is a Univercœlum about which not one word can be spoken, or one thought can be conceived. If all the sublimest thoughts of the inhabitants of the earth were combined, their magnitude would be naught in comparison to the extent of the beauty, greatness, and grandeur, of the celestial heaven. Nay, all thoughts, save the thoughts of that Being whom these things represent, would be as *one atom* in comparison to that which is above, beneath, and around those things of which I have spoken. The human race can not conceive of this immensity; but O! how beautiful, how pure, and how enduring, are these truths!

Yet, the restless mind of man leaves earth and soars off into the regions of the celestial spheres; it strives to familiarize itself with all the creations thereof, and brings into its employ all the mathematical skill that can be of service in marking out and mapping out the structure of the Universe; and while it is striving to comprehend these things, the thoughts expand to their utmost tension, and doubt and dread repulse it back to earth. It finds no resting-place, and returns to its narrow encasement unsatisfied. Hence, again, I say, were all thoughts of this nature that ever have been conceived by man, combined together, they would not be adequate to a comprehension of the grandeur even of the *Third Sphere* of human existence.

I perceive, then, that we have just entered the *vestibule* that leads to apartments too vast and immense to ever be described. Yet I am permitted to ascend to the FOURTH SPHERE, and observe the comparative perfection that there exists, in reference to that of the subordinate habitations. Thus I ascend to, and am immerged into, the *fourth* habitation of the spirits and angels that were once of the human race.

§ 200. I now perceive the *order* of the spheres; which is in this wise: The first Sphere is the Natural; the second is the Spiritual; the third, the Celestial; the fourth, the Supernatural; the fifth, the Superspiritual; and the sixth, the Supercelestial.

I am now permitted to speak of matters pertaining to the *Supernatural Sphere.*

In this sphere are also three societies and three distinct degrees of Love, Will, and Wisdom — each society being unfolded from the one next below.

I perceive that an incessant transition is also occurring from the Third to this Sphere, and also an as immense transferation from this to a still higher.

In this Sphere everything is still more lovely: and even here all things appear to have attained the highest possible loveliness and exaltation. So true is this, that the inhabitants of the sphere next below, in all their sparkling purity, appear even as undeveloped. The beautiful emanation that surrounds and clothes each society, is of such an intense light that it is impossible to approach it, or to search into the interiors of the inhabitants. Colors of every conceivable description surround their local habitation, each being a bright indication of purity, goodness, happiness, and wisdom. Every form and thing is constantly growing lovelier and lovelier, and every sphere more beautiful and pure. Each indicates a spiral progression, and that they are ascending nigh unto the throne of the Alpha and Omega. Each thing shows forth its own purity, and speaks its own celestial language. Each object is distinct in its proclamations, and every lesson of instruction is as a word of the Most High!

The first society is in numbers almost infinite: and from them flows spontaneously an element of love that is clearer than the clearest water, and brighter than the brightest crystal; and its reflection clothes the higher societies with a garment of whiteness pure as the jewels that adorn the crown of the King of kings and the Lord of lords.

And from the mediatorial society flows a constant stream of passive and active Will, subject at all times to the life-giving promptings of Love, and receiving the high approbations of Wisdom. This is constantly descending and ascending, as the light goeth forth from the sun to enliven the earth, and returns to he revivified.

Wisdom in this supernatural Sphere, is as a fount that is constantly springing up and flowing over all the subordinates. It is like a great receptacle in which are deposited the choicest thoughts and memories of the angels and spirits of this exalted Sphere. It is like a treasury whose contents are depositions for the lower angels, who ascend to and unlock it, and extract from its depths beautiful thoughts, and upon them ponder and meditate. They have contemplations so exceedingly immense, that the Love and Life of the Universe appear open to their thoughts, and they drink of their depths and thirst not.

In a more exalted degree I behold those *plains*—decked with life and beauty inconceivable; and over them is diffused an omniprevalent element of purity that appears as life, and by this they live and bloom in beauty.

In a different and higher degree, also, I perceive those ceaseless *streams of living water*. Their gentle flowings speak only of tranquillity and unending happiness; while the inexhaustible Fount from which they spring proclaims the constitution and infinity of the Divine Mind.

Also those undulating *valleys*, or wave-like variations, appear, presenting grandeur and loveliness indescribable. They transcend all possible conceptions of the lovely and beautiful; and their united voices sink into the recesses of the soul, yet they are silent and unheard. They are penetrating as the electric fire, yet gentle as the mountain-air. They are dignified in their tone, and are withal impressively pensive. They do not *compel*, but cause a *voluntary* submission to their undying teachings.

And again those *groves* are presented—and appear in a more exalted degree of loveliness. They are as the tree of Righteousness, budding and blossoming as the rose. They proclaim glory and honor even in their refreshing shade, and inspire the reposer therein with thoughts worthy of such a celestial home.

And the *inhabitants* are of the most exquisite purity and loveliness; and they, with one united voice—a voice that arises not from *speech*, but from *action*—proclaim glory, honor, immortality, and eternal life. They are wending their way up to the city of the living God. They are illuminating the vestibule of truth and the archway that leads to immortal life. They are pervading all below them with the holy influences of wisdom, and with the most simple love. Gentle as the unsophisticated dove, they send forth a welcome to all below their exalted state; and with a kind, peaceful, and inviting smile, they call all to come away, and go with them to the Fount of purity on high!

The *atmosphere* of this spirit-home is rainbowed and clothed with resplendent brightness, such as reflects the goodness of all things, and the use to which they are applied. Yea, it is a mirror in which are represented the living beauties of heaven and earth—even of all things beneath this exalted state of perfection.

Such is the loveliness, goodness, and wisdom of the Divine Mind, that nothing is made in vain; but everything is as a living thought, and every thought is as a representative of perfect Wisdom. Everything is thus admired, appreciated, and applied, in every degree of material and spiritual existence; and in this Supernatural Sphere this truth is especially and perfectly manifested.

---

§ 201. Inasmuch as life is universal, death can not mar the divine constitution of things; and by virtue of this, the inhabitants of the Fourth Sphere, like those of others, repose for a moment in silence, and awake as beings of the FIFTH SPHERE or *Superspiritual* habitation. And by and through this process, I am enabled to behold the vast possessions of the fifth department of the great Temple of Truth.

It is almost impossible to approach, yet I draw nigh and behold with humility the extended landscape and living happiness, which are here so exceedingly enchanting, that all I have previously beheld appears clouded with comparative imperfection. The vast landscape of this spiritual habitation is reflected on the perceptions of my spirit with an impressiveness that renders all speech inadequate to express the beauties thereof.

The first society, as in the third and fourth Spheres, is a child of the highest society in the Sphere below. And here Love, Will, and Wisdom, present a more attractive loveliness. Love appears as the perfection of Wisdom, while Wisdom appears greater and more extensive than all the Love and Wisdom heretofore described, combined.

And it is well to relate, that as the Spheres approach the Divine Mind, they become more simple, more lovely, more unassuming, and more pure. The nearer they approach the Fount of purity, the more transparent they become, and the more do their inhabitants appear to exist as it were without body and without external and artificial habiliments. They appear unclothed, and eminently purified.

There is an exhalation from each society that forms an encompassing halo of glory, which surpasses all brightness of the material sun and all brilliancy that illuminates any portion of the material Universe.

Each spirit seems so pure, and the thoughts of all seem so celestial, that it is almost impossible to resist the attraction thus presented. There is such a commingling of thoughts, and such an affection manifested for each other, as seems beyond all captivations imaginable. Every mind is like an opening flower, and every thought is like the fragrance thereof. Every love is like a bud, and its expression is like the rose. Their wisdom is as the fountains of heaven which dry not, and which perpetually flow to all that thirst, and heal all that are wounded, and cleanse all that are not purified. I behold their Wisdom in every thought, in every movement, and in every expression of Will and Love. It is indeed beautiful!—and what is to be lamented is, that language must be employed to speak of that which defieth utterance. O may expressive silence breathe forth an eloquence that will penetrate the souls of men, and duly elevate their understandings; and may they be induced to abandon expression where speech is vain, and extend their conceptions to the bright spheres of everlasting love!

Here, in the Superspiritual Sphere, the scenery possesses a redoubled grandeur and loveliness. Still more perceptibly are the thoughts of the Divine Mind impressed on all created things. The plains, and valleys, and groves, and streams of living water, are all instrumental in the great work of purification and refinement. They are all bright representatives of spiritual industry and universal love, and are also living advocates of the perfection of Him who breathed them and all living creations into being.

The spirits here are so lovely and attractive, that it requires an effort to prevent being, as it were, absorbed into and becoming a part of them. Here I perceive another truth vividly manifested, and that is, that all things possess mutual affinities, and that things differ only as to degrees and states of development. Thus is established, what has been before declared, that opposites or antagonistic principles can not exist; that all things were created and are animated by one living Essence; and that it is injustice to the character of that Divine Essence for men on earth to say or believe that there is a principle or habitation existing opposed to the general happiness, or to that celestial purity which joins in one all created things.

This Sphere is so closely allied to the Spiritual Sun, that it becomes incomprehensible to the inhabitants of the earth—whose sphere of existence is nothing more than one atom in the great Body of material and spiritual constructions.

§ 202. As has been related of the transition of the spirits and angels of the Spheres below, so do those of the Fifth Sphere ascend to, and become inhabitants of the SIXTH, or the *Supercelestial* habitation.

Here is the consummation of all conceivable perfection! Here is the sublimation of all purity, of all goodness, and of all refinement, as appertaining to the spirits of every human race in the Universe. All spirits and angels are of the human races, and these occupy earths innumerable, from which they ascend through all the Spheres to this, the Supercelestial habitation. Here they have combined all the perfections that have been uniformly unfolding while passing through the ascending Spheres or stages of eternal progression. This Sphere is the great ultimate of all beauty, and the crown of all loveliness and purity. Yea, it is the highest point of angelic loveliness.

Countless millions dwell in each society in each Sphere—more than numbers can express. Yet the combined numbers dwelling in all subordinate Spheres would not form any comparison with *one half* of *one* society that dwells in this supercelestial home! How inconceivable, therefore, must be the immensity of each society in this Sphere, inasmuch as the *half* of *one* society comprises more individuals than all the created forms that animate all the subordinate Spheres of universal space! Yet creation has *just begun*: Love is just born, Will is just conceived, and Wisdom is in the germ yet undeveloped!

Here are the fields of Paradise; and on them is erected the house of many mansions. Interior splendor and gorgeousness is penetrating to all the spirits and angels thereof, and shines through them with a brilliancy of celestial light, as the light of the Divine Mind penetrates his whole material Structure. And the exterior beauty, grandeur, and magnificence of this celestial mansion, express in unequivocal language that it was not made by hands, yet is eternal in the heavens. It is the great Asylum where all are taken in, and loved, and breathed upon, and made perfect. It is the home of all celestial things.

All things are divine, both in the material and spiritual Universe; and all become celestial. So every created spirit is invited by the progressive law of the Father to its home; and when it enters and becomes sensible of the loveliness and purity thereof, it glorifies the Father, not in prayer, but by *thought* and *deed* for ever and ever. Each one, then, is an undying child of the Eternal One, who is the Father of all: and no one is so low but that it is the highest of some still lower, and no one is so high but that it is the lowest of some yet undeveloped. One spirit can not say unto another, " I need thee not;" for each one is the sustainer of another, and the mutual dependence constitutes the harmony and wisdom of all things.

In this Supercelestial home are all the beauties of earth and heaven combined, developed, and perfected. It is thus removed from human comprehension, and it can not therefore with profit be dwelt upon, or impressed on the memory for meditation. Notwithstanding what might be said concerning it are legitimate truths, they are too high and refined to be comprehended by the human race—nay, even by those in the *Third Sphere* of wisdom and knowledge. No one can say with propriety, " Why not tell us all ?" if he will but consider his incompetency to comprehend that which has already been related.

The brightness in this state of celestial purity exceeds all conception—and the elegance, majesty, power, grandeur, goodness, and happiness, transcend all human thought. And here spirits and angels rejoice with exceeding joy and thanksgiving : and this by *action*, and not by speech—by *Wisdom*, and not by Love. Still Love is the all-animating and life-giving element.

Such, then, is the immensity of these things, and such the greatness and glory of the Supercelestial habitation. And it is proper not to confide in that which is opposed to this high degree of angelic purity, but to encourage hope when born of Wisdom, and belief when well conceived; and then those things will descend to and illuminate the human mind, and give eternal life to that which now seems mortal and changeable.

§ 203. From the position now occupied I can perceive, and in a degree comprehend, the SEVENTH SPHERE, or the Infinite Vortex of Love and Wisdom, and the great Spiritual Sun of the Divine Mind that illuminates all the spiritual worlds.—And behold, the natural sun is the sun of the *natural* Universe, while the Spiritual Sun was and is the Sun of the *spiritual* Universe! The *material* can only illuminate the *natural*, and the spiritual illuminates the spiritual. Of the Body and constitution of the material sun, the Univercœlum was born into being, and caressed, nourished, illuminated, and perfected, in universal order and harmony. From the constitution of the Spiritual Sun, all the *heavens* were created; and by it they are sustained, controlled, purified, perfected, and illuminated: and every spontaneous breath of light and love is as a smile of the all-pervading Father and Creator of all that is, and of all that is not, developed.

Thus the Spiritual Spheres are allied to the Spiritual Sun, while the natural spheres approach the material sun. Thus the spiritual is as a soul, and yet a garment, to the natural, while the two are joined together as one creation. And the *second* or Spiritual Sphere sustains a relation to the fifth Circle of Suns, and their innumerable planets — and is as a soul to it, and comprehends the whole as one creation. So the third Sphere is allied to the fourth Circle; and the fourth Sphere to the third Circle; and the fifth Sphere to the second Circle; and the sixth Sphere to the first Circle: and the SEVENTH SPHERE is the Great Sun and Centre of all power, and the Vortex of all creations!

This displays the order and harmony of the Divine Mind, and this is one Body of one Immortal SOUL!*

Much might be said of the Seventh Sphere, or the Spiritual Sun of the Universe — yet all would be inconsistent with the order and power of the human mind. For speech is vain, and all that might be said of the incomprehensibility, the magnitude, and the infinitude of the truth centred in the Spiritual Sun, would consist only of *words;* and these it would be useless to speak and impress upon the human mind. Neither would it be proper to speak of the essences, qualities, and attributes, dwelling within the Vortex from which rolled forth the Universe, inasmuch as each possible atom comprehends more than the human mind is able to grasp. More, then, would be superfluous and unprofitable. For the word "*incomprehensible*" falls far short of conveying a definite idea of the immensity thereof; and

---

* On the next morning after the above was delivered, the clairvoyant was thrown into the abnormal state for the purpose of examining some patients who were under his medical treatment: but after the manipulations were completed, he remained motionless and speechless for some fifteen minutes, when, in a faint whisper, he uttered the words "It is painful." He was then speedily restored to the normal condition. At the close of the subsequent lecture he alluded to this circumstance, and said that owing to the excitement remaining on his mind from the previous lecture, his mind was, on the occasion referred to, elevated to such close proximity to the Sphere of the Spiritual Sun, that the light was beyond endurance; and that had he not been quickly relieved from his condition, his faculties would have been for a time deranged.

even this word implies the impossibility of human understanding. This much only can be said: It is an inexhaustible Vortex of Life and Light which are Love, and of Order and Form which are Wisdom — which flow not only into Heaven, but into the material Universe: and everything is thereby breathed into being. And the Great Centre and Spiritual Sun is the habitation and throne of the Divine Mind, the Great Positive, Central Power of the Universe, and of all eternal movement! And it is a Fountain in which nothing exists but what is pure, divine, everlasting, and infinite!

---

§ 204. The natural Universe corresponds to the spiritual; and one is related to the other as intimately as the body is to the soul. For every spiritual Sphere is the creator, sustainer, and pervader, of a natural Sphere; and this order is preserved in every department of creation.

A mind was sufficiently illuminated to have an actual knowledge of the relation and affinity existing between the natural and spiritual Spheres, and of the Spheres to one another, and this was Emanuel Swedenborg. He, however, employed terms to express the same things that I have endeavored to impress by terms of a different and more congenial character. He put forth the truth that there were different degrees of goodness, and that the lowest was so imperfect when compared with the highest, that the one seemed evil and the other good; the one perfect and the other imperfect. Hence he describes the first three Spheres as three *hells*, inhabited by lower spirits and angels; while the three higher Spheres were the three heavens in which the higher spirits and angels dwelt. He represented the first Spheres as being under the disapprobation of the all-wise Judge, yet as being loved with an unfailing affection — while the higher Spheres were near the Great Spiritual Sun, and their inhabitants dwelt under the smile of Divine approval. And he also related the truth that the inhabitants of these Spheres could not approach each other, because of the dissimilitude in their positions and degrees of refinement — any more than evil can approach goodness, or darkness can approach light.

All this, I can affirm, is true, not in the *absolute*, but rather in the *comparative* sense. There is a seeming difference between the lower and the higher in all things; yet the highest, as has been proved, is an unfolded representative of what the lowest has in substance, undeveloped. It is, then, the use of *terms*, and their particular application, that presents the apparent discrepancy existing between his relations and these. And I can with assurance affirm, that the conceptions are the same in substance, and *true* — as is demonstrated by the order and harmony of all visible things; and that a unity of thought has arisen, by independent processes, from no other cause than the influxations of the truths of visible and invisible Nature. From this, as a common source, and from an illumination of the same, has the relation of each been derived; and the two accounts from this cause mutually substantiate each other. Concerning this, then, I say no more.

§ 205. The spirits of the various planets in our solar system are in different stages of refinement. And those that are on the higher have the privilege of descending to the lower planets, and immersing their thoughts into the spirits of the inhabitants at will, though the latter in many cases know it not. In this manner do spirits descend to, and dwell on, the earth, when they have a peculiar attraction to some relative or friend; and they are ever ready to introduce into his mind thoughts of higher things, and suggestions that are pure, though these may seem to the person to flow independently from the workings of his own spirit. Spirits from any sphere may, *by permission*, descend to any earth in the Universe, and breathe sentiments into the minds of others which are pure and elevating. Hence it is that there are times when the mind appears to travel in the company of those it knows not, and has visions in its dreams that are actually true, and sometimes come to pass with remarkable accuracy. At other times, dreams are incited by the influx of thoughts from spirits, but are not *defined*, because they are not duly directed. There is, however, a species of dreaming which is uncaused by anything except an excitement of the nervous medium or consciousness of the body. Such dreams are only unquieted thoughts, and wild and fantastic formations of thoughts pre-impressed into visions and fancies.

It is a truth that spirits commune with one another while one is in the body and the other in the higher Spheres — and this, too, when the person in the body is unconscious of the influx, and hence can not be convinced of the fact; and this truth will ere long present itself in the form of a living demonstration. And the world will hail with delight the ushering in of that era when the interiors of men will be opened, and the spiritual communion will be established such as is now being enjoyed by the inhabitants of Mars, Jupiter, and Saturn, because of their superior refinement. Concerning these things and their details, a knowledge can be had by perusing the relations made by Swedenborg during the period of his mental illumination.

---

§ 206. The structure of the Universe is now presented to the mind, and all its living beauties, together with the Divine Essence that gives it life and animation. It presents an indestructible basis of hope and faith, and a corresponding foundation of human action. It is as a mirror in which are reflected all corresponding beauties yet uncreated, but proved to be in embryo by the universal teachings of natural law. The whole is BEAUTIFUL. The whole is as ONE BODY, and GOD the SOUL and FATHER of all living and unliving things. Everything is perfect in its way and state of being. Everything is necessary — even *indispensable*. Everything is pure, even divine and celestial. Everything teaches harmony, and universal reciprocation by an unfailing manifestation of the same. Everything is of, in, through, and to, the Divine Mind. All things are parts of Him; and these are as one Whole, even Nature, Man, and Heaven.

The earths, or the first Sphere, constitute the germ; the second Sphere is the roots; the third, the body; the fourth, the branches; the fifth, the buds; the sixth, the blossom; and the seventh is BEAUTY — beauty that blooms with an immortal fragrance. Here is the Tree of *Righteousness* — righteousness because all is right and nothing wrong. It is the Tree of *Goodness* — because nothing is evil. It is the Tree of immortal *Life* — because there is no death. It is the Tree of divine *Perfection* — because there is nothing imperfect. It is the Tree of *Truth* — because there is no falsehood in the divine creations. It is the Tree of eternal *Causation* — because nothing *is* but what was in another form before. It is the Tree of *Love* and *Wisdom* — because there is no confusion or disunity; for all things are working together for good, and that good is the elevation of all low and undeveloped things to a high degree of refinement from which a Universe yet unborn will be ushered into being to breathe the breath of heaven.

Here, then, is the Tree whose foundation rests in the depths of Time, and whose top extends to the heights of Eternity. It puts forth branches throughout the lengths and breadths of the Universe, and casts a refreshing shade over the labyrinths of space whose limits no thought can define.

Further contemplations upon these inconceivable creations would be taxing the mind beyond its powers of thought, and would not tend to usefulness. Yet a word fitly spoken, by way of admonition, may not lose its influence until some of the most desirable results are accomplished. Remember, then, that the *germ* of this great Tree is in the *First Sphere*, which comprehends all earths and their inhabitants. Knowing this, let every one strive diligently to cultivate the germ, and to make perfect its unfoldings. Strive to give its properties and essences a proper and truthful direction. Put forth all love, and energy, and wisdom, to effect that which is most desirable — that, the principles of which are found in the nature of all men, and that which prompts them to profitable action; and, remember, that is UNITY : and unity is HAPPINESS.

In view of these things, the importance and truthfulness of the saying is manifested, that " The things which are seen are temporal; but the things which are not seen are eternal :" and, also, that the things which are visible are terrestrial; while the things which are invisible are heavenly. While these truths present themselves in bold relief, the human mind should put forth efforts to comprehend their signification and importance. In doing this, mankind will discover that the mind must be *refined and perfected*, and that when this is properly accomplished, the social world will be correspondingly elevated, and thus be advanced to honor, goodness, and UNIVERSAL PEACE.

END OF THE SECOND PART.

PART III.

THE APPLICATION;

OR,

A VOICE TO MANKIND.

THE HUMAN RACE is composed of *three distinct parts, classes,* or *societies.* The poor, ignorant, enslaved, oppressed, and working classes, constitute the *lower stratum* of society. The semi-wealthy, learned, enslavers, oppressors, and dictating classes, form the *second* or *transition stratum;* and the rich, intelligent, enslaving, oppressing, and idle classes, form the *third stratum,* and serve to complete the body of Mankind.

The *poor* are distributed among all the nations of the earth, They are those who are born amid circumstances opposed to their nature and its requirements. They are those who have necessities unsupplied, desires ungratified, and affections uncared for. They are the degraded, the down-trodden, the forsaken and unappreciated of the land. They are the despised, the weak, the wretched, and the repulsed, of all others that compose the human race. Inferior circumstances produce inferior effects; hence the poor are also ignorant. And because they are uneducated, they are the more easily chained in the degrading shackles of superstition, and enslaved by laws imposed by government. They are imbecile, and hence are fit subjects to bear the burden and weight of the upper classes; and feeling impressed that they are performing their duty, they submit to arbitrary and tyrannical government.

Inferior circumstances not only create these effects, but also *slavery*. Millions that belong to the first part of the race, are existing under the most oppressive slavery, and are compelled to do honor to those who oppress them. Their thoughts are restricted, and their innate powers are crushed by those who hold them in bondage for the purpose of perpetuating the darkness of degradation to which they are subject. They are also sorely afflicted, and with the most inhuman and unnatural afflictions. The symmetry of their forms is marred; the constitutional qualities of their being are obstructed in their proper development; and their spiritual faculties are clouded from birth to the grave by vice, misery, superstition, and all manner of impositions possible

The poor are thus oppressed (yet the oppressed are not always poor); and oppression is a protective policy employed by those occupying a higher position in the scale of social circumstances.

The poor are also the *laboring* and *productive* classes. The wealth of the world has been accumulated by the incessant toil of those who are compelled by the hand of oppression to work constantly to gain a subsistence: and yet their labor is not duly rewarded. In every portion of the world it is a general fact that he who labors the most, receives the least in return. And the more laborious the thing in which men engage, the more are they enslaved, degraded, and unrewarded.

The poor are the *sustainers*, because they are the *industrious*. They are the producers of wealth, and of all the blessings that circulate through other and higher societies; and yet they are the forgotten, the despised, and the uneducated!

Poverty is such a universal affliction, that many are led to believe that it is a means ordered in the providence of things for the purpose of causing a submissiveness in the nature of man whereby he may receive ultimate reward and consolation. Some men are striving to console the poor by these deceptive prospects; and such being impelled by interest, are anxious to have such an opinion prevail among them, so that poverty and ignorance may be perpetuated, and that thereby the permanency of their despotic and tyrannical control may be secured. In every portion of the earth the poor are uncared for, and their circumstances are very seldom relieved. Still they are the foundation of all that blesses the human race, and of all which mankind enjoy.

The *semi-wealthy* are those who are situated amid *superior circum-*

stances; and being thus situated from birth to death, they become the *mediatorial* classes, learned in every department of art and agriculture. These are the direct employers and governors of the lower classes. They exert a continual influence on those in their employ, and press them to labor not agreeable to the constitution of man, and for this labor give them little reward. The mediatorial class thus enslave and oppress those beneath them. They are compelled to do this by an *interest* which actuates all their movements; and they are thus afflicting those striving for a subsistence, because their welfare and all their interests consist in a vast amount of labor and little reward. They are exceedingly oppressive, because society is so constituted that the interest of every man is in direct *opposition* to the interests of others: and thus what is one man's interest results in another's misfortune.

The *higher* class are the *wealthy* and *powerful* — holding within their grasp the productions of those beneath them, and distributing happiness only as it is extracted from them by the unceasing calls of those who are oppressed and degraded. They are the *capitalists;* for the wealth which the poor create is accumulated by them, and held within their grasp. Wealth that rightly belongs to those who create it, is thus given to those who earned it not, and hence have no natural title to it.

The higher classes are those who rest upon the toil and labor of the mass of mankind. They are thus both enslaving and oppressing, because of their dependence and yet their controlling influence, which is both unjust and destructive to the peace and happiness that otherwise would be enjoyed by the lower classes of community. They are the *enlightened;* for being situated amid superior circumstances, they have the advantage of all superior attainments and superficial accomplishments existing in the world. This intelligence is the only pledge for the world's ultimate amelioration from vice, misery, and degradation. But this intelligence is at present improperly directed; and instead of illuminating the mass of mankind, it is shrouding the whole race with bigotry, superstition, and prejudice! It is making more ignorant those classes which are ignorant, and confirming them in their low and unfortunate situations. Meanwhile it is dividing the human family into sects and exclusive classes, and is also creating every species of disunity and dissatisfaction.

The *poor* and *moderate* classes are not the governing, but the governed. They are not the enslavers, but the enslaved. They are not *in themselves* the impure and unsanctified, but are *made* so by those above them. They are not the unfortunately constituted, but become weak and deformed by the burden of the responsibility universally imposed upon them.

The wealthy being the *powerful*, from them flow all arbitration, oppression, and absolute misery, that prevail in the world. It is from this class that exclusiveness and sectarianism take their rise, and flow like an ocean-tide over all the classes beneath them.

The rich, as to their *favorable situations*, are examples of what the *Race* will be, when equal wealth and equal justice pervade the social world. *Intelligence* will then be the governor and administrator of all laws and principles required by the constitution of the human family. Then all may drink at the fount of Knowledge, and thirst not. But owing to the disunity that prevails in society, the wants of the lower classes are not supplied, and the desires of those in the higher classes are supplied with such a profusion, that they are unable to appreciate the blessings of life, and the natural enjoyments flowing from a well-ordered desire and its adequate gratification.

These three classes constitute the Human Race; and each of them will exist in its present condition so long as intelligence is exclusive, labor is unrewarded, and wealth is possessed by those who have it unjustly.

---

§ 2. The poor are those who have desires unsupplied. Thus they are rendered miserable, and their existence is entirely unappreciated. They are those who have all the pressure and the afflictions of the race; and by their ignorance they are compelled to remain thus situated. They can not set forth with moving eloquence the vice and misery that prevail among them; they can not free themselves from the shackles which bind and crush them to the earth. They can not escape the prison of sectarianism, nor raise their voice against the many inhuman proceedings that are instituted against them. The poor lie at the lowest point in society, and are therefore sustaining, by their perpetual industry, the great weight of the world that rests upon them. They have no means to extricate themselves, or to advance where everything opposes their progress and arrests their ascension. They can not accumulate force and power of themselves, because each person is striving for a subsistence, and laboring to supply his increasing wants. *General* power is thus lost and dissipated among *individuals;* which prevents them from acting as a *body* to ameliorate their condition.

The highest society exists as if they were not in possession of feeling and affection for what is just, and good, and righteous. They seem to be unconscious of sympathy, and unable to discern the *cause* of the evil and misery that prevail. They are *seemingly* striving to benefit all; yet in that which appears to benefit most, a greater injury is done to the working-classes. And every *isolated* act of benevolence, though *meant* for good, ends in affliction; and every effort toward amelioration creates sectarian hostility, and terminates in depression of the most tyrannical character!

Society is thus constructed. It will preserve its structure in *form* for ever; but its constitutional developments will change ere long, materially — the result of which will be distributive justice and harmony.

The cause of all human action is centred in these three things: *Love* (or desire), *Necessity*, and *Interest*. *Desires* are created by the *love*, or bodily requirements. *Necessity* is the desire ungratified, or the requirement unsupplied; and *Interest* is the spring of action, and is a means by which love is rewarded, by which desires are gratified, and necessities supplied.

Interest, then, is the *mode* of human action, and is the ultimate cause of all industry, all invention, all movement, and intelligence, in the world. Interest is the means employed to supply the necessities of the human body. Where there is no interest, there can be no action; where there is no desire, there can be no interest; and where there is no love, there can be no desire.

It is impossible for a man to act without an *interest*. His interest may consist in self-gratification or emolument; in sectarian advancement; in local usurpation; in general benevolence, brotherly kindness, and charity; in universal love, or in the attainment of knowledge. But in whatever thing his interest is centred, for that will he act alone; and while thus acting, he will, as society now exists, injure some and benefit others, please some and excite indignation in others. — And thus it is that interests (being the cause of human action) will, if not directed aright, produce unhappy consequences.

The interests of the *poor* consist in rendering themselves and their families happy. To this end they exert all their abilities to extract from the earth, and absorb from the higher societies, a sufficient reward for their labor. Their interests are opposed to the interests of those who employ them; and this creates an antagonism between the laborer and him for whom he labors. One is diametrically opposed to the other. Thus it is that while industry becomes fatiguing and disgusting to the laborer, the employer is pressing him to more and heavier action, and meanwhile reduces his reward to the lowest possible amount. The laborer is thus discouraged from laboring cheerfully, and the employer is discouraged from rewarding abundantly. The interest of the laborer consists in the *reward;* the interest of the employer consists in the *amount of labor* accomplished: therefore one is absorbing from the other; and the absorption creates distinction, obstruction, and disunity. They are thus existing in direct opposition to each other.

Thus labor is despised and shunned by the human family, because it is unappreciated. Hence *poverty* pervades the world; and this is perpetuated by disunity of interests and a want of sympathizing feelings and affections between man and man. The poor have no regard for the situation of the rich, nor the rich for that of the poor; and they thus despise and repulse each other. The unfortunate circumstances that surround and embarrass the poor from birth, encourage the monopolies of the higher classes, and the interests of the latter consist in the distinction thus created. It thus becomes impossible to discover harmony between the interests of the poor and rich, or affinity between their respective situations.

Men may have their *judgment* convinced of what is their *duty;* yet their *interests* consist in that to which their duty is *opposed*. Hence the world is immoral and disorganized. It is proper that all should be so situated as that industry may become a *necessity*, and that its reward may be legitimate and proportional.

If universal industry existed, all would be wealthy, and all would appreciate and glorify their existence. Neither would there be so much labor needed; for a little labor, if properly directed, would contribute more to the general wealth of the world than twice the same amount in the present condition of the human race. *One third* of the present amount of individual labor, if equally distributed and rendered profitable, would contribute more to the happiness and wealth of mankind than the amount of individual labor now performed; and then rewards would be equal, interests reciprocal, and all action universally beneficial. As interests now are opposed to each other, all action of laborer and employer must necessarily be in corresponding opposition. Hostility is constantly being generated by the disaffection for each other's welfare, arising from this cause. Every one has desires uncared for by others, and necessities which none but himself knows, and for the relief of which no one but himself provides. The provision is *extracted from*, not *freely given*, as it ought to be, by others, or the body of the human race. Thus one's interest consists in that for which no other has an affinity.

And so conflicting are the situations of men in the lower strata of society, that there is nothing but vice, misery, discontent, hostility, and retaliation, existing. Their interests are like conflicting elements, which in meeting, destroy each other's power. Hence the harmony that would exist, if interests ran gently into each other, is dissipated. Hence he is immorally situated whose duty tells him one thing and his interests another.

§ 3. The laborer, feeling an interest in the amount of reward given for his toil, has no interest in the general improvements in *machinery* that are made to relieve and curtail labor. Labor must be appreciated and duly remunerated, before there can be either a pleasure in industry, or a general interest taken in mechanical and agricultural improvements. That inactivity may be repulsed from the earth, industry must command increased rewards. There must not only be a higher value set on industry, but a higher regard must be manifested to him who labors, in order to make all feel an interest in activity, and that no one may feel an attraction to idleness and speculation. The laboring-classes support those who are idle, and the idle in return despise and oppress those who labor, because their interest is not in industry, but in unfeeling speculation.

The interest of the laborer should consist in the thing on which he is employed. Then he would press onward in his physical and mental exertions to improvements of the most valuable character, such as would not only ameliorate his own condition, but would send forth a blessing over the whole world. As things are now existing, the laborer feels an interest in the *reward* only, and not in the employment itself. Therefore labor is disgusting and tiresome, while its reward alone actuates the worker; and thus the proper development of his physical and intellectual powers is discouraged and obstructed. The laborer feels no interest in the advancement of his employer's interest, but merely in the amount of reward he may extract from him, and which is necessary to his subsistence. He who employs feels no interest in the poor and their necessities, but exerts his power and ingenuity to press the laborer to every possible extreme, and then remunerates him agreeably to his own interests. The employer does not reward the laborer because he feels an interest in his and his family's welfare. On the other hand, after compelling him to labor excessively, he pays him only as a man would feed his herds at night. Nay, the classes who speculate upon the poor and the oppressed, in many instances do not scruple to force them from their families at an hour which all the laws of the human system have appropriated to rest, into the field of labor or the workshop of toil, and after compelling them to work without cessation until their energies are exhausted, reward them as their own power and interest may dictate — even as a man would drive a mule from his stable, oppress him with heavy burdens during the day, and at night requite his labor, and hunger, and prostration, in proportion to the amount of food he has garnered up for all his extensive herds.

The poor are thus oppressed, and the laborer is thus not justly rewarded. They not only have no interest in mechanical improvements, but have none in the cultivation of their own powers; for all their physical energies are concentrated, day after day, on gaining a subsistence, and their mental powers are circumscribed to the limited circle of their degraded occupation.

Men should be rewarded in proportion to the *amount of labor* they accomplish, and then they would feel an interest in *industry*, and not merely in its *reward*. At present, however, he who labors most and suffers the most oppression, receives the least reward; he who is idle and subsists upon the labor of others, is both abundantly rewarded, and extensively appreciated for supposed goodness and virtue.

It is true that virtue exists only where vice is not; and it is, moreover, true that he who is idle, is necessarily *vicious* — and is no more than an unnecessary particle (or person) in the constitution of the human family. Such a one is an excrescence to society, and is an injury to the welfare and happiness of the laboring and industrious. Nothing can be more injurious to the human race than an inactive population, or a class of persons who despise, and yet subsist and speculate upon, the labor of others — of those who are degraded.

The beehive of industry typifies what the race should and will be. In the economy of the beehive, one thing is particularly to be remarked: and that is, that every inactive bee is considered a drone to the community, and therefore all interest and affection are withdrawn from it; and they all decide that the bee is thus an injury to the welfare of the whole, and that it must be cast from their midst for ever. Every bee is obliged to contribute its share to the wealth and elevation of the whole mass; and they are taught to feel an instinctive affection for the universal welfare. And having their interests thus centred, nothing can thwart their activity for the benefit of each other and the whole; nothing can prevent the accumulation of wealth, or destroy the happiness which they universally enjoy. Here, then, the philosophy of social harmony is represented; and all that is necessary for the human family to do, is to adopt a corresponding system.

Poverty is necessity unsupplied; and therefore this indicates disease in the organization of society.—For if all men were properly situated, want would not exist in any *part*, while an abundance belongs to the body as a *whole:* and absorption would not exist while every one created his *own* happiness and meanwhile the happiness of *others*.

Vice, degradation, necessity, and misery, pervade society only because there is no unity in the interests and movements of men. He who has a family to support, seeks to serve some person who may give him a reward adequate to his wants. But if there is no sympathy extended to his necessities, he drowns his crushed feelings and his domestic embarrassments in the depths of intoxication. He goes to every extreme in this vice for no other purpose than to sear his sympathies against the cries of his children, and his sensibilities to the supplications of his wife! He becomes unnerved and incapable of laboring, even if labor is procured; and anticipating a most wretched dejection in his own family, he lays his hands on the possessions of others, and ingeniously conveys something to his family. Thus a *theft* is committed; and now the community is for the first time aware that such a miserable being existed! They appeal to conventional laws, investigate his case, and employ unfeeling magistrates to seal his imprisonment. No one feels an interest in his welfare; but all are pleased at his capture, condemnation, and repulsion from the bosom of society, and the light of the sun that smiles on all, that all may be happy!

Not long from this and a family is thrown upon the institutions, destitute of all bodily requirements, physical strength, and mental energy. The children are situated among circumstances of the most vitiating and corrupting character. The mother is unable to perform her duty toward them, and they are led into the paths of vice, ignorance, and prostitution. Nay, every invention is sought out by them to relieve their immediate wants, and improve their external condition. Under various circumstances, those children advance to maturity, and are then thrown upon society to find employment by which they may live, if they are fortunate and successful in their movements. It may be that some one of them will advance to a position tending to unfold the physical and mental powers, and such a one may bring forth living evidence of innate genius and magnanimity of soul.

Another one may seek domestic labor, but being incapacitated, is unsuccessful, becomes disheartened, and is cast out by the employer, uncared for, upon the disunited and conflicting world! This one will flee for refuge into the paths of vice and misery — will seek shelter where no human being should lie, and drown all sensibilities in the abundance of vice into which he or she is immersed — and perhaps end where the father did, a dishonor to society, and an outrage to the moral sensibilities of the human race!

Another may be situated differently, but still where influences are corrupting and opposed to the proper direction of the faculties. This one may be selfish, ferocious, and barbarous in the extreme — even to the destruction of a fellow-being's life — and finally swing before the gazing world as a *representation* of its *own corruption, ignorance,* and *fanaticism!*

Another one, being a female, and because of unfavorable birth being despised, may seek seclusion from the scoffs of an unfeeling world in the sinks of iniquity and prostitution — and there live as a representative of social disunity, discord, degradation, and conflicting individual interests.

Here, then, is a family unknown to the world, until some one of them, pressed by poverty, commits a depredation; and then the community takes an interest, not in the *unfortunate*, but in him who loses for the benefit of that desolated family! Then one member after another becomes known and *despised!* Every innate energy is crushed by the withering frowns of the social world! Every pure aspiration is pressed back upon the soul, because it needs an atmosphere of light, liberty, and social happiness. The light of genius is clouded by the inferior circumstances surrounding and obstructing its development. Nay, every pure and innate quality of the human soul is arrested in its growth, because society smiles not on its tenderness, nourishes not its roots, and assists not, by superior circumstances, its growth. Everything tends to darken the sun of vivacity and future prospect; and where the light and heat of this dwell not, the human soul can not bud and blossom, for its soil is barren and uncongenial!

§ 4. Interests are thus mutually opposed; and the effects of the opposition are the evil and misery that prevail in the world. No man would be evil in action if he had not an *interest* in being so. No man would touch the wine-cup were it not to gratify some unhealthy desire, created by influences and situations in which men are often existing. No man would defraud his neighbor and plunder his possessions, if all wants were supplied and desires gratified. No man would injure or destroy the life of his neighbor, were it not to accomplish some end, being actuated by a necessity unknown to community. Neither would man injure his neighbor, if his interests consisted in his neighbor's welfare. No man would deceive or falsify, if his interests consisted in honesty and unrestricted benevolence. Finally, no man or woman in the human race would do an unholy deed, if their interests consisted in the interest of the *whole*, so as to comprehend both individual and universal happiness.

Community are aware of all unholy deeds *when* they are committed; and they manifest no sympathy toward the unfortunate perpetrator, but have an interest in his condemnation and imprisonment. If society felt an interest in the welfare of its individuals, then men would not be in situations that are vitiating, but would be placed amid superior circumstances, and thus benefited and rendered useful to the requirements of the community at large.

All these evils arise from this one fact—that labor is unrewarded and unappreciated; and hence that labor is disgusting to him who is compelled to perform it, and absolutely abhorred by those who subsist on the industry of the poor and oppressed. No interest is felt in labor itself, but merely in its emoluments. No interest is exercised for the general good, but all interests are isolated, corrupting, enslaving, and disorganizing. No interest is centred in the general advancement and happiness of the race, but merely in individual acquisitions of wealth, and power, and aristocratic rank. No interest is felt in the condition of those who are unhappily situated from birth to the grave, but everything is against the cultivation of their powers, the enjoyment of their existence, and the profitableness and utility of their lives. No interest is exercised in behalf of those who are unable to assist themselves and enjoy the rightful blessings of life; but all are striving to advance to individual power, and honor, and emolument — are even willing to exert a commanding influence over those who are depressed and unable to resist the tyrannical domination thus exercised over them. No interest is universal, but all are isolated, individual, and corrupting: and all this is existing because labor is not appreciated as a universal blessing, and esteemed in proportion to its tendency to elevate the human race.

The laborer is entitled to something more than arising at daybreak, going forth into the field and toiling till dark, and then returning to his couch of straw, and awaking again with body prostrated and suffering with hunger. Industry is entitled to more than this; for activity is the wealth of the world, and the use and destiny of man. Yet it is a truth that in various portions of the world, laborers are confined to the meanest subsistence, and their bodies are sacrificed to the enslaving and degrading speculations of idle men. They are forced almost from their cradles to the plantation or the manufacturing establishment, and are compelled to work as long as sunlight will permit, then to return to their desolate homes fatigued and unrewarded! While they are obliged to lead a life like this, those subsisting upon their labors pass on regardless of the destitution spread before them.

Interests are so conflicting, that men sacrifice their real dignity of character and moral worth, by engaging in every species of fraud, imposition, and cruel speculation — and that, too, as practised upon a multitude of uneducated beings who are confined to labor of the most oppressive character, both in the field and in the workshop. He who, by the workings of social circumstances, happens to be born where this oppression and slavery exists, knows no use of his own being, nor of the enjoyments to which he is entitled by Nature and her extensive provisions.

In the various countries and kingdoms of the earth, monarchical governments and exclusive and arbitrary laws are instituted as a protective policy and safeguard to aristocracy and despotism. And they are also as walls, defending the accumulated wealth of idlers against absorptions by the poor within their dominions. Every kingdom, with all its wealth, owes its birth to the incessant industry of the injured and unrewarded poor. The most stately lord is nothing more than a drone, supported by those compelled to till the soil and bring forth its wealth and excellences.—And while the land is burdened with lords and inactive men, the poor *must* be degraded and deprived of their just dues; and where such useless materials exist, vice, poverty, and wretchedness, will also dwell. These latter are unfailing representatives of indolence, lordly aristocracy, and despotic governments. Where suffering most exists, there the burden of idle and useless materials is. And this suffering in society is always an unfailing indication of conflicting interests, which are constantly producing violations of the injunction, "Thou shalt love thy neighbor as thyself."

It is impossible to find a radical distinction between the natures or the requirements of different men : but there is a difference only in the *degree* in which these are manifested. Some men require *more* than others in the way of physical or mental *food;* yet all are entitled to as much as they desire, especially when that desire is governed by a well-ordered Wisdom.

§ 5. As he who *tills the soil* feels no absolute interest in its productions, but only in the paltry sum given for his labors, so the *science of agriculture* has not advanced to that degree of perfection of which it is capable. All improvements are such as result from isolated effort, and therefore they are not such as to visibly benefit mankind, but their benefits are dissipated by vain speculation.

MECHANICS feel no interest in the improvement of *machinery*, any further than it conduces to individual wealth. There is no general interest manifested for the relief and consequent reward of the laborer. Hence, if mechanics improve in arts and sciences which abridge manual labor, they also take the food from him whose employment is destroyed. It is clear, then, that the interests of the laborer are opposed to those of the mechanic; and the conflict creates hatred and local persecution.

Every new invention *should* be hailed with shouts of joy by all, as conducing to the relief of laborious employment, and to the advancement of the race. But instead of this, every new invention is frowned upon with all the jealousy of disunited interests. Thus genius is crushed, and the poor man's energies are prostrated by the non-reception of his invention and the non-appreciation of his ingenuity.

If a man should invent a floating battery as a means of *destruction,* or plan any other new mode of destroying human life and the interests of nations, then would the public encomiums be warm and enthusiastic. Any new and deathly instrument is hailed by all as a reliever of national hostility, and an indirect benefit to the poor and unfortunate. This is an expression of a public feeling characterizing every nation of the earth; and how unholy are the conditions which give rise to this feeling! These conditions breathe hatred and wretchedness into the bosom of every excitable being, and deposite the poison of envy in each neighbor's cup; and when they drink, all descriptions of prejudice, hostility, strife, persecution, and fanaticism, flow from their intoxicated minds!

The community is thus disordered, even in its departments of mechanical industry. Every new invention for the destruction of *life* is smiled upon by the mass; but every new invention for the destruction of *degrading toil*, and for the elevation of the interests of the race, is only hailed with delight by a few good and benevolent minds, while the *mass*, feeling conscious that it crosses their interests, scout at and frown it down, that it may not go forth to *their injury*. The laborer is thus opposed to mechanical improvement. Any exertion in the way of such improvement is the commencement of hostility and persecution between the inventor and the mass of laborers.

TRADESMEN are all engaged in isolated pursuits, diametrically *opposed* to each other. Each one establishes a capital and a business where the most advantage can be taken of his neighbor and of the community. Thus isolated business among the tradesmen is leading to the most ingenious deception and falsehood. He who can converse with the most freedom, and present the most external inducements, has the advantage over his neighbors in his accumulations of wealth as derived and extracted from the community; while he who is less competent in these respects, ultimately fails in his enterprise, and then receives for his consolation the fiendish exultations of his neighboring tradesmen.

It is right and profitable to unveil the corruptions of society, and to present a mirror in which the actions and situation of every person may be visibly and justly represented. Nothing is more injurious to the morals of community, and more enslaving to the poor man, than the vast congregation of tradesmen, whose interests are as much opposed to each other as the darkness of midnight is to the light of noonday. More vice exists among this class of community than in any other department of society. They are connected with each other locally, and are joined externally, to extract an unreasonable profit from him who buys—yet they are *internally* bitterly opposed to each other's welfare; and each one is compelled by interests to overreach and deceive his neighbor. The fact of their being thus impelled by misdirected interests, generates every species of vice and disunity among themselves and in society. The buyer enters the establishment of the tradesman with the full conviction that the latter will *deceive* him if *possible*. Therefore the interests of the *buyer* and of the *seller* are in direct *opposition* to each other. And what is worse than all is, that there is a distrust of virtue and morality deposited in the bosom of every man toward his neighbor and the world!

As society is existing, men are considered *uneducated* if they have not an acute perception of their neighbors' faults and follies, or if they are not at all times prepared with deceptive plans to overcome the intrigues and deceptions of others. If a man has grown up from the cradle to manhood, in a little community where peace and harmony dwell, having no suspicion of evil or deception as pervading society, and having an implicit confidence in the purity of the dealings of mankind with each other; and if he should go forth into a community of desperate and unfortunately-situated men, he would be deceived in the most cruel manner. His property would be taken from him for one half its value; his pure spirit would be corrupted; his confidence would be betrayed, and his natural genius smothered: and for all this loss, he would receive the fiendish sneers of the tradesmen, because he was not *educated*, and aware of their ingenious expertness! Thus no men are more viciously situated than *tradesmen*, and none are doing a more direct *injury* to the social requirements of *all mankind*.

The poor man is entitled to food and clothing in as great abundance, and even greater, than he who subsists upon the poor man's labor. But what a hopeless adventure it is for an honest man to prefer this claim, or to endeavor to procure suitable garments for his person! In the first place, the article from which clothing is made is gathered from the earth which he cultivates. Its owner demands and receives a profit from the manufacturer—who presses the operatives to labor for little reward, that his profit may be greater when he transfers his produce to the tradesman. By the time the tradesman receives the cloth, the *profits* consume more than its *original value*. The tradesman is, however, entitled to a profit *also*, and this the *buyer* must pay. The poor man then receives of the tradesman his garments, and is compelled to pay the combined tariffs and profits of the agriculturist, the manufacturer, and the tradesman!

Thus from the labor of the poor man are all these various and conflicting situations sustained, and the many persons therein engaged constantly supported. Surely it is not strange that poverty exists where capital is so isolated and interests so discordant.

Tradesmen are also striving to succeed at the sacrifice of *each other's* interests; and while doing so, they affect the manufacturer, the operatives, the agriculturists, and those who toil from early dawn till evening without reward.

There should be no local, isolated establishments, such as are now existing; but there should be a *general storehouse* for every community and every city; and this should be *abundantly supplied* by the united industry of the whole community. Not a tear should be shed in consequence of hunger; no bosom should throb with pain or sink with disconsolation. No child should be left to shiver from cold, or suffer deprivation of natural wants; no mother should lament her children's, her own, or her husband's destitution. Nor should there be a life sacrificed at the altar of want, or destroyed by the hand of fearful starvation; for those stores of wealth and abundance should yield a subsistence to every one who moves and dwells in the human form. Then tradesmen's interests would consist merely in assisting others to their natural demands, and not in keeping from them every article of comfort and subsistence which they may hold within their own grasp, as at present.

§ 6. The LAWYER's interest is opposed to *general peace* and *righteousness*. Lawyers are in situations which make them interested in the *disturbances* that prevail, and not in the general tranquillity of community. They have their interests centred in the numerous *litigations* caused by persecution and hostility. Where vice exists, poverty prevails to an equal extent; and where vice and poverty prevail, the lawyer is most powerfully attracted. Instead of being *peacemakers*, they are *peace-destroyers;* inasmuch as the settlement of every legal question must be for or against the individuals concerned. The result of this is latent envy, and a secretive determination to have their demands satisfied, and that, too, when the laws of society can take no cognizance of their plans to deceive and injure. Every act of adjudication among the legal profession is the commencement of interior hatred and hostility. And besides this, every man seeks refuge in the laws of society and the state, against the injuries of his neighbor; and this is the strongest indication of disease in the constitution of society. For local quarrels and conflicts are blemishes that affect society as ulcers affect the diseased body; and it is clear that blemishes would neither affect society nor the body of man, if the interior qualities and particles of the constitution were pure, united, and circulating throughout the whole form with a perfect equality. Evils that exist in society are like diseased parts of the body; and the open contentions manifested through the workings of vice are like pains that affect the body: and both testify of internal corruption. And he is the true *peace-maker* who strikes at the root of social evil, and who destroys the fruit of the contaminating tree.

If the poor of the earth were *educated*, and their feelings were *refined*, there would be no stooping to the vice of deception and falsehood; neither would there exist so much disunity which lawyers are employed to settle according to the established codes of the land. And every legal decision is a virtual protest against the prevalence of morality and unity of human interests. If the mechanic labored in connexion with the tiller of the soil, and their enterprises were mutually assisting to each other, such a thing as contention and lawsuits between them would not be known. Did tradesmen act in accordance with the requirements of the mechanic and the laborer, then would their reciprocal action create harmony, and the lawyer would have no occupation.

The lawyer's interest is therefore decidedly opposed to this state of things; and as they are exerting an undue influence in society, their opposition will retard the progress of social, moral, and universal reform. Their interests consist in the prevalence of ignorance and imbecility, in the greatest amount of strife, contention, and deception, and in every species of corruption and degradation that now render society a disgusting body — even as a whitened sepulchre, full of dead men's bones!

Lawyers, *as men*, are good and honest, like all other men; but how deplorable to reflect on their corrupting situations! From these situations spring the most unhealthy influences into the bosom of society; and instead of reforming and equalizing mankind, and amicably settling their difficulties, they are merely casting a veil over blemishes by an external legal process, while that which they conceal is rife with all sorts of evil, extortion, and excess. No verdict is given without violating as many feelings as it gratifies. Hence a great portion of the counteracting and conflicting feelings that are in the world, are because the verdicts of conventional laws are in favor of or against the established interest or prejudice of some person or persons. It can not be said that they are *relieving* the evils of society, so long as verdicts are isolated and superficial in their character. The laws of *Nature* are unlike this. *Their* verdicts are manifested to all beings, and all acknowledge their justice, and are encouraged by their unfailing distribution of justice to every created form.

The lawyer's interest therefore consists in the amount of vice and misery that prevail, and not in the peace, and unity, and happiness, which the world is striving to enjoy. The lawyer's situation is thus the most unenviable of any except that of the *clergyman*. But lawyers are to be relieved from their positions ere long, by feeling a thrilling conviction of the truths of Nature, and by her unceasing demands for social reform and distributive justice. It is pleasing to contemplate the day when men will forsake theory, sect, philosophy, prejudice, and situation, for the sole purpose of fulfilling their use in the nature of things, and thereby to establish happiness in every portion of the world: for each will have a position created by his own industry.

§ 7. The PHYSICIAN's interest consists in the amount of organic violation that occurs, and in the abundance of distress and physical wretchedness that are found in the sick-room, the hospital, the asylum, the prison, the army, and throughout the nation. Physicians, as men not professionally employed, will express the most unbounded benevolence, and actual sympathy, for the suffering that exists. They will express all the yearnings of noble minds for the improvement and education of the poor and ignorant, and for superior situations to bless the poor man's home and the rich man's constitution. But a physician, in his *occupation*, feels no interest in any new invention, or system, or compound, that might be effectual in curing disease. He feels no interest in the advancement of intelligence on the subjects of anatomy and physiology, because a general knowledge of the organic structure of man would lead to a great amount of health, inasmuch as then all would strive to avoid violation. He feels no interest in the prevalence of physiological knowledge, nor is he interested in any degree of reform leading to a destruction of vice, debauchery, and physical violations. Disease and pain exist because the science of life and the necessities of the human body are unknown to a majority of the human race.

The poor man is obliged to exert all his physical energies to gain a subsistence for himself and family. He is thereby subject to exposures of every possible description, and to sufferings that are intolerable. The atmosphere may change, and bring disease to his exposed body. Labor may be excessive and disproportionate; and its results may be deformity, contractions, inflammations, and muscular prostration, some or all of which are a portion of the poor man's reward. Thus exposed, he sinks under disease; and when prostrated on his couch, amid his family whose wants are unsupplied, he ventures to raise his voice to the wealth and philanthropy of society in supplication, and humbly solicits relief. What is the reply which he receives? It is the frowns and silent abuses of the community— and he can see that the world regards him not. Thus forsaken, he languishes and departs unappreciated! Such examples are, in modified forms, visible in every portion of the world. The physician feels no interest in the health of that sick man, and it is a matter of indifference to him whether his pains are soothed or his situation relieved. He seeks not the poor man, because the little *attraction* (which is insignificant indeed) is not in the poor man's possession. Therefore the poor man is neglected, because the physician's interest consists, not in the prevalence of health, but in the extent of disease among those able to reward his labors.

The wife and children of this poor man are also exposed to inclement weather, and to every description of destitution possible to conceive. The wife, exercised by grief and depressed with sorrow, becomes weakened and emaciated, and finally occupies the bed just deserted by her unfortunate and neglected companion. She, too, is encompassed with sorrow, and is afflicted with privations, which society perceives not. Amid the cries of her children, she is depressed beyond the possibility of a resurrection; and she soon closes her eyes upon the world with a fear, and dread, and sorrow, unknown to any but herself: and the last vibration upon her ear is the cry of hunger arising from her infant child! She thus dies a sacrifice to human injustice and social disorganization!

The children, one by one, are taken and placed in the asylum, and there cared for in proportion to the reward given to the physician and the overseer. There they are treated as *strangers;* there they grow like the plant uncultivated, and finally become a burden to the community and the keeper of the almshouse who supports them all.

If the physician were well situated and properly rewarded, he would seek the afflicted, relieve their pains, and strive to inculcate physiological truths whereby disease might be avoided, and unnecessary violations escaped. If the physician were rewarded in proportion to the amount of *health* that exists, then would he feel anxious to have vice, and misery, and degradation, and debauchery to cease, and health to bless the existence of every man. These corruptions gyrate through all portions and classes of society, and the physician is *interested* therein. And where *disease* is in abundance, *there* he is attracted, not because he feels interested in the *health* and *prosperity* of his patients, but in that which he *receives* for his medical attentions.

Nothing can be more dishonoring to the convictions of the physician than the corrupting situation which he occupies; for he is compelled to follow the promptings of his interest, while his convictions of duty and his higher sensibilities weep over his ill-directed proceedings. The physician's duty, like that of the lawyer and the clergyman, is sensibly impressed on his judgment by Nature, and he would cheerfully comply with its dictates, were he not so viciously and unhappily situated. But *interest* is the governing principle of human existence; and the object to be attained is so to *change* the *situations* of men that their interests may correspond with the admonitions of their enlightened judgments.

The physician has an internal conviction which he can not suppress, that what he is obliged to do in his profession is directly opposed to his duty. He can not resist this conviction; and the same is true of the lawyer, mechanic, and the laborer. And this truth unfolds the fearful and horrible fact in the condition of the human race— that men are not only contending with each other in their social occupations, but that there is a constant antagonism existing between *interest* and *duty* in every bosom. Men's *interests* tell them one thing, and their *duty* another. Interests are created by the necessities of the body and its propensities; and men, to supply these necessities, are compelled to smother conscience in the blackest clouds of social warfare and conflicting interests.

One third of the earth's population are bound by the hand of disease, merely because they are uneducated, inferiorly conditioned, and unjustly treated by the exclusiveness of classes and aristocracies.

And this one third are also crushed by poverty, caused by ingenious speculations on their labor. These come into being, live unhappy and useless lives, and finally die, not knowing the destiny of their creation. They live, moreover, in a wilderness of pain, starvation, and discontentment; and it is conspicuously true that physicians never venture into that wilderness of despair! They never explore the regions of pain, distress, and wretchedness, because their *interests* speak, and their steps are directed to the bed of the rich man, whose wealth consists of the accumulated productions of that wilderness of despairing and diseased beings! Terrible indeed is the unrighteousness of these things: and they are truths that need unveiling, though they will thrill the soul of every enlightened person with an overwhelming conviction of their truth and importance!

The *human race* is afflicted with disease. Mankind as a body are *sick*, and need a *physician*. They need effectual attention and permanent restitution to health, and energy, and happiness. The race, then, must be *educated*. The rudiments of this education must consist in each one *knowing himself*, in every anatomical and physiological particular; and then the world will not be cursed with ignorance, vice, disease, and misery. Then physicians will be *useful* and beneficial; for their time and talents will be concentrated in the great work of social and moral reform, and their interests will not only consist in the amount of *health* enjoyed, but in the destruction of ignorance, violation, and local wretchedness.

§ 8. Of all professions and situations occupied by men, none is absolutely more unenviable and more corrupting than that sustained by CLERGYMEN. It is a deplorable fact that all the miseries, the conflicts, the wars, the devastations, and the hostile prejudices, existing in the world, are owing to the corrupting situation and influence of clergymen. From the beginning of the human race to the middle of this century, nothing has been more prominent than sectarian enthusiasm and theological warfare. And from the lowest period of the race, there have been successive modifications of clerical power: but each modification has only contributed to consolidate the error, and make the evil more impregnable. Clergymen have (like other professional men) smothered their consciences in the gloomy cloud of sectarianism. They are all *good in spirit*, but *unholy* in *situation* and *influence*. And nothing can be more disgusting and depressing, even to their own clouded judgments, than the unrighteousness proceeding from the influence they exert over an ignorant and imbecile race.

Each clergyman, like the physician, is opposed to every new system of practice and model of profession. Physicians do not countenance *new* modes and systems of practice, because this would be stepping from the consolidated systems established by early generations. And their system is so defended by a wall of Latin and insignificant terms, that no one can pass through and become initiated without spending a large sum in some medical or technical institution. The wall is so unsurpassable, that the majority of mankind are obliged to remain on the outer, uninformed of their nature and the paths that lead to health and happiness. The *clergyman* is still a little *more* unfortunately situated, and is as effectually defended against the invasion of natural intelligence, and the discoveries of any researcher into the truths of Nature and her God, that clergymen speak of so much. They also have a consolidated system of error — which error, however, is concealed by the assumed cloak of " orthodoxy," which means " the *right way*."— But it is only the right way in one sense, and that is to defend sectarianism against its foes !

Clergymen have a *system of practice* which is guarded by commentaries so vast, and sentinels so numerous, that the practice in general can not be overthrown, or new systems be built up in its stead. They have not, however, succeeded *fully* in this particular, inasmuch as new systems of theological practice are being conceived and instituted in nearly every generation. The world at the present day is a striking example of this truth. It displays many systems of sectarianism, and modes of curing the diseased soul.— And there are also clergymen practising in each mode and system of " salvation." Some have more expedient and plausible ceremonies than others, and such generally receive more patients ; and in this way new sects and new forms of sectarian prejudice are established.

Their interest consists in smothering the consciences of men, as the physician's interest consists in general violation of the organic laws. If clergymen can have a general psychological ignorance prevail, they are well pleased. If they can have a general effeminacy and mental submission, then their occupation is prosperous and their reward proportional. If they can have a submissive sectarianism, and a moderate yet ignorant prejudice for exclusive sects, then they entertain no fears as to the perpetuation of their reward, and the success of their professional enterprise. Clergymen *can not deny* that their interests consist in the prevalence of *ignorance* and *sectarian prejudice*, and *not* in *free* and *unrestricted thought* and *theological investigation.* They are aware that the unrestricted exercise of the mental powers would seal an everlasting destruction to all sectarianism, and consequently to their professions. If the human mind were free from the shackles imposed by prejudice, it would not rest until every vestige of chimerical philosophy and theology was banished from the earth. The clergyman's policy proclaims his consciousness of this fearful truth. He shrinks childishly from the investigation, and strives to protect his situation by a more sanctimonious life, and a deeper devotion to the sectarian prejudices of his parishioners!

Previous research into the condition of man and society has demonstrated that man, having been well situated, amid many cultivations of his own industry, began to exercise his mental powers on spiritual subjects, and upon the most profound mysteries. His thoughts were at first confined to his social condition and to the things near and about him that were pleasurable and profitable to the requirements of the body. And after having removed all influences that excited pain or displeasure, he lived happily, being abundantly nourished by good and congenial productions. Soon, however, the mind deserted visible things, and soared in search of that beyond its comprehension.—And what is remarkable is that the first adventurer in celestial imaginations was a chieftain who was what at the present day would be called a *clergyman*. He, like others after him, felt inspired with novel conceptions, and, not perceiving their origin, supposed they were *divine*.

From the first, these chieftains were adored as celestial teachers, and true expounders of every (without them) inexplicable mystery. It was found necessary to establish a distinction between those thus elevated, and the enslaved admirer. Moreover, it was deemed a virtue, and an evidence of divine religion, for the poor, depressed laborer to give all his super-productions to the priests and chieftains. The priests, thus elevated and pauperously supported, exerted an influence over those beneath them, which established at once despotic government and sectarian usurpation.

Clergymen have been so long engaged in their profession—in perpetuating the primitive doctrines among the people, carefully preserving every mystery — and in establishing lines of demarcation between the good and evil in society — that the bright functions of reason in them have become completely beclouded; and they feel conscientiously employed, and impelled by a sense of duty to continue to promulgate their hereditary doctrines. Their conceptions of duty are at the present day moulded in their profession. Hence the most brilliant mind, the most sensitive conscience, the most worthy man, is pursuing his profession under the deepest convictions of a mysterious duty enjoined upon him. They feel it impossible to be mistaken in their work. They feel that as the profession was established *many centuries ago*, it is no more than consistent with the highest *reason* that it should be perpetuated.

Their interests consist in the prevalence of *ignorance* on psychological subjects. They are evidently conscious of this truth; for when a new discovery is presented which is unfavorable to their leading principles, they are impelled by a sense of duty and religious interest, to defend their profession against such an unholy invasion. It is with them as with the physician. — All new systems in his profession, all new discoveries and newly-invented medicines, he *opposes;* for these are against his interest and professional education. The success of any new medicine would reduce his practice, and conflict with his prejudices. So clergymen, in whatever situation they may be placed, are anxious that new discoveries and truths should not prevail, inasmuch as every new truth would convey a light into their midst, which would reveal the hideousness of their corruption and imbecility to a confiding world.

§ 9. From the influence of such ignorant despotism, the world is thus disorganized, and existing amid conflicting elements of the most corroding and corrupting character. The clergy exert power over the prejudices of every society throughout the world. From the cradle their doctrines exert their influence; at youth they become instamped, and at manhood the mind is hampered with a confirmed prejudice to some sectarian faith, and to some formal observance, barren of benevolence. The laborer, the mechanic, the tradesman, the lawyer, and the physician, are all under the immediate control of clerical influence; and all of them yield to this influence as slaves yield to the imperious commands of a potentate. Like the Medes and Persians with reference to their secular laws, they dare not move and raise their voice against the corrupting restrictions imposed by the clergymen. For an open denunciation of them, or a serious expression of a conviction of any new and higher truths, would bring down upon them the fearful threats of the religious profession, and it would not be long before the general prejudice would crush them to the earth. Let any man speak sentiments *irresistibly* received, derogatory to the religion of the world, and the whole clerical army would be arrayed against him. All sects would instantly combine their forces to repulse and crush the untrammelled mind! His voice would be hushed, his influence would be arrested, and his benevolent teachings overwhelmed in the clouds of ignorance and religious fanaticism!

When the laborer is nourishing the vegetation; when he is engaged in beautifying the earth and perfecting the harvest; in short, when he is connected with the teachings of Nature and her requirements, he conceives of a benevolent Creator, who is good unto all, and is no respecter of persons; and who, in his impartiality, has made the same provisions for the Christian, the laborer, and the cannibal. The experience of the poor man is more closely connected with truth than that of any other, because he is constantly associating his thoughts with Nature, her laws, and her evident bestowments upon him. His convictions are irresistible when free from the clergyman's philosophy, or from any conventional doctrines. But when he leaves the field and turns to society, his better convictions are instantly crushed by the gloominess of the doctrines and impressions of the theological world! He is not only subject to all the vicissitudes of life, but to the contaminations of sectarian belief. And if his natural convictions are too strong for the admission of sectarian doctrines, the clergyman beholds him as an outcast, because he can not believe his inconsistent teachings. Nay, the clergyman would smother what little hope he has derived from Reason, and throw him and his family into consternation and despair. Being impelled by *interest*, the clergyman seeks the laborer, and endeavors to rescue his blemished soul from ultimate destruction. He first tells the man to *believe*. He questions the faith presented. He is told it is a sin to employ his "*carnal reason*" on such a subject. He inquires *what to believe*. The clergyman presents to his mind a profound mystery, not surpassed by the invention of the Chaldeans or of the priests of the Juggernaut! He discovers he *can not* believe. Then the clergyman's hope for his salvation is lost. He utters a drawling invocation for the lost soul, and, for the especial consolation of himself and family, deliberately consigns him to an inviting gulf of *unending torment!*

Clergyman, see what you have done, and behold your iniquity! The man you have visited was unsophisticated by the corruptions of sectarianism. He enjoyed his communions with Nature; for in her he saw the smiles of a divine Creator. But now he hesitates whether to return to his field of pleasure, or seek the dens of iniquity to smother his disconsolation! Behold, you have driven him to desperation! He no longer loves his neighbor, his family, or his nation. With indignation he curses the earth which gave him life, and the God who exposed him to such fearful destruction! He curses Nature, man, and Heaven; for all appear dark, and inconsistent with what you have called "*divine revelation.*" See, then, how he flies for refuge to the alehouse! And now his joys and sorrows are lost in a stupor, while his body is obstructing the wayside! His joys are buried in intoxication. His despair is drowned in insensibility. His physical energies are lost—his forces are expended. He has violated every law of his being, and now, writhing in pain, he breathes out a curse on society, and dies in degradation! His family are all infected with the epidemic; and they, too, are distributed in the asylum, in the prison, and in the grave!

Such examples have existed in every generation. And who has caused this misfortune, and destroyed the natural enjoyments justly belonging to this family in common with all men?

The *mechanic*, being engaged in his occupation, can not devote his thoughts to the various *causes* existing in society that oppose his happiness and contentment. So he labors intensely during the week, deserts his business (which has become disgusting), and seeks the sanctuary, to gain if possible some consolation to relieve his anxieties and bless his existence. He is led by the clergy, and dares not to think or speak that which they do not sanction. The minds of mechanics are generally enlightened concerning the rudimental principles of Nature and of mechanism, but they reason not concerning the theology of their forefathers. They are submissive to sectarian restrictions, and are thus a *mentally-enslaved* though a *worthy* class in society.

The *tradesman* is obliged to lull the admonitions of his conscience into silence during the days of his business; for then he is compelled by *interest* to invent all manner of deception in order to succeed in his occupation. Certainly he violates his duty by following his interests. He darkens his judgment by intensity of application. He, however, can arouse his slumbering conscience when he enters the sanctuary, and drink in every agreeable expression from the clergyman that would heal his wounded conscience and encourage him to proceed in his business.

The tradesman also contributes liberally to the support of local sectarianism, and this secures him a high seat in the synagogue; and he is generally considered as one of the "*elect.*" This, however, is a matter of suspicion in his own mind, and even the clergyman dares not reveal his deepest doubts. The clergyman is thus obliged to deceive those who hear him, merely that he may be sustained in his occupation. And so long as he can procure submissive converts to the mysteries which he promulgates, he is pleased; for this is one of the manifestations the world requires of religious purity and prospective salvation.

Men go to church with their interests closed and their reason open. They hear good and practical principles taught, and admire them. They are told to love their neighbor, and do unto others as they desire others to do unto them. These are good and moral principles, and men admire them. But let them return to their business, and they find those principles impracticable; for they remember the maxim of early tradesmen, that "*he who is honest can not succeed.*" Hence mechanics, tradesmen, and lawyers, admire and preserve those moral teachings in *theory*, but continue the old maxim in *practice*.

Thus clergymen teach that which is good occasionally, but not that which is practicable. They tell what men should do with an eye to their *profession*, but are not willing to follow their own advice. They will encourage the laborer, but shun labor. They encourage the mechanic, but have no sympathy for his occupation. They advise the tradesman, but assist not in reforming his unholy situation. They sanction the legal profession, but are deeply convinced of the vitiated practice. They admonish among themselves, and sometimes disagree, but they are careful to preserve their *profession* by strenuously opposing the light of knowledge. They fear the electric fire of intelligence, and shrink from its penetration. They are conscious of their misty foundation, and of the innate barrenness of their system. Hence the torch of wisdom is too bright, and the benevolence of the human heart is too expansive, for their contracted systems of religion.

§ 10. Clergymen are exceedingly unfortunately situated. They deserve the sympathies of the whole world, while their occupation should be changed as soon as possible. And their influence should be tending to wisdom rather than ignorance, to benevolence rather than restriction, to light rather than darkness, to Nature rather than a book, and to God rather than the devil, who is at the present day one of the most important personages engaged in sustaining and protecting their tottering systems against the invasions of natural morality and human intelligence!

Clergymen have manufactured a theology whose author is a God of inconceivable attributes, yet which are beneath the natural characteristics of *man*. The God whom they have invented is only a huge human potentate, who is susceptible to pain and pleasure, to impulse and reason, to justice and injustice, to exclusiveness and benevolence. The *devil* whom they have manufactured is no less human except in his *anatomy*. His passions are as strong as their God's; his reason and ingenuity are transcending, and his influence over the human race is far more potent. While the administration is divided between them, the *devil's* is the *greater;* for the majority of mankind are supposed to court his presence, and finally to animate his illuminated abode!

Here, then, are the creations of man: a God after his own image, a devil after his own likeness, a theology after his own interest, and a system of practice after his own prejudices!

Clergymen feel interested in the restriction and suppression of thought; and in order to defend themselves against it, they call their devil to their immediate assistance. And by his influence the voice of reason is hushed, their sanctuaries are filled, their financial departments are supplied, and their profession is thrown into a flourishing condition. Can you not, reader, perceive that you are compelled to love their God because you are frightened by their devil? Can you not see that your love is born of hate, and fear, and a mysterious consternation? Can you not see that your thoughts are crushed, and that the exercise of your reason is prohibited because it is called *carnal* by the clergyman? Do you not see that it is their *interest* that prompts them to restrict the spontaneous aspirations of your bosom for communion with Nature and Heaven? Do you not see that the clergy are *immorally situated*, notwithstanding they profess the *highest* morality and the highest spiritual enlightenment?

Reader, *your* interest consists in the free exercise of your moral and intellectual endowments — in unrestricted inquiry and unceasing intellectual progress. Your happiness consists in the light, and unity, and happiness, of the whole world. Your interest consists in being free as the mountain-air — in being as free to utter thoughts as the sun is to bless the vegetation of the earth. *Your* interests, then, are *opposed* to the interests of the *clergyman;* for he *restricts* your inquiries, and strives to crush the spontaneous aspirations of your benevolence. He tells you you must believe and move in the circle which he has marked out. That circle is a mere denomination, characterized by local hostility, *apparent* purity, and corrupting prejudices. He binds you within that circle with the chains of *sectarianism,* which he locks with the key of *fear,* and attaches to a monument of *imagination.* That circle is walled about with prejudice, ecclesiastical tyranny, oppression, and despotism. Only one gate is open through which an escape may be effected, and there is stationed — *the devil!* He frowns as you approach, and you fly to the sanctuary and the shepherd for protection! Reader, *your* interests are *without;* the *clergyman's* interests are *within.* It is with you and your convictions to decide whether a *sectarian bondage* shall oppress the freeborn mind, or whether *knowledge* and *universal happiness* shall bless the earth.

But there is one great consolation for the enslaved mind who ventures to escape through the gate of this great sectarian wall and city — and to enjoy this consolation, remember that the chain which binds you, with its lock, is only *fear;* the monument only *imagination,* and the satanic gate-keeper only a sectarian phantom! Nothing, then, prevents your escape. Press onward! — and after you have gained the field of Nature, raise your thoughts to Him whose essence is love, and whose wisdom is universal justice, benevolence, and reciprocation!

Clerical and sectarian despotism encompasses the inhabitants of the earth. Like a mantle it extends over all nations; and thus the world is in bondage, not knowing the kingdom of heaven, which is peace on earth and good-will to men. Prejudices are so enstamped upon every being that the world is in a confused condition. Men approach each other only as their prejudices coalesce. This is following too much the inclinations of the *body,* and not the directions of the *intellect.*

All evil sprang from a source intimately connected with the influence of chieftains and religious potentates. — And these are still sustaining and modifying this evil, and consolidating it in different degrees in every portion of the earth. Men are self-deceived. They first admit, through fear, the teachings of their chieftain, potentate, or clergyman, and finally cherish the faith which they have adopted with great affection, and are ready at all times to defend it by bitter anathemas and unholy denunciations of their neighbors. Men are first deceived, and then delight, as it were, in conscientiously deceiving others. After they have admitted a faith, whether congenial with their reason or not, they feel anxious to *sustain* what they have adopted. Hence there exist in society religious strife, contention, and prejudice. Every nation has all these combined; and they are manifested whenever approached or invaded by an antagonism.

---

§ 11. Reader, suppose yourself among the followers of Mohammed. Wander forth into the desert, and there lift your voice against the Koran. If you wish to see the sectarian Genius, just utter these words: "I disbelieve the Koran;" and behold in the distance a dark and fearful cloud, from which is emerging a chariot drawn by infuriated steeds, and in which is seated a huge, gigantic form, whose countenance is as black as midnight, and whose garments are the wealth of nations. See! it approaches with a frightful speed. By its side is seated a darling child whose name is *Ignorance;* and on the brow of that huge monster is written in characters of fire— "*Mohammedanism*"! It rushes by, bearing down nations in its course. War and persecution are its attendants, and misery, desolation, and ruin, complete the train: while over the whole is waving the flag of fanaticism; and beneath, blood is as a river!

That form has departed. The desert is clear, and you are deserted. Reader, meditate upon the *cause* of all this, and give forth your convictions to the world. Was it not by denouncing the Koran that you excited the prejudices of the nation, which in return breathed wrath, ruin, and indignation? And was not that prejudice an attribute of the great Genius of sectarianism, established and sustained by a religious chieftain? Did you not see how earnestly the nation engaged in crushing and arresting your thoughts? And was not this because they considered you an enemy to what *they call* truth and religion? Think of these causes, and let reason display her verdict to the world.

But you forget, reader, that you are a *Christian*, or a resident of a *Christian* land, where the inhabitants are *civilized*, where the *true* religion exists, where such fanaticism *can not be*, and where such ruin, dismay, and prejudice, *can not possibly exist!* You are convinced of this—and to demonstrate its truth, go forth into the fields of science and knowledge spread before you. Drink in the streams of knowledge that are springing up about you in every direction. Supply every natural want—every passion for which food is there offered; and now open your mouth and utter these words: " I believe not the theology of the land;" and behold in the distance an army of infuriated and exasperated clergymen, armed with spears of indignation and battle-axes of—*Christian purity!* Their steps are hurried, their movements confused, and their countenances darkened with fear, while their mouths proclaim, " Think no evil." See how they march and erect a battery of *commentaries*, and prepare for battle! How strange that every one is armed so differently! Each one has his peculiar mode and plan of fighting, yet they all combine and are arrayed against you. Behold again! Just as they were prepared to demolish you and your thoughts, a *disturbance* sprang up in their midst; and see what a wretched confusion is presented! Instead of fighting you, they are quarrelling and fighting with each other; and what is stranger than all is that their firearms do not perform their office! Now they are again at peace in those portions where the confusion was created, and they are again prepared to fire a volley upon you. Alas for your reputation, your happiness, your life! for now the torch is at the priming. Now is the explosion— and where are you?

You are now recovered from your consternation; and you perceive that the whole fire, and all the opposition, is only a cloud of dense and disgusting *smoke!* Not a shot has done execution. Every cannon of wrath and spear of destruction was pointed at your person, reputation, and life; and is it not strange that you are not destroyed? Meditate.—Now the reason appears plain: they had *powder*, but no *balls!* Your destruction was doubtful to them, and they began to quarrel among themselves. And you perceive that notwithstanding everything was aimed at your breast, nothing has harmed you; for you are *immortal*. Their battery was destroyed by its own explosion; and what before was war and contention, is now the remains of that old corrupt sectarianism, which you may deposite in the grave of fanaticism, and erect over it a monument of ignorance to be interrogated by generations yet unborn!

The war is over; you have fought the good fight; you stood alone—*and are unharmed!* And now that all is clear, and the fields of science and knowledge are blooming before you with beauty and living happiness, you can repose and contemplate the strength of that power which preserved you. You now perceive on reflection that you were clothed with a garment through which their spears and bolts of sectarianism could not enter. What was that garment?—Reader, with delight you exclaim, "It was immortal Truth!"

A religious strife and party antagonism has pervaded the earth ever since the early stages of the human race; and each successive generation has only modified and confirmed the previous doctrines, until at the present day there exists a universal discord. This discord is owing to the promulgation of doctrines heretofore conceived, to the exclusion of all others, or of new truths that would enlighten the world. Among the early nations a distinction of classes was made by those who directed their religious sentiments and governed their thoughts. These were chieftains, who were supposed to exert a mysterious influence over the subjects under their respective dominions. In all ages and countries this sectarian distinction has been the most prominent feature in society; and this is at the present day engendering new and more corrupting prejudices.—And all this is the work of popes, bishops, rulers, and clergymen.

Some men have conceived that it is their privilege to exercise their *reason*, and believe whatever *it* sanctions: but those who have conceived this truth are compelled to smother it for the want of an atmosphere of light and liberty. Such men are also compelled to arrest their thoughts, and confine their influence to a limited circle, because sectarian hostility and local prejudices cloud the atmosphere of free thought, and render their existence dark, dreary, and uncongenial.

There are nations upon the earth so shackled with the chains of sectarianism imposed by religious and despotic governors, that they are obliged to think only what their priests permit, and thus are slaves to religious tyranny and fanaticism. No one among them dares to express the deepest convictions of his judgment; for before him is erected the fearful prison, the rack, and the stake, around which consuming flames are created, to compel submission and arrest the thoughts of his freeborn mind! Inquisitions, then, are recognised as a form of converting souls to religion and love to one another! It is known that in generations past these inhuman tortures were imposed by apostle-endowed chieftains—whose business it was to rule the people and compel submission, if not by enslaving mandates, then more effectually by the rack or the boiling caldron. It is certainly not natural for the human mind to be converted to religion by lacerating and disorganizing the body—much less to be made to love the pope and his commands by being *burned* or *boiled* into submission.

§ 12. The mussulman is seriously devoted to the teachings of his chieftain, and deliberately denounces all dissenters as infidels and unconverted beings. He has a prophet whose life is clothed with miracles, whose teachings are unsurpassed for mystery, and whose whole career has never been equalled. The mussulman can appeal to the miraculous power of Mohammed, and on its authority he demands conviction and faith from others. He tells you that his inspired lawgiver traversed the sun and its brilliant atmosphere without casting a shadow, and deliberately separated the moon with a knife, and traversed ninety heavens in one night, on an animal that was one half woman and one half horse! The mussulman will tell you that you must visit Mecca once in your life, give one tenth of all you have to the priest, and that by so doing you will escape an ocean of inconceivable flames, by passing over an enormous bridge, whose immensity almost exceeds that of one human hair!—and that thus you will finally dwell in heaven for ever, where all good *mussulmen* will preserve an eternal youth! No miracles can be more inexplicable than these; none more inconsistent with the laws of Nature; and, reader, you do not *believe* them: for they are written in the Koran by Mohammed, and in the productions of his followers!

But remember you have also a book that proclaims mysteries almost as inconsistent, and *them* you *believe!* Reflect one moment, and you will discover that the mussulman disbelieves the claims of *your* religion, and *its* miracles, because it is written *in the Bible*, and that by authors unknown. The mussulman calls you an "*infidel dog*" with great self-complacency, and with a serious approbation of conscience; while you reciprocate the favor by calling him an *ignorant Arab*, having no hope or light in the world!

But the convictions of the Mohammedan, the Chaldean, the Persian, and the Christian, are all derived only from hereditary impressions, and from circumstances not worthy of distinct veneration, or of exclusive sectarian faith. All are seriously *convinced,* and all are as seriously *deceived.*

War, and bloodshed, and cruelty, and persecution, are all the legitimate effects of sectarian usurpation and priestly government. Clergymen are indeed most unrighteously situated. Their influence is corrupting to the morals established immutably in Nature, and the distributive benevolence contained in the constitution of Nature's God. Men who are laboring to reform the race by destroying all sectarian distinction, are sanctimoniously opposed by the theological shepherds of the land, who profess to be teachers of the highest morality, and advocates of the most universal reformation. Let one free mind express his convictions, and the clergy of the land piously denounce him as an "infidel dog," the same as the mussulman would denounce the *clergy.* Inconsistent indeed are the social and general conflicts arising from sectarianism, with the teachings of Nature and her divine requirements. For the clergy teach that exclusiveness whereby sectarianism is preserved, and religious hostility is engendered, whose fruits are local disunity and social confusion. Even domestic happiness is turned to misery, and the affections of parents and children, and brothers and sisters, are all crushed and disunited. They no longer love each other, for the clergy have made them *bigots!*

Reader, have you a companion? If so, when the day arrives to visit the sanctuary, do you not, after having enjoyed years of social bliss and domestic happiness, walk side by side from your dwelling, and separate on the corner of some highway, and go to different temples of worship? Are you not united at your peaceful homes, and in everything but the religious impressions of your youth, and their confirmations to your minds? Do you not separate and seek different modes and sanctuaries of worship? At the same time, do you not withdraw friendship and affection from each other, and are you not in your spiritual predilections disunited by a wall of partition built by the *sectarianism* of the land? And was not that wall established by the *clerical profession?* And have they not told you that you should forsake each other, your homes, your country, your companions and children, for the sake of a more strict devotion to what they teach you to consider as a holy and righteous life?

Families should be as *one* in their search after truth, and their obedience to the morality of Nature; but instead of this, families are fearing to approach each other, because of their religious convictions!

The son, surrounded by different circumstances from those surrounding the father, is impressed with a different religious doctrine, and therefore a dread of the presence of each other is created between them; and they are no longer congenial or affectionate. The mother, too, is opposed to the father, and the daughters are in like manner thrown into confusion, and no longer love each other with the same strength of affection that previously bound them in peace together.

Society is thus disorganized, both in its general and particular departments. The corrupting influence of clergymen extends to families, to all the professions of the day, and to all the governments; and consequently the whole race is as a flock of sheep whose direction is undefined and whose relations are no longer congenial. This condition of society will exist so long as the clergyman's interest consists in the prevalence of ignorance on psychological subjects, and the general testimonies of Nature. Their interests must be changed so as to be in favor of knowledge and intellectual progression. Their influence will then be elevating, and their position in society will be both useful and industrial. They must be made to feel the importance of unrestricted inquiry into the *causes* of *evil*, and of a general investigation of all principles that govern Nature and man with an *unerring* government. They must understand and cherish those principles, and apply their teachings to the necessities of society — and thereby establish a morality that is as indestructible as the laws that govern the Universe. Thus they will improve the race; and this will bring happiness and peace.

§ 13. What is the cause of the ignorance that shrouds the world? — the barbarous despotism that exists among the nations? — the war, bloodshed, persecutions, and intolerance, that have existed in every empire and portion of the earth? For what purpose was the dungeon established, the rack constructed, and the stake and flame invented? What is the cause of the religious wars, and tumults, and contentions, that have so sorely afflicted the nations in every age and generation? What is the cause of cities, once well constructed and beautiful, and displaying all the splendor and wealth of the land, now lying in desolation? Why is it that where once throbbed the cheerful heart, and where was heard the sweet voice of affection and friendship, are now heard only the hideous yells of the beasts of the forest? Why is it that where all was once beauty, opulence, and splendor, is now a mass of ruins, inhabited only by the reptile and other forms that disgust the human eye? What is the cause of vast empires, after being established and living in abundance for a while, sinking to be known no more except as the cold steel of the long-forgotten warrior, or the spear of some infuriated potentate is exhumed from among the ruins? What is the cause of the expedition of the Israelites, and of the laws given by Moses in the mount?—of the unalterable laws of the Medes and Persians?—of the worship of the sun and of the Juggernaut?—of the origin of Catholicism and of Protestantism, which at the present day are exercising their omnipotency over the societies and nations under their respective influences? What is the cause of all this dissimilarity, this confusion, war, persecution, fanaticism, and religious intolerance? What is the cause of even *families* separating, and their members despising each other? What is the cause of poverty, of vice, and of all infractions upon the physical and moral laws of human nature? What is the cause of aristocracy, and pride, and arrogance? What is the cause of the fiendish exultations of one man or one sect over the destruction or unsuccess of another? What is the cause of your prejudices, and why do you tremble and shrink from investigation? Reader, speak and proclaim the causes of these. Fear the frown of no legal practitioner. Smile at the stake and flame. Face the rack unmoved: fear not the rod of persecution, for truth and purity will protect you. Speak boldly and fearlessly your earnest and serious convictions: and Nature will smile upon you with her divine approbations; the angels will rejoice, and the Divine Mind will bless your mind with celestial knowledge. Fear no clerical practitioner (for they, like the physician and lawyer, have various modes of practising), for although he may be well versed in the learning of his profession, he can not quell the testimonies of a divine Nature, or the corresponding convictions of a noble mind!

The clergyman may become more devoted to his denomination, and assume a more sanctimonious countenance, but, reader, remember that the *external* is not the *reality*, and that the inside of the platter may be full of extortion and excess! New councils may be organized, and new conventions called. Fearful resolutions may be passed, and solemn prayers may be offered for your destruction, and also your salvation. But remember those prayers are sometimes the spontaneous desires of misdirected *passion*.—And, moreover, remember that homage is done to the Divine Mind, not in prayer and unmeaning supplication, but in harmonious industry and universal ACTION.

Theory may be the profession of some, but *practice* must be the manifestation of *all*. Search well, therefore, into the causes of these evils; and after the investigation is completed, ask those religious teachers who piously oppose you, whether sectarian despotism and prejudice have not shrouded the race as a "veil of covering cast over all nations"? And then tell him that that covering is now *removed*, and that you see the corruptions of the whole world. Know no fear—no doubt; but press onward and search the field of science and the unerring book of Nature. And let this one thing be your consolation and your hope—that the tide of intelligence is rising, and is flowing to and over all nations, even as an immense ocean of truth and knowledge. It will flow on to its destined universality; and remember—IT EBBS NOT AGAIN!

The lines of sectarian distinction are so visibly drawn in families, societies, states, and nations, that the whole world can not fail to perceive them, and freely admit their deleterious and corroding influence upon true and divine morality. Nation wars with nation; and one subdues the other and confiscates its most precious wealth, such as gives to nations honor, and to their cities elegance and beauty. And the destruction by one nation of the wealth and existence of another, is from the impulse of local prejudice and religious usurpation. So likewise is society divided into castes, groups, exclusive sects, denominations, and institutions, all of which inculcate different principles of faith and morality. The influence of these extends also into the bosom of families and divides their members one from another.

All of these national wars have sprung legitimately from local impressions disseminated by the clerical profession. These various sects and institutions in society are also living offspring of the same parent; for each one of them is an open expression of sectarian affection, and love of party distinction and aristocracy.

Ask the poor man whether the sympathies of the higher classes are extended to him in his inferior condition? Ask the traveller who has deserted friends and home, whether he meets with sympathy in society, or finds a general willingness to supply his wants? And ask the mechanic, also, whether he can move in the higher circles, or whether they descend to and favor him with their smiles and approbation?—or whether he is not rather shunned and unnoticed by him who has his footmen in livery, and whose coffers are filled with the products of the laborer's and mechanic's industry? In the present order of things, one man desires to gain, if possible, the ascendency over his neighbor. He desires to display more dignity, and to accumulate more wealth, so that he, thus defended against poverty, may look down upon him who labors with a species of triumph and exultation not worthy of an existence in the human breast.

---

§ 14. In every nation, there exists to some degree the same exclusiveness and the same depression and bondage. This exclusive, sectarian, and prejudicial feeling, is created by the clerical practitioners; for they preach the doctrines of partiality even in the nature of the Divine Mind. They, with an audacity unparalleled, call a class of their brethren "*sinners*," while those under their immediate influence are esteemed as "*the righteous*," or "*the elect*." They have established two distinct classes in society, which they call "*good*" and "*evil*." Those who are good (in *their* sight) are admonished to spurn the evil and degraded, and to leave them to their sinks of desolation. Thus he who is called *evil* becomes exasperated, and, for the sake of retaliation, seeks an unrestrained indulgence in his own animal inclinations. Thus a distinction is created by the clergy, the influence of which fills the prison, and gives employment to the legal profession and to the *hangman!* It also establishes prostitution, fills the almshouse and the asylum, casts the poor upon society uncared for, causes them to forsake their home and friends, and go down to the grave through the paths of misery, despair, and intoxication!

Clergymen create this distinction. They draw a line between good and evil, and, with an apostolic license, consign one class to the regions of darkness, wretchedness, and pain, while the other is elevated to the highest seat in the celestial heaven, to have their enjoyments enhanced by contemplating the miseries of damned souls! So long as there exists a sectarian distinction between good and evil, so long will war, persecution, ignorance, vice, misery, and degradation, exist. Meanwhile there will be the self-righteous, the self-sanctified, the "born again," and the religious hypocrite, whose imperfections will be obscured from the gaze of natural eyes by a cloak of gorgeous wealth and pretended piety. So long as sectarian interpretations are confided in, so long will governments continue to be exclusive in their enactments and privileges. And with them the church will coalesce, and thus confirm a most unrighteous despotism which will enslave and corrupt the morals of society, and misery will everywhere raise her hideous head, weeping in anguish unutterable!

Party prejudice and isolated denominations will remain and enslave society so long as the clergyman's interest tells him to preserve ignorance and repress the light of knowledge. A latent cupidity is generated by their profession, which penetrates through all the recesses of society and pervades the whole nation. Nay, it is self and universally deceptive.—And this, too, is the offspring of clerical policy, and the first-born of Ignorance and Hypocrisy.

Most deplorable is the state of society all over the world! Every home is desolate of that pure morality which recognises all as brethren, and barren of those elevating principles which are taught by Nature as the laws of God. Every denomination "*knows*" that its own doctrines are right, and each one is earnestly engaged in denouncing and exposing others; and thus strife and sectarian warfare are perpetuated. And who are the champions of the battle? Are they not the theological gladiators, who exert an influence on your minds and affections while claiming to be teachers of *peace* and divine *purity*? Are these not the shepherds of the land, whose flocks are the societies over which they preside? But alas! the flock is sheared of their wealth and the fruits of their industry, and that, too, to support an army of useless and *injurious* persons in splendor and elegance. For such men are useless in their *present* occupation—even injurious to the peace and health of community. How much therefore do they need the sympathies of the world, who at the same time should strive to *change* their situations and render them useful to the human race!

So long as clergymen preach distinction, so long will *vice* exist; and so long as they array the mind of the community against the free exercise of the mental faculties, so long will prejudice remain, and mankind will continue to despise and abhor each other. So long as men presume to say, "I am holier than thou," so long will bigotry and fanaticism continue to destroy the happiness of mankind. So long as clergymen continue to say, with their usual application of the language, " The good shall be on the right, and the evil upon the left," so long will a corruption continue to prevail in society, and so long will local hostility clothe the beauties of Nature with blood and carnage. So long as men preach truths and not practise or assist others to practise them, so long will there exist a degeneracy in the moral condition of the race which all preachers and systems can not regenerate and make perfect.

As society is existing, it is impossible for a man duly to love his neighbor, or to feel an interest in the universal elevation of the race. Nor can one do unto others as he would have others do unto him; for every law and sectarian doctrine opposes, and therefore the interest of every man is in direct opposition to such a manifestation of benevolence. Men may preach to the race and exhort them all to be happy, while they do nothing to accomplish this end, and while it is plain that every circumstance opposes such a universal peace. But as well might the clergy preach to the great river with the intention of arresting its tide or changing its course — or to the vegetation of the earth, that it may come forth in all seasons and under all circumstances alike — or tell the black man that it is with him to say whether his color shall remain as it is, or whether he shall become white — or tell the poor man that he may be wealthy at pleasure — or the rich man that he may be good or evil at will. In all of these teachings the clergyman would fail to accomplish the thing for which he labored. For it is impossible for men to be moral and good when all influences are corrupting and vitiating — or for men to be evil when all influences are elevating and purifying. Nay, clergymen should learn this truth: that mankind can not be what they would at pleasure, in any possible particular; for they are existing from birth to the grave amid uncontrollable circumstances, such as are being created by every profession, every government, and every hereditary impression upon the physical and mental constitution of man. Moreover, clergymen must learn that these circumstances, which govern the world, are the creations of *man*, and that *he* possesses power to seal their everlasting destruction, and to create superior ones in their stead, to bless his existence. Therefore it is more than folly to proclaim that which is absolutely impracticable, from the pulpit to a race misled by the circumstances of their own creation. Men should not cherish prejudices against each other, so long as the sun shines to bless the earth and all men, and while the laws of Nature are unchangeable and ever impartial in their displays.

§ 15. One portion of the earth is called a "Christian land." It is thought to be blessed with celestial truths that no other country enjoys; and this is the constant saying of those who are most engaged in the promulgation of sectarian doctrines. But, reader, in this "Christian land" exists error consolidated and sublimated; and there is also inherent hostility that would burst out and flow over the nation were it not for the freedom guarantied to the public mind, and the political privilege of unrestricted thought. These considerations are startling, but they are true, and are evidently demonstrated in every department of society in that civilized land.

A more conspicuous manifestation of intolerance is yet to come: for behold yon chapel, and enter it, and listen to what is said. Every seat is filled, and all look to the pulpit with emotions of awe and fear! All are silent, and each one is seemingly in deep meditation. Just now one arises and remarks to the audience as follows:—

"Perhaps many of you have heard of the audacity and boasting presumption of one in our community who has professed to work miracles, and to reveal truths which we know are false and damning," &c.

Reader, this man is followed by another man by his side, whose looks indicate age, and countenance erudition. His deportment reveals his superficial enlightenment, and his general appearance bespeaks devotion and seriousness. He now addresses the audience, saying:—

"Many of you, my beloved, have read and heard it said, that in the last days false prophets will arise; that they will be as wolves in sheep's clothing, professing to do many marvellous things, thereby endeavoring to corrupt the people of God. Lately such a one has appeared. He is sowing the seeds of disunity, corruption, and infidelity, in the world; and it becomes us as Christians and righteous men to spurn this teacher, and reject all disseminators of his errors, from our tables of communion and from a seat in our sanctuary. For, my beloved, it is written that 'false Christs and false prophets shall arise and show great signs and miracles, insomuch that, if it were possible, they shall deceive the very elect.' My beloved friends, how strikingly the prophecy is fulfilled even at this day, among us! Let us strenuously oppose the invasions of all such anti-Christian principles, by meeting frequently, and invoking the strength of our God, who will visit such deceivers with a *consuming vengeance!* And let us repulse this man's sayings from our families, lest they pollute the rising generation, and thus damn their souls for ever."

Reader, this speaker has concluded, and is again seated.—And now do you see the audience delighting and exulting among themselves that they have overcome the spirit of the evil one? See with what an air of circumspection they arise and depart. They approach their homes and retire, each having a *misty* impression upon his mind, the cause of which he perceives not, and is thus deceived. Believing that their devotion to the teachings of their clergyman is purity and safety of soul, and believing that what they have heard is all truth, they are hence *afraid to see* what their clergyman denounces as error.

Such are and will be the manifestations of clerical influence in this "*Christian land.*" Certainly if it were not distinguished by the term "Christian," no one would suspect it of Christianity. So indeed it is with those who are converted to any sectarian faith. They *call* themselves "*righteous;*" and were it not for this expression, their nearest neighbors would have no knowledge of their righteousness. In almost every instance, the most safely-converted are obliged to tell the fact before a person in community is aware of it. Is it not strange that men are "born again" so mysteriously, and yet their friends discover no visible change in their deportment?

Then what are men converted to? It is to sectarian prejudices; to a mysterious faith; to an undefinable impression, and to an open enmity to their unconverted brother without the denomination of which they are members. They are converts to *sectarianism*, then, and not to divine morality; converts to *prejudice*, and not to the *free* and *unrestrained* exercise of the spiritual faculties; converts to exclusiveness, and not to universal benevolence; converts to a mysterious faith, and not to the open revealments of Nature, which is an expressed thought of the Deity!

Men are thus self-deceived, and they are constantly suspecting others of practising deception. They perceive that they are constantly being deceived themselves, and hence are compelled to deceive others. Such men often become misanthropists, and ultimately forsake society, because they are suspicious of its purity and disgusted with its conflicting elements.

Clergymen, what are the causes engaged in producing and perpetuating these things? What are the causes of "evangelical" distinctions, and the belief that one is evil and the other is good? What are the causes of these disunities in society? What were the causes of the crucifixion, the inquisition, the crusades, and of the martyrdom of good and enlightened men? What were the causes of the massacre of St. Bartholomew? What are the causes of war, devastation, and national poverty? Why do men in each nation love their own local associations and despise all others? Why are vice and misery existing?—and why are ignorance, prejudice, and restriction of thought? Why are *you*, clergymen, fearing that the "*carnal reason*" will discover too much truth? Why do you admonish your hearers not to think or read much on subjects of a high and elevating character?

Clergymen, consider these interrogatories? Remember the world requires a *full* and *candid decision;* and remember, too, that language is inadequate to express the importance of these questions, and their answers. If you do not *candidly* decide for the world, the world will for you ere long; and then your situations will be changed: your influence will be arrested, and your personal existences made useful. And then if you will not cheerfully consent to be happy, you will be compelled to breathe happiness, by your unceasing industry, to the inhabitants of the whole earth.

§ 16. "What!" you exclaim, "would you have us abandon our spiritual efforts to elevate the degraded, and to reform a sinful race? Would you have us withdraw our sympathies from this great work of spiritual reformation, and desert the requirements of men, that they may become more evil and contaminated? Would you have us desert our sanctuaries and temples of holy worship, consecrated to God and his divine revelation, and open the floodgates of infidelity, that this may drown the religious world and desolate the earth? Would you have us sanction unrestricted investigation concerning that of which men are ignorant—the effect of which would be universal presumption and blasphemy? Would you have us arrest our benign labors in the great spiritual vineyard, and leave all the vines, and flowers, and shrubbery, to wither and decay? Have we not visited the widows and fatherless in their afflictions, shed tears over and prayed for them, invoking the blessings of our Father to rest upon them and bless their existence? Have we not mourned for the condition of the poor and necessitated? Have we not encouraged them by offering the balm of Gilead to their wounded and lacerated bosoms? Have we not proclaimed from our pulpits— 'Blessed are they that mourn, for they shall be comforted: blessed are the peace-makers, for they shall see God'? Have we not offered hope, and rest, and consolation, to the barren bosom? Have we not unfolded the blessings of heavenly bliss, and specifically pointed out the strait and narrow way that leads unto eternal life? Behold these things," you again exclaim, and ask, "Are we not most impiously misrepresented? For our labors have been unceasing; we have suffered deprivations and perils by sea and land. We have deserted our friends and homes, and travelled as missionaries to foreign lands, to instruct and inform the poor heathen of his imminent danger, and of the means to escape it? We have made an estimate of the saved and lost souls among them. We have come to the conclusion that fifty thousand are sinking to hell every day! This mathematical calculation we have presented to an enlightened and Christianized world, and called upon them to bestow means for our support, that we may labor for these poor, ignorant, and abandoned souls. We have missionaries distributed in every portion of the earth, seriously and incessantly devoted to their appointed labors. They suffer cruelties and persecutions of the most inexpressible character. They forego all pleasure and experience all pain, that they may accomplish the great work of spiritual reformation." With surprise you again exclaim, "Would you have us withdraw our sympathies from the heathen, and leave them to irretrievable destruction?"

Then, again, you say, "You misunderstand our holy religion, and call it '*manufactured*,' while we know it is an express revelation from God to man. The effects of our holy religion (as you informed your readers) are evidently righteous, from the great dissimilarity between the heathen and Christian nations. The Hindoos are exceedingly ignorant. They have long pilgrimages; they expose themselves to imminent danger—prostrate themselves in the sand, and let men and horses walk over them; they crawl upon their hands and knees, and draw themselves, with the most idolatrous veneration, toward the temple of Juggernaut. The ponderous car of their heathen god rolls over and crushes their bodies. They undergo all this with a confidence in, and devotion to, their religion, unparalleled by any nation upon the earth. And when a loved husband dies, an altar is erected, on which he is placed, and the widow is obliged to accompany the dead body as a sacrifice on the burning pile. The babes are placed with their parents; the torch is applied, and the consuming flame destroys the living with the dead!—And all this because they have not the *Christian religion!* Then," you say again, "reflect—for the whole heathen world are like these in their sensuous devotion to a polluted and unmeaning system of idolatry."

You also refer to the heathen philosophers, and point out their infamous iniquities. You represent that their morals were debasing to the lowest degree; that all principles of virtue were crushed; that all privileges enjoyed by the female sex were restricted; that their chastity was polluted, and their existence rendered miserable. You say that no teacher ever lived who promulgated the same morality, virtue, and high principles of celestial purity, as those who penned the book whose truths you proclaim from your pulpits and in your sanctuaries of divine worship and moral instruction.

Again, you say, "Our labors are misinterpreted, and our high calling improperly spoken of: for behold what our religion has done! On emerging from the heathen into the Christian world, we perceive wealth, wisdom, and happiness, distributed in every direction. Well-constructed and opulent cities, governed by our principles of morality, are visible, and happy villages are blessing the land, whose lofty spires bespeak Christian purity and a righteous nation. Every art is cultivated; every privilege is granted tending to advance the agriculturist in his pursuits; every facility is offered for establishing and perfecting navigation of all descriptions, and all modes of expedite travel. Every man has the freedom of his own mind, thoughts, and sentiments, except the black man, who is in slavery, because slavery is sanctioned by our religion. And behold the wealth and prosperity of the American nation! Everything in its possession has flourished from the beginning, and continues to thrive, with all the blessings a nation can desire. See, then, what our religion — our principles — our high calling — has done for the civilized nations of the earth! — And in view of all this, you rise in rebellion against our efforts and our profession! You misinterpret our most holy intentions, our deepest yearnings, and our serious devotion to the principles of morality and of human improvement!"

The voice of Nature replies: Abandon your *present*, but establish *new* efforts, whereby the social world may *harmonize*, and morality bloom as a rose, from the superior situations of mankind. Do not cultivate the *flower* of morality, before you have planted the *seed* of human industry. Do not begin at the *top* of a building, before you have laid its foundation in the earth. Open the floodgates of infidelity to all the *useless* and *unrighteous professions* of the age, and thereby establish a *fidelity* to the indestructible laws of Nature, and to her divine morality. Cease your mourning for the widow and the fatherless, and go forth and *labor to supply their necessities*. Cease your long and unmeaning prayers and invocations, and honor the God of your being by laboring in the vineyard of a fertile earth, and thereby bless your own and your neighbor's existence, with abundance and happiness. An instance can not be shown in which a sigh has healed the injured breast, or a prayer has given food to the hungry.

Brethren, you *mean* well, but your labors are useless and impoverishing to the human race. You repose unlimited confidence in the Divine Mind and his providence toward his creatures—and you are anxious to have your Father in heaven do that which you can do yourselves. You call for assistance when you are depressed with the afflictions of those around you. Your supplications are *pure*, but alas! they are *unavailing*; because, clergymen, though you are *seriously* you are *immorally* employed!

---

§ 17. Moreover, learn this truth: that morality is not in your systems of religion, but is immoveably established in Nature and in Man; and if you desire to elevate the race, strive to establish conditions adapted to its proper development. Verbal prayers are insignificant, ineffectual, and unprofitable.—But every true and righteous prayer consists in an unchanging devotion to the principles of Nature, and the teachings of a benevolent Father. Then pray in *action* and in *deed*, but not with your *tongue*, though seriousness may prompt the utterance. Be religiously devoted to *practice*, and not to *theory*. Tell no more what men *should* do, but go forth and *assist* them to do it.

The voice of Nature replies again, that your system and profession are *not* misrepresented: for in them are concealed the elements of evil and disunity.—For behold how much the more devotedly the Hindoo is attached to *his* religion, because he *hates yours!* He despises your sanctimonious offerings, and repulses all your missionary innovations. It is this *antagonism* that retards his abandonment of all heathenish and idolatrous worship. He beholds other nations smothered in a sectarian faith imposed by a God he knows not. Thus he loathes and despises them. Heathens thus centre their affections in, and restrict their thoughts to, the deified principles of their speechless god—and all this to manifest an increased devotion by way of *retaliation* upon all Christian invaders and mysterious teachers.

The heathen philosophers taught some *good*, but more *evil*. They believed all they taught to be the highest morality, but as they descended into sensuous observation, they drew conclusions that were both erroneous and impure. Their minds had just emerged from an immense ocean of ignorance and fanaticism; and they rushed impetuously to the indulgence of unrestrained animal gratification. Their wisdom was uncultivated; their perceptions were acute, but their moral faculties were undeveloped.

Between these two extremes sprang up the modified and rational system contained in the book which you, clergymen, are promulgating. Hence this book contains more real and useful principles than any collection of manuscripts on the earth. Those who wrote them were enlightened, because the extremes of the heathen ignorance and philosophy were an unfailing index from which central and useful truths could be deduced. Nothing is contained in these manuscripts but what is of the highest importance to the human race; and this is especially true of those portions indicating the morality derivable from universal industry and reciprocal justice. They are plain—all can read them—they need no expounding. They are intended as incentives to an end which all should be employed to accomplish—even love to the neighbor, and peace on earth, and good-will to men. *Preaching* will never effect this: *action* will accomplish it in a brief period.

The voice of Nature again replies, that the effects of your system, and of its promulgation, have *not* been righteous. But how is this to be proved? Is not the distinction evidently visible between the heathen and the Christian world?—and can it be denied that Christianity has produced the great elevation of the one, which renders the degradation of the other conspicuous?

Reader, in the distance a form is visible.—It is an aged man, whose countenance indicates purity and benevolence of soul. He seems like one of the primitive inhabitants. His pace is slow and firm; his form is well proportioned; and with a smile upon his countenance, he approaches you. Just inquire of him concerning his birth and experience, and concerning his knowledge of the heathen and civilized nations—and of the *causes* engaged in producing the manifest dissimilarity between them.

In answer to your question, he replies that he is an Anglo-Saxon; that he is acquainted with the causes of civilization, and can give you some wholesome advice, so that you may recognise and perpetuate the causes, that their effects may hereafter be more conspicuous. Listen, now, while the venerable man utters his experience:—

'From the beginning, man had necessities, which he labored to supply. His increasing wants led to the development of his physical and mental attributes; and this enabled him to accomplish many useful inventions. Impulsed by a powerful desire, he perpetuated his species, not knowing the wisdom of this purpose of Nature. Each new being, however, was made useful in tilling the earth. Natural desires were gratified, social requirements abundantly supplied, and man's domestic happiness was in a measure complete from his own industry, invention, and development.

"It was not long after this period that man launched his mind on the ocean of imagination! Having no wisdom as a helm to guide his thoughts, he ran upon shoals and bars, and among icebergs, rocks, islands, and strange regions, until, alas! his mind, like a vessel, stranded upon the beach of a dark and gloomy philosophy, from which *theology* had its birth.

"The nations thereafter continued their physical improvements and industry, meanwhile cherishing and fostering the various remnants of the mental wreck which constituted their peculiar modes of chimerical and imaginative worship. Each succeeding generation confirmed the opinions of the preceding ones, until the various nations were prejudiced and infatuated, being devotedly attached to their peculiar idols and forms of religious veneration. They sacrificed their lives, their homes, and their peace, in defence of their religion. Sectarian hostility raged like a consuming fire throughout the earth, which led to the invention of warring implements, and of all plans of personal and national destruction. The moral and social faculties of man were crushed and perverted. Their little wisdom was turned to ingenuity and deception — their affections to bitterness and vindictive vengeance. Then it was that the whole world was divided by the walls of sectarian envy and religious fanaticism. The heathen, exasperated, fought those who were more fortunately situated, and apparently blessed with a better God and a better religion. Those who had cultivated their intellectual faculties, and abundantly supplied their physical necessities, founded cities characterized by wealth and splendor; and they believed that their *God* caused this prosperity, and not themselves. With this conviction, they rushed against and strove to subdue the heathens and their systems of social government and religious devotion. In this manner, nation after nation was destroyed, and new ones were established. Each nation was as a sect; each dominion as an exclusive world; and each one pointed the sword of vengeance at its neighbor's breast. Men became so suspicious of each other, that forts, and castles, and monasteries, were erected, and cities were built with walls about them impossible to be demolished.

§ 18. "Thus the world was interiorly degraded—the exterior expression of which consisted in all these exclusive institutions, castles of defence, cities of suspicion, and walls of forbidding vengeance, on whose heights were stationed cannons of destruction. All of these were outward representations of the condition of the mental world.

"While the world was in this condition, a number of manuscripts were collected from the writings of different historians and of persons interested in the social welfare of the race. After their collection, they were voted and revoted as celestial, by various councils. They were ultimately adopted as canonical: and from that moment to the nineteenth century, their contents have been deposited in the *affections* but not in the *judgments* of men. Inasmuch as the affections are *passionate*, they gave forth a religious *prejudice*, which it was and is almost impossible to subdue by the genial light of Wisdom.

"Such," continues the aged man, "was the condition of the religious world, that the Persians, the Hindoos, and the Mohammedans, loathed the Christians, as the Christians did them. This established the lines of demarcation between the interests of nations and families of the earth; for all were opposed to each other, because Prejudice wielded her sceptre, and the nations bowed in submission.

"The Christian religion was far the most acceptable to the enlightened, because of its pure maxims, and principles of truth and sympathy. Soon after it was adopted, it became blended with the social relations of those who received it; and local hostility began. Sects, creeds, and denominations, sprang from the many interpretations of the Bible. The latter, like a tree, has put forth branches which extend into the mental atmosphere, and absorb the feelings, interests, and affections, of men. But the nations continued to be industrious; and hence a portion of the world became greatly advanced.—And so it was when *my* nation was confirmed in its present condition.

"So things were situated, when a man proposed to discover other portions of the earth. At this time, navigation was greatly perfected; and Christopher Columbus, impulsed by a disposition to explore, discovered the American continent. The first settlement in the New World became established. Immigration thereafter was immense. The families having good social habits, made the land fertile in useful productions. Not long, and religious intolerance and potential tyranny endeavored to crush the free and equal rights of the Americans, and to destroy their peace and prosperity by imposing unjust claims upon their property. The inhabitants, being inspired by a sense of justice and love of freedom, prepared to defend their rights. A council was called, and a noble mind was intrusted with the execution of its mandates. He was called the Son of Liberty, and is known and loved for his vigilance and his unfailing prosecution of the work assigned him.

"The council decided that 'all men were born free and equal, and were endowed with certain inalienable rights, among which were life, liberty, and the pursuit of happiness.' Thenceforward they proceeded to break the chain of despotism, and to conquer the opponent of their freedom. They succeeded. Republican government was adopted by the voice of the people, and the race was made happy and united. Meanwhile the various sects sprang up, and endeavored to divide the affections of the nation. They have in a measure succeeded: for a proof of which behold the civilized nations of the earth!"

Reader, notice the puritan father, how he turns pale and his voice falters in uttering this last sentence! But listen;—he speaks again:—

"Brethren and clergymen, your system *did not* cause this civilization; but it was caused by primitive invention incited by necessity, and by subsequent cultivation of the social and intellectual powers. It was *actual industry*, and *not preaching;* it was a knowledge of physical necessities, and the supplying of them, that erected your beautiful cities, accumulated your wealth, distributed your splendor, and developed your elegance and your fertility of mental powers. It was this that unfolded the genius of your natures, and that gave you your worthy citizens. But all your *disunity, conflicts of interests, prejudices, fear of thought,* and *sectarianism*, are owing to that system which you are locally promulgating, and endeavoring to extend to the heathen nations.

"Brethren, I have only one question to ask, and to this I demand an answer: Are the causes of civilization owing to the prevalence of Christian principles?—or to the actual industry of those who could hardly read them? Were those wars caused by industry, or by religious intolerance and fanaticism? If industry was and is the cause of civilization, will the promulgation of your principles assist this cause to advance, or arrest it? If not, then can you say that the heathen is sinful because he has no religion? and that you are righteous because you are blessed by the *partial* favor of a *universal* Father?"

The old man has turned his face and departed. His experience, and knowledge of civil and religious history, are valuable to the race. Reader, ponder well upon these revealments—and then decide whether the clergy and their system are misrepresented.

§ 19. Many people believe that evils in society are referable to personal vices and individual constitutional tendencies, and thus they impose on man a responsibility which is unjust, because he can not assume it. He may cherish the above belief, but he can not practise the principles of his conviction, because they are not found in Nature, nor in Man, nor anywhere in the constitution of divine creations. Owing to the ignorance of parents concerning their own nature and its laws, the rising generation are made imperfect, because they imbibe vices or improper inclinations from their parents *hereditarily*. In this defect only are the evils of society referable to personal vices.

But it is a truth that human character is unfolded, either favorably or unfavorably, perfectly or imperfectly, by the influence of the social and religious conditions that surround it. The human character is always a representative of the soil that gave it birth, and the atmosphere in which it was developed. Inasmuch, then, as man can not make his own being, character, or disposition, it is impossible for him to assume the responsibility of an unactuated free agent.

Mankind are all composed of the same materials, differently combined, and of the same essences differently distributed; and these different combinations constitute the varieties of mankind, and the dissimilarities of their passions, necessities, and spiritual possessions.

Man can not think what he chooses at will; for he is compelled to create influences, or court them, before he can arrange and concentrate his thoughts. In order to read, a man must have a book; in order to converse, he must have another to hear and respond. In like manner he is governed in all his physical and mental tendencies. He can not love and dislike at will; for he is compelled to love that which is lovely, and he can not love that which is disgusting or uncongenial with the susceptibility of his affections. He can not believe or disbelieve by desire; for his mind invariably decides *for* or *against*, according to the preponderance of *evidence* presented to his spirit by the senses. Therefore man can not be good when influences are *evil*. He can not be *perfect* when he is *imperfectly* constituted. He can not love when his affections are displeased. He can not *think* without internal or external causes being engaged in inciting and evolving thought. He can not believe when there is not sufficient evidence; he can not *disbelieve* when evidence preponderates. Thus man is a child of Nature, as Nature is a child of the Deity. He is governed by her principles; for they run into and constitute his being. Man's only *free agency* or *free will* is subject to the promptings of Wisdom, which is his peculiar endowment. This he is enabled to exercise over his own feelings, inclinations, and all things below him on earth. So far as this sanctions, he is free to act or not to act; and this makes him a passive being, subject to influences from within and without.

Then it is proper for all mankind to know this important truth: that man in nature is *passive*, because of his Wisdom, which is a counterpoise established against the Life and Love of all created things; and that to make man *moral*, all influences from within and without must correspond to the nature of his constitution, and the highest suggestions of an enlightened Wisdom. Such is man; and such is his relation to Nature, her laws, and the Divine Mind.

Reader, if you are elevated to a seat of honor to govern and direct your brethren the people, your interest *now* consists in an exclusive distribution of favors and privileges to those under your government. To be in accordance with the laws of Nature, your position should be determined by your superior constitutional qualifications. And your government should contemplate the interests of all living creatures, and your privileges should be distributed according to the peculiar wants of each one. Thus you should assist all; and that by a feeling of unrestricted benevolence, and a wise and impartial distribution of justice, liberty, and equal rights.

Reader, if you are a representative of your state or portion of the earth, your interest consists in advocating those measures which would benefit those who gave you the office, and in legislating for the exclusive classes and their aggrandizement. To be in accordance with Nature, you should be as an unblemished mirror in which would be vividly reflected everything existing in the state or portion of the country which you came to represent. Then your government would be equal, and one person would have an unbounded confidence in another.

Reader, if you are a *wealthy* man, your interest consists in establishing a monopoly which no other person can overcome, thereby to accumulate more wealth. Hence you are doing injustice to the rights of men beneath you, notwithstanding you subscribe liberally to the support of the institutions of education, in which literature, and art, and elegance, are taught; also to sustain asylums, and almshouses, and prisons. The support of all these may be derived from you; and yet you are doing injustice to the interests and rights of your subordinate brethren. To be in accordance with *Nature*, you should feel no monopolizing disposition, nor should you expend so much wealth on local institutions. Each one of these being isolated, costs at least one third more than the same education, privileges, and benefits, would if they were arranged according to a system of reciprocal interest and the promptings of a benevolent soul.

Reader, if you are a *clergyman*, your interest consists in limiting thought, and restricting the spontaneous investigations natural to the human mind. You are also compelled to smother your own convictions beneath the prejudices of your own congregation, and the society in which you move. You dare not express the highest convictions of your judgment; for in that case your influence would sink, and your occupation would no longer afford subsistence and emolument. To be in accordance with Nature, you should be teaching that which Nature teaches, and should expound that upon which mankind are ignorant. You should unshackle the human mind by cultivating its Wisdom. You should inculcate no mysteries that the human mind can not solve; for rest assured that whether such mysteries are imaginative or true, they are unnecessary to the inhabitants of this sphere. You should teach those who need to be educated; and teach them only that which is practicable, and tends to benefit the whole. Restrict no mind that is capable of reason; and if men's thoughts are not well directed, it is your duty to cultivate their Wisdom, so that they may think properly. You should take your text from the simple and well-written Book of Nature, whose language all understand, and whose teachings all will receive; and thus you will be teachers indeed.—And then your influence will purify and elevate the spiritual elements of the whole human race.

Reader, if your profession is the *law*, your interest consists in the numerous vices and disturbances occurring in society. You are not devoted to *justice* so much as to *favoring* him who rewards you most liberally. To be in accordance with Nature, you should be constantly engaged in equalizing the movements of society, and teaching the world justice and love. You should be earnestly engaged in giving justice to those who need it most, by elucidating its principles to all. And then you would be a blessing to society, and would be honored with the title of " peace-makers," which can not *now* be applied. You should be interested in *peace* and *universal justice;* and then the principles of Nature would fully correspond to, and sanction, your useful labors.

---

§ 20. Reader, if you are a *physician*, your interest consists in vice and sickness, and in all manner of infractions of the physical laws, and in the prevalence of abuses in society, whereby disease is generated and your profession is rendered eminently flourishing. To be in accordance with *Nature*, you should be as the *good physician*, interested in the health of the whole world, earnestly studying the interests of others, improving their minds, unfolding the mysteries of their constitutions, and daily engaged in curing and preventing disease. Then you would breathe an impartial favor, and a healing influence, to all about you; and you would thus be blessed while you were blessing the existences of your brethren.

Reader, if you are a *mechanic*, your interest consists in all inventions that tend to reduce and depreciate the labor of man. You feel desirous of obtaining knowledge of art sufficient to establish your monopoly, and to insure your success over the competitions of your neighbor. Therefore your studies and inventions are selfish and isolated. To be in accordance with *Nature*, you should study the geometrical attributes of, and the mechanism manifested in, all things. You should apply your discoveries to machinery, and to all things profitable to the human race universally. Labor should not be *isolated*, but *general*. No strife should exist, but on the contrary there should be a constant desire to advance the interests of the world. Thus your own wants and the wants of others would be supplied, while your existence would be a blessing, your labor attractive, and your occupation happiness.

Reader, if you are a *poor* man, your interest consists in a hurried and inferior tilling of the soil; for even the movements of your labor are governed by the amount of reward which you receive. You feel no interest in labor itself, in improvement, or in the occupations of others: therefore your existence is displeasing and unhappy. To be in accordance with *Nature*, you should feel an attraction to labor as arising from its just organization and distribution. You should be interested in all the inventions of others, and in all things tending to beautify and render the earth productive.

Mankind, your interests are opposed to each other: and hence all the innumerable evils that prevail in society, and which are marring the beauty and usefulness of the human race. You are as a Man whose organs are diseased, and whose requirements are opposed to each other. You are as a body diseased *internally*, and whose disease is not visible to the sensuous perceptions of men. You are striving to keep the surface healthy, and to make it appear sound and perfect, while the disease is raging among the organs invisibly, and these are absorbing each other's strength, and each one is striving to transcend and govern another.

But it is impossible to continue this policy of superficial healing much longer. The disease and corruptions of society are bursting forth and contaminating the body with sores of filth, and with unhealthy abominations. An effort to heal these outbreaks and running sores would be like a physician striving to heal a bile when the blood is diseased. Mankind as one human body must have a constitutional cleansing and renovating. Then the body will rise to the fulness of the stature of a perfect man, and all will be health within and peace without. Strive, then, to feel these truths and apply their teachings. Do not exert yourselves to keep the *surface* whole, while the disease is *constitutional*; but renovate your system, equalize your situations, and thus harmonize one with another. Be as a brotherhood, and love each other. Do this by making all things attractive, and existence a blessing. Do this by fulfilling your destiny, and thus honoring the creation of your Father which is in heaven. Do all these things, and you will be a *moral* race, united in your feelings, elevated in your affections, refined in your sentiments, and perfected in wisdom. Do this, and you will know no distinction; for your interests and personal existence will be blended into one harmonious Whole. Do this, and goodness will be the result of your efforts, and righteousness the temple of your habitation.

Thus it is proved that society and the human race are *diseased;* and I now proceed to prescribe the REMEDY.

§ 21. There is a constitutional and mutual affection manifested between every particle and compound in being. This is the *law of association* — which is the rudimental principle of Nature established by God, who is Love. This law creates, develops, and perfects, Man — and distributes the race, together with all created things, to portions of the earth congenial with their respective natures and qualifications. Every form in the vegetable world is distributed by this law of mutual affection. The huge trees are rooted in soil and grow in climates where the delicate flower can not subsist. A garden can not exist where the wilderness is, at least until the soil is cultivated and rendered fertile. Neither can the delicate forms in the animal world exist among those that are huge, gigantic, and possessing dissimilar habits. The fish can not live with the bird, nor the bird with the quadruped. That is, one can not subsist upon that which sustains the other: but each requires different food, and this distinguishes their individual necessities and habits.

So with the human world: They are distributed in various portions of the earth, and in different climates, all surrounding things in Nature being adapted to their peculiar constitutions, and congenial with their physical requirements. The law of association being the rudimental law of Nature, and flowing into and uniting all things, is fully developed in the human form. It constitutes men differently, gives them different passions, inclinations, and essences and properties of soul. It creates the diversity, the multifariousness, manifested in the human world. But although it makes men unlike each other, the variety is necessary to harmonize and unite the whole. The diversity manifests the order of development. It is the mode of perpetual progress, the cause of happiness, and the spring of all life and energy, of all passion and its gratification. Therefore the diversity is the order of Nature, the requirement of man, and the foundation of harmony.

Mankind inherit their diversified attributes from the womb of Nature, these having been there deposited and impregnated by the Love and Wisdom of God. These attributes constitute the affinity which man sustains to Nature, and to her provisions to which he is entitled. There is no passion or desire of man which Nature has not provided means to gratify, especially when such passion or desire is governed by *Wisdom*, by which also its gratification should be regulated. Man is entitled to liberty, plenty, and happiness, by Nature. She bequeaths these to him, and presents her larder stored with bounteous provisions, and invites man to receive, enjoy, and cultivate them, and be what she intended he should.

This inseparable relation between man and Nature and the Principles of God, is established by the law of association. There is no possible way to annul this reciprocal relation, or to escape from the obligation to bow in obedience to the laws which govern it. This law of Nature is divine, because it is the Love and Life of the Deity. It distributes impartial blessings to all, and for every action it dispenses an adequate reward or punishment. There can be no denial of the absoluteness of the connexion, and there is no escaping the effects accomplished by the workings of these principles.

Man is, then, a child of Nature, caressed, and guided into all wisdom, by her unchangeable possessions. Man is well formed, well constructed, and well distributed, on the bosom of Nature; and he, as a dutiful child, should acknowledge the relation and submit to her wise commands and dispensations.

As the law of association thus unites Nature and man, and establishes diverse and multipotent characteristics in the race, it is upon this indestructible basis that rests the law of reciprocal justice and consequent morality and happiness. Every being, then, is entitled by Nature to liberty and happiness; and if every one does not receive these, injustice is done in some portion of the human world. If the desires of a single being are not gratified, then there is an unjust and isolated absorption in some parts of the great Body, which is an injury both to the absorber and to those subject to the absorption.

All men have not the same desires, and do not need the same gratification. Each one has peculiar wants, and the wants of each one differ in their degrees of development. Hence it follows that happiness should be dispensed by bestowing blessings in proportion to the capabilities of men to appreciate and enjoy them. Those who have superfluous gratifications are as miserable as those whose wants are not adequately supplied. In the one instance, desires become morbid, unhealthy, and corrupting; while in the other, they are impetuous and constantly generating vice, disease, and unhappiness. It is therefore an injury for any one to have more than he can well employ, appreciate, or make useful; while on the other hand, it is unjust to deprive any one of that which is necessary to his existence, or of any blessing to which he is entitled by Nature.

To prevent absorption in any part of the great human Body, therefore, the Wisdom of men must recognise the divine law of *Association*. This law must be applied by making all situations and all degrees of human industry correspond to its uniform requirements. Here, then, is the *first* item in the remedy for the disease of the social world.

Mankind, remember you must become acquainted with your nature, your Creator, and the laws which inseparably unite and harmonize all created things. You must become *enlightened*, and feel the force of this divine truth; and in doing this you will remove a part of the disease which now corrupts your mental constitution.

The law of Association, then, establishes *harmony*, and imperatively forbids injustice to anything which it comprehends within its dominion; and this is only limited by the expanse of inconceivable space.

Another truth, then, is necessarily evolved, and must be acknowledged; and that is, that every man is not only entitled to liberty, plenty, justice, and happiness, but he has an important office to fulfil, an end to accomplish, and a destiny to fulfil. Hence each man must have a distinct position in the great structure of human society; and that position must be determined by his constitutional qualifications, and his ability to discharge the obligations it imposes. He must *gravitate* to his own peculiar centre, as this is determined by the law of association: that is, to whatever soil, climate, occupation, and situation, may be most congenial with his natural inclinations as modified and governed by Wisdom.

Men *now* occupy situations which they are not capable of filling; and therefore everything they do is injurious to some, beneficial to others, and disgusting to themselves. Being compelled to engage in that which they are not qualified to perform, creates discontent in the mind, and does injustice to all dependent on their labors. But every one is entitled to a position determined by the quality and abilities of his constitution.

---

§ 22. Each man is but an *organ* of the great human *Body*. In the present condition of things, one organ is opposed to, and absorbs the strength and happiness of, another. This generates every species of evil, pain, wretchedness, and disorganization. But it is proper that each individual, as an organ of the body, should occupy a position agreeable with the demands of his own nature and the nature of others; and thus distributive and impartial justice would be generated, which would remove the disease, renovate and perfect the body, and promote unity and happiness.

Suppose a man to have a disease which affects each organ by obstruction, absorption, and a disturbance of the equilibrium in their forces and essences: would it not be proper to remove the obstruction, destroy absorption, and equalize the forces and essences, so that they might create health? Then if this is the correct process, is it not equally correct to remove all absorption, obstruction, and want of equilibrium in society—so that every man, like an organ of the body, may perform his appropriate functions, and not only be happy himself, but generate happiness for others?

One effect of the law of association is known as *harmony;* and *harmony* is the soul and element of *music*. Music is a representation of divine *Order;* and *Order* is the Wisdom of the Deity. To establish *harmony*, therefore, in society, every man must be well instructed and properly situated, so that his movements may accord with the movements of the whole; and thus the movements of the human race will be in concert.

Suppose a musical instrument well constructed, and capable of giving forth perfect and beautiful melody. Suppose also that the notes it is capable of sounding all accompany it, but are *confused*. Think you that harmony can proceed from that instrument? Notwithstanding the notes are all there, if they are not well placed, well timed, or properly concerted, the consequence will be that the most disgusting and frightful discord will proceed from the instrument. So with the human race: the *structure* is *perfect;* the notes are *all existing;* but they are *misplaced:* and vice, antagonism, and immorality, are the consequences.

The instrument of society can not be tuned except by an enlightened *Wisdom*. Wisdom may arrange society, and place every man in a position congenial with his own nature and the universal requirements of the race. After mankind are so situated, *discord* can not arise, but most happy harmony, morality, virtue, and righteousness, will prevail.

Man has no desires that can not be gratified. He has no peculiarities but what some position would render agreeable and proper.—And these peculiarities must be considered as a musician would consider the notes used in the composition of a tune; and Wisdom must arrange them in concert, so that *melody* may be fully developed. There is not, nor will there ever be, one being too many. But in order to make man fulfil his destiny, place him in a *situation* to do it. Make industry *attractive;* make every dispensation just, and determine every position by specific qualifications. Advance the lower strata of society by pervading them with Wisdom and pure influences. Then every man will perform the use for which he was destined, and all contention that now prevails will be lost in the harmony of the whole.

Mankind must be so distributed, and every person must be so situated, as that the position of each may correspond to, and harmonize with, divine Law, such as is established by God in Nature and in Man unchangeably. Every individual must *gravitate* to the position suggested by his nature and its necessities, and also by the requirements of others, above and below him, in the Brotherhood. There should be no restriction to individual movements, especially when all movements are determined by the wisdom and righteousness of the supreme governor and director of human society. Every person should be as harmoniously situated as the notes in a well-arranged piece of music; and then all feeling, inclination, judgment, industry, progress, and intellectual attainment, would completely correspond to the law of uniform development and the combined interests of the whole.

No person upon the earth should exist inferiorly situated, because such is not in accordance with the nature and order of divine creations. No faculties should be crushed for the want of mental liberty; no powers of a mechanical, mathematical, or philosophical tendency, should be obstructed; for Nature prescribes liberty and unrestriction of thought. Hence man should be so situated as that all his spiritual qualities and faculties may be uncontrolled, and their unfoldings unbounded. That these things may be so, men should occupy those positions *only* which they are capable of filling, and in which they are happy and at home. But at present, some are teachers who are not so capable of teaching as many of their pupils. Some are occupying important offices by a voice of the people, and yet are not so capable of governing as those who are governed are to control themselves.

And one truth prominent among all nations and in all ages of the world is, that the most useful, pure, benevolent, and intelligent men, are those who, receiving a perfect constitution by birth, and being naturally situated, have unfolded a teeming intellect, such as never proceeds from any institution or any mode of obtaining superficial education. Hence it is clear that all those who are good and perfect, and have the most truth, are the unsophisticated offspring of Nature. Such minds possess all the qualifications of mechanics, philosophers, and philanthropists, and love truth and wisdom for their own sakes only, and not to acquire the character of being learned, and thus be advanced to honor and emolument. It is proper, then, that all should be perfectly arranged and well situated, so that all the movements of men, whether industrial or mental, may accord with their own nature and the interests of the whole society.

Men must become acquainted with the law of association and its distributions, before they can concert an harmonious brotherhood on earth. And after men are well situated, so that the whole will correspond to a system of undisturbed harmony, then will be developed the law of *Order*. This Order will unite them, and also represent the same displayed in the structure of the Universe. And thus the lowest and most imperfect will occupy the lowest point in society; and a graduated development will characterize the ascending groups, until they rise to the highest point of human perfection. And then he who is the most perfect in his physical and spiritual constitution, will occupy the highest position in society, as governor, and will pervade the whole by Wisdom, and direct them righteously according to divine harmony and universal order.

§ 23. Then there will be an order in human society, in which every group may represent a *planet*. And the groups may be so arranged as that their interests will revolve around the central object of their own industry and the Temple of Knowledge. Let the Sun of the race be the centre of all human wisdom, whose enlivening influence may generate industry, abundance, and happiness. Let each group, society, or state, be a planet; and let the whole give to and receive from the central Sun congenial reciprocations, so that there may not exist any *inertia*, restriction, poverty, or unhappiness. Moreover, let each group, as a planet, revolve within or around the orbits of others, according to their relation to the Sun of Knowledge and Centre of pervading happiness.

Each group will occupy such a position in relation to the Centre or Sun of society as is determined by its degree of progress, and its department of industry, so that its movements may be profitable and well defined. And there will be a uniform movement of all the groups, both within themselves and in their revolutions around their central governor or Sun of attraction.

And the various departments of society will represent the Solar System also in their mutual exchangings of purified and perfected particles. In other words, persons in the first society who advance and become capable of associating with the second, must be permitted to ascend and occupy the positions in the scale of progressive development for which they have become qualified. And let this mutual exchange be continued through all the groups, even up to the central power. And he who arrives there first by natural qualification, will succeed to the throne of government. And so there will be a constant supply of particles (or persons), both at the seat of government and at the extremities of society.

Individual advancement, to be pure, must be unceasing and perpetual. A person in the lowest society will gyrate through all the positions he is there capable of occupying, and ascend in like manner through all the societies to the Sun or seat of Wisdom. A perpetual reciprocation will be an inevitable consequence of the arrangement of society according to the divine law of association. Therefore an incessant progression will characterize human society and its component parts.

This mutual exchange of particles, or individuals, will result naturally from the order of refinement in each group or society; for their degree, or nearness to the centre, must be determined by their innate capabilities, and their absolute relation to the centre of Wisdom. So every individual will feel an inclination toward the centre of attraction; and all his efforts will be concentrated to gain the lofty seat. Also his interest will consist in the *purity* of his progress; for deception and *impure* enlightenment would only render a person more gross, and cause him to remain in a lower society longer than he otherwise would. Besides this, persons will mutually assist each other, inasmuch as a reciprocal assistance, without any isolated absorption, will materially accelerate the purification of all, and accomplish it more in accordance with natural law.

Each group will of itself constitute a little world, or a congregation of affectionate and inseparable individuals, laboring for each other's welfare. They will accumulate wealth for each other's enjoyment, and exchange favors one with another, for the purpose of making their group exceed as much as possible the lower, and approach in refinement the higher; and thus a lower and higher interest will be established. Each group should be like a planet in every particular; for each planet is an accumulation of mutually-agreeable particles, all assisting to effect a universal refinement. And thus associated, they revolve with unanimity around the Sun or Centre of their existence; and so should each group in the Solar System of mankind on earth. Each group, society, or state, as a planet, should be constituted of mutually-assisting particles (or persons), congenial with each other and with the sun or centre around which all societies should revolve in their movements and efforts to advance and become perfect.

This, then, should be the order of society. Then mankind would represent the harmony of the Solar System, in which no disturbance is discoverable, because the great central Sun is both the parent and governor, whose pervading influence sustains an indestructible equilibrium.

After having established this *Order*, a *Form* will be developed. This will be an expression of human wisdom, and will indicate the beauty of developed social happiness. This form will be as a *human body* in its arrangements and interior movements, but will correspond externally to the structure of the Universe. By *Form* is meant the mode of preserving and perpetuating Order, serving as a chart upon which will be impressed the situation of each person in society, and the relation of each to the central power. This Form will not only be the mode of preserving external Order, but of perfecting interior industry and individual character. It will be the Body of Mankind—a perfect representation of interior order, harmony, and association. It will be the means by which all mankind can associate with the beauties of Nature and the laws of God, even as a man associates with external things through the senses of the organization. And the human race will have a Form that will be a perfect representative of interior purity, harmony, and spiritual loveliness—that will be a perfect likeness of its interior, even as the human body is an image of the soul.

Mankind always had and always will have a Body, and that will represent the interior; and therefore a knowledge of the *Soul* of society may be had by carefully viewing its *Form*.—And at present this is very imperfect and very much disconcerted.

This, then, should be the plan of reorganizing society and the human world: First, develop *Light*, or the law of association. Unfold its teachings and apply them to the race. By this means, *Life* will be established, which is industry, harmony, and happiness. Then perfect *Love* will reign; for Light and Life are Love.—And association and harmony are the legitimate effects of Love, and Love is God.

After having developed these, an Order will be displayed in the structure of the race. This order will be the standard and law of human industry and mental qualification. It will confirm a unity of interest, and an unchanging reciprocation of feeling, affection, and mental associations, from the lowest to the highest degree of human advancement.

From this the human world will receive a *Form*—which will be the fulness of the stature of a perfect Man. And this Form will be the great exterior representative of interior love and industry, and also the mode by and through which the great Soul of Mankind will commune with the excellences of higher Spheres. Then Order and Form will be established, which are representatives of *Wisdom*—such as will emanate from the centre of social government, and spread distributive justice over the earth.

Then society will be in this condition: Perfect *Light* and *Life*, which are association and harmony, the whole of which will constitute Love perfectly developed:—and *Order* and *Form*, which are movement and mode, and which will constitute Wisdom, perfectly developed. Thus the human race will display Light and Life, which are *Love*, and Order and Form, which are *Wisdom*. Thus will be established *universal happiness*—because the whole race will represent the harmony of all created things, and typify the express majesty of the Divine Creator.

§ 24. Not only can human society be made to represent the harmonious movements displayed in our Solar System and in the Universe, but it can be made to correspond in every possible division and particular to the uniform kingdoms and creations of Nature. The lower stratum in the human world will, when properly arranged, take the lowest point, and correspond to the primary stratification of the earth. And the strata or groups of society may be uniformly situated one above another, as relative innate purity and capability may determine, and as is represented in the geological formations of this terrestrial sphere.—And the highest group may, in all its intellectual and brilliant excellences, correspond to the bosom of Nature, or the last stratum of the earth.

But human society may be organized on a more definite plan even than this. The first or incapable group of society may be so constructed as to represent the *mineral world*. That is, it may have three divisions: the first being the lowest, the second being the mediatorial, and the third being the highest—and the whole composing a perfect structure, and meanwhile naturally immerging into the society or group next above. Every particle in the mineral kingdom is incessantly engaged in activity, whereby the good of each is mutually established, and a reciprocal interest is caused to pervade the whole. So it may be with the first group or lower stratum of society. One may assist to sustain and develop another, which in return will act upon others; and thus will be established an interior industry so perfectly organized that no person will be compelled to labor excessively, to sustain unjust responsibilities, or be in any way deprived of his physical and mental requirements.

The second group may be made to correspond in its structure to the *vegetable kingdom*: and this can be accomplished by understanding the mutual relations existing between all plants as individuals, and how they are inseparably engaged in promoting a general good, observing a righteous reciprocation among themselves. Society, then, in its second department, would be a representative of the vegetable kingdom.

The ascending group may correspond to, and typify in every department, the *animal world* and its harmony. So may the highest or *central* group correspond to *Mankind*, in their relation to Nature and the various kingdoms. And as man is lord over of all subordinate creations; as he possesses the wisdom of love, and is a crown of material perfection, it is suggested that the central group of human society should manifest all the intelligence and perfection of the whole race concentrated. It may be the throne of human government, and the unfailing source of justice, benevolence, and liberty. This may be the centre of attraction to which all should be inclined, and by which all will be assisted to attain any degree of eminence possible for Wisdom to desire.

Society may be divided and subsided into as many groups or families as may be suggested by Wisdom and existing circumstances; and each individual group may correspond to the infinite variety contained in each kingdom in Nature. That is, the lower stratum of society may comprehend as many towns, counties, or states, as may be determined by general desire, and by a just estimate of human character and its qualifications; and these again may be subdivided into a variety of families or associations. And then they will correspond precisely to the specific compounds that are contained in the mineral kingdom. There is an infinite variety in this kingdom, and all have distinctive existences. So society may be constructed: and harmony will be the inevitable consequence, inasmuch as harmony is invariably manifested in the mineral kingdom, as a result of its structure.

So also the *second* stratum may comprehend as many portions of towns, counties, or states, as will harmonize with the situation of the lower; and this may represent the *vegetable* kingdom. Yet it should only be distinguished from the lower and higher by a different structure, though one calculated to perpetuate individual progression.

So with the *third* stratum; and so also with the *fourth*, which may be the centre of the human family, either on one continent or on both, and situated where all facilities exist, or can be made to exist, by which its influence may descend through all the lower strata and contribute to their health, happiness, and advancement. From this centre, a just administration must and will proceed; for no one can be the governor, emperor, or lord, of the human race, unless he has attained the highest possible degree of human wisdom. Such a one will be calculated to rule and govern all the departments of human industry, direct and perfect the establishment of all conveniences, explore and investigate all phenomena, and distribute peace, justice, and harmony, to all without distinction.

Society may be thus organized, inasmuch as the structure and laws of Nature suggest the plan. Moreover, the latter constitute a foundation upon which the superstructure may be erected indestructibly. And all its parts may be united by the same laws, actuated by the same general interests, and be preserved in the same undisturbed harmony.

Such is the *anatomy* of society presented for human contemplation and analysis. It is merely a *general* suggestion; and although *true*, it may be deemed *impracticable* by many good and intelligent minds. Such must analyze the features of this suggestion; and if it is not found to be true, and more suggestive than it would at first appear to be, it should lead to a *better* structure; and then its impulse will be pure, useful, and remedial of the present disorganized state of all human society.

Such is the cure for the corroding disease dwelling in the vitals of the human race, and existing in every society, state, nation, and empire, upon the earth. The disease has been revealed unexaggerated; its remedy is simple and will be effectual, if properly applied.

Having presented society in its disorganized condition, and the principles to organize it, it is proper to explain how these principles may soon be comprehended, and their teachings applied—and how men may proceed, without much destruction of interests or violence to local prejudices, to accomplish the reorganization. This can be done without changing the component parts of present society, and also without dislocating men from their present positions, or destroying their situations, except in a qualified degree, to which they will cheerfully accede, and thus effect the general millennium. Remember that all this harmony may be established without creating any serious conflict or disturbance in the present organization of social affairs. But in order to accomplish this, a living energy must inspire every philanthropist and every enlightened teacher, and they must be unceasing for a little time in preaching to the inhabitants of the earth, "Repent ye, for the kingdom of heaven is at hand." For all must repent, or, in other words, receive the conviction that distributive justice must pervade the social world before God's kingdom can come, and his will be done on earth as it is in heaven—or throughout all the higher spheres of celestial happiness. Keeping this in memory, I will now proceed to direct how the great remedy may be obtained, how the disease may be arrested and the system renovated, and how the divine kingdom may be established, and the new heaven and new earth wherein dwelleth righteousness may be understood, acknowledged, applied, and established, throughout the human race.

§ 25. To SUCCEED, the primary movements to elevate social relations, and to establish individual industry, may be commenced on this wise: Six agriculturists, inspired with the principles of charity and the spirit of improvement, and having a desire to associate, may form themselves into an association or corporation, with combined interests and desires for prosperity. They must fully understand each other, both as to their physical and mental qualifications, and must know how near they can approach a unity of interests, and how much each can contribute to the interests of the association.

They may enter into an agreement, such as will constitute them a corporation. This agreement must be based upon a plain diagram representing their individual possessions, interests, intentions, and proposed mode of condensing and organizing labor. This instrument of agreement must be as a map, representing their farms, with their value, their situations, their qualities of soil as to fertility or barrenness, their various locations, and the positions which they respectively occupy in relation to the nearest village, to the rivers or ports of commerce, and the existing facilities of effecting an access to the most populous and opulent cities. Moreover, it must represent every kind of soil, with its precise condition, as productive of vegetables, oats, rye, wheat, barley, corn, and also state the amount and condition of meadow and wood lands. A clear and lucid investigation, calculation, and statement, must be made in reference to the amount of labor necessary to bestow upon each division of one or all of the farms in order to render it fertile, productive, accessible, and remunerative.

Each individual must make a clear and truthful statement of the embarrassments, obligations, and expenses, to which he is at present subject; and also of the probable amount of money required to advance the condition of his farm to a high state of cultivation.

This agreement must be the spontaneous expression of their benevolent and united minds, impregnated with the desire and intention to remedy their own estrangement in industrial pursuits, and to correspondingly benefit community.

Six men, possessing farms in proper relations to each other, would be the least possible number who could concentrate and produce power among themselves, such as would be sensibly felt by all surrounding them. To this number any additional number may be joined, if the land occupied by them is in close connexion, and unbroken by any opposing landholder or agriculturist.

After deciding on the structure of their corporation, one of the members, who is most competent, should be chosen to officiate as governor, or president, and recording secretary. He should be qualified to suggest improvements, and to decide upon the most proper mode of organizing and distributing labor advantageously. This person should be the centre around which the rest should revolve or act in unity, and to whom they will look for justice in his dispensations and propriety in his suggestions and plans of labor and improvement. This one will manage the affairs of the association, and be as a standard to the corporation.

After having spiritually associated, devised their plan of agreement, and having all arrangements in order, agreeable to the situation and interests of each one, it is proper to institute the most searching investigations as to what may beautify their land, and restore fertility to the barren portions—and as to the most feasible plans to arrange and condense their labor for the accomplishment of this end. They must understand the science of organic chemistry in all of its ramifications, so that they may restore to weak soil its required equilibrium of organic matter, and thus fertilize and render it productive. They must also understand and apply in the tilling of their land the teachings of modern geology and magnetism. They must learn never to exhaust the soil of its requisite chemical properties, which is now frequently done by uninformed farmers. Soil can only retain its thriftiness and capacity of vegetable production by having restored to its bosom as much elementary matter as is taken from it. To sustain the fertility of the soil, then, it is necessary to understand the principles of geology and chemistry; the qualities of marine and alluvial deposites; the action of decomposed vegetable and animal compounds; the constitution of the earth and atmosphere, and the mutual relation which exists between them, and their co-operation in rendering fertile a parsimonious soil. Understanding these important principles, and perceiving their practicability, they will be enabled to devise the most agreeable means of applying them, so as to make them profitable in promoting their individual wealth and general advancement.

Then they must inquire into the various modes and plans of organizing and combining labor; how much labor it is proper to bestow upon any given object; at what time it should be bestowed, and how many can labor profitably to accelerate its accomplishment. Knowing these things, and adopting the proper plans of proceeding, they should call to their assistance as many laborers as can properly and profitably be employed.

They should not work *over* three quarters of the period of sunlight; and the employment of each one must be of such a character as will agree with his constitutional abilities and his desire to be engaged.

Thus organized, the distribution of labor for each week may be determined at the close of the previous one; and in this way each person will understand the portion assigned him, the position he is to occupy, and the amount of labor he is to accomplish. The laborers should be distributed in *groups* of numbers and strength sufficient to perform within the week the amount to them allotted.

Each member of the association must keep a strict account of his personal and general expenses, of the amount of labor accomplished in each six days on his farm, and of the number of men by whom it was accomplished. Thus each one, at the end of the week, should bring to the governor a truthful register of labor received from the groups of the association.

The quarter of time not devoted to the field may be set apart for individual diversion, instruction, study, and contemplation. Let it be exclusively devoted to all things pertaining to mental and moral improvement.—And thus he who labors will labor with a pleasure and profit to his physical being, and will change manual labor for mental advancement in every department of science, art, agriculture, and spiritual truth.

In this manner can labor be condensed, made attractive, profitable, and elevating. And this is the rudimental step toward establishing among the tillers of the land a reciprocal movement, and a privilege of assisting themselves and community to a more congenial and useful existence. This may be called an "*Agricultural Association.*" They will discover that they have the advantage over all individuals of like occupation in society, and that they will be enabled to supply the requirements of a populous village with more ease and profitableness than any dealer, merchant, or speculator.

§ 26. The Firm, in some thriving and populous village, town, or city, should erect a large and capacious *Storehouse*, which should be wisely constructed and adapted to the reception of their various productions. It should be situated conveniently, and made in every possible manner suitable to receive their abundant productions, which may be distributed according to the wants and requirements of the people. In this storehouse they must deposit in order the various creations of their industry, which should be valued at the same price which the community are compelled to pay for the same articles to merchants and grocers under the present system of trade. This storehouse and its abundant possessions, belonging to the Agriculturist Firm, would be a living illustration of the advantages of organized and rewarded labor, and a blessing to community.

This establishment may be conducted by any well-qualified person chosen by the association, and his assistants may be of his own choosing; and they all should belong to the association, and to a greater or less extent have an interest in its stock and wealth, so that each individual may have an interest centred in the prosperity of the Firm, both in respect to the farms and the establishment. Thus a unity of action would exist as a spontaneous result of the situation of each individual; and this would remove all deception, and develop justice and honesty in each being.

Each farmer should receive credit in proportion to the amount of stock by him deposited, and should be rewarded in proportion to its increasing revenue. A value must be placed upon each article of produce by the united voice of the whole Firm. This should be a standard by which each parcel should be valued as it enters the establishment; and credit should be given the depositor accordingly. The amount of stores in the establishment will be governed by the productions of the farms, and the reward of each laborer will hold a relation to the amount of produce in, and the benefits derived from, the establishment. Thus there will be a reciprocal exchange of interests, which will secure the permanency of the association, and render inexhaustible the capital of the Agriculturist Firm.

The contents of the storehouse may be sold to the community as they demand, at a price determined by the benevolence of the Firm, — who under such circumstances can sell at least fifteen per cent. cheaper than the same articles can be sold by individual tradesmen in villages and cities. And even then the productions will yield the producers at least twenty-five per cent. profit. And according as the distribution of labor is advantageous can this ratio be increased, even to double.

There will be a mutual deposition of capital, and a corresponding interest, which will constitute the whole association an established monopoly, and which will compel a change in the present order of industry, trade, and commerce. The influence of such an association, properly situated, would extend to adjoining townships and counties, and would be sensibly felt in various portions of the state. This would attract one farmer after another into the association, to arrest the depreciation of his land, and the decrease of the inflow of wealth from its productions. No individual farmer could compete with the association, and consequently its influence would continually widen by taking more into its constitution. And an influence, corresponding to that exerted on all members of the association, would be exerted on the inhabitants of the adjoining towns and counties; so that by a gradual yet permanent expansion, this system of agricultural labor would ultimately comprehend a whole state. Then other states could not resist its tranquillizing influence, and would adopt a similar mode of combining wealth with industry, and interest with energy and knowledge.

At first it would be best for associations of not less than six to form in various parts of towns, counties, or states, where all necessary facilities are existing, and all circumstances are such as to justify the enterprise. These small associations being once established, would enlarge until the interest of one would run into and become the interest of another; and ultimately a whole state would be combined as one Firm, governed by the same principles of justice and industry, and actuated by the same interests to all physical and intellectual improvement.

The first good object of such an association will be to combine interests, wealth, power, sympathy, and benevolence, and to bring men in closer relations as to their social and intellectual natures. Their interests will consist, not in the accumulation of needless wealth, but in *happiness*—which each person will enjoy, from being so situated as to render *others* happy. Not for the purpose of speculating upon community will the association labor, but to ameliorate the condition of the mechanic and the various professions, by supplying their wants abundantly, and at a price which falls within their resources.

The second object will be to combine labor so judiciously that one man, by working no more than under the present system, may produce twice the amount of labor, and create more food for general consumption. And thus it will be proved that organized industry is the only proper and effectual means of supplying the requirements of consumers, and making labor agreeable, healthful, instructive, and remunerative.

Another object will be to increase the demand for laborers, and advance the reward of labor—thereby giving employment to those who are now idle, and providing a proper subsistence for those foreign immigrants who are becoming citizens of the United States, and are being distributed in various portions of each state, destitute of property, health, and food. By increasing the demand for labor, and augmenting its reward, industry will become *attractive* to those who are compelled to labor for a subsistence. And by having this labor well distributed, and applied wisely and scientifically, it will make the soil productive, so that under any atmospheric vicissitudes it will yield enough to supply the wants of the whole association, the laborers included, and supply the storehouse with sufficient to redeem all expenses, and dispense an adequate and agreeable reward to each member.

Another valuable object will be attained; and that is, that *six* farms of ordinary size, conveniently situated in reference to the ports of commerce or towns and cities, would be made to produce as much as *ten* farms of equal size and quality of soil under the present system of cultivation. Three fourths more may be derived from one farm than is under the existing crude system of labor and agricultural science. An application of the principles and teachings of chemistry in the cultivation of the soil, would restore to it the most surprising thriftiness and richness of production. It could in a little time be made to produce sufficient to preserve its equilibrium of moisture and fertility, and also to supply the increasing wants of the association and the community.

§ 27. If six farms, then, can be made to yield as much as ten do under the present system of agriculture, is it not reasonable to suppose that the various vicissitudes of the seasons can not destroy more than the amount ordinarily produced by four farms? And then the productions of six would yet be preserved, which would afford an ample reward to the laborer and the capitalist. No season, however unfavorable, ever destroys more than one half of the ordinary productions of the soil. And even what would remain in such a one would, in association, more than supply all wants, and leave untouched all individual investments.

Men who engage in this enterprise must not feel that the accumulation of *money* is their object, but the greatest amount of *happiness*. Therefore the six agriculturists must be men having a high sense of justice, benevolence, and sympathy, not only for each other, but as respects the social condition of the community at large. They must feel that *money* is not valuable as productive of happiness; that it is no security against the invasion of disease, poverty, or destitution; that it is no benefit to their children, to community, or to the world. They must feel that money is now but a subject of individual and general infatuation — and that it is a most useless substance, and should not attract the attention of the noble mind, nor command the obedience of that dignified soul who feels that he lives for *wisdom* and *happiness*, and not for slavish degradation. With these feelings, they will come together and join their individual possessions, for the purpose of increasing power, charity, benevolence, and happiness. They must not join for the purpose of increasing individual wealth, or speculating on the laborer or the community; but for the purpose of increasing the demand for, and the reward of, labor, and to beautify the soil by applying scientific principles, and thus perfecting its fruitful qualities.

These men must well understand the depths of their own judgments, and of their feelings of benevolence and desires for unity. — And if each can arrive at the conclusion that they are living here to live again, and that their true desires and destinies are to procure *happiness*, then they may form an association impervious to all selfish and aristocratic innovations. They must not join their farms for the purpose of receiving as much interest as under their present mode of cultivation, but for the purpose of feeling as *one family*, united in their interests and enterprise, and one in their intentions to benefit the laboring classes, themselves, and the community at large.

In justice, there is no right to claim a stipulated interest for the appropriation of any portion of land, inasmuch as the soil is a bestowment and dispensation of Nature, unmerited by the existence, ingenuity, or industry, of any human being. In truth, *labor* is the use and destiny of man on earth, especially when that labor is attractive, well distributed, and well compensated. Then the association must exist on this wise :—

The existence, person, or body, of every laborer, must be considered as the only *real* and *natural* investment in the capital of the Firm. The industry of each individual is the personal bestowment of capital, for which each is entitled to every blessing and real requirement of life, and for the bestowment of which the association as a body is accountable. In this way, each individual would feel an interest in the amount of labor accomplished, and its results, and therefore an interest in the action of the whole. *Labor alone* must be remunerated; *capital* should be considered as an auxiliary — as a dispensation of Nature — and the foundation upon which the proposed superstructure can rest and be successfully established.

The object of having a standard price to each article, and a conventional rule as regulating the creation, deposition, and distribution, of the productions, is to facilitate the preservation of *memoranda*, and to conform as much as possible to mercantile arrangements that are existing; and also that there may be a definite value affixed to each article, to labor, and to the goods or property which each member appropriates to himself from the productions of the whole. These rules of procedure would be proper, in order to conform in a measure to present usages and cherished prejudices, and to a distaste for a too sudden transition from the present system to such an association of labor and interest.

Labor must have a reward prescribed in the rules of the compact; and that must be in proportion to the amount and kind of work performed, and the circumstances under which each one labors: each having a position assigned him in the field, which he is qualified to sustain. And this rule must apply to all, from the one who digs the trench, to the governor of the association; and the reward in all cases must be graduated according to the labor accomplished by the individual, and must be determined by the wisdom of the enlightened members and the sanction of the governor.

Remember that each one must be situated *advantageously* in the field and in every other department of the Agriculturist Association. Let *Wisdom* govern the distribution and compensation of labor, and not *desire* or *impulse*. Things being situated in this wise, labor could be rewarded justly and proportionally; and this by a conventional sum established by the *wisdom, justice*, and *benevolence*, of the first associates. And these must be careful not to have more interest in self-emolument than in the cheerfulness and happiness of the laborer.

Understand, then, that each man is to labor three fourths of a day, for which he is to be credited, and is to have as much as is necessary for his comfort, for which he shall be charged. At the end of each season, a general statement of affairs must be made and presented to each member, stating the amount of labor performed, its reward, the amount of produce received, and the balance of its proceeds after expenses are defrayed. And after each laborer is duly rewarded, the unexhausted wealth must be justly distributed to each primary depositor of property, as the just interest on his investment.

Labor is the *first* and *only* thing absolutely demanding reward. An interest must be paid upon *its* outlay; and after this the capitalists may receive the remaining sum, more or less, as interest on their primary deposition of property. The land can not be destroyed—

will not lose its value — will never fail to be a substantial guaranty against poverty or destitution. The human *body* — the *laborer* — is the only *real* capital demanding an interest from the wealth, strength, and opulence, of the association. And it is the *man* and his *efforts* that must be appreciated, and not the *unmerited soil,* to which no man by nature has a just and exclusive claim.

---

§ 28. And in order to conform to the present state of education, and to existing social movements, it is proper to commence a new heaven and a new earth with as much caution, gentleness, and judgment, as can be brought to bear, in reference to the present and a better system of social and intellectual affairs. And hence the necessity of having *good* and *benevolent* men to give the *first* impetus, and to consequently compel the remaining portions of the community to adopt a new system of social organization. A sacrifice must be made for the purpose of attaining a glorious reward, and a more desirable state of things.

The generality of minds will oppose this benevolent system, and believe it to be impracticable; but this will not arrest the efforts of six well-associated agriculturists, and the influence which they will exert over all the portions of each town, county, state, kingdom, and continent.

These are the incipient movements necessary to institute or create from the *old* a *new* world in respect to social interests and happiness. These first movements, after having been in operation for a few seasons, will resolve themselves into systems already conceived and partly established. New suggestions will be made, leading to improvements in every department of agriculture, science, social reform, and happiness. After being thus organized, each person will conceive how he can improve and advance his individual interests, and also the objects of universal benevolence. Therefore the community will glide imperceptibly from this crude system of association to the highest point of physical, social, and intellectual cultivation; and ultimately they will arrive at that eminence of perfection which will establish peace on earth, love to the neighbor, and good-will to all men.

On this rudimental principle may the association be conceived and established. And it will resolve itself from one system into another, and incessant progress will exemplify the constitutional tendency of human nature, until the earth will yield abundantly; until the farms appear like gardens; until industry is appreciated as a blessing; and every member, participating in the goodness thereof, will fulfil the destiny of his creation. And all being associated in interests and wisdom, will exercise distributive justice, and be HAPPY!

Love, unity, peace, power, wisdom, wealth, and happiness, will be the inherent attributes of the constitution thus formed. And these attributes will spring up and flow forth among the various and higher branches of art, science, and mechanism. Once establish such an association, and the demand for the invention, perfection, and manufacturing, of agricultural implements, will be increased. This will arouse the genius of every inventive mind, as men will see the need of instruments to till, beautify, and make fruitful, the soil. The influence of this will extend to all mechanics and their various objects of pursuit. Consequently a corresponding association must be formed among them, so that they may supply the demands of the farmer, and so that the two associations may freely exchange productions and wealth with each other.

An association of MECHANICS for the purpose of perfecting and utilizing machinery may be composed of from *fifteen* to *thirty* members. An article of agreement must join them in unity, and specify all their various investments, their proposed distribution of labor, the kind needed, the qualifications of the members to perform the various and specific branches of mechanical labor, the number of hours to work in one day (which should be with them not more than two thirds of sunlight), the advantages which they will have in respect to commerce, and the proposed location of their association, which should be in a convenient and accessible place. These things must be all clearly stated upon their articles of agreement. They must have their principles of mechanism distinctly impressed upon each laborer; and in the same things must all their novices and apprentices be instructed. They must comprehend the requirements and demands of the farmer. They must understand the relation which exists between chemical and mechanical principles; they must study well to adapt each movement in their employment to the various occupations and labors instituted by the agriculturists. They must learn well to perfect and condense labor, by inventing and establishing machinery within the circumference of the farmer's interests, in the form of saw-mills, flour-mills, manufactories, and establishments for the construction of agricultural implements.

An association of mechanics may so diminish their individual liabilities and expenses, as to render machinery available to all demanders, and that at a price corresponding to the cheapness of the soil's productions. As mechanics are now situated, they lose all the advantages of invention and wealth, because they are existing isolatedly, each striving to compete with, or take advantage of, his neighbor. They have power and wealth immense, but this being distributed among individuals, loses in influence and profitableness: and thus they are weak, though strong; and are contending, though one in occupation.

An association will remedy all these evils; for instead of each mechanic having an establishment incurring individual expenses, they may conjoin, combine their power, wisdom, and wealth, unite their movements, and organize their laborers; and then the expenses of a large association will not exceed those of five individual establishments as these now exist. Instead of having workshops disconnected, they may have them all combined in one well-constructed establishment erected by the association, sustained by their united wealth, and supported by the immense productions of the Agricultural Association. Every laborer could obtain provision for himself and his family with ease and without fear of destitution, because provisions would exist in abundance. Thus cheerfully impelled onward, each mechanic would gravitate to the establishment of the association, and enjoy a pleasure in industry. His mind would be unclouded with the fear of poverty and domestic necessities. He would work the time allotted, and devote the remainder of the day to amusement, instruction, contemplation, and investigation. He would feel an interest in labor, both for his own personal and for the general welfare. He would not be fatigued with gratification or monotony — but the hours of labor would be a relief from other pursuits in which he might be engaged; and the variety would make existence desirable and render it a blessing. Such would be the situation and condition of each member of the association.

§ 29. Each member must be interested in his own success and the success of the whole establishment. Each one must consider his person — his body — as living capital invested: his labor will be the interest of that capital, which will supply his individual necessities, and conduce to the wealth and emolument of the whole association. For remember that labor, when justly appreciated, organized, and remunerated, will yield more *absolute* wealth than it now can, under the present system of fatiguing and disgusting employment. One man would accomplish as much in two thirds of one day, thus situated, as three would at present. Then the reward of that labor, being proportionate, would more than supply his necessities, and would contribute to enrich the treasury of the association besides.

As labor is distributed at present among mechanics, at least one third of the labor apparently accomplished results in no good, but an absolute injury. Among mechanics, there are some who obstruct the process of business and counteract the efforts of others : for what one does is undone by another. They are like a machine disabled, and unmoved by any adequate power, foreign or inherent. The parts of this machine are the laborers. They, as cogs in a wheel, should be situated with reference to each other so as to produce harmony in their motion, and power in their action and influence. Each man, as a cog-wheel of the machine, must be relatively and wisely placed, in order to realize all the harmony and accomplish all the labor desired.

On this principle must labor be organized : In the mechanical establishment, each member will have his position and labor allotted to him by the judgment of the governor or qualified judge of justice and industry. Each member, then, will assume a position in the living machine of human industry in which he may assist those below and above him, and contribute to the wealth, strength, and harmony, of the whole.

This establishment should be near some thriving village or opulent city, and accessible to some seaport, so that they may hold commerce with regions where their materials exist, and with all manufacturing establishments in the state or states of the continent.

Their chief object must be to assist the agriculturist in his ennobling enterprise. They must feel an interest in beautifying and perfecting the soil, so that all wants may be supplied. An association thus constituted would not long exist before their interests would run into and inseparably unite them with the Agriculturist Association. For farmers, being enlightened in the *science* of cultivation, would feel the immediate importance of mechanical invention, and of the application of mechanical principles and machinery in the cultivation of the earth. They would discover that machines, not yet in their possession, would be useful as auxiliaries. Thus their demand for mechanical labor would be increased. This would stimulate the association to study, construct, and perfect, machinery to suit the requirements of the soil and its cultivators. This would give them labor immense; and hence they could not resist the feeling of interestedness in the welfare and improvement of those requiring their inventions. Thus the mechanic would feel an interest in the agriculturist — the result of which would be a combination and condensation of wealth and power; and thus the whole would become an *Agri-mechanical Association*.

The bodily necessities of the multitude thus employed would create a substantial centre of interest for the various tradesmen and mechanical producers that now exist individually in society. The abundance of cattle and herds produced would contribute very largely to the interests of the *manufacturers of leather*; and they, by following similar suggestions and improvements, would concentrate and combine their occupation in a form so as to compete and correspond with those who supply them with business, at a price in inverse proportion to the abundance of the stock produced. The leather-manufacturers would soon discover that the articles of their creation can be supplied with more abundance and ease under this system than under the present, and their processes would be so greatly improved and accelerated as to enable them to manufacture their leather with more promptness and pleasure, and then to afford the community their productions at a price corresponding to the price of that which they receive.

The *shoe-manufacturers* would then find it proper and profitable to form themselves into a similar association. One association in this branch may be composed of from seventy-five to one hundred members. With an equal distribution of labor according to individual ability and desire, they may combine their stock, labor, and movements, and produce one third more than the same number of men at present, under the most favorable circumstances. Each one may have his peculiar branch allotted to him, and not be compelled to do any more than his interest may dictate — remembering that his interest must be the interest of the association. Similar principles of labor and investment must be adopted as in the other associations; and the object of their labor and productions must be centred in the desire to supply as abundantly as possible the demands of the Agri-mechanical Association and the poor in society. Inasmuch as their expenses will be decreased from one third to one half, thus associated, it is agreeable to reason to suppose that what they may produce will flow forth and supply all demands with a spontaneousness that will encourage every laborer and bless every destitute being.

In like manner may an association of *hatters* be formed — the number of members being the same. There should be with them the same investment of body, interest, and labor, and the same reciprocal and harmonious movement should be established. And the object to be attained must in every particular be similar to that of the shoe-manufacturers.

So likewise may the *clothiers* or *garment-makers* be joined, and be producers of wealth and happiness upon the same reciprocal principles.

And there are minor occupations, all of which should be comprehended within the three great associations. They may be so situated as to have their interests parallel with the interests of the organized bodies, which will be planned and elucidated by those who will study the principles of social industry, interest, wealth, and power.

Men may pass from the present into this system without any material sacrifice, and with the full assurance of retaining their present personal possessions; and if vigorous in their enterprise, they will acquire much more.

§ 30. There is no means at *first* to ameliorate the condition and curtail the labor of *females*. At present, each female parent has as much labor to accomplish in her household as three can with propriety do. The reason is clear: Every woman having a family is obliged to struggle through isolated labor unassisted, and with domestic embarrassments which are frequent and increasing. And the labor of every family is as much as the labor of *three* would be if they were situated nearer to each other, so that one large and well-constructed machine, by the assistance of a few females, would do all the washing of a large number of families. And baking, sewing, embroidery, horticulture, and all labor suitable to each qualified female, may be performed with more ease, less embarrassment, and with delight. These are among the progressive steps not as yet well to urge, inasmuch as they will be the spontaneous effects of the primary movements herein recommended for the farmer and the mechanic.

The order, form, and influence, of these co-operative associations, will legitimately extend to the *manufacturers of cotton and woollen fabrics;* and the action upon them will be effectual and salutary. They will find it impossible to subsist under their present system of labor: for the opulence and strength of the Agri-mechanical Association will indicate the possibility of establishing manufactories of a more agreeable and productive nature. The manufacturers, then, will be driven to the exercise of reason and justice, a conformity to which, however, will be found more profitable and agreeable than their present isolated operations. The result will be a reorganization and condensation of labor among this class; and its remuneration will create an interest and happiness among the operatives.

Of the cotton and wool manufacturers, the proprietors of from four to six establishments may associate, unite their wealth, combine their strength, and become a powerful monopoly whose influence will extend through every state and into other kingdoms. They, like other associationists, will discover the proper means of establishing their interests and organizing their labor in due relation to the interests and labor of the agriculturist and the mechanic.

In foreign kingdoms, operatives are compelled to labor from two thirds to three fourths of every twenty-four hours unrewarded. Their physical energies are prostrated, their labor is misdirected, and their productions are not much honor to the employer, being associated in the mind with poverty, disease, and death. An association may so direct the movements of the laborers as to make them all productive, pleasurable, interesting, and remunerative. Those who engage in, and become members of, the association, may have their respective positions assigned to them in the various branches of labor in the establishment. So well may they be arranged in forms, series, and groups—in positions, movements, and qualifications—that all united will be as a moving machine, exceedingly productive of the various articles they conjoin to create. In the manufactories, this system of labor has already arrived to some degree of perfection. Manufacturers exercise more wisdom in the distribution of labor than do most other men. Yet they are laboring under disadvantages and monopolizing influences, foreign and immediate, which compel them to enforce the operatives to more labor than they in justice can be required to perform, and to reduce their compensation—and all for the purpose of overcoming, and yet sustaining, monopoly and competition.

Their form of association will be derived from those established before them. The most active means must be instituted, the most enlightened ingenuity must be exercised, and the most benevolent and just feelings cultivated; and these will secure harmony in their proceedings, success in their enterprise, and unity in their stock, strength, labor, wealth, and benevolence.

Their interests are so intimately allied to those of the *wool and cotton growers*, that it will be impossible for one to thrive without affecting the other correspondingly. The perfection of agricultural science, and the knowledge of the constituent parts of the vegetable and animal forms, will give to the cultivator of the soil a controlling influence over the mechanic and the manufacturer. He will learn to produce well, cheaply, and abundantly, and even not to feel the expense of the production. The wool, selected in parcels of various degrees of refinement, may by the Agriculturist Association be made suitable to enter the machine to come forth in cloth for the community.

If manufacturers will not unite their operations with those of the cultivator, the mechanics, so intimately connected, will unite in establishing a manufactory for their own benefit and objects of benevolence—and thus drive those, who are not willing, to organize themselves correspondingly without, to flow into, and become members of, the united Establishment. Once join the farmer and mechanic in unity and benevolence of action, and the whole social world will be obliged to follow their example, or form a close relation to the associations that will be already established.

Thus the sympathy will be communicated from the agricultural association to the various departments of trade, mechanism, and manufacturing. And the germ once deposited on the bosom of the soil, will grow up unimpeded, until all other departments of society will come into corresponding unity of action and interest.

§ 31. The next and most important movement will be among the various *professions*. The great load of corruption and social disease arising from their vitiating situations will then be nearly removed, and every member will become a useful wheel in the great machine of humanity. The immediate effect of the preceding associations will be felt among the *legal profession*. For men will have learned to exercise the principles of legal and moral justice in their own lives, and in the affairs of their various establishments. There will be no necessity for long and tedious suits concerning personal or real estates. The business of chancery will be diminished. The exercise of *su-*

perficial justice will be discarded and despised; and the profession will glory in the downfall of that which they are *now* convinced is neither righteous nor beneficial in its influence.

There may then be an association of this profession consisting of from seventy-five to one hundred and fifty members—each member to contribute capital of valuable *information* to the treasury of *knowledge*, which the chief and best-qualified mind must preserve. They must not confine their attention exclusively to the principles of legal and social jurisprudence; but they must investigate, and accumulate valuable information to benefit the farmer, the mechanic, and the manufacturer. They must promote justice in the discovery and application of *practical principles;* and this should be the *chief* object of the legal association. They may devise, according to their associated wisdom, the most agreeable social constitution similar to those already established.

And it is proper for each member to have his field of investigation allotted to him: and all should observe the various changes of occupation necessary to sustain physical and cultivate intellectual health.

Their labor, then, may be distributed in this manner: Four hours of each day may be devoted to the demonstration of the practicability of discovered principles. Their work should pass through the various Series, one being higher than the other, for criticism, until it reaches their governor, who shall reject or sanction their conclusions. In one association there may be six Series. The first or rudimental Series should be engaged in the useful departments of elementary science and literature. The labors of this should be modified and corrected by the second Series, enlarged by the third, demonstrated by the fourth; their various ramifications may be unfolded and their practicability determined by the fifth; the whole may be rejected or sanctioned by the sixth, which shall consist of the governor and his associates.—And thence the discoveries or principles will flow perfected to the farmer and the mechanic, and their application will enrich the soil, bless the farmer's industry, inspire the mechanic with confidence in the foundation of his movements, and make his efforts successful; and their general influence will be adapted to the wants of the community, and the results will be honoring to the legal profession, as displaying distributive justice and harmony in their highest modes of manifestation.

This association must be watchful of, and interested in, the various movements of the associationists. They must elucidate and explain all principles of justice and amicableness to each member; lecture to them, and instruct their minds in the mysteries of Nature, her beauties, her bestowments, teachings, and requirements, and in all principles which are necessary for each individual to comprehend, for happiness.

Four hours of each day should be thus occupied by the various Series of the legal association. The governor must be the supreme judge of equity and harmony, which he must freely dispense among the various groups of each association when required. He and his courtiers or associates must be the just jurors or judges of every apparent discrepancy that may occur. Every one should repose confidence in them, because their objects and interests must be reciprocal. They must not rest when there are any elements of dissatisfaction in any of the various groups of the community. They must not, as they now do, wait until such disturbances involve families and estates in long and tedious discussions; but they must be *peacemakers*— and go and extinguish all corrupting disaffections ere they are fanned into a dissolving flame of passion and social contention. Thus they will not only *teach*, but *practise* the principles of distributive justice, the tranquillizing influence of which will advance them to honor, and elevate every member in the various associations.

Thus labor is to be distributed in this association for four hours of each day. The remainder of sunlight will be devoted to the cultivation of the floral kingdom, to the fine and refining arts, to amusements, to *any* diversion, so long as that benefits the physical and elevates the moral being.

An association can not long exist on this wise before they will be attracted to the beauties of the soil. They will appreciate its blessings, and resort to it as a diversion and pleasure, and as a relief from the incessant fatigues of wealthy gratification, and the depression of mental attention and emulation. They will discover in labor an attraction; and they will devote themselves, as inclination may dictate, to the farming, mechanical, and manufacturing employments. Some will be predisposed to the invention of *machinery*, to which a portion of their time will be with pleasure and profit devoted. Others will be interested in the artistic pursuits, employing themselves in sculpture, portrait and landscape painting, and also in expressing their instincts, affections, genius, and intelligence, in the multifarious creations which will spontaneously flow from their association and general unity of interest.

All that should be done in the way of legalizing and demonstrating the principles of justice to the community, can be accomplished in the brief period of four hours in each day. And in whatsoever additional pursuits they engage, their time and talents will be remunerated in proportion to all their physical and mental wants, remembering that *Wisdom* is to be the administrator. Their existence will be useful, honored, elevated, and generally purifying to all the lower yet happy laboring classes.

Immediately will the fire of this association be communicated to the *physicians*—who will form a similar association or institution, constituted of a similar number of congenial and well-qualified members. The medical institution will be devoted to the *discovery* and *arrest* of disease, and not to the tiresome practice of *curing* diseases which are already contracted, as is the mode at present.

This institution must also be composed of six Series, or states, or parts, the centre of which will be their Professor and Judge. Labor is to be distributed among each Series such as they are qualified and willing to perform. Their interests, as a whole, will be the interest of the other and subordinate associations.

The labor of the first Series must be to explore the physical condition and structure of every individual, and to communicate their discoveries to the *second* Series. These are to investigate the facts and place them in a proper juxtaposition to the name of the diseased or defective individual, and the group of which he is a member. The statements in this form must be given to the *third*; analyzed by them and given to the *fourth*; the proper remedies and treatment must be stated by them and given to the *fifth*—who will decide upon the appropriateness of the remedy to the cause and nature of the disease. The *sixth*, consisting of the Judge and Professors, will sanction or disapprove the proposed treatment, and despatch the proper members to officiate in the application of their remedies to the patient.

In this way may every disease be discovered, properly understood, and most permanently cured—which never can be done under the present system of isolated investigation and practice. Then all professional discussions, anathemas, and denunciations, will be abolished, and conflicting systems of practice will not exist: for all will be combined as one true system, taught and established in the nature of things.

§ 32. Four hours of each day may be thus employed. Let the chief object and interest be to keep the people from violation by teaching them the constitution of their being, the necessity of obedience, and the propriety of cleanliness, exercise, and judgment, in all their individual and social relations. Each individual must learn the importance of exercising a clear and potent *wisdom* in his living and occupation; and the various associations must construct all the conveniences for bathing, washing, and thorough cleansing, as they are directed by the physicians. They must be governed in their household relations, in their diet, in *all* things relating to health, according to the dictation of the physicians. Such must be the labor of the physicians; and such must be its results.

Each association will reward the legal and medical institutions in proportion to the good they accomplish in their four hours of industry, which will be vast and appreciated. For talent will be deeply esteemed, and proportionally remunerated. Each association will discover that they can not succeed without the existence of the legal and medical professions; for the first will disseminate the principles of justice, and the latter the blessings of health and the knowledge of personal physiology. One will be indispensable to the other; and thus they will approve, assist, and bless, each other's movements.

Another object of the medical institution must be to investigate the principles of chemistry, physiology, allopathy, homœopathy, hydropathy, magnetism, atmospheric and solar electricity, and all things appertaining to the human body, either directly or indirectly. They will discover that each one of the various systems of medical practice at present existing contains some, but not *all* truth, as is claimed for each one by its respective professors. They will discover that each system recognises some principles susceptible of the most beneficial application. They must combine all the medical discoveries and sciences, and, from a searching investigation, produce one grand and unequivocal System of medical practice. Let their superior wisdom direct the application of each discovery, principle, prescription, rule of regimen and therapeutics. And by the conventional sanction of the judge and professors, an incontrovertible system will be established, which will arrest, overcome, and dispel, every species of organic and functional disease.

Each Series and Degree of members must have their field of labor and investigation so wisely adapted to their abilities as to make the distribution of industry in the whole institution to precisely correspond with that of the associations upon which they depend, and among which they officiate.

The remainder of the day may be devoted to social festivities and all species of gymnastic exercises calculated to promote physical vigor and energy of intellect. Or they may participate in the various and agreeable branches of agriculture, mechanism, and art. They may enter into every species of amusement, so long as an unclouded *Wisdom* sanctions the justice, propriety, and profitableness thereof.

On this wise may one legal and medical association be established; and they will constitute an established central and attractive power, such as can not be resisted. Its influence will extend over all the relative professions, and form them into a similar community of wealth and elevation.

And now will the highest profession be compelled (for they will not make the move without compulsion) to form a similar constitution, for the unrestricted dissemination of knowledge, the crushing of prejudices, and the advancement of the moral and intellectual world? The CLERICAL profession must form an institution for the purpose of moral culture and spiritual progress. And inasmuch as they are, or at least *should* be, the most worthy of all professions and individuals in the constitution of society, it is necessary to explain the most feasible and congenial plan of reforming them, so that they may reform society.

Clergymen, associated in numbers of from fifty to seventy-five, may organize an institution in which each member (the whole being distributed in classes) may occupy a position according to the requirements of the institute, and the use it is intended to accomplish. This institution is to be arranged upon principles similar to those controlling others — with members so arranged as to produce an harmonious movement, both among themselves and with reference to the community. It is to be the seminary for instruction, especially for instruction in the higher branches of knowledge. It is to have concentrated all the combined literature, science, philosophy, and theology, that now exist in the universities and collegiate institutions of the land. Their object must be to understand the depths and widths of natural law and science; to bring forth and analyze all the theological *isms* of the land; to reject the evil and preserve the good out of the vast congregation of systems; to understand the theology of Nature, and the manifest constitution of the Divine Mind, and to blend science, and theology, and reason, and philosophy, into one grand system of education. They must discard all restriction of thought and investigation, all circumscribing prejudices, all unholy teachings and systems, that now pervade the mental world; and finally, they must discard all things tending to establish sects, or to promote distinction or prejudice, and receive only that which flows spontaneously from the indications of Nature, and the sanctions of a free and well-constructed judgment. This must be the object impressed upon such a number of clergymen before they can effectually reform the social and moral world, and form an immoveable institution of knowledge and righteousness.

With this object duly in view, the institution may be established in this order and form, to succeed, and bless society: Seventy-five members are as many as should enter into one association. These may be divided into six classes. To preserve form and order, they should be situated in progressive relation to each other, so that the six Series may be so many *steps* of literary, scientific, and theological development, commencing at the primary class, and ascending to him who presides in the sanctuary of the people.

The first class must be composed of qualified individuals whose degree will be above the office of the highest physician in the previous institution. They are to be the transition-step from the legal and medical field into the scientific and philosophical. They must take up the various subjects where the physician leaves off. And the results accumulated by them must be transferred to the *second* degree—and so onward and upward to the sixth, who shall be the emperor of social righteousness. Thence their vast scientific and spiritual accumulations will flow to the lower associations, be comprehended by them, well adapted to their wants, actualized, and made eminently useful and practical.

§ 33. The six Degrees are all steps of relative perfection. Each person, according as he has advanced, may be designated by the peculiar brilliancy, taste, and elegance, of his habiliments. A distinction must thus be established, in order that there may be an attraction for the situation of every individual that will extend to and elevate the lower classes. The members in the various degrees are to be situated in positions agreeable to their most wise desires, and according as their abilities to sustain and render themselves useful may suggest.

The *establishment* to be erected by this institution may in its architectural qualities display all the superior combinations of beauty, use, order, form, adaptation, agreeableness, and magnificence. It may be decorated with examples of every mechanical and architectural invention. It may represent in structure externally the combined contributions of art, science, and architecture, and be a standard of magnificence: and all this for the important purpose of representing the advancement of this age beyond those that are gone by, and for the purpose of indicating the progress of the race. The structure should be such as to captivate all tastes and affections, and to suit all desires in respect to order, form, and splendor; and it should be a standing representative of the wisdom, wealth, strength, opulence, and refinement, of the whole nation.

Interiorly, it should possess the attributes of cheerfulness, fascination, splendor, convenience, and refinement, and should imbody all the architectural conceptions of what should be the sanctuary of human wisdom and righteousness.

It should have six apartments, which must, in structure, correspond to the degrees of their respective occupants. Each chamber, or apartment, should possess all the conveniences suitable to the department of the association to which it belongs: and the appearance of each member must fully correspond to the position occupied. Thus the building, both internally and externally, must be adapted to, and must correspond with, the use and end contemplated—as also must its occupants to the offices respectively assigned to them; and thus the whole institution will display the harmony of Wisdom in actual demonstration.

The emperor and his courtiers and counsellors are to legislate for the several associations within the circumference assigned to their institution. They are to disseminate, irrespectively, justice and judgment to every individual—and to be the governors, presidents, kings, or lords, to exercise justice and wisdom as derived from science and the savings of combined systems by them accumulated, analyzed, refined, and practically applied. They are to be the governors in respect to all which subordinate classes require to bless and make them happy. They are to have perfect confidence in the people, which the latter, as brethren, will desire and reciprocate. The lower associations will represent the successive developments of the great human machine of industry and happiness; and the *highest* or *clerical* institution must be the pervading power to penetrate and start into unceasing activity all the subordinate departments of society. They must legislate for, and apply the principles of morality, science, and refinement, to every individual who requires, and thus sustain a watchfulness over the whole flock, feeling desirous to perfect and perpetuate social unity, and thus contribute to the interests and requirements of the Whole.

Seminaries and universities at present existing, are not such as disseminate the *kind* of knowledge that mankind require. And as they are isolatedly and conventionally situated and supported, they are not accessible to those classes who need education and refinement. Therefore, to prevent the perpetuation of this educational system, let an institution be formed as has been proposed. Let the reward which is now given to pastors by their congregations, the wealth lavished upon the erection and gorgeous embellishment of the churches and systems that are now individually or collectively supported, within a given territory, be combined and concentrated, with the strength and intelligence of the people, into just one institution of seventy-five members. It may be supported by the same amount of contributions that are now made to individual societies, clergymen, and universities.

This project can be easily accomplished by presenting the public mind with a clear calculation and statement of the funds required, the movements necessary, and the amount of good to be legitimately derived therefrom by all. In each county, shire, state, or kingdom, there is wealth expended sufficient to organize and sustain more institutions of this character than will be found absolutely necessary. Then collegiate technicalities will be bestowed upon those who are qualified to justly appreciate and apply the immense and useful attainments which they will denote.

But the identity of these several institutions now existing will be lost, and their isolated wealth will be distributed among deserving individuals. It will extend to the almshouse, to the asylum, to the hospital, to the mariners' association, and to the poor of every town and state; and it will not lose its force until it descends, by the industry of every restored and elevated being, to the soil, whence it will send forth an abundance to all in return. This all may be done without seriously depreciating the capital or riches of one person in society. On the contrary, it will enrich and advance them to honor and happiness.

The change must be only in this particular at present, viz., that the various sects, with their clergymen, should, instead of dividing, unite their strength and wealth, with their bestowments upon missionaries and upon isolated institutions of education; and thus an alliance should be effected between all sects. Their clergymen should meet, assisted by the same as they now receive, or *any* proper sum, as a reward for their industry, and form an institution upon the principles of distributive justice and wisdom. And those who now support religious systems and benevolent institutions will find it much to their advantage to cast their bestowments into the treasury of such an enterprise; for all would be correspondingly enriched and elevated thereby. On this wise, then, may clergymen be improved in situation, and be advanced to personal and general honor, wisdom, and righteousness.

---

§ 34. The form and structure of society is now made manifest. The formation of the agricultural, mechanical, and manufacturing degrees or associations of industry, strength, and wealth, are the three movements necessary for society, that it may preserve its identity, and establish a foundation on which to exist and thrive immensely. These are the *rudimental* forms necessary to establish. They, as one, constitute the body of Love, or of reciprocal movement. The *farmer*, *mechanic*, and *manufacturer*, are a *trinity* composing one body of industry and equal distributions of labor. They are at the bottom, and support all else, and hence correspond to the principle of Love contained and demonstrated in the nature of the divine creations.

Then the *legal*, *medical*, and *clerical* associations, are a *trinity* forming one Whole, which corresponds to Wisdom. The first arrange all conventional movements on the principles of equity, harmony, and practicability. They restore all deranged or defective personal and conventional bodies to a state of health and harmony, and consequently are those who recognise justice and display it without distinction in their various administrations. The *second* seek out and restore all the subjects of disease, whether personal or general, to a state of health and strength; and thus assist the legal profession in their occupation and influence. The *third* accumulate science, art, theology, and philosophy, which they make perfect and practicable. These they disseminate among, and freely apply to, the members of each association, as they in wisdom desire or require. Hence the clerical institution will be the great court of justice, the temple of liberty, and the sanctuary of knowledge and righteousness. Their influence, in practice, will proclaim, " Fear not, for behold we bring you glad tidings of great joy which shall be unto all people." The response will be, " Glory to God in the highest, on earth peace, good-will to men."

Thus the legal, medical, and clerical associations, are three parts of one whole system, which corresponds to Wisdom. So the structure of society will be an imitation of the structure of the Universe; and its Soul will be like the structure of the Divine Mind, which is Love and Wisdom. The kingdom of heaven will be on earth, and under its dominion each one may repose in undisturbed confidence, fulfil the destiny of his being, and glorify the unbounded blessings of higher spheres.

Family forms, sympathies, and relations, it is proper to preserve— inasmuch as it is not necessary to change any of the conjugial attachments that now exist, to successfully establish the principles and movements of an association. Directions concerning these things will naturally arise from the wisdom and investigation consequent on such a social organization.

But education, both primary and scientific, needs to be essentially changed: that is, there must not exist so many and dissimilar modes of impressing youthful minds with doctrine instead of practice, and with useless instead of practicable principles. There must exist a *unity* in education, and a progress in administering instruction to the young. And, agreeably with the sympathies and present prejudices of every family, the present system may be essentially and profitably modified in the following manner:—

The Agricultural Association may have a department and system of rudimental instruction for their young, in which may be taught the primary rules of orthography, etymology, syntax, and prosody. These should perfect the instruction in this department.

The Mechanical Association may have a system in unity of plan with the latter, taking from this lower branch into their own hands the charge of the education which may be given to their children. This stage of education should range from the primary, through geography, arithmetic, and mathematics, comprehending all the primary principles of mechanism, and the general principles of the whole Agri-mechanical Association.

The *manufacturers* will likewise adopt a system of educating their young—which will proceed from the general education of the latter class into its various ramifications, and will also consist in practically demonstrating the principles impressed on their children in the school of the mechanics.

The *legal* association may have a seminary for taking up the various instructions of the last system, and carrying them on through the rudimental branches of their own attainments.

And so the *medical* and *clerical* associations must proceed—the latter to bestow every species of valuable information in possession of the race. They are to teach none other than sound, unprejudicial, and practical principles of life and happiness. And the instructions in this department are to be considered the completion of every proper and useful education.

The various associations may have systems thus successively established, so that in the ascension from the farmer's to the highest institution, one perfect system of education may be completed.

It will be discovered (according to various writers on education) that children should not be mentally fatigued with instructions derived from books, a monitor, or anything that may interfere with the *natural* process of the development of their tender faculties; and that an age of from six to eight years is necessary for each child to attain before being introduced into any school of education. In this way all fatigue may be escaped, and all youthful interest for instruction be preserved.

At the age of eight years, the natural predisposition and mental and physical qualifications of each child will be sufficiently unfolded to indicate to the parent the *kind* of education or employment which would be agreeable and proper. It will be found that some children will pass from the farmer's family through all the systems, until they attain a high seat in the people's sanctuary. And this will be determined by the innate aspirations of the mind indicated even in childhood. If the child is born amid the circumstances of the agriculturist, and if, as the faculties unfold, he indicates a disposition for science and philosophy, and manifests a general veneration, he should pass directly from the primary school to the legal, and thence to the clerical. If a child is inclined to the medical profession, let his inclinations be cultivated, and let him pass directly from the primary to the medical school, where he will receive his required instruction. A pre-qualification and predisposition should never escape the observation of a parent, in any of his children. His convictions must be communicated to the institution to which the child is by nature attracted, and by which its education will be freely given.

---

§ 35. It will also be discovered that some children born amid the circumstances of the legal, medical, and clerical profession, will be disqualified for any of these, and by nature will gravitate to the mechanical or agricultural employment. So there will be an equal and just exchange of desires and attractions among the children of each association, which will gratify their parents, and banish all social disturbance from the community.

On these principles will education of every low and high degree be perfected — distributing equality or preference to all according to innate ability and natural attraction.

As men are *at present* situated, education does violence in many instances, both to body and mind. Some who are now debased, digging the trench, laying the wall, or slavishly tilling the earth, are better qualified by nature to be physicians, or teachers of science, than many of those who are thus situated. Many who are now clergymen would be in their element if in the workshop or in the field. So with many physicians, lawyers, manufacturers, and mechanics. Men are now compelled to engage, for a subsistence, in that in which it is neither their nature nor desire to engage. This is the reason why the various professions have men who dishonor their employment and prostitute their superficial education. And so men in the various branches of farming and manufacturing who do not succeed in their employment, being always dissatisfied, striving to escape from their situations, and being finally compelled to remain, lose all interest in their avocations, and are neither useful to themselves nor to society. Details concerning these important truths may be found in the writings of valuable men who have thought upon and investigated the causes of social disunity, and unfolded the errors of present education. But it would not be important to multiply examples in this place. Yet these can be perceived by every enlightened mind who can distinguish the relation between cause and effect.

Association would remedy all these evils — would not only cultivate all the good interests of the human soul, but give them a truthful and proper direction. Men who are now engaged in the various modes of employment, would at once gravitate to that which is most congenial to their nature and qualifications. Children would inevitably do the same; and therefore an equality would be the highest result of such a social and educational organization. Every facility must be conceived and practised by the superior association, for the purpose of instructing and refining each child and parent.

Women, in each association, should exercise as much taste as the men — inasmuch as they suggest all the life-imparting impulses to the male department. They must cultivate and display their conceptions of the beautiful as manifested in any of the delicate arts and sciences, which must be among the chief objects of the ascending and superior associations to cultivate. The floral kingdom can be greatly advanced in beauty, order, and instruction. All the high degrees of beauty which may be displayed in dress and ornament, and the various possessions sanctioned by the wisdom of the governor, can be derived from the delicate textures of flowers. This may be the primary field of the females.

Thence they may ascend to the refined arts of painting, embroidery, and all the higher branches as relating to beauty and grandeur, and cultivate all the lovely conceptions of Nature and art. These things must be the essential attraction of the female. And she will receive all the accomplishments which a superior wisdom can dispense, and which well-constructed institutions abundantly possess.

Thus the education of youth, male and female, may be conducted; and the result will be a total destruction of all disunity now caused by individuals occupying situations for which they by nature are in no wise qualified.*

Such must be the *Body*, and the movements within must be the *Soul*, of society. The superior or clerical association should thus be the seat of justice, legislation, and dispensation; and all subordinate ones will perform the important offices assigned them. And from the harmony and unity of the whole, will proceed SOCIAL HAPPINESS AND SPIRITUAL ELEVATION.

One facility, one most powerful engine of freedom and of the distribution of thought, must be attached to the superior association, and thus be a part of it, and that is THE PRESS. This wields an omnipotent sceptre over the public mind, and is a rightful vehicle for the dissemination of personal, local, scientific, and general information. A printing department, then, should be composed of a congregation of present proprietors, and conducted upon the most expeditious principles which the science of mechanism can without difficulty supply. A multitude of presses may be governed by one well-constructed engine, and labor may be so distributed as that as much labor as is at present accomplished may be performed in one third of the time.

This must form an important part of the superior association. The interest of printers must be concentrated on the great end of *social unity*, and on the *equal distribution of knowledge*. Until they agree to this, there will exist as much disunity in their pursuits as now exists. Those who are competent to preside at the editorial table should perceive at a glance the consistency of this proposed system. They, moreover, should exert their influence in promulgating the high principles of magnanimity and benevolence of soul.

One truth, however, is particularly impressive, and that is, that if he who wields the pen to inform the public mind through journals and books of the day, does not perceive the importance of these principles of social reform, he is most certainly not qualified for the office which he is compelled by circumstances to occupy. A movement can not be depended upon as commencing in this class, but only among the laboring classes — the *farmers* and the *mechanics* — who, when once organized, will draw the social world into their consociable embrace.

The *mercantile* business as now existing will be essentially changed. The provisions sold by the grocer will be procured from the Establishment of the farmers. And this will consequently compel those of this branch to congregate into a large association, or submit to be attracted into the various employments adopted by the six associations. The same destiny awaits those who are now engaged in the retail of manufactured goods : for the manufacturers will also have an Establishment for their productions — which will be distributed according to increasing demands. And this will be more convenient and profitable than to have their productions gyrate through the hands of the tradesmen, which is nothing more nor less than advancing the first profits to a price almost equal to the cost of the goods primarily.

The detached mechanics in villages and cities will be drawn into the associations, for they can not exist separate from them.

§ 36. Finally, the rudimental movements of the association must begin on these gentle principles ; and then they will gradually modify the present system, until it is resolved into a new one. This plan will not offend established prejudices, nor disturb the present relations of families, friends, and social organizations; but it will address itself to those who are advanced and prepared to enter immediately on this grand and elevating enterprise of social and moral reformation.

I am not impressed to enter into *details* concerning the *advanced stages* of the reorganization, nor of the movements required — as these will be for future consideration, and the careful investigation of their promulgators. *Wisdom* and *circumstances* will govern the *details* of the several associations; and therefore it would be premature to attempt now to unfold the subject.

The machinery, the structure, the primary movements have thus been suggested and explained; and if they are in their essential teachings obeyed, the legitimate consequences will be the peace and happiness which the race desires.

This will be the era of peace. And remarkable as it may appear, it is true that the most prominent writers, from the time of Confucius and Zoroaster to the present century, have spoken of this period with a great deal of prophetic delight. Each one has contributed some principles that are true and practicable. They descend from the heathen philosophers, and flow through the Old and New Testaments, and are presented in various forms at the present day.

SWEDENBORG has done more than any other person to accumulate, sift, and preserve, the useful productions of each nation: and he has formed them into a system that is practicable and serviceable to every mind. Yet they can not now be understood or applied so extensively as when the superior Association is formed, and their wisdom is concentrated for the purpose of accumulating and applying all truths.

Heretofore I have referred to the several revelations that have been given by men in every century within the limits of national chronology. Their teachings in the main are important. They can only be proved so, and applied with a benefit, after society is formed into a closer and more agreeable relation.

Now it is made manifest that the teachings of Jesus were descriptions of *effects* to flow legitimately from such a social organization. And likewise the prophets indulged in the same delightful anticipations of glorious *effects* to be one day enjoyed on earth. Men have not distinguished properly, in examining the teachings of Jesus, the nature and relation of cause and effect. These they have *confounded*, and generally the *effects* described by him are taken for primary *causes* to reform society. The golden rule, the feeling of brotherly love, love to the neighbor, and such like, are not *causes*, but *effects*, which will be realized and consummated ere long on earth. He taught what *should* be, not that which would *produce* it: he spoke of *effects*, not *causes*. He spoke of *unity*, and *spiritual consolation, elevation,* and *happiness;* but not of *social evils*, their *causes*, and the *means* to remove them.

Then he who loves and admires the doctrines of this great and glorious Reformer, should abandon immediately the preaching of *effects*, and exercise his wisdom to reconstruct society — to introduce *causes* which may harmonize social interests, so that those very desirable *effects* may be realized. He who would honor his Master (or the type of the human race, which is Jesus), must abandon mere *speech*, and proceed to *action*. Preach in *deed*, and not in *speech*. Cease unmeaning prayers, and go forth into the sinks of social wretchedness and desolation, and offer an *assisting hand*, which is a prayer divinely manifested. Discrimination must be made between the causes of social evil and the effects of brotherly kindness and charity, which latter *only* were described by the elevated moral Reformer. This being done, no man will be called a *heretic* if he proposes movements of reform not intimated in the teachings of Jesus; for one thing is certain — that no man can transcend the principles of these teachings in his most active imaginations of social unity and peace, inasmuch as they are the highest principles of social and moral reciprocation. This once acknowledged, and it will be conceded that *he* honors the teachings of Jesus, who is active in instituting principles and movements of reform, so that the grand *effect* of love to the neighbor may be fully and unchangeably established.

Recurrence to the writings of Charles Fourier is necessary for the purpose of bringing his social system before the world, so that mankind may investigate it, and give a just verdict as to its truth, morality, and practicability. It is impossible to escape the conclusion that he revealed many truthful causes and principles of reform that must be in some degree practised before the kingdom of heaven can be established on earth. I am impressed, then, to suggest that those who engage in the reform should accumulate the various principles and suggestions of moral and philosophical writers. They must discover how much *real* truth each author imbodies, its relation to present existing evils, the extent of its application, and the results if practised.

The great movements of the day are all advancing the public to this desirable consummation. The efforts for the abolition of slavery; those for the repeal of capital punishment; the reform of prison-discipline; the temperance reformation; the liberality of the various sects; the general open demand of the public mind for some relief from social and mental embarrassments; the agitations in various portions of Europe; the elevation of the public morals; the manifest sympathies toward the poor and degraded; the excitement among the inhabitants of Scotland for the relief of their poor; the general condition of France; the liberal investigations of Germany; the researches among the tombs and monuments of Egypt, revealing the truths of national antiquity; the absolute predominance of *facts* over *imagination*, and truth over error; the general condition of the heathen world; and finally the movements among every nation of the earth, both social, scientific, and spiritual — all proclaim the approach of this sublime era.

Our country, its interests, wealth, and government, are fearfully involved in a peace-destroying war, the result of which will be a powerful reaction on every mind; and this will accelerate the insinuation of these principles, and their practice. The era is nigh: the judgment-day, when wisdom shall predominate, will soon arrive; and this will banish ignorance, error, prejudice, and fanaticism, from the earth. A general revolution is at hand. It is already kindled — Wisdom will fan the sparks into a flame, and this will consume contention and sin, and all will come forth purified, elevated, HAPPY! This is the flame of LOVE — the consuming vengeance of TRUTH and GOODNESS. For it is a fact that whatever new truth is presented to the world, no matter how gentle, lovely, and fascinating, it may be, it is to *establish a prejudice* like a consuming fire of vengeance. Hence it is opposed: and the conflict demonstrates the difference between truth and error, reason and fanaticism. But the prospect is clear — the purifying fire of Love, Truth, and Knowledge, will consume all else, and vengeance will only be manifested in the conflict of established prejudices.

§ 37. Such is the era foreseen by David, Isaiah, Jeremiah, Ezekiel, Daniel, Zechariah, and Malachi. Such was the period impressed upon Confucius, Zoroaster, Brama, Jesus, Mohammed, Fourier, and upon male and female writers of every century down to the present day. It was sung in the Orphic hymns of Egypt, described in the writings of heathen poets and philosophers, preached and anticipated by Paul, and metaphorically described by John in the Apocalypse. It is that which gives consolation to every writer who feels the importance of a social reformation; and it is that which inspires the bosom of every philanthropist, gives consolation to the depressed, hope to the disquieted, promise to the philosopher, and an asylum to the admirer of Nature and worshipper of her manifestations.

Unspeakable inducements have been presented to an aspiration for this sublime consummation: for behold the deepest and most secret recesses of Nature have been searched, and their immense possessions revealed. The magnificence of the material Universe; its undying energies, qualities, essences, and combinations of beauty — have been unfolded and brought forth unexaggerated. From the central power of terrestrial creation, the successive degrees of development; the manifestations of each step; the results of each creation; the unvarying tendencies of all, their teachings and their practicability, have been shown forth in their enchanting grandeur. The creation of the earth; the form, essence, and production, of each kingdom; the general concentration of power in the creation of man; his attributes; his social and spiritual qualifications; his unlimited and righteous exercise of power over the various created things beneath him; the relative positions and offices which he and the subordinate creations sustain, and the unity, order, wisdom, grandeur, and excellency of all divine developments, have all been unfolded to man. More than this, the stupendous grandeur of the spiritual habitations has been reflected upon his spiritual vision. Their celestial attractions, their dispensations, their requirements, have been presented to the lively and willing intellect of man. The grand architecture of all terrestrial and celestial things has been presented in a true form for the purpose of impelling man onward and upward in the improvement of his natural life and spiritual being.

The laws of Nature have been clearly unfolded, from which may be drawn a code of just and righteous laws of social government. These have been applied to society, and directions have been given for their practice. Society has been arranged so as to represent the material and spiritual creations of the Divine Mind — so that an equal harmony may pervade it, which may restore the disunited and conflicting race to the bosom of Nature, to her principles, and to the love of God.

Then, tillers of the soil—*agriculturists*—who among your vast number shall be the *first* to deposite the germ of social happiness, and bless your brethren? Multitudinous as you are, are there not *six* among you ready in social and moral culture to enter upon this glorious enterprise? *Mechanics*, who among you shall first manifest the righteousness of your cause, your industry, your art, as the art of Nature? Who among your number shall be the advocates of distributive justice, attractive labor, and a proper compensation? *Manufacturers*, will you not concentrate your wealth and power to effect a general good, and assist all co-workers in the vineyard of industry and happiness?

Lawyers, who among you shall give the *first* impulse, and promulgate and establish these principles of association, of justice, of human brotherhood? Who in your vast numbers is qualified to ascend to the honorable seat of government, to be a supreme judge? Who shall bring forth his energies, his mental strength, to accomplish this desirable end? *Physicians*, in your midst, who is the one to be the grand professor and governor of your elevated and useful occupation? Who shall ascend to the various degrees of honor and usefulness? *Clergymen*, what one among you is qualified to be the grand king and lord of social righteousness, such as shall be derived from the laws of Nature, and shall flow to and comprehend every being of the earth? Who shall be the number to congregate and legislate for the people? Who shall prove by actual demonstration that he is a nobleman by nature, and a philanthropist in action? Who among you shall go forth and disseminate the principles of social reform, preach the kingdom of heaven, dispense intelligence, and elevate the depressed? Upon you and your holy proceedings depends the success of those teachings which it has been the burden of every intelligent mind to conceive—and *suppress*, for the want of mental liberty.

Agriculturists, mechanics, manufacturers—do you not feel the importance of changing your own and your laborers' situations?—of supplying all wants, and establishing universal industry? Lawyers, physicians, clergymen—do you not feel the omnipotence of Nature's truths? Do you not see that they are immortal and can not die? Give ear to her proclamations and her admonitions, and proceed to change your situations in life, and strive to represent the heavenly societies on earth. Nature demands obedience. Upon her and her laws depends your misery or happiness. She everywhere proclaims this truth: that at her hand is the punishment of every vice, and the reward of every virtue; that in her bosom is nourishment and inexhaustible provisions for all her creatures—but that they must bow in submission to her commands to receive her spontaneous bestowments.

Finally, I will leave you all to interrogate Nature and the Divine Mind, to determine whether error shall reign instead of truth, vice instead of virtue, misery instead of happiness, or contention instead of harmony. I discover that your inquiries will be fully and satisfactorily answered, your reason convinced, your minds elevated, your movements righteous, expeditious, and immediate. And the results thereof will be the destruction of all sorrow, and the ushering-in of joy unspeakable and blessings immense. This once accomplished, and behold—your uncultivated fields, dense and fearful forests, untraversed morasses, barren deserts, gloomy wildernesses, are all beautiful gardens, yielding the choicest productions of earth. Happy villages are visible in every direction. Valleys are teeming with all the excellences of life and industry. These bespeak prosperity and happiness. Even your valleys are exalted, your rough and impassable places are made smooth, the crooked and fantastic are made straight and beautiful, and all nations rejoice in social unity and righteousness!

Innumerable contributions of science and art are derived from every village. In every continent, nations converse through the medium of the electric fire. Powerful engines are in motion perfecting commerce, convenience, safety, wealth, and science. Every port is thrown open, and each county enjoys the blessings of unrestricted intercourse with all others. Mutual exchanges are made, reciprocal justice is displayed, and a halo of peace is the crown of every nation. The deserts are cultivated and bring forth abundantly. The wilderness blossoms as the rose. Earth is a terrestrial heaven, peopled with superior beings, typifying in their lives the grandeur and holiness of Paradise. All contention, all strife and national animosities, have for ever ceased. The flag of Liberty is unfurled, and the ocean of Truth is rising, and the fount of Love is on earth, springing up unto everlasting life. Behold—every child of the Eternal One is laboring with pleasure in the field, in the departments of science, in the courts of justice, in the temple of health, or in the sanctuary of peace and brotherly love! Each one is situated as is prescribed by Nature and her Creator. His kingdom has come, his will is done on earth as it is in heaven.—And all rest even while they are beautifying and gardenizing the soil. Strength, opulence, grandeur, and glory, are visible in every department of social life. None are weak, depressed, diseased: all are strong, elevated, healthy. The *milennium*—the day of peace—the era of righteousness—is established. Everything proclaims glory, and honor, and immortal life. Nothing is lost—all are saved. He who rules omnipotent hath spoken from the solitary deserts, and from the monuments and persecutions of ages bygone. He has revealed his character in every particle, leaf, flower, and tree, and arched the heavens with his glory. He has impressed on man the express image of his nature and attributes. He has crowned him the lord of creation. He has elevated, refined, and perfected, the formerly-misdirected race of man, and brought the whole to the fulness of the stature of a PERFECT BEING!

Such will be the appearance of the earth ere long! The vision indicates prosperity and peace. It is an object for which all should labor; it is an end yet to be accomplished; it *will* be: but who among you, brethren, shall deposite the *germ*, establish the *nucleus*—the central power—of righteousness? Your reason—your unclouded intellects—will decide. To prove your superiority, your innate magnanimity and goodness of soul, do not rest in pain while you may be active in undying pleasure. All that has been promised in every age to this century, will be fully realized. When distributive justice pervades the social world, then virtue and morality will bloom with an immortal beauty. The sun of righteousness will arise in the horizon of universal industry, and shed its genial rays over all the fields of peace, plenty, and human happiness!

THE END.

www.ingramcontent.com/pod-product-compliance
Lightning Source LLC
Chambersburg PA
CBHW080050190426
43201CB00035B/2156